An important and fascinating book which both develops existing theoretical ideas and breaks new empirical ground. It will generate debate and hopefully inspire further research in a similar vein.

Nick Crossley, *University of Manchester*

By focusing on class differences in the way that social agents relate to and invest in their bodies, Vandebroeck provides the English reader a fresh look at the way the body exists, is experienced and perceived: a path breaking study that I think will become an instant classic.

Muriel Darmon, *CNRS/EHESS, Paris I – Sorbonne*

This is a fantastic book, throwing fresh light on topics of profound sociological and political significance, from eating disorders and the meaning of beauty to the relationship between class and gender. In so doing Vandebroeck weaves together astute theoretical reflection with forensic empirical scrutiny in a manner recalling the best works of Bourdieu himself.

Will Atkinson, *University of Bristol*

Distinctions in the Flesh

The past decades have witnessed a surge of sociological interest in the body. From the focal point of aesthetic investment, political regulation and moral anxiety, to a means of redefining traditional conceptions of agency and identity, the body has been cast in a wide variety of sociological roles. However, there is one topic that proves conspicuously absent from this burgeoning literature on the body, namely its role in the everyday (re)production of class-boundaries.

Distinctions in the Flesh aims to fill that void by showing that the way individuals perceive, use and manage their bodies is fundamentally intertwined with their social position and trajectory. Drawing on a wide array of survey-data – from food-preferences to sporting-practices and from weight-concern to tastes in clothing – this book shows how bodies not only function as key markers of class-differences, but also help to naturalize and legitimize such differences. Along the way, it scrutinizes popular notions like the "obesity epidemic", questions the role of "the media" in shaping the way people judge their bodies and sheds doubt on sociological narratives that cast the body as a malleable object that is increasingly open to individual control and reflexive management.

This book will be of interest to scholars of class, lifestyle and identity, but also to social epidemiologists, health professionals and anyone interested in the way that social inequalities become, quite *literally*, inscribed in the body.

Dieter Vandebroeck is an assistant-professor of sociology at the Free University of Brussels (Vrije Universiteit Brussel) and a former visiting fellow at the Centre for Research on Socio-Cultural Change (CRESC) at the University of Manchester.

Culture, Economy and the Social
A new series from CRESC – the ESRC Centre for Research on Socio-Cultural Change

Editors
Professor Tony Bennett, Social and Cultural Theory, University of Western Sydney; Professor Penny Harvey, Anthropology, Manchester University; Professor Kevin Hetherington, Geography, Open University

Editorial Advisory Board
Andrew Barry, University of Oxford; Michel Callon, Ecole des Mines de Paris; Dipesh Chakrabarty, The University of Chicago; Mike Crang, University of Durham; Tim Dant, Lancaster University; Jean-Louis Fabiani, Ecoles de Hautes Etudes en Sciences Sociales; Antoine Hennion, Paris Institute of Technology; Eric Hirsch, Brunel University; John Law, The Open University; Randy Martin, New York University; Timothy Mitchell, New York University; Rolland Munro, Keele University; Andrew Pickering, University of Exeter; Mary Poovey, New York University; Hugh Willmott, University of Cardiff; Sharon Zukin, Brooklyn College City University New York/Graduate School, City University of New York

The *Culture, Economy and the Social* series is committed to innovative contemporary, comparative and historical work on the relations between social, cultural and economic change. It publishes empirically-based research that is theoretically informed, that critically examines the ways in which social, cultural and economic change is framed and made visible, and that is attentive to perspectives that tend to be ignored or side-lined by grand theorising or epochal accounts of social change. The series addresses the diverse manifestations of contemporary capitalism, and considers the various ways in which the 'social', 'the cultural' and 'the economic' are apprehended as tangible sites of value and practice. It is explicitly comparative, publishing books that work across disciplinary perspectives, cross-culturally, or across different historical periods.

The series is actively engaged in the analysis of the different theoretical traditions that have contributed to the development of the 'cultural turn' with a view to clarifying where these approaches converge and where they diverge on a particular issue. It is equally concerned to explore the new critical agendas emerging from current critiques of the cultural turn: those associated with the descriptive turn for example. Our commitment to interdisciplinarity thus aims at enriching theoretical and methodological discussion, building awareness of the common ground that has emerged in the past decade, and thinking through what is at stake in those approaches that resist integration to a common analytical model.

Series titles include:

Objects and Materials
A Routledge companion
Edited by Penny Harvey,
Eleanor Conlin Casella,
Gillian Evans, Hannah Knox,
Christine McLean, Elizabeth B. Silva,
Nicholas Thoburn and
Kath Woodward

Accumulation
The material politics of plastic
Edited by Gay Hawkins,
Jennifer Gabrys and Mike Michael

Theorizing Cultural Work
Labour, continuity and change in the cultural and creative industries
Edited by Mark Banks, Rosalind Gill and Stephanie Taylor

Comedy and Distinction
The cultural currency of a 'good' sense of humour
Sam Friedman

The Provoked Economy
Economic reality and the performative turn
Fabian Muniesa

Rio de Janeiro
Urban life through the eyes of the city
Beatriz Jaguaribe

The Routledge Companion to Bourdieu's 'Distinction'
Edited by Philippe Coulangeon and Julien Duval

Devising Consumption
Cultural economies of insurance, credit and spending
Liz McFall

Industry and Work in Contemporary Capitalism
Global models, local lives?
Edited by Victoria Goddard and Susana Narotzky

Lived Economies of Consumer Credit
Consumer credit, debt collection and the capture of affect
Joe Deville

Cultural Pedagogies and Human Conduct
Edited by Megan Watkins,
Greg Noble and Catherine Driscoll

Culture as a Vocation
Sociology of career choices in cultural management
Vincent Dubois

Topologies of Power
John Allen

Distinctions in the Flesh
Social class and the embodiment of inequality
Dieter Vandebroeck

Coming Soon:

Film Criticism as a Cultural Institution
Crisis and continuity from the 20th to the 21st century
Huw Walmsley-Evans

Unbecoming Things
Mutable objects and the politics of waste
Nicky Gregson and Mike Crang

For a complete list of titles in this series, please visit www.routledge.com/CRESC/book-series/CRESC

E·S·R·C
ECONOMIC
& SOCIAL
RESEARCH
COUNCIL

Centre for Research on
Socio-Cultural Change

Distinctions in the Flesh
Social class and the embodiment of inequality

Dieter Vandebroeck

LONDON AND NEW YORK

First published 2017
by Routledge
2 Park Square, Milton Park, Abingdon, Oxon OX14 4RN

and by Routledge
711 Third Avenue, New York, NY 10017

First issued in paperback 2018

Routledge is an imprint of the Taylor & Francis Group, an informa business

© 2017 Dieter Vandebroeck

The right of Dieter Vandebroeck to be identified as author of this work has been asserted by him in accordance with sections 77 and 78 of the Copyright, Designs and Patents Act 1988.

All rights reserved. No part of this book may be reprinted or reproduced or utilized in any form or by any electronic, mechanical, or other means, now known or hereafter invented, including photocopying and recording, or in any information storage or retrieval system, without permission in writing from the publishers.

Trademark notice: Product or corporate names may be trademarks or registered trademarks, and are used only for identification and explanation without intent to infringe.

British Library Cataloguing in Publication Data
A catalogue record for this book is available from the British Library

Library of Congress Cataloging in Publication Data
Names: Vandebroeck, Dieter, author.
Title: Distinctions in the flesh : social class and the embodiment of inequality / by Dieter Vandebroeck.
Description: 1 Edition. | New York : Routledge, 2016.
Identifiers: LCCN 2016004651| ISBN 9781138123557 (hardback) | ISBN 9781315648781 (ebook)
Subjects: LCSH: Human body–Social aspects. | Social classes. | Equality–Social aspects.
Classification: LCC HM636 .V36 2016 | DDC 305–dc23
LC record available at http://lccn.loc.gov/2016004651

ISBN 13: 978-1-138-59876-8 (pbk)
ISBN 13: 978-1-138-12355-7 (hbk)

Typeset in Times New Roman
by Wearset Ltd, Boldon, Tyne and Wear

 Printed in the United Kingdom by Henry Ling Limited

For Leen

Contents

List of figures	xiv
List of tables	xv
Acknowledgements	xvii

Introduction: vulgar object, vulgar method   1
The absent 'class body' 3
Beyond the 'topical body' 6
Questions of method 8
The structure of the book 10

PART I
Social order, body order   13

1 The body in social space   15
'Analysis situs' 16
An 'order of coexistence' 18
Probable class, actual class 22
Distinct distinctions 24
Gendered bodies 27
Social space, sexual space 30

2 Classifying bodies, classified bodies, class bodies   38
Incorporation 39
Comprehension 41
History-in-bodies 44
A sense of place 46
A 'class unconscious' 49
'Modus operandi' and 'opus operatum' 52
Being and seeming 53
'I can', 'it can', 'I must' 56

The two bodies 59
Transcendence and negation 62

3 The body in social time   66
Time for pain 66
Pain and prevention 68
The causality of the probable 73
Investment 77
Time-perspective and self-control 81

PART II
Modes of embodiment   85

4 The perceptible body   87
Sociology's fear of fat 89
Deconstructing the "obesity epidemic" 91
Social class and body-mass 95
The social perception of body-weight 98
Average and norm 103
Diet and diaita *106*
Hysteresis-effects 108
Current body, dream body 111
Hexis and cathexis 115
A moral physiognomy of class 118
A "disease of the will" 124

5 The hungry body   126
The (social) sense of the senses 128
Substance and function 130
Style and form 139
Matter and manner 143
Elective austerity and conspicuous consumption 147
The social inertia of food-tastes 151

6 The playful body   156
Semantic elasticity 156
The need for sports 159
A social morphology of sporting-preferences 163
Form and force 167
Hard and soft 171
The sacred and the profane 175

PART III
Class bodies 179

7 Relaxation in tension 181
Conspicuous simplicity 183
'Askesis' and 'aesthesis' 186
Negative cultivation 190

8 Tension in relaxation 194
Inner tension 195
Body-images 198
A Protestant aesthetic 203
Doxa and orthodoxy 205
Being-perceived 207
Situating reflexivity 210

9 Necessity incarnate 212
The labouring body 214
A body-for-others 217
The de-narcissized body 221
The "unregulated" body 225

Conclusion: the visible and the invisible 228
A view from nowhere 229
Expansion and compression 230
Negative discrimination 233
Distinctions in the flesh 234

Methodological appendices 237
Appendix 1: description of primary and secondary data sources 237
Appendix 2: constructing social space 241
Appendix 3: figure rating scale 244
Appendix 4: additional tables and figures 246

References 261
Index 271

Figures

1.1	Diagram of social space	20
1.2	The distribution of gender-ratios across social space	34
4.1	Distribution of body-mass by gender and educational capital	104
4.2	Distribution of body-mass by gender and social class	105
4.3	Current, ideal and most disliked body by social class (*men*)	112
4.4	Current, ideal and most disliked body by social class (*women*)	113
4.5	Classification of male silhouettes by social class *(% and type)*	119
4.6	Classification of female silhouettes by social class *(% and type)*	120
A3.1	Diagram of male and female body-types	245

Tables

4.1	Body-size characteristics by gender, level of education, income and professional status	93
4.2	Body-size characteristics by gender and class fraction	97
4.3	Weight-concern and body-mass by gender, educational capital, economic capital and professional status	99
4.4	Weight-concern and body-mass by gender and class fraction	100
4.5	Satisfaction with weight and appearance by gender, educational capital, professional status and social class	116
5.1	Attitudes towards food and dining by gender, educational capital and class fraction	134
5.2	Ranking of favourite dishes by social class, *men*	140
5.3	Attitudes towards food and dining by gender, social class and social origin	152
6.1	Participation in sporting activities by gender, educational capital and class fraction	160
6.2	Sports-preferences by educational capital, class fraction and social trajectory	165
6.3	Gym-attendance by gender, educational capital and class fraction	170
8.1	Women's consumption of various types of printed and visual media	200
8.2	Relationship between women's media-consumption, body-image and physical size	201
A1.1	Sociographic composition of the sample for *Body Survey 2010*	238
A1.2	Summary of secondary data-sets	239
A2.1	A taxonomy of social position	243
A4.1	Indices of dieting and weight-concern by gender, educational capital, professional status and social class	246
A4.2	Selection of current, ideal and most disliked body by gender and social class	248
A4.3	Selection of class bodies by social class	250
A4.4	Annual average household-expenditure on food (*upper class*)	252

A4.5 Annual average household-expenditure on food
(*middle-class*) 255
A4.6 Annual average household-expenditure on food
(*working-class*) 258
A4.7 Total time devoted to meals 260

Acknowledgements

Many people have contributed, directly and indirectly, to making this book possible. Throughout my research I was always able to count on the intellectual and emotional support from colleagues and friends at the Department of Sociology and the TOR Research Group at the Free University of Brussels. I owe a special thanks to Ignace Glorieux for his kind support and the quiet confidence he exuded throughout the entire project. The daily conversations with Kobe De Keere, Jan Claeys, Jessie Vandeweyer, Wendy Smits, Bram Spruyt and Maaike Jappens were crucial to maintaining both my sense of sociological and emotional sanity, for which I am immensely grateful. Patricia Van den Eeckhout and Dimo Kavadias both offered insightful and constructive commentary on earlier drafts of the manuscript. Many thanks also to Sven Sanctobin who provided invaluable assistance with the coordination of the survey and Reg Carremans, who lent his graphical talent in helping to develop the visual methodology. Toon Kuppens and Alan Quireyns provided much welcomed sorties from the seclusions of academia. My research was able to benefit immensely from a stay at the School of Social Sciences of the University of Manchester and a visiting fellowship at the Centre for Research on Sociocultural Change (CRESC). I owe a sincere debt of gratitude to Mike Savage and Nick Crossley for making this stay possible, as well as for providing insightful comments on the manuscript and invaluable assistance in getting it to a publisher. Felix Bühlmann, Ebru Söytemel and Josine Opmeer made my stay at Manchester both intellectually challenging and emotionally rewarding (*Danke, teşekkürler, dankjewel!*). My work also benefited from lively discussions with members of the Network for the Study of Cultural Distinctions and Social Differentiation (SCUD). Special thanks are due to Annick Prieur, Lennart Rosenlund, Johs Hjelbrekke, Magne Flemmen and Predrag Cveticanin. A "*grand merci*" also goes to Muriel Darmon for her kind support of the manuscript. Thanks also to Tony Bennett who received the original text with much enthusiasm, provided constructive criticisms and kindly assisted it throughout the editorial process. At Routledge and Wearset, Alyson Claffey and Ashleigh Phillips responded to my many editorial whims with generous support and much patience. The research presented in this book was made possible by a generous grant of the Flemish Foundation for Scientific Research (FWO). Finally, this book would never have seen the light of day were it not for my partner Leen, who remains both my fiercest critic and most ardent supporter. I dedicate it wholeheartedly to her.

Introduction
Vulgar object, vulgar method

> Although it has, in order to constitute itself, to reject all the forms of that biologism which always tend to naturalize social differences by reducing them to anthropological invariants, sociology can understand the social game in its most essential aspects only if it takes into account certain of the universal characteristics of bodily existence, such as the fact of existing as a separate biological individual, or of being confined to a place and a moment, or even the fact of being and knowing oneself destined for death, so many more than scientifically attested properties which never come into the axiomatics of positivist anthropology.
> (Bourdieu, 1990a: 196)

If it is true that 'the point-of-view creates the object' (De Saussure, 1966 [1907]: 8), then it should also follow that it is the point-of-view which helps to create the *value* of the object. That the academic standing and broader public relevance of any research-topic owes as much to the prestige of the discipline that makes it into an "object", than to any of its intrinsic properties becomes particularly clear when one deals with an object that appears "superficial" at best and "vulgar" at worst, namely the physical, visceral and sensuous *body*. While it is the distinct privilege of more prestigious disciplines – like philosophy or history – to be able to transform the most "common" or "trivial" topics into "distinguished" and "singular" objects of investigation, less prominent branches of science – like sociology – are often bereft of such a Midas touch. If the former are often seen as elevating their object – one of the surest signs of social consecration (for groups as much as individuals) is to have one's "history" written – then the latter is all too often accused of reducing it. The case of the body shows with particular clarity that the specific task of *de-naturalization* – i.e. of robbing the social world of its self-evidence and its apparent foundation in the "natural" order of things – which is inherently that of all of the *social* sciences, is always more difficult to perform in the case of sociology. In fact, at least part of the argument that will be developed throughout this study – namely that one of the apparently most intimate, personal and natural aspects of being, namely the relationship to our body, is fundamentally shaped by impersonal, objective and social conditions – could be (and indeed *has* been) buttressed using historical or ethnographic methods. For instance, the analysis could have singled out one of the most universal and natural imperatives of physical being – the need for food – and have traced its historical evolution over the past centuries. In this manner, it could have demonstrated that what is deemed "gross" or "sickening" today, was considered quite "normal" and even "tasteful" just a few generations ago and hence have concluded that the apparently most automatic of bodily reactions (desire and disgust, appetite and revulsion, etc.) are profoundly *social* in origin. Alternatively, this study could have fixed on another aspect of human physicality – say sexual desire – and have compared its particular mode of expression across various social systems in order to show that this "universal" need is gratified in shapes and hues that are often as variegated as these systems themselves.

While undoubtedly leading to similar conclusions, such approaches would nonetheless be considered infinitely less reductionist than the one adopted here. In fact, when tackling the visceral realities of the flesh with the interpretative tools of her trade (statistical analysis, interviewing, ethnographic observation, etc.), the sociologist can benefit little from the neutralizing effect of *distance* that – by virtue of studying an object that is remote in time or space – is granted to the historian or the anthropologist. It is precisely this distance that enables the latter to engage with the physicality of the body in a manner that would be deemed nothing short of voyeuristic or obscene when contemplated by sociologists. In fact, the same reader who chuckles at detailed historical descriptions of flatulence and defecation in the medieval dining hall or indulges in vivid examples of the poor hygienic standards and bizarre sexual mores at the court of Louis XIV, is generally less amused when it is his own dinner table and sense of hygiene that are being scrutinized. Similarly, those who frown at ethnographic accounts of the West-African "fattening rooms" – where tribal chiefs invest in their own status by increasing the girth of their daughters – are often less inclined to recognize a similar social logic in their own weekly trips to the gym.

In fact, the traditional resistance that sociology tends to provoke – being a science that is all too often accused of "reducing" the Individual to the Collective, the Subjective to the Objective or the Natural to the Social – is in a sense *doubled*, when it takes as its object the one thing that we not only tend to experience as the most familiar and natural, but which we also claim as being irreducibly our own, namely our *bodies*. This leads any attempt at uncovering the common regularities and shared features of this most personal of relationships to be easily perceived as an attack on individual choice and freedom, a dispossession or denial of ownership and self-control (or in more contemporary jargon: of 'agency' and 'reflexivity') and this all the more so, the more agents' position in the social structure tends to reinforce their own sense of freedom and singularity. Worse yet, when dealing with an object that constitutes the most 'tangible manifestation of the "person"' (Bourdieu, 1984: 192) and hence cannot but be taken as "personal", a simple *description* of a particular practice, property or opinion (a 'value-reference' in Weber's terminology) can quite easily be mistaken for a subjective *evaluation* or *judgment* of such properties and beliefs. This is only compounded by the fact that the very categories the analysis uses as instruments of classification, comparison and characterization – such as "ideal body", "overweight", "*petit-bourgeois*" or even more seemingly neutral oppositions such "heavy" vs. "light" or "large" vs. "small" – are also used by social agents themselves, albeit more often with the purpose of condemnation, stigmatization or caricaturization. If the following chapters are marked by a (more than) profuse usage of quotation marks, this is precisely to constantly highlight the difference between the *descriptive* and *prescriptive* applications of terms, between their uses as instruments of *definition* or tools of *defamation*.[1]

This (mis)perception of the sociological method as a form of reduction is even more likely when the analysis arms itself – as is the case here – with one of the most cruelly objectifying techniques in the sociological arsenal, namely *statistical analysis*. Contrary to the ethnographic description or the interview-excerpt which still "flesh out" individuals with a given degree of existential detail or at least allow them the ownership of their own words, statistics reduces them to those properties, *and only those*, that are deemed pertinent from the point-of-view of the analysis. If it does so, however, this is only to underline the fact that in as far as sociology deals with *individual* agents (or individual bodies), it never does so in their capacity as 'empirical individuals' – i.e. as singular subjects with their proper name and their irreducible properties – but always treats them as constructed or 'epistemic individuals' which are 'defined by a finite set of explicitly defined properties which differ through a series of identifiable differences from the set of properties, constructed according to the same explicit criteria, which characterize other individuals' (Bourdieu, 1988: 22). This distinction becomes all the more important to highlight when dealing with *physical* properties which, despite having all the characteristics of 'social facts', are necessarily incarnated in individual bodies.

The absent 'class body'

At this point, the discerning reader might question the relevance of yet another study devoted to the body. At first glance, there is indeed little that such a study could add to a sociological genre that has already produced a veritable outpouring of literature on all things corporeal. In fact, the body has long managed to escape from what Marcel Mauss called the 'obnoxious rubric' (*vilaine rubric*) of the "Miscellaneous", to which it was still confined when he wrote his famous *Techniques of the Body* (1973 [1934]: 70), retrospectively canonized as one of the founding texts of the sociology of the body.[2] Ever since its eruption onto the sociological stage at the end of last century, the body has been cast in a wide variety of roles: a living metaphor for the organization of social systems (Douglas, 1996a [1970]), the object of various modes of social and personal governance (Turner, 1996), an integral component of a 'reflexively organized narrative of self' (Giddens, 1992), a 'project' harnessed to the demands of an increasingly individualized self-identity (Shilling, 2003) or an analytical category providing the means to re-conceptualize some of the classical divisions of social theory (Crossley, 2001), to name but a few of the variegated perspectives on the subject.

Together, these different perspectives have managed to place the body squarely on the sociological agenda. However, in as much as the body has been used to shed new light on the perennial problems of order and change, cognition and identity, structure and agency, there is one topic that is often remarkably absent from the long list of sociological issues that the body has been made to address, namely that of *social class*. When browsing through the numerous tomes that have cropped up under the heading of 'sociology of the body', one is often struck by the silence with which its authors brush over the thematic of class-relationships and social domination. Stronger still, even if one leaves aside the contended and contentious nature of 'class' as an analytical concept, one is often hard-pressed to find *any* developed account of social differentiation within this otherwise quite impressive body of literature. In fact, sociologists seem to have largely broached the 'problem of the body' from two opposite directions. On the one hand, they have looked at it from the point-of-view of the body politic *as a whole*, that is, from the perspective of *a* social system, *a* culture or *a* time-period, be it 'post-industrial capitalism', 'Western consumerism' or 'late modernity'. On the other hand, they have treated this problem from the perspective of the *individual* agent as, for instance, a way of rethinking traditional questions of agency and cognition, a central element in the construction of the self, a source of 'existential anxiety' and uncertainty or the object of ever-increasing possibilities of individual stylization. The role that class occupies in such accounts tends to range from that of an ancillary issue to that of an altogether obsolete explanatory factor, a 'zombie category' (Beck and Beck-Gernsheim, 2002) characteristic of an outdated brand of social analysis.

The relative negligence of processes of *class*-domination within the literature becomes even more apparent, when compared to the myriad discussions on the body's role in the reproduction and legitimization of *other* forms of social domination, most notably those inscribed in the sexual division of labour, ethno-racial relationships or even the struggles between different age-groups. In this manner, it is quite common to see sociological compendia on the body to carry separate headings for gender, age and race but curiously enough, *not* for class. Feminist and black scholars in particular have been pivotal in not only highlighting the profoundly corporeal nature of social life, but also for showing how traditional, universalistic accounts of 'embodiment' very often reflect the particular bodily experience of white men (see for instance; Henley, 1977; Slaughter, 1977; Connell, 1987; Young, 2005 and Fanon, 2008 [1952]). Similarly, considerable attention has been devoted to the biological reality of ageing and the ways in which age-groups struggle to impose their own definition of "youth", "midlife" or "old age", while attempting to resist those imposed by others (see Featherstone and Hepworth, 1991; Turner, 1995). While such work has been crucial in elaborating traditional concepts like the 'lived body', 'embodiment' or the 'body scheme' by showing how they are fundamentally differentiated along sexual, ethnic or age-divisions, efforts to show how the experience of the body is equally circumscribed by the realities of class are still few and far between.

The central aim of this study is to address this gap in the literature by attempting to demonstrate the centrality of class-dynamics to our understanding of the social *production* and *perception* of the body. More specifically, it will attempt to show that body and class are implicated in a mutually reinforcing relationship. On the one hand, class-positions define the *social conditions of possibility* for the inculcation of particular ways of using, perceiving and treating the body which, in turn, contribute to shaping the body in its most tangible of features. On the other hand, it is precisely because class-differences become incorporated into the biological body – that is, are at once individualized *and* naturalized – that the body delivers a crucial contribution to the process whereby such differences become 'misperceived as natural, individual, moral dispositions instead of socially mediated forms that relate directly to cultural relations of domination and exclusion' (Charlesworth, 2000: 158). This study will attempt to demonstrate that this dual logic is central to understanding how the cardinal divisions inscribed in the social order come to be perceived as "natural", in the twofold sense of the term, namely as both "self-evident" or "second-nature", as well as rooted in the biological order of things and hence endowed with all the ineluctable necessity of Nature.

This concern with both the *symbolic* and *embodied* dimension of contemporary class-relationships also guided the choice for the theoretical perspective that informs the analyses presented in this study. While these analyses take their theoretical cues from a number of different authors (such as the processual sociology of Norbert Elias, the phenomenology of Merleau-Ponty or the cultural theory of Mary Douglas), they derive their main inspiration from the sociological oeuvre of Pierre Bourdieu. In fact, long before the body became a particularly fashionable object of sociological theorizing, Bourdieu's analyses of social practice already assigned it a key role as a central vector in the (re)production of the social order. From his early, quasi-phenomenological descriptions of the 'bodily habitus' of the peasants in his native Béarn (Bourdieu, 2008) or his analyses of the body's role as a 'practical operator' of the central divisions and oppositions of Kabylian mythology (Bourdieu, 1977a), through his discussions of the importance of the 'body scheme' in understanding the sociolect of the different social classes (Bourdieu, 1977b) or his recognition of the body as 'the most indisputable materialization of class taste' (Bourdieu, 1984: 192) in his now seminal *Distinction*, to his later reflections on the role of bodily emotion and symbolic violence (Bourdieu, 2000a), Bourdieu's intellectual trajectory reveals a keen sensitivity to the fundamentally *embodied* nature of social divisions. As such, his oeuvre contains a compelling research-programme for a sociology of the body whose analytical potential remains largely untapped (the important work of authors like Wacquant [2004] or Darmon [2009] notwithstanding). Since the first part of this study is devoted to elaborating the relevance of Bourdieu's concepts for sociologists of the body, while the second and third part will aim to provide a *practical* demonstration of this relevance, I will not elaborate too much on it here. As the opening quote to this introduction suggests, this book will aim to show that only by 'tak[ing] into account certain of the universal characteristics of bodily existence' (Bourdieu, 1990a: 196) is it possible to fully grasp the logic of contemporary class-dynamics. In addition, it will try to demonstrate that Bourdieu's oeuvre allows us to tackle (and potentially overcome) some of the cardinal oppositions that divide the field of "body-studies", a field that, despite being one of the youngest of sociology's many sub-disciplinary provinces, shows no lack of internal division.

Beyond the 'topical body'

In fact, contrary to what the opening paragraphs might suggest, the obstacles to a properly *sociological* understanding of the body are not located exclusively (or even primarily) on the side of sociology's reception. Sociologists have in fact been quite good at throwing up their own obstacles to such an understanding. One of the most formidable of these obstacles is undoubtedly the wide gap that separates *theoretical* reflections on the body's role in the production and reproduction of social life, from actual *empirical* research on the numerous 'thoroughfares between body and society' (Freund, 1988). On the one hand, the field of 'body studies' abounds with efforts to craft a unified theoretical programme for sociological studies of the body. Such efforts have given rise to a wide variety of analytical typologies and conceptual schematics that are often so diverse in their scope and intent (let alone their proper definition of the body), that they can only be somewhat grudgingly subsumed under the heading of 'sociology of the body'.[3] While these various attempts at 'theorizing' the body have undoubtedly contributed to securing its place on the sociological topic-list, fact remains that they all too often remain perched on the lofty heights of theoretical speculation and rarely descend to the humbler plains of empirical analysis. In fact, most often they take the form of purely scholastic synthesis of the writings of a diverse body of canonical authors which results in conceptual contraptions that are neither designed *for*, nor particularly compatible *with* the exigencies of empirical research. More importantly, the various attempts at *theoretical* synthesis clash with the fragmented manner in which the body is made into an actual object of *empirical* research. In fact, the study of the different ways in which social agents relate to their bodies remains balkanized across a host of disciplinary specializations, including the sociology of health, the sociology of food, the sociology of sports, the sociology of the family or gender-studies. While such an advanced division of labour might have led to progress in each of these particular domains, it has also given rise to a somewhat prismatic understanding of the reality of embodiment, what Csordas (1994: 5) has dubbed the view of the 'topical body'. In fact, by isolating particular modalities of embodiment (the hungry body, the body in pain, the ageing body, the body at play, etc.), such specialization has pushed the question of the *interrelationships* between these dimensions and, above all, the degree to which they constitute a relatively coherent *system* of bodily practices and beliefs to the margins of sociological interest. More specifically, by carving up the body into a series of distinct topics or domains, such sub-disciplinary divisions tend to skirt the question of the *homologies* between the different ways in which social agents relate to their bodies – as manifested in such (seemingly) disparate domains as fertility-strategies, food choices, sexual practices, medical beliefs, clothing-styles or sports-preferences – and especially of the way in which these are, in turn, intelligibly related to positions in social space.

To show that different class-positions engender quite systematic orientations towards the body, meant first of all to break with the conventional positivistic wisdom which equates scientific rigor and analytical precision with the study of a single, clearly delineated research-topic ("*Sports preferences among young, working-class men*"; "*Eating habits of unemployed single women*"; etc.). Instead, this study has chosen to pursue the question of the social logic of embodiment across three different fields of practice, namely bodily care (with a particular focus on dieting and weight-concern), food-habits and sports practices. This relational approach hinges on a double conviction. First, that only by systematically observing, analyzing and comparing different *types* of bodily practices and beliefs does it become possible to adequately reconstruct the type of "unwritten grammar" that governs the manner in which different social groups or classes relate to their body. In fact, the "rules" that structure this relationship are, as Boltanski (1971: 217) has already argued (and as Chapter 2 will develop more clearly), rarely ever constituted as such, that is to say, as an explicit normative "code" of regulations, prescriptions and prohibitions. Instead, they are more akin to the principles that govern the social uses of language (and the mother tongue in particular) which are largely mastered in a pre-reflexive, implicit manner and do not require the explicit knowledge of grammar and syntax to produce meaningful and structured utterances in a wide variety of situations. From this it follows, that the only way to systematically uncover these "rules" is to study the concrete practices and beliefs *in* and *through* which they are expressed and to do so in a plurality of different contexts.

A second reason for adopting this comparative perspective is that, contrary to the abovementioned methodological precept, such an approach actually allows for a more controlled and hence rigorous analysis of the object of study. In fact, by studying the relationship to the body as it is manifested *across* different fields of practice, the analysis is effectively forced into a 'methodic circle' (Bourdieu *et al.*, 1991: 65) in which each new observation in a *particular* domain – the judgment of a particular dish, the choice of "ideal body", the preference for a specific sport, etc. – automatically triggered a re-evaluation of the significance attributed to the entire *system* of practices and representation, which in turn led to a re-interpretation of the meaning previously assigned to the practices/beliefs in all the *other* domains. Instead of therefore simply piling a sociology of food onto a sociology of sports and a sociology of bodily care, the analysis questioned these three domains for the homologies (and dissimilarities) they contained and hence for the insights into the *overall* relationship to the body that they could provide. What this approach has inevitably lost in depth and detail, it will have hopefully gained in an understanding of structure and systematicity.

Questions of method

Needless to say, such lofty theoretical aspirations are bound to clash with the reality of existing research on the topic. Given the specialized nature of empirical (and especially 'quantitative') studies on the body, the different ways in which social agents relate to their bodies are rarely the object of one single survey. This meant that the analysis was forced to cull its material from a wide range of existing sources, including health-surveys, household budget-surveys, value studies and lifestyle-surveys. Overall, the results presented in this study draw on data from seven different studies, a full overview of which can be found in the methodological appendices (Appendix 1). Constructing indicators on bodily practices and beliefs from such a diverse corpus of material – originally produced to satisfy divergent theoretical and practical needs – inevitably raises issues of comparability and compatibility. Since each study usually contained information on only one aspect of the relationship to the body (weight-satisfaction, food choices, medical opinions, etc.), it often proved difficult to *directly* compare the relative explanatory weight of different indicators of social position (occupation, level of education, income, etc.) *across* different domains. In addition, the range and type of these indicators often varied considerably from one survey to the next. This proved to be particularly true of occupational taxonomies which were often the only means of locating individual agents in the class-structure. The surveys that were used in fact wielded a variety of occupational schemes, which were not only animated (knowingly or not) by different views of class-status, but also proved at odds with the particular *relational* conception of social structure as a 'field' or 'space', which is at the core of this study (see Chapter 1). In practice, this often meant that specific subgroups or 'class-fractions' could not be isolated for analysis, especially when the survey in question used a 'closed' coding scheme. However, for those surveys that *did* allow for a more a finely graded classification – i.e. those that provided information on individual occupations *and* had a sample-size that was large enough to construct specific categories, while maintaining a sufficient level of statistical aggregation – the analysis devised its own classificatory scheme to facilitate comparisons across surveys (for the particular theoretical rationale behind this classification, as well as a rudimentary conversion-scheme linking it to the other occupational taxonomies, see Appendix 2). To further ensure a certain degree of uniformity between the different sources, the selected studies were deliberately limited in both time and space. All of the surveys that were used for the statistical analysis were conducted between 2003 and 2010 on representative samples of adult members (i.e. 18 years old or older) of the Belgian (or Flemish) population.

While such *technical* obstacles proved important, they were by no means insurmountable and, more importantly, were often secondary to the infinitely more subtle, but often more fundamental ways in which the use of *existing* data shaped the construction of the research object. In fact, when drawing on surveys that were originally produced in relationship to a quite *different* theoretical problematic, the analyst needs to be especially vigilant to avoid inadvertently importing the particular (and often partial) constructions of the object that animated such studies in the first place. This is not just the case for the abovementioned indicators of social position, but also applies to the particular ways in which indicators of bodily practices and beliefs were *themselves* constructed. For instance, many questionnaires often defined particular practices – e.g. "*going to the gym*" or "*visiting a restaurant*" – in a manner that effectively obscured the *secondary* social differences linked to the specific *type* or *modality* of practice, such as "*body-building*" vs. "*fitness*" or "*Italian food*" vs. "*French cuisine*". Since different social groups confer different, even opposite meanings to the nominally identical categories provided by the questionnaire (a problem that will discussed more fully in Chapters 5 and 6), the polysemic character of such broadly defined categories inevitably has the effect of artificially attenuating class-differences in these particular domains.

Such methodological reflexivity became even more imperative when dealing with surveys whose primary goal was not that of generating a better *theoretical* understanding of certain practices and beliefs, but above all to provide *practical* instruments for monitoring, managing and, if possible, modifying such practices and beliefs. A good example are public health-surveys (see Boltanski, 1969: 57ff.). Deliberately crafted to gauge the diffusion – throughout a given population – of those techniques, practices and forms of know-how that medical science recognizes as legitimate – and *only* those – one of the main goals of such surveys is to separate the "normal" from the "pathological" and hence to identify those fractions of the population whose behaviour is in need of "intervention". However, because they are primarily interested in the social distribution of *officially* recognized ways of treating the body – tacitly inscribed in the questionnaire as the norm – their logic often emulates that of the scholastic exam with its "good" and its "bad" answers and, consequently, its good and its bad pupils. Especially when read through a medical lens, the relationship to the body of those whose answers most often deviate from this norm (i.e. those situated at the bottom of the class-structure) are grasped almost exclusively in *negative* terms, namely as being characterized by an intrinsic "absence" or "lack" (of knowledge, exercise, nutrition, etc.). It is hence very easy to slip from the observation that members of the working-class often do not adhere to the principles and guidelines established by medical science to the conclusion that their manner of perceiving and treating the body does not adhere to *any* principles at all. In this manner, through their very mode of questioning health-surveys tacitly help to perpetuate the popular fiction of the working-class body as inherently undisciplined and uncultivated (an issue discussed at length in Chapter 9).

Even if the analysis tried as much as possible to avoid the obstacles that inevitably arise from working with existing surveys – which often implied a quite laborious process of statistical recoding – any secondary reading of the available statistics is ultimately confronted with the impossibility of mining existing data for answers to questions they were never meant to address in the first place. That is why, in addition to the available surveys, the analyses presented here also draw on the results of a smaller study (891 respondents), conducted in

2009–2010, that was specifically designed to tackle the key questions that this book will set out to answer (see Appendix 1). While this study is by no means based on a representative sample of the population, the participants in this survey did vary enough in terms of social position and trajectory to provide some tentative insights into the embodiment of social class.

The structure of the book

Finally, a word on the structure of the book. I have chosen *not* to introduce this study with an encyclopedic review of the different theoretical perspectives (phenomenological, post-structuralist, Foucauldian, etc.) that define the contemporary field of 'body studies'. The reason for this is twofold. First, because the sociological literature already abounds with volumes devoted to the body's position within the conceptual architecture of the discipline's most consecrated authors (some good examples are Turner, 1996; Crossley, 2001; Shilling, 2003 and more recently Cregan, 2006). To further add to these various compendia on the body lies well beyond my ability and ambition. Secondly, because the text tries, as much as possible, to retain the unity of theoretical argument and empirical analysis. So while I will engage with other theoretical perspectives throughout the following chapters, I have chosen to do so within the context of the specific problems raised by the analysis, whether it be the construction of a particular variable or the discussion of a particular (statistical) relationship. This is also reflected in the structure of the text. Rather than presenting "Theory" and "Data" in separate chapters or sections, I have aimed to integrate them as much as possible. The central line of argumentation is presented in the main body of the text, while the indented sections (in smaller print) provide the specific analyses on which this argumentation is based.

The first part of this study (Part I: Social Order, Body Order) outlines the key concepts and central theoretical principles that inform the analyses presented in the second part. The theoretical core of this study is comprised of a triple analytical stance, which can be summarized as: (1) a *relational* conception of social structure, (2) an *embodied* or *dispositional* understanding of social cognition and (3) a focus on the inherently *temporal* dimension of the relationship to the body. The first three chapters are each devoted to elaborating one of these principles. Chapter 1 outlines the conception of social structure that will animate this study, a view that is condensed in the concept of 'social space'. Chapter 2 focuses on the various ways in which the body is 'in-corporated' into this social space, highlighting its role as both the generative principles *behind* routine acts of 'class-ification' as well as the materialization *of* the logic inscribed in particular class-conditions. Chapter 3 hinges on the simple proposition that the relationship to the body is inextricably tied to that other fundamental dimension of social existence, namely the relationship to *time* and that a sociology of the body is also, necessarily, a sociology of temporal dispositions.

Together, these three chapters lay the groundwork for the analyses presented in the second part (Part II: Modes of Embodiment), which tackles the three abovementioned topics, namely body-weight and body-image, the relationship to food- and sporting-preferences. Each of these three topics was chosen, because they highlight distinct aspects of the way in which class-differences shape how social agents come to perceive, use and care for their bodies. Chapter 4 focuses on the role of class in shaping both the production and perception of the *physicality* of the body (its size, shape and appearance) and will demonstrate that class-divisions are, in a quite literal sense, "inscribed" in the body. Chapter 5 shifts the attention from the body's 'exterior' to its 'interior', focusing on its tastes and appetites, its revulsions and disgusts by analyzing how class-differences shape our relationship to food and drink. Finally, Chapter 6 uses the case of sporting-practices to show how the more playful uses of the body provide key insights into the unwritten principles that govern the way the body is used and perceived by different social classes.

If the second part of the book in a sense 'de-composes' the relationship to the body into three of its key-aspects, the third part aims to 're-compose' this relationship by showing how it functions as a fairly coherent *system* of bodily practices and beliefs. Drawing on the analyses presented in the second part, Chapters 7 to 9 then present a series of 'composite images' which correspond to the three main classes – i.e. dominant, middle and working-class – that are identified in the study.[4] While undeniably ideal-types, each of these chapters nevertheless aims to condense the most distinctive features and to outline the organizing principles of the relationship to the body that characterizes these three regions of social space and show how these principles can only be understood in relationship to one another. The central argument that will be developed throughout is that our bodies not only come to bear the markers of their position *in* and trajectory *through* social space – embodying, quite literally, the divisions and oppositions that define this space in their postures, gestures and features – but in turn contribute to naturalizing these divisions by transforming them into the product of an individual and immutable nature. The ultimate goal then is twofold: to both contribute to a sociology of the body that is more attuned to the everyday realities of class, as well as to develop a more *embodied* understanding of the formation and operation of class-identities. In which of the two, if any, I have succeeded best, will be up for the reader to decide.

Notes

1. A quick note on the use of quotation marks. Single quotations are reserved for citations from other authors or used to denote *scientific* concepts (e.g. 'habitus', 'physical capital', etc.). Double quotations are used to refer to the everyday, normative uses of terms (e.g. "vulgar", "refined", etc.) and for research statements / propositions (e.g. "I like familiar food the best").
2. While Mauss' essay is rightfully considered to be a pioneering text, in reality, it was another member of the "Ecole Française", namely Maurice Halbwachs, who more than two decades earlier had already addressed the question of the relationship between social norms and physical embodiment in his doctoral thesis *La Théorie de l'Homme Moyen: Essai sûr Quetelet* (1912).

3 Considerable controversy is already generated, as Synnott (1993) ironically observed, by the correct *number* of bodies that should be analytically distinguished. So whereas Douglas (1996a [1970]) suggests we look at the interrelationships between the 'two bodies', namely the individual and the social body, Scheper-Hughes and Lock (1987) argue we need to take into account at least *three* bodies (the individual body, the social body *and* the body politic), while Turner (1996) wields a typology distinguishing four distinct 'body problems' (reproduction, regulation, restraint and representation) and O'Neill (2004) even ups the ante to five bodies.
4 It should be noted that this tripartite division (working/middle/upper) mainly serves as a presentational device and that the actual model of class-structure that informs this study – as discussed in Chapter 1 and Appendix 2 – is considerably more complex.

Part I
Social order, body order

1   The body in social space

> Is the skin the wall enclosing the true self? Is it the skull or the rib-cage? Where and what is the barrier which separates the human inner self from everything outside, where and what the substance it contains? It is difficult to say, for inside the skull we find only the brain, inside the rib-cage only the heart and vitals. Is this really the core of individuality, the real self, with an existence apart from the world outside and thus apart from 'society' too?
>
> (Elias, 1978: 24)

When it comes to studying the social world, there are few things that presents themselves with a more spontaneous sense of singularity than the human body. Self-contained, isolated, distinguished by a visible and tangible boundary that separates the "Individual", the "Subjective" and the "Personal" from its "Environment", "Society" and "Others", the body provides the natural template for any type of autonomous, self-regulating system. This is not only true for the natural and the life sciences, but equally applies to the social sciences where, from Hobbes' 'Leviathan' to Luhmann's 'systems theory', the body has served as 'the prototypical entity of modern social thought' (Abbott, 1995: 860). An entity that, furthermore, constitutes the sole mode through which social agents present themselves as "individuals", occupying a discrete and singular position in time and space and endowed with physical, visible features that define each and every one of them as indisputably "unique". This spontaneous perception of the individual (body) as a self-sufficient unit harbouring a singular and irreducible essence, the 'homo clausus' as described by Norbert Elias' (1978) in the opening quote, is further reinforced by a host of social conventions that not only ratify (often legally), but *sanctify* this singularity and effectively transform the body into a Durkheimian 'sacred object'. Conventions which dictate, for instance, that one can only offer one's body to others, partly or wholly, within social relationships that have been purged of economic or other "profane" interests, as when one "donates" (never "sells") one's blood or organs in a purely altruistic gesture or gives one's body to another in a sexual act that is deemed to be the ultimate expression of love and commitment (and hence fully opposed to the fleeting, interchangeable exchanges of the "market"). Conventions which also clearly define the legitimate manner and circumstances in which the body's

16 *Social order, body order*

sacred boundary can be transgressed, as shown by the highly revealing example of the gynaecological exam, so skilfully dissected by Henslin and Biggs (2007 [1993]), in which male physicians' contact to female sexual organs is subjected to a highly ritualized act of 'depersonification and repersonification' which, in order to safeguard the sacred character of female sexuality, transforms female patients from subjects (*patient-as-person*) into objects (*patient-as-pelvis*) back into subjects.

'Analysis situs'

This self-evidence of the isolated body is in fact one of the most powerful obstacles to sociological objectification. First, because it provides the seemingly most solid basis for the *personalist* belief in the irreducible uniqueness of each individual. In fact, those who tend to equate sociology with the sinister quest for "iron laws" and immutable "determinisms" and are hence quick to denounce its truths as affronts to human dignity and freedom, only have to invoke the blatantly obvious fact of the morphological singularity of each individual (body) to demonstrate the futility of any attempts at classification or generalization. Secondly, it forms the foundation of a *realist* or *substantialist* vision of social reality, which only tends to consider as real or relevant that which it can see or touch. The *relational* vision of social reality, which always runs up against the fact that this reality tends to present itself in a "thing-like" fashion – in the form of discrete individuals, groups, classes, institutions, etc. – is therefore perhaps nowhere as difficult to apply as when it comes to the sociology of the body. This relational vision in fact hinges on the counterintuitive proposition, that in order to adequately grasp the social logic that shapes bodies in their apparently most singular and spontaneous of features, one needs to move beyond their (all too) visible and tangible reality to construct the system or network of relationships – the 'figuration' in Elias' terms – *in* and *through* which they are formed and *from* which they derive their most distinctive and distinguished properties.

It is in fact Norbert Elias who can be credited for being one of the first to not only demonstrate the full *sociological* significance of such apparently trivial or vulgar uses of the body as eating with a fork or blowing one's nose, but for doing so within a properly *relational* conception of social structure and historical process (and this, one should add, long before either 'embodiment' or 'relationality' became particularly glossy terms in the sociological lexicon). His seminal *The Civilizing Process* (2000 [1939]) does not only provide a comprehensive genealogy of changes in Western attitudes towards the body and bodily processes – like eating, drinking, spitting, urinating or defecating – tracing their evolution from relatively unproblematic aspects of everyday life to areas of existence that became increasingly subjected to social taboos, but it explicitly ties such changes to more encompassing transformations in the social fabric of Western societies. Crucially, he located the dynamics of such change not in the mechanical determinations of the "environment" (be it in the form of an economic "infrastructure" or a cultural "Zeitgeist"), nor in the atomized actions of individual agents. Instead, he situated them in the changing pattern of relationships or 'figurations' in which these agents or groups of agents find themselves enmeshed. As Elias himself puts it: 'The "circumstances" which change are not something which comes upon men from "outside": they are the relationships between people themselves' (2000: 402).

With the aid a formidable synthesis of a Weberian perspective on state-formation, a Durkheimian take on the division of labour and Freud's work on the structure of the psyche, Elias retraces the long-term process whereby an agglomeration of small, self-contained 'survival units' (Elias, 2000) developed into the complex web of interdependencies that characterize modern societies. These interdependencies not only locked more and more social groups together in chains of mutual dependence – themselves defined by shifting balances of power – but also served as the conduits which facilitated the 'impregnation of broader strata by behavioural forms and drive-controls originating in court-society' (Elias, 2000: 427). Propelled by the incessant dynamic of distinction and pretension, forms of bodily control and self-censorship that were originally developed within the tight-knit figuration of the courtly aristocracy gradually spread, first to an ascending bourgeoisie eager to adopt these forms of 'civilized' conduct and from there to ever-wider branches of Western social figurations. While Elias' work hence provides valuable insights for sociologists of the body, the biggest strength of his approach – i.e. its focus on the *historicity* of the body as the product of *long-term* social developments – might also be its greatest drawback. In fact, the keen sense for the often subtle social differences in comportment and etiquette that informs his historical analyses – like his skilful dissection of the mannerisms and power-dynamics at the court of Louis XIV (Elias, 1983) – often stands in shrill contrast to the rather offhand manner in which he brushes over *contemporary* social differences in bodily self-control. While he is by no means oblivious to such differences, the focus on the long-term perspective often leads him to downplay their significance.[1] When read through the lens of the past, contemporary contrasts in "civilized" behaviour will undeniably appear as less sharp and extreme as those of previous generations:

> Seen at close quarters, where only a small segment of [the civilizing process] is visible, the differences in social personality-structure between the upper and lower classes in the Western world today may still seem considerable. But if the whole sweep of the movement over centuries is perceived, one can see that the sharp contrasts between the behaviour of different social groups – like the contrasts and sudden switches within the behaviour of individuals – are steadily diminishing.
>
> (Elias, 2000: 383)

Elsewhere he writes:

> The pattern of self-constraints, the template by which drives are moulded, certainly varies widely according to the function and position of the individual

within this network, and there are even today in different sectors of the Western world variations of intensity and stability in the apparatus of self-constraint that seem *at face value* very large.

(Elias, 2000: 369, *my emphasis*)

However, he then rushes to add:

But when compared to the psychological make-up of people in less complex societies, these differences and degrees within more complex societies become less significant, and the main line of transformation, which is the primary concern of this study, emerges very clearly.

(Elias, 2000: 369)

Elias is in fact quite insistent that the gradual diminishing of class-contrasts in civilized comportment is not a matter of analytical perspective alone. In fact, he takes it to be 'one of the most important peculiarities of the "civilizing process"' (2000: 383) that the dynamic of functional differentiation, which ties dominant and dominated groups into ever-tighter webs of interdependence, produces a gradual attenuation of differences in their comportment. If dominated groups aim to emulate and adopt elements of the lifestyle of dominant groups, it is equally true that the latter increasingly assimilate forms of behaviour of those who occupy dominated positions within the figuration. Hence, inasmuch as contemporary 'differences and gradations in the conduct of lower, middle- and upper-classes' are still considered important, Elias relegates them to a 'set of problems of their own' (*ein Problemkreis für sich*) which he leaves it to others to tackle.[2] However, as indicated in the introduction, it is precisely these 'differences and gradations' that form the subject of our particular inquiry. What we therefore need is an analytical perspective that shares Elias' insistence on the primacy of *relationships* in the study of social phenomena, but is at the same time more attuned to the role of *contemporary* class-divisions in shaping the everyday uses of the body. In this chapter, I will aim to show that such an approach can be found in the work of an author who developed a sociological perspective that is highly similar to that of Elias and is in some ways indebted to it, namely Pierre Bourdieu.

An 'order of coexistence'

The 'subterranean affinities' (Paulle *et al.*, 2012) between the sociologies of Elias and Bourdieu are manifold and in themselves worthy of more attention than they have thus far received. At the most general level, their work has produced a number of conceptual tools (habitus, field, figuration) that deliberately aim to transcend some of the cardinal oppositions that continue to haunt modern social thought (individual/society, micro/macro, mind/body, conflict/consensus, structure/agency, etc.). The expression 'tools' is moreover not chosen lightly, since their concepts did not arise out of a purely theoretical synthesis of a selective body of canonical authors (in the vein of Parsons' 'structural functionalism' or Giddens' 'structuration theory') but were crafted *in* and *for* the confrontation with a particularly broad array of empirical objects. More substantially, their respective brands of sociology are animated by a highly similar social ontology. Like Elias, Bourdieu treats social agents as fundamentally characterized by a 'double historicity'. According to this view, each individual agent is at once the product of a collective history (*fylogenesis* or *sociogenesis*), defined as the totality of manners of seeing, acting, feeling, etc. that have emerged from the historical struggles of past generations, which is in turn acquired, either partly or wholly, within the particular course of an individual, social trajectory (*ontogenesis* or *psychogenesis*). It is this doubly historical conception of the social agent that also informs their mutual interest in the relationship between social and mental structures, that is, in the homologies between the structural organization of social systems and the cognitive schemata of those who constitute such systems. This is no doubt one of the main reasons for their mutual appropriation of the concept of 'habitus', even though Elias tends to develop the notion more strongly along the lines of an historicized psychoanalysis of affective regulation and libidinal sublimation, while Bourdieu tends to continue in the Durkheimian tradition and its interest in the problem of 'primitive classifications'. Finally, and more relevant for the case at hand, Bourdieu's sociology is similarly rooted in a thoroughly *relational* vision of social reality.[3] In fact, he proposes to treat sociology as a 'social topology' (Bourdieu, 1985: 723; Bourdieu, 1989: 16; Bourdieu, 1996). This topological perspective is rooted in the methodological principle that the analyst, before plunging head over heels into the particularities of a specific object, should first attempt to construct (within the limits of the available data) the system of relationships *in* which this object is entangled and *from* which it derives its particular characteristics. These relationships are themselves irreducible to the fleeting conjunctures of face-to-face interaction, but instead take the form of *objective* power-relationships (of the type professor/student, employer/employee, man/woman, etc.) which 'possess a reality existing outside individuals who, at every moment, conform to them' (Durkheim, 2013: 44) and hence effectively structure and constrain the manner in which their concrete interactions unfold.

As such, they form a particular configuration of social positions that are linked to another 'through relations of proximity, vicinity or distance, as well as through order relations, such as above, below and between' (Bourdieu, 1996: 11). Together, this system of relative positions constitutes what Bourdieu coins a 'field' which, when referring to the social order in its entirety, he specifies as the 'field of social classes' or more generally as 'social space' (Bourdieu, 1984: 228). The principal forces that structure this space and determine the relative position of agents or groups of agents within it are the different types of social power or 'capital'. Taking his cues from Weber's (1978 [1921]: 302ff. and 926ff.) multidimensional view of social status, as expressed in his conceptual trinity of 'Klasse', 'Stand' and 'Partei', Bourdieu distinguishes between three basic forms of social power, namely *economic, cultural* (or *informational*) and *social* capital. To these three basic forms, which are themselves further differentiated according to the particular type of field (scientific, literary,...), Bourdieu adds a fourth type, namely *symbolic* capital, which is the particular form that each type of capital takes when it is perceived and recognized as "legitimate" and as such ceases to exist as "capital", namely as accumulated *social* labour, but instead comes to function as a sign of innate, natural quality such as "class", "success", "intelligence", "talent" or "charm".

Using these different forms of capital, it becomes possible to situate agents within a multi-dimensional space (see Figure 1.1). The first, and most important dimension of this space discriminates between social agents on the basis of their overall 'capital-volume' or the totality of resources that determine their relative degree of power *in* and *over* the space. On the basis of such differences in total volume, Bourdieu distinguishes between three 'major classes of conditions of existence' (1984: 114). Those who are situated at the top of the space, the *dominant class* (or the 'field of power'), are most well-endowed with the different types of profitable resources and are as such furthest removed – objectively *and* subjectively – from those who occupy positions at the bottom of the space, the *working* or *popular classes*, who tend to be most deprived in this respect. Between these two extremes, Bourdieu situates an intermediate social category, the middle-class or *petit-bourgeoisie*, who derive a considerable number of their characteristics precisely from this "halfway" position in social space. In fact, their practices and representations find a dual point-of-reference

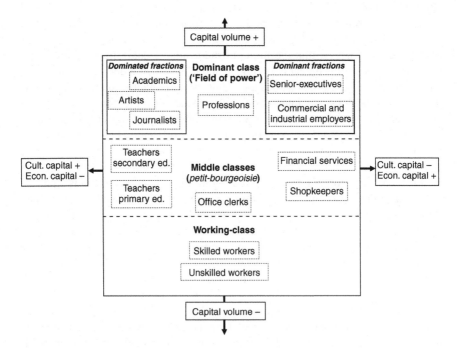

Figure 1.1 Diagram of social space.

The body in social space   21

in the lifestyle of the working-classes, *against* which their own lifestyle is defined and *from* whom they try to distinguish themselves, and in the dominant lifestyle *towards* which they tend to aspire. This division of the social hierarchy in a "high-middle-low" is in itself not particularly original and can be found, in form or another, in most conventional taxonomies of "socioeconomic status". Bourdieu's particular contribution lies in the fact that he identifies a *second* classificatory principle that he deems crucial to adequately grasping contemporary differences in social practice and lifestyle:

> The differences stemming from the total volume of capital almost always conceal, both from common awareness and also from 'scientific' knowledge, the *secondary differences* which, within each of the classes defined by overall volume of capital, separate *class fractions*, defined by different asset structures, i.e., *different distributions of their total capital among the different types of capital*.
>
> (Bourdieu, 1984: 114, *my emphasis*)

These differences in capital-*composition* help to position agents along a second dimension according to the particular *type* of capital that dominates in their complete structure of assets. More specifically, it opposes groups of agents or *class-fractions* on the basis of the relative weight of *economic* vs. *cultural* capital within this structure.[4] According to Bourdieu, this opposition reflects the fundamental structure of the French dominant class which, far from forming a unified, homogenous group (often implied in terms like "elite" or "upper class") is itself organized as a fairly autonomous space or field. This 'field of power' (Bourdieu and Wacquant, 1992: 229) opposes fractions that are strongly engaged in fields of *cultural* production (artists, writers, academics, etc.) and are therefore richest cultural capital (while being, relatively speaking, least endowed with economic capital) to those who are positioned within the economic field (senior-executives, commercial employers, industrialists, etc.) and hence have an inverse capital-structure, where economic capital dominates vis-à-vis cultural capital. Situated between these *dominated* and *dominant* fractions of the dominant class is a group that has a fairly "symmetrical" capital-structure which combines high volumes of cultural capital with high incomes and which Bourdieu identifies with the members of the professions. This same opposition is also found at the level of the middle-class or *petit-bourgeoisie*, where it similarly opposes fractions that are *culturally* dominant (teachers in primary and secondary education, for instance) from those who are most well-endowed with *economic* capital (shop- and small business-owners or, more recently, the providers of financial services such as those working in insurance or real-estate). Together, these two dimensions define the fundamental structure of the social world as 'the set of constraints, inscribed in the very reality of that world, which govern its functioning in a durable way, determining the chances for success of practices' (Bourdieu, 1986: 242). A world which is, moreover, far from static, but allows for change and displacement. Bourdieu conceptualizes this as the *transformations* in the capital-volume and/or

– structure of individual agents or groups of agents. These changes constitute the third dimension of the social space and take the form of individual or collective *movements* throughout this space. Movements which are analogous to displacements in physical space in that they 'are paid for in work, in efforts and above all in time' (Bourdieu, 1985: 725), the time that is necessary to either increase the overall volume of one's capital-structure (i.e. *vertical* movements, as when the daughter of a primary school teacher becomes a university lecturer), to alter the composition of this structure by converting economic into cultural capital and vice versa (i.e. *horizontal* movements, as when the son of a high school teacher starts his own business) or to change both the volume *and* composition of this structure (i.e. *diagonal* movements, as when the daughter of a primary school teacher becomes a senior-executive in a large private firm).

Probable class, actual class

The space thus outlined constitutes the totality of actual and potential positions – an 'order of coexistence' (*Ordnung des Nebeneinanderbestehens*) in Leibniz's phrase (2006 [1715]) – that social agents can occupy, either synchronically or diachronically. A "coexistence" that tends, furthermore, to be far from peaceful, but is itself the basis for the different and antagonistic perspectives that oppose social agents or groups of agents. Again, there are analogies to physical space in that one's "location" (*position*) *in* the space is at the basis of one's "point-of-view" (*prise-de-position*) *on* the space, which will present itself in a similar manner to those who occupy neighbouring positions, while taking on a different, even opposing form for those who are located at opposite ends of the space. In this manner, those who occupy similar positions in the space constructed on the basis of capital-volume and -structure are exposed to similar conditions and similar condition*ing* experiences and hence, through the mediating role of the 'class habitus' (see Chapter 2), tend to have a high probability of sharing similar properties, attributes and qualities. The closer agents are therefore located in this space, the more "properties" – *including*, as the analyses to follow will aim to show, their visible, physical features – they will share, while the further they are apart, the more they will differ on a wide range of social practices and representations. More importantly for the topic at hand, these differences in social position are not only at the basis of the different "points-of-view" on the social world and those within it, but also structure agents' relationships to the other fundamental dimensions of social existence, namely to the *body* and to *time* (something which will be discussed in more detail in Chapters 2 and 3, respectively).

Using this principle of relative social distance, it becomes possible to demarcate "regions" within the overall space which group neighbouring social positions, and hence agents endowed with similar properties, into a distinct "class". The smaller the region that is outlined, the more homogenous the class in question will be. Moreover, the meaning of "class" within this perspective (which is also the one that will be used throughout this study) is that of a *logical* or *theoretical* class that as such only exists "on paper", constructed by the analyst on the basis of a limited number of classificatory principles and within the limits of the data available, which 'insofar as it is the product of an explanatory classification, entirely similar to those of zoologists or botanists, makes it possible to *explain* and predict the practices and properties of the things classified' (Bourdieu, 1985: 725, *original emphasis*). In fact, the theoretically constructed nature of these classes by no means implies that the individuals they group are lumped together in a purely arbitrary fashion. However, while Bourdieu insists on the reality and objectivity of the affinities and solidarities that are engendered by a shared location in social space, he also stresses that such affinities are rooted in a largely *practical* understanding of social identity or difference. While this practical 'sense of one's place' (Bourdieu, 1989) enables social agents to intuitively recognize "one of their own" and distinguish between what is and what is not "for them" (see Chapter 2), it by no means implies the explicit and mutual recognition of a shared identity as members of a clearly-defined "group". It is in this point that Bourdieu most clearly parts ways with the Marxist conception of class, which he not only criticizes for its tendency towards "economism", but also for falling into the double trap of theoreticism and substantialism. The latter consists precisely in treating the "paper classes" drawn up by the analyst (the 'class-*in*-itself') *as if* they were real groups endowed with a full consciousness of their own boundaries, interests and goals (the 'class-for-itself'). A consciousness, which is itself either treated as the purely mechanical product of objective, external conditions (the proletarization of the middle-classes) or, inversely, as the result of a wholly voluntaristic "waking of consciousness" conceived as a mental or intellectual emancipation. In this particular respect, Bourdieu's own conception of class seems much closer to that of Weber, who not only warned that 'to treat "class" conceptually as being equivalent to "group" leads to distortion' (1978: 930), but also argued that the 'emergence of an association or even of mere social action from a common class situation is by no means a universal phenomenon' (ibid.: 929). Even if the lasting experience of similar social condition(ing)s tends to produce a practical orchestration of ways of acting towards the social world – the 'generation of essentially *similar* reactions' or of an 'amorphous social action' as Weber put it (ibid.) – which is in itself an objective *potential* for collective mobilization, this still does not warrant the analyst to treat the theoretically constructed class as anything more than a virtual or a 'probable class' (Bourdieu, 1985: 725). In fact, to ignore the distinction between the *probable* and the *real* class is not only to overlook the specific role of the symbolic labour of political 'representation' – which helps to create the group or class by endowing it with spokespersons, manifestos, banners, insignia, etc. – but also (and more importantly) to ignore the difference between the *practical*, embodied knowledge of social structure that each agent acquires in the course of his or her own trajectory through social space and the *theoretical* understanding of social classes and class-relationships acquired by the sociologist on the basis of those characteristics, and only those, which he or she deems relevant from the point-of-view of the analysis.

Distinct distinctions

If I have presented a somewhat scholastic exposition on the concept of 'social space', this is not only because it will play such a crucial role in informing the analyses to follow, but also because discussions of this concept often prove remarkably absent from commentaries on Bourdieu's oeuvre, both critical *and* sympathetic. This seems especially true of the manner in which his writings have reached the shores of Anglophone social science, where they have often been (and still *are*) subjected to a particularly selective and piecemeal appropriation (see Wacquant, 1993; Sallaz and Zavisca, 2007). The importation of his ideas into different national contexts has often centred on particular ideas ('social reproduction'), individual concepts ('cultural capital'), if not single texts (*Distinction*) which have often been somewhat artificially wrenched from the broader conceptual architecture in which they were meant to function. His views on social structure and social class – as condensed into such concepts as the 'field of power', the 'field of social classes' or 'social space' – prove to be a particular case in point. While these concepts were deliberately crafted to break with static conceptions of classes and class-cultures by treating them as dynamic arenas of contention in which opposing class-*fractions*, endowed with different types of capital, vie over the very definition of the class itself and (hence) over its boundaries, subsequent interpretations have often presented a considerably stripped-down version of this model. In fact, it is not uncommon to find Bourdieu's spatial conception of social structure reduced to the very one-dimensional schemes of social and symbolic stratification – compressed in such binary alternatives as "elite vs. popular", "highbrow vs. lowbrow" or "dominant vs. dominated" – it was specifically designed to overcome (on this point also see Bennett *et al.*, 2009: 11ff.).

A good example is Michele Lamont's (1992) comparative study of the culture and ethics of the French and American upper-middle-classes. While claiming some sympathy for Bourdieu's views, she nevertheless makes little mention of the internal divisions that structure the upper-middle and upper-classes. In fact, she even explicitly rejects Bourdieu's notion of 'power field' [*sic*] on the grounds that it 'requires defining the limits of groups which is most often an arbitrary decision because few groups have absolute natural boundaries' (1992: 276, n. 49), a somewhat curious observation, since it is precisely one of the functions of the concept of 'social space' to highlight both the *constructed* and *contended* nature of class-boundaries. Ironically enough, her own analyses suggest 'that the boundary-drawing activities of the members of the upper-middle-class varies with the degree to which their occupation is instrumental to, and dependent on, profit-making' (Lamont, 1992: 152) with those who are engaged in sectors of cultural production and transmission (artists, teachers, scientists, etc.) 'placing more value on cultural or moral standards of evaluation' (ibid.), while those who are employed in the private, for-profit sectors (accountants, bankers, senior-executives) are 'more likely to value socioeconomic standards of evaluation' (ibid.), an observation that seems perfectly compatible with the concept of social space. Critical engagements with Bourdieu's multi-dimensional conception of social structure are also remarkably absent from the numerous studies that have cropped up around the concept of the 'cultural omnivore' as originally coined by Richard Peterson (see Peterson and Simkus, 1992). While quick to criticize Bourdieu's views on (dominant) tastes as overly static, and homogenizing, they curiously fail to address the one principle that helps to account for both the variations *within* 'highbrow' or 'elite' tastes as well as the logic of their transformations (for a similar critique see Lizardo, 2006). Such omissions are far from trivial. In fact, to overlook or to ignore the role of capital-*composition* as a secondary, yet equally fundamental principle of differentiation is to effectively strip the model of its most distinctive and potentially most insightful features. What makes the absence of references to this second dimension – both in theoretical commentary *and* in empirical research – all the more puzzling is that it hardly constitutes a 'residual category' (Alexander, 1987), but is integral element of Bourdieu's social ontology. Not only is it absolutely central to his understanding of the synchronic distribution of practices, properties and beliefs across the class-structure, but it is also key to the way in which he conceives changes in this distribution over time. According to Bourdieu, the true dynamic of changes in tastes is not only (and perhaps not even primarily) located in the symbolic struggles between dominant and aspiring social groups (the "vertical dimension" in accordance with the traditional model of "chase-and-flight"), but also takes places between the different fractions of the middle and upper-classes that are themselves armed with different *types* of social power. If notions like "high culture", "elite taste" or "dominant lifestyle" have their merit in so far as they point to general similarities in the lifestyle of those who occupy dominant social positions (such as the disinterested concern with form and stylistic originality, the refusal of the "common", the "popular" and hence the "vulgar" and the search for the most exclusive, distinctive properties yielding the highest symbolic profits), they easily become mystifying if it is forgotten that the very definition of these terms is itself an object of struggle.

A struggle between two competing principles of distinction, two distinct ways of asserting distance from necessity and the "vulgarity" of those who are condemned to necessity, corresponding to the two opposing poles of the dominant class or the 'field of power'. On the one hand, there is the self-imposed asceticism of the *dominated* fractions of the dominant class – the artists, cultural producers and academic professions – who assert their cultural authority through an ethos of elective restraint and ostentatious simplicity, which forms the basis of a lifestyle that is centred on the rejection of "materialism" in all its forms. On the other hand, there is the conspicuous consumption of the *dominant* fractions of the dominant class – the private-sector executives, the commercial and industrial employers, etc. – whose economic wealth is expressed in a 'hedonistic aesthetic of ease and facility' (Bourdieu, 1984: 176) and whose lifestyle centres on the consumption of products, properties and practices that largely derive their distinctive value from their economic cost.

Hence, far from constituting a unified system, as more stenographic readings have suggested, "highbrow", "elite" or "dominant" tastes are marked by internal divisions which manifest themselves in choices for practices, properties and products that are often 'so different in their style and object and sometimes so antagonistic [...] that it is easy to forget that they are variants of the same fundamental relationship to necessity' (Bourdieu, 1984: 176). While the dispositions towards the "disinterested" and the "gratuitous" can only take root in conditions that are marked by ease and relative luxury – i.e. by distance from necessity and freedom from the constraints it imposes – the distinct sources of social power that define this distance (material wealth or cultural competence) are themselves at the basis of considerable differences in lifestyle. Differences which Bourdieu even deems 'comparable to the gap between two "cultures" in the anthropological sense' (ibid.: 283), that is, a gap between two distinct cosmologies or "worldviews". In fact, if everyday disputes over taste, especially as they pertain to the uses, presentation and management of the body, often take such a violent form and provoke such intense reactions, this is because the stakes in these disputes are far from "cosmetic". Behind such disputes lie fundamental disagreements over the legitimate principle of domination, namely economic success or intellectual authority, "materialistic" or "spiritual values", "innerwordly" or "outerwordly" status.

None of the above is in any way meant as a call for conceptual orthodoxy, nor is it inspired by the typically hermeneutic desire to define the "correct" or "legitimate" uses of an author and his works. The ultimate test of Bourdieu's theoretical pudding must lie in its empirical eating and in this sense the burden of proof falls fully on the analyses presented in the second and third part. These remarks merely serve to point out what in my view are important lacunae in subsequent applications of Bourdieu's ideas. Lacunae which have not only led numerous critics to engage in a good deal of conceptual "shadow-boxing", but also caused them to overlook an entire series of pertinent social differences. In fact, against all forms of positivistic glorification of Data, it should be stressed that differences *between* and *within* classes have all the chance of passing unnoticed, if they are not introduced into the inquiry from the very start, that is, not only inform the construction of 'independent' variables that allow for the identification of the specific effects of capital-volume *and* -composition, but also of 'dependent' variables that enable such differences to be expressed, instead of dissolving them behind general and generic categories ("*classical music*", "*going to a restaurant*", "*doing sports*", etc.).

Whether or not the opposition between culture and economy, "art" and "argent", intellectuals and executives is indeed a "peculiarity of the French" or can instead be generalized (within the limits imposed by national history) to *all* social formations that have advanced market-economies and strongly developed systems of higher-education, is ultimately a matter of comparative, empirical research. That the particular form and strength of this opposition will vary considerably from one national context to another seems only natural. However, the real question is whether this differentiation in the dominant sources of social power is so weak that one can simply dispense with its study altogether. At any rate, to reach such a conclusion already implies that the role of capital-structure as a differentiating principle merits more attention than it has thus far received. In this respect, it is quite promising to see that every time that empirical analyses are actually geared towards such a multi-dimensional conception of social status, significant differences have been found. This has been the case for Prieur *et al.*'s (2008) study of class-differentiation in tastes and lifestyle in contemporary Denmark, Stempel's (2005) analyses of sports-preferences in the United States or Lizardo's (2006) work on the role of gendered occupational identities to name but a few.

Gendered bodies

There is however another, less obvious reason why the concept of social space will play such a central role in the analyses to follow. In the remainder of this chapter, I will aim to demonstrate that this concept enables us to capture another crucial aspect of class-relationships, namely their fundamentally *gendered* nature. In fact, any discussion on the role of class-dynamics in the production and perception of the body is bound to remain incomplete, if it does not take into account the ways in which bodies are implicated in that other set of power-relationships, namely those defined by the *sexual* division of labour. It is these power-relationships and the structures of masculine domination they serve to uphold, which are at the basis of the fundamentally different ways in which men and women come to perceive and experience their own bodies. As already mentioned in the introductory chapter, it is in no small part due to the work of feminist scholars that the body has come to occupy a more prominent place on the sociological agenda. The analyses of authors like Iris Young, Raewyn Connell, Nancy Henley, Susan Bordo or Sandra Bartky have shown how by ignoring the role of the body in the study of the social world, classical social theory has managed to neglect central aspects of the ways in which at least of half of its inhabitants experience this world. While an exhaustive account of the role of sexual domination in shaping the practical experience of the male and female body would provide material for a book in itself, I will limit myself to outlining three distinct ways in which this particular form of domination circumscribes embodiment.

First, it effectively transforms the female body into the legitimate object of the male gaze and male desire. In fact, one of the defining features of female bodily experience is the manner in which women come to experience their social being as inherently a 'being-perceived', which as such exists largely *for* and *through* the judgments of men. Crucially, the work of authors like Henley (1977), Connell (1987) and Young (2005) has been instrumental in showing how sexual domination does not just work upon the body through discourse, representations or explicit norms of appropriate femininity and masculinity (i.e. the 'body-image' of social psychology), but fundamentally defines the manner in which women and men come to *use* their bodies, inscribing its logic at the level of motor-habits and postural schemes. Henley (1977: 124ff.) and Young (2005: 35ff.) in particular have shown how women's 'bodily self-reference' – i.e. their

28 Social order, body order

constant awareness of their own bodies as objects-for-others – often prevents them from using their complete bodily potential and from fully committing themselves to the most mundane physical acts. This in turn endows their actions with a reticence and gaucheness which makes women appear as less powerful, less adept and more fragile, both in their own eyes and those of men. Connell (1987: 66ff.), whose work will be discussed in more detail in the following chapter, even argues that by defining the appropriate male and female uses of the body, the sexual division of labour fundamentally contributes to *producing* the very physical reality – i.e. the strong masculine body and the frail feminine physique symbolizing the "natural" superiority of men over women – it merely purports to *express*.

A second, closely related manner in which the sexual division of labour circumscribes the relationship to the body is by assigning women with the task of the social production and management of symbolic capital, that is, with the specific labour of presentation and representation (see Collins, 1992; Bourdieu, 2002: 99ff.). Conditioned to perceive and judge themselves in terms of their own beauty and looks, women are also deemed to have a "natural" interest in the things of beauty and an "innate" concern for form, formality and appearance. This not only defines their role within the domestic sphere – where women are (held) responsible for the public "image" of the family, that is, the appearance of their children, their husbands and their homes – but also defines the functions they take up in the labour market, where they are over-represented in occupations that centre on what Collins (1992: 214) coined 'Goffmanian labour', namely the specific task of organizational representation and impression-management, such as secretaries, receptionists, sales clerks and nurses. Thirdly and finally, the sexual division of labour shapes the manner in which men and women come to experience their bodies by situating them at opposite sides of the Nature-Culture divide. Within this perspective, which Ortner (1972) has argued to be quite trans-cultural, women are perceived as being closer to Nature and treated as more intimately linked and more "coextensive" with their bodies, that is to say, are not only viewed as more impulsive, more emotional, but also as more exposed to the vagaries of biological existence. Men, on the other hand, are resolutely placed on the side of Culture, that is, of mind and rationality and are deemed more capable of the emotional restraint and self-control that is thought to be the basis for social success and social power (also see Young, 1990: 122).

The role of sexual domination in shaping men and women's practical experience of their own bodies has by now been extensively documented and there is little that this study could add to what is already an impressive body of literature. The main thrust of our analyses will instead be to show how this form of domination rarely imposes itself in a uniform manner and is itself strongly modulated by men and women's overall position in social space. As Bourdieu notes:

> Because the classificatory schemes through which the body is practically apprehended and appreciated are always grounded twofold, both in the

social division of labour and the sexual division of labour, the relationship to the body is specified according to sex and according to the form that the division of labour between the sexes takes depending on the position occupied in the social division of labour.

(Bourdieu, 1990b: 77)

In fact, if the analyses to follow will consistently show that women are more conscious and anxious about their body, devote more interest, time and means to its presentation, management and cultivation and are more receptive to the dominant norms of appearance and demeanour than men, they also reveal systematic and considerable differences *within* both sexes, which separate (and *oppose*) men and women who occupy different positions in social space.

What empirical analysis uncovers is not a fixed structure of masculine domination and feminine subordination, but a range of masculinities and femininities that are themselves rooted in relationships of force that vary in terms of the volume and type of capital that agents have at their disposal. In fact, there is perhaps no better proof of the *arbitrary* foundations of the sexual division of labour and the pattern of masculine domination it serves to uphold, then to observe the quite *systematic* variations that the relationship between the sexes undergoes, when one moves from dominated to dominant social positions (and, among the latter, from the dominant to the dominated fractions of the middle- and upper classes) *within* one and the same social structure. More specifically, both the *degree* and *manner* in which men and women invest in their sexual identity – that, is symbolically highlight or euphemize their biological sex through demeanour, clothing or cosmetics – is itself strongly determined by their access to the social resources (i.e. capital) that provide the basis for an officially recognized and valorizing social identity. If, as our analyses will attempt to show, the gap between men and women tends to systematically *widen* – in both practices and representations – as one moves from dominant to dominated social positions – shifting from a finely graded continuum to an increasingly clear-cut dichotomy – this is because, as Schwartz reminds us, 'sexual identities are at once the most readily available and [provide] a specific source of valorisation for each sex' (1990: 206). In social conditions that are marked by the fundamental absence of the forms of capital that provide the basis for a consecrated identity (educational degrees, job titles, etc.), sexual identities are often one of the few ways of ascending to a valorized and valorizing sense of self. This is one of the reasons why the relationship to the body becomes increasingly differentiated along gendered lines as one moves down the social hierarchy. In fact, where other classes can construct their identities around the *symbolic* competences (entrepreneurial success, intellectual achievement, etc.) provided by the possession of economic or cultural capital, members of the working-class are often forced to draw their own sense of social worth from the one form of capital they have at their disposal, namely their labour power, that is to say, from their bodies as a source of strength and embodied skill. This is one of the reasons why they are more inclined than other classes to view the relationships between the sexes (and social relationships in general) primarily as relationships of physical force, a form of classification in which men are perceived as "naturally" superior. Schwartz continues:

> If socially dominated groups hold so strongly to these [sexual] divisions, it is because they provide its members with a privileged access to the mastery of a space and a projection of the self. The canons of virility and femininity can only be relativized if individuals can exchange them for other socially consecrated modes of being: it is precisely this [exchange] which is far from self-evident for members of the working-class.
>
> (1990: 206)

In fact, as one rises in the social hierarchy and agents increasingly have access to *other* sources of social status, the strict divisions between the sexes tend to loosen. Not only do women increasingly adopt roles and develop interests (in politics, culture, etc.) that among dominated groups are most often reserved for men, but men from the middle and dominant classes also increasingly display a concern with the body's form and appearance – in matters of diet, clothing and cosmetics, for instance – which their working-class counterparts tend to perceive as overly "effeminate" and often delegate wholly or partly to the women of their class. If the logic of sexual domination can therefore not be considered independently from that of social and *class*-domination, it is equally true that an understanding of the latter remains incomplete as long as one does not take into account the *sexual* dimension of the relationships between the classes.

Social space, sexual space

That class-differences are in fact imbued with sexual qualities was already clearly acknowledged by Paul Willis (1977) in his seminal study on the formation of working-class identity among adolescent boys. According to Willis, one of the main reasons why his "lads" not only came to accept, but actively embraced a dominated position in a division of labour that defines mental work as more exacting, more valuable and hence as superior to manual work (which it equates with simple and mind-*less* execution), is because they interpreted this division in inherently *sexual* terms. In fact, while they recognized the hierarchy of the mental and the manual, they effectively inverted its terms by equating the former with the feminine and the effete and hence the inferior and insignificant (i.e. as mere "pencil-pushing", not "real work"), while associating the latter with the physical skills and competence that testify to the natural superiority of men:

> For 'the lads', a division in which they take themselves to be favoured (the sexual) overlies, becomes part of, and finally partially challenges the valency of a division in which they are disadvantaged (mental/manual labour power).
>
> (Willis, 1977: 148)

It is hence through a patriarchal conception of the relationship between the sexes that the lads came to accept a given state of the relationship between the classes. There are at least two important ways in which the working-class valorization of masculinity (and its devaluation of femininity) contributes to the reproduction of class-differences. First, by equating "education" with "emasculation", it actively reinforces the mechanism of self-exclusion that results from the gradual adjustment of educational aspirations to their objective chances of success (a mechanism that will be discussed more fully in the following chapter). It does so, more specifically, by enabling such self-exclusion to be lived in the positive mode of male self-assertion in which 'the authority structure of the school becomes the antagonist against which one's masculinity is cut' (Connell, 2000: 135). Secondly, by imbuing manual labour with a meaning and quality it does not intrinsically possess (and even runs counter to its reality as physically demanding, dangerous and ill-remunerated), this ethos of virility enables the 'brutality of the working-situation [to be] partially re-interpreted into a heroic exercise of manly confrontation with *the task*. Difficult, uncomfortable and dangerous conditions are seen, not for themselves, but for their appropriateness to a masculine readiness and hardness.' (Willis, 1977: 150, *original emphasis*). If working-class men so readily come to accept the realities of manual labour, this is because even the most demanding and exploitative type of work still provides them with 'the materials for an elemental self-esteem' (ibid.) and enables them to demonstrate their ownership of the one capital they can spend and spend freely, namely their physical strength. This means that, for those who are situated at the bottom of social space, physical capital and the types of status it provides ("strength", "toughness", etc.) occupies a place that is quite analogous to the importance attributed to cultural and linguistic competences by others classes, a situation that is succinctly summarized by Charlesworth: 'Growing up working-class and effete is like growing up petit-bourgeois and stupid' (1999: 260).

Willis' observations are of specific interest here, because they touch on a more general point, namely that 'where two sets of divisions [i.e. a *social* and a *sexual* one, DV] are lived out in the same concrete space, they cannot remain separate.' (Willis, 1977: 148). While it is in fact possible to *analytically* distinguish between the socially and sexually qualified aspects of a particular practice, property or person, our analyses will attempt to show that everyday social life, especially in matters pertaining to the body, rarely draws such clear-cut distinctions and instead 'establishes all sorts of practical equivalences among the different divisions of the social world – divisions between the sexes, between the age groups and between the social classes' (Bourdieu, 1990b: 71). Bourdieu even considers it as one of the defining characteristics of the 'practical logic' that organizes the everyday perception of the social world, that it establishes homologies between the different social hierarchies, so that the language and logic of social domination continuously draws on and merges with the logic and imagery of sexual domination:

> The oppositions through which the dominant taxonomy [...] conceives the opposition between the classes are [...] more or less perfectly congruent

with the taxonomy which organizes the divisions of the sexes. *The dominant qualities are a twofold negation of virility*, because acquiring them demands docility [...] and because that docility is applied to dispositions that are themselves feminine.

(Bourdieu, 1977b: 661–662, *my emphasis*)

This observation is interesting for two reasons. First, because this merging of social and sexual qualities in the everyday perception of class-differences helps to account for the fact that, from the point-of-view of the dominated, men who are situated higher-up in the social hierarchy are increasingly viewed as effeminate and effete (i.e. as not "real" men), whereas from the perspective of the dominant, women who are situated at the bottom of the class-structure are often seen as loud, vulgar, promiscuous and unruly, in short, as "unfeminine" and endowed with all the properties that the sexual division of labour tends to assign to men (see Skeggs, 1997; Skeggs, 2005). Secondly and more importantly, it suggests that the different types of capital, far from being "gender-neutral" forms of social power as some feminist critics have suggested (McCall, 1992), can in a sense be conceived as *doubly* gendered, that is, both in terms of the dispositions that favour their accumulation, as well as in the specific type of symbolic power they provide (intellectual prestige vs. material success, cultural authority vs. economic power, etc.).

In this sense, cultural capital cannot only be defined as a "feminine" type of capital, because it produces a proclivity for practices and properties that are traditionally associated with women (literature, art, the concern with form and appearance, etc.), but also because its accumulation objectively demands a type of "docility", that tends to be associated with a dominated position in the sexual hierarchy.[5] This docility applies to both its acquisition within the formal setting of the educational system, as well as its more informal and diffuse transmission within the family unit. In the former case, it demands a type of obedience to pedagogic authority (the "ear'ole conformism" described by Willis' lads), that is diametrically opposed to the masculine imperatives of active, confrontational and public self-affirmation. In the latter, it is often acquired in the course of practices and activities that tend to be similarly incompatible with an agonistic and assertive type of masculinity, the paradigm of which is undoubtedly *reading*, a solitary, domestic and physically passive form of leisure.

This is also why, paradoxically, the same dispositions that are the product of a dominated position in one hierarchy – i.e. that defined by the sexual division of labour – can facilitate mobility in another, namely that of social class (and cultural capital in particular). 'Mobility', as Bourdieu notes 'is, as it were, the reward for docility', to which he immediately adds, 'a docility in one of the most essential dimensions of social identity, the relation to the body' (1977b: 661). In fact, the doubly gendered nature of capital implies that such mobility often comes at a different price for men and women. While identifying with the dominant culture is always liable of being perceived as a form of disloyalty to the dominated (*"Who does she think she is?"*; *"Does he think he's better than us?"*; etc.), for working-class *women*, who are situated in a socio-sexual cosmology that more than any other class defines (and devalues) the "refined", the "cultivated" or the "intellectual" as typically feminine qualities, such identifications are less likely to be viewed as a radical break with class-identity (on this point also see Collins, 1992).[6]

For working-class men, on the other hand, adopting dominant traits is often synonymous with renouncing the most visible markers (both at the level of appearance and bodily hexis) of an ethos of virility which provides them with one of the few (and hence heavily invested) sources of a valorized and valorizing identity. As such, the development of social, and especially *educational* aspirations, is not only likely to be perceived as an act of social treason, but also (and perhaps more importantly) of sexual transgression, exposing boys to the risk of being branded as "poofs", "fags" and "wimps" (see Connell, 2000: 131ff.). Hence, when working-class boys *do* cultivate such aspirations, they often find themselves in a particularly pernicious double bind. On the one hand, by identifying with the (feminine) culture of the educational system, they run the risk of becoming alienated from their (male) peer-group and hence of condemning themselves to social isolation. On the other hand, by defying pedagogic authority, which is one of the central ways of attaining and maintaining status within their peer-group, they threaten to undermine one of the few avenues of upward mobility. It is no wonder then, as Reay (2002) already observed, that such contradictory status-demands often generate considerable psychological tension and hamper the development of a stable and integrated sense of self-identity among academically aspiring, working-class boys.[7] From the above, several things follow which are crucial to the rest of our argument. First, that those factors that favour the development of feminine dispositions, or perhaps better, obstruct the adoption of masculine roles are an essential element in promoting the upward mobility of working-class boys and men. Secondly, that the type of identity provided by working-class masculinity – which is defined in simultaneous opposition to the "feminine" and the "bourgeois" – offers a degree of protection against the imposition of the dominant definition of appearance and demeanour and the lifestyle in which it originates. From this it also follows, third, that working-class *women* find themselves in the most contradictory position. In fact while their position in the sexual division of labour renders them more susceptible to the dominant definition of the legitimate body and judge themselves accordingly, the necessity that defines their conditions of existence leave them most dispossessed of the means to realize this definition.

The reason for elaborating on this *gendered* dimension of capital and the dispositions that facilitate their accumulation is not only that sexual identities – and the relationship to the body they engender – play a crucial role in the reproduction and naturalization of differences *between* the classes, but also contribute to the social production and perception of differences *within* classes, particularly between their fractions richest in cultural and economic capital:

34 *Social order, body order*

> [T]he dominant fractions of the dominant class always tend to conceive their relation to the dominated fractions – 'intellectuals', 'artists', 'professors' – in terms of the opposition between the male and the female, the virile and the effeminate, which is given different contents depending on the period (e.g. nowadays short hair/long hair; 'economico-political' culture/'artistico-literary' culture, etc.).
>
> (Bourdieu, 1978: 826)

In fact, whereas cultural capital tends to be associated with a form of symbolic power and a set of dispositions (i.e. aesthetic sensibility, linguistic competence, etc.) that are coded as feminine and effeminate, economic capital provides the

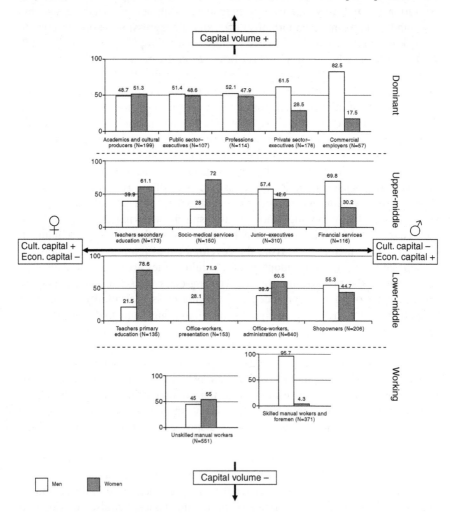

Figure 1.2 The distribution of gender-ratios across social space
Source: BNHS '04

basis for the "real", temporal power that remains the distinct privilege of men (the natural "wage-earners"). This is particularly evident in the type of dispositions that favour its accumulation, which are themselves a sublimated form of the traits that accompany a *dominant* position in the sexual division of labour, namely competitiveness, a desire for confrontation and domination, toughness and emotional detachment, the strategic-instrumental rationality that defines the "business-sense" and, more generally, an agonistic conception of the social world as inherently defined by conflict and struggle ("dog-eat-dog"). While less overtly sexist and patriarchic than working-class masculinity – being able to assert their dominance symbolically, rather than physically and hence privileging 'rationality and responsibility rather than pride and aggressiveness' (Connell, 2000: 140) – the dispositions that define the corporate habitus are often no less androcentric.

This not only applies to the ethos of the "old" economic bourgeoisie (the industrial and commercial employers), with its patriarchic conception of the family and its glorification of "anti-intellectual" virtues such as prowess in sports, patriotism and militarism, but is also the case for what Connell identified as an emerging 'transnational business masculinity' (2000: 52ff., also Connell and Wood, 2005). While more liberal in sexual and ethical matters than the traditional bourgeoisie, this new economic elite (personified by the executives in international finance) is often equally male-centred, as shown by its tendency to commodify its relationship to women ("trophy wives", high-end prostitution, etc.), but also by the masculine tropes that pervade the language of the "new corporate culture", which often fuses the logic of management with that of athletic competition and team-sports (see Kay and Laberge, 2002). The patriarchic dimensions of this ethos are especially clear in its relationship to the dominated fractions of the dominant and middle-class. In fact, the same logic that leads men, increasingly so as one moves down the social hierarchy, to claim their own labour as "real" work, demanding "real" skills and producing "real" results – i.e. as more important, more relevant and more central to the functioning and survival of the economy, both domestic and (inter)national – while devaluing the work of women as superficial and superfluous (especially in everything related to the management of "appearances"), also re-emerges in the paternalistic conceptions that the dominant fractions of the dominant and middle-class have of intellectuals, artists and teachers, whom they often mock for their naïve "idealism", their lack of *sérieux* and distance from the "real" world:

> [I]n the field of power, there is the opposition, deeply scored in the objectivity of practices and properties, between industrial and commercial employers on the one hand and intellectuals on the other, and also inscribed in people's minds, in the form of explicit or implicit taxonomies which make the 'intellectual' appear, in the eyes of the 'bourgeois', as a being endowed with properties entirely situated on the side of the female – lack of realism, otherworldliness, irresponsibility (as is clearly seen in situations in which the temporally dominant take the opportunity to call the intellectual or artist to order and, as men so often do to women, explain 'how the world works').
> (Bourdieu, 2002: 105–106)

This shows how the struggle to impose the legitimate lifestyle and definition of the body and, through it, to impose the legitimate principles of vision of the social world is also a struggle to impose a masculine or feminine vision of that world (see Wacquant, 2010: esp. 201ff.). The main reason for drawing attention to this "sexualization" of social and class-differences (or "*class*-ification" of sexual differences) is twofold. First, because it helps to account for the unequal distribution of men and women across the structure of social space (as shown in *Figure 1.2*). In fact, as one moves from the dominant to the dominated pole of the middle- and dominant classes, the gender-ratio tends to shift from class-fractions that are strongly male-dominated (the employers, the senior-executives, those providing financial services such as insurance and real-estate, etc.) over those that are more balanced in terms of gender (the professions, the office clerks in traditional administrative functions) to those that are predominantly feminine (teachers, therapists, dieticians and other socio-medical services). Secondly, it will help to account for the observation (which we will encounter time and again in the second and third part of this study) that as one moves from dominated to dominant social positions and, among the latter, from the dominant to the dominated pole of the middle- and upper classes, that men display interests, subscribe to opinions and are endowed with properties that are traditionally coded as feminine, while movements in the opposite direction reveal that women increasingly display tastes and properties that are traditionally seen as masculine. How these two observations play out in the everyday uses and perception of the body will be illustrated in more detail in the second part of this study. In the following chapter we will look more closely at the way in which the body is – quite literally – 'in-corporated' in this social and sexual space.

Notes

1 In fact, on the very first page of the German edition of *The Civilizing Process* he already points to 'numerous and easily obtainable observations' which show that 'the standards and patterns of affective control in societies at different stages of development and *even in different strata of the same society* can be quite different' (1997: 9, *my emphasis*). Further in the book he notes that 'Classes living permanently in danger of starving to death or of being killed by enemies can hardly develop or maintain those stable restraints characteristic of the more civilized' (ibid.: 310, *my emphasis*). These examples and others throughout the book seem sufficient to acquit Elias of the charges of having produced a "classist" theory of behavioural change, as suggested by Cregan (2006: 27ff.).
2 Here, a quite important nuance seems to have been lost in the English translation of the original German text (both the 1982 and 2000 Blackwell editions). While the original reads: 'Die viele Fragen, die sich aus den Unterschieden und Abstufungen im Verhalten van Ober-, Mittel- und Unterschichten ergeben, bilden einen Problemkreis für sich.' [1997/1939: 353] ('*The many questions that arise from the differences and gradations in the conduct of lower-, middle- and upper-classes constitute a set of problems of their own*' DV), the English translation has simple turned this into: 'There are, of course, many unsolved problems raised by this vista.' (1982: 251; 2000: 382).
3 This common relational vision and the use of relational concepts can be traced back to a shared intellectual sympathy for the work of Neo-Kantian philosopher Ernst Cassirer (see Bourdieu and Wacquant, 1992: 97; Goudsblom, 1995).

4 The role of *social* capital remains curiously absent from this discussion and while Bourdieu devoted several theoretical pieces to the concept (see Bourdieu, 1980 and Bourdieu, 1986), it seems to have never played a particularly prominent role in his empirical research.
5 The term "docility" is here used in the original etymological sense of the Latin *docilis* meaning "easily taught".
6 This of course by no means implies a minimization of the often intense feelings of alienation and exclusion that the experience of higher-education still generates for working-class *women*, as has been extensively documented by authors such as Skeggs (1997), Bufton (2003) and Reay (2009). It merely aims to show that educational aspirations, *from the point-of-view of the dominated*, are more compatible (or at any rate less *in*compatible) with the socially ascribed sexual identities of women.
7 Richard Hoggart, in his seminal *The Uses of Literacy* (1957), also noted how for working-class boys the development of educational aspirations often goes hand-in-hand with a gradual withdrawal from *male* peer-groups and an increasing absorption into the domestic world of women: 'He is similarly likely to be separated from the boys' groups outside the home, is no longer a full member of the gang which clusters round the lamp-posts in the evenings; there is homework to be done. But these are the male groups among which others in his generation grow up, and his detachment from them is emotionally linked with one more aspect of his home situation – that he now tends to be closer to the women of the house than to the men. The boy spends a large part of his time at the physical centre of the home, where the women's spirit rules, quietly getting on with his work whilst his mother get on with her jobs – the father not yet back from work or out for a drink with his mates. The man and the boy's brothers are outside, in the world of men; the boy sits in the women's world.' (1957: 295).

2 Classifying bodies, classified bodies, class bodies

> It is a feature of the destiny of social existence that the essential elements that are uniformly inherent to all individuals of a certain group almost never manifest themselves as the highest, but often rather as the lowest motives and interests of these individuals.... What everyone possesses can obviously always only be the possession of the least well-endowed; and since it is always the lot of humanity that the higher can indeed sink down to the lower, but that the latter cannot so easily rise to the former, so in general the level on which everyone meets must lie very close to the level of the very lowest.
>
> (Simmel, 1997 [1910]: 130)

Having outlined the basic conception of social structure that will inform the analyses to follow, this chapter will look more closely at *how* social agents can be said to 'embody' this social space. It will focus especially on the body's role as the primary means 'through' which social agents come to inhabit, know and navigate this space, but also as the material tangible substrate for social and especially class-identity. It is in fact in our capacity as embodied, 'fleshed out' subjects that we come to be fundamentally affected, impressed and modified by the structures of the physical and the social world. As *physico-material* beings we are not only confined to occupy a discrete location in time and space, but are also exposed to the forces, frictions and inertias of physical existence, all of which tend to leave their mark on the body, either momentarily (bruises, scratches, etc.) or permanently (scars, disfigurements, etc.), visibly (burns, cuts, etc.) or invisibly (inflammations, fractures, etc.). As *biological* organisms, we are traversed by a host of visceral processes – respiration, digestion, circulation, excretion, etc. – that impinge on our existence "from the inside" and do so in a manner that is often as autonomous as it is anonymous. Finally, as *socialized* bodies, we are equally "affected", "driven" or "moved" by the forces that inhabit the social world. Forces, that also leave their physical traces *in* and *on* the body and often impose themselves with an equally ineluctable necessity, but which do so in a manner that has little or nothing to do with simple *mechanical* determination and through 'a mode of inclusion irreducible to simple material and spatial inclusion' (Bourdieu, 2000: 135).

This chapter will aim to show that there are at least three ways in which the observation that we *are* and *have* bodies is relevant (if not crucial) to an adequate understanding of class-relationships. First, because the body provides the foundation for a pre-discursive, pre-reflexive mode of social cognition and identity. The following paragraphs will in fact argue that a good deal of what constitutes *class*-identity is not situated at the level of discourse or ideology, but instead exists primarily in practical or *embodied* form, that is, as encoded in body-techniques and postural schemes and somatized in physical states of attraction and repulsion, desire and disgust. Secondly, because the body itself is to a considerable extent the materialization of the necessity that is inscribed in a given social position or trajectory which durably mar(k)s its perceptible features such as its size, shape and musculature. Thirdly and finally, because it is through our bodies that we are subjected to the *universal* imperatives of physico-visceral being, which impose themselves on *all* of us, regardless of social position, and hence throw up their own challenges to the production and maintenance of class-boundaries.

Incorporation

In order to better grasp the distinctive manner in which embodied agents are shaped by the rhythms and structures of the social world, one can again turn to one of the key properties of social "fields" or "spaces". In fact, one of the central tenets of a 'field-theoretical' perspective, both in the natural *and* the social sciences (as discussed by Martin, 2003), is that fields can *only* exert their particular force on "bodies" that are endowed with properties which render them susceptible to this force in the first place. A good example would be the manner in which sawdust or iron filings behave radically different when brought into a magnetic field. The crucial (if not cardinal) difference between the type of "bodies" that are generally dealt with in the natural sciences and the *embodied* agents studied by the social sciences, is that for the latter these properties, or better *dispositions*, are rarely ever present "ab ovo" and are instead the product of an individual and collective *genesis*. A genesis which, furthermore, cannot be considered independently from agents' exposure to the regularities, rhythms and determinations of a particular social field. To borrow a metaphor from Lahire:

> The sugar has not constituted its 'disposition to dissolve' by way of a history of past contacts with water, whereas the actor is the product of his or her multiple past experiences, multiple acquisitions – more or less complete – made in the course of situations that have been lived previously.
>
> (2011: 53)

Unlike iron particles which already "have" and do not "acquire" their disposition towards magnetism from their prolonged exposure to a magnetic field, the dispositions of *socialized* bodies are always the product of a process of social formation. Such a genesis is only possible, because as *biological* organisms, human agents are distinguished from non-human animals by their degree of *conditionability*, that is, by their 'natural capacity to acquire non-natural, arbitrary capacities' (Bourdieu, 2000b: 136). This innate capacity – which Plessner (1975) coined 'the anthropological law of natural artificiality [*natürliche Künstlichkeit*]' because it constitutes one of the few anthropological *in*variants – not only enables humans to appropriate a dizzyingly wide range of skills (from tying a shoelace to hunting buffalo, using a keyboard to performing open-heart surgery), but also renders them susceptible to an extremely broad range of environmental cues. It is precisely one of the distinguishing features of humans that they can be "moved" by a virtually endless range of stimuli providing the body with an 'immense plasticity in its response to the environmental forces at work on it' (Berger and Luckmann, 1967: 48).

This diversity of *abilities* and plasticity of *susceptibilities* are ultimately two sides of the same analytical coin. In fact, it is precisely *because* agents can acquire a wide range of skills and competences, that they can in turn become affected or "determined" by an equally wide array of environmental cues. Where the modern urbanite merely sees an innocuous-looking broken branch forming part of an equally innocuous scenery, the trained huntsman is able to read the size, direction and speed of his potential prey. Similarly, the same Bach cantata or poem by Baudelaire that can move a cultivated audience to tears will leave the philistine wholly untouched. Phrased in somewhat more general terms, it is only because their exposure to a given socio-cultural environment has endowed agents with more or less durable dispositions, that they are in turn capable of being determined by this environment, that is to say, become receptive to the various cues for action it contains.

From this it follows that the relationship between agent and world always presents itself in a dual aspect, namely as both a *relationship of conditioning* and a *relationship of construction*. Acquiring her everyday skills from the social world, the agent in turn invests these skills in making sense of this social world. While both aspects of this relationship are therefore equally central, more weight is given to the former since 'the relationship of knowledge depends on the relationship of conditioning that precedes it' (Bourdieu and Wacquant, 1992: 127). Crucially, this 'relationship of conditioning' cannot be reduced to the mere inculcation of explicit social norms, ethical codes, linguistic skills, collective representations or theoretical know-how and hence extends well beyond what is traditionally defined as 'socialization'. In fact, because the relationship to the social world is one of *total inclusion*, the individual agent is not only exposed to its rhythms and regularities by means of her *mental* faculties (i.e. those of explicit reasoning and conceptual thought), but through her entire range of sensory capacities. As Marx famously asserted: [M]an is affirmed in the objective world not only in the act of thinking, but with *all* his senses' (2007 [1844]: 108, *original emphasis*). This implies a more comprehensive type of social conditioning, which does not stop short at shaping the structures of the mind, but effectively transforms the body – its movements, compulsions and features – defining a type of socialization or acculturation that is effectively an

Classifying bodies 41

incorporation. What this chapter will attempt to argue, is that some of the most deep-seated features of class-identity are not located at the level of consciously held opinions, but are instead carried in bodily postures and gestures, in physical reactions and "gut feelings".

Comprehension

If the focus on embodiment leads us to expand the traditional conception of socialization, this also applies to the structur*ing* aspects of this relationship, namely to the process whereby embodied agents constitute their everyday world as "meaning-full". In fact, the type of "comprehension" that is engendered in the relationship between agents and their social environment tends to elude the conventional, scholastic definition of "understanding" or "knowledge". It is a form of comprehension that several authors working in different theoretical traditions, but with a similar analytic intent have attempted to define. The pragmatist philosopher John Dewey, for one, referred to it as 'habit' to indicate a 'system of beliefs, desires and purposes that are formed in the interaction of biological aptitudes with a social environment' (1922: i). The anthropologist and linguist Edward Sapir spoke of 'intuition' to describe the manner in which social behaviour is structured according to 'deep-seated cultural patterns' whose distinctive property is that they are 'not so much known as felt, not so much capable of conscious description as of naïve practice' (1949 [1927]: 548). Gilbert Ryle (1949) described this particular type of understanding as a 'knowing *how*' (which he opposed to a 'knowing *that*'), while Merleau-Ponty speaks of a 'knowledge in the hands' to describe a type of understanding that is 'forthcoming only when bodily effort is made and cannot be formulated in detachment from that effort' (1996 [1962]: 144). Finally, Bourdieu coins it 'practical sense', 'practical knowledge' or 'corporeal knowledge' (the terms are used interchangeably) which forms the basis for a 'practical comprehension of the world quite different from the intentional act of conscious decoding that is normally designated by the idea of comprehension' (2000b: 135). While each of these authors approached this type of understanding from different angles, highlighted different aspects and often took it to different conclusions, they nevertheless largely agree over its fundamental principles.[1] First of all, they all used it to define a type of understanding that is largely acquired in and for *practice*. This not only means that they treat it as fundamentally oriented towards the achievement of practical ends and hence endowed with a 'projectile power' (Dewey, 1922: 25), but also as a type of knowledge that is developed, maintained and refined by way of *doing* rather than *thinking*, through active engagement with the social world, rather than through detached contemplation and therefore as largely *procedural*, rather than *propositional* in character.

From this it follows, second, that it is a form of understanding that is largely *habitual* in character, that is to say, acquired through the gradual, repeated and sustained confrontation with a particular pattern of (inter)actions, problems and obstacles. As Ryle put it:

> Learning *how* or improving in ability is not like learning *that* or acquiring information. Truths can be imparted, procedures can only be inculcated and while inculcation is a gradual process, imparting is relatively sudden. It makes sense to ask at what moment someone became apprised of a truth, but not to ask at what moment someone acquired a skill.
>
> (1949: 48, *original emphasis*)

This not only endows practical understanding with an important *temporal* vector – defining it as a gradual and on-going *process*, rather than a fixed *state* – but also serves to distinguish it from a simple collection of "habits" or a set of conditioned "reflexes". In fact, when Dewey or Merleau-Ponty speak of "habit", they are careful to distinguish it from its common-sense definition as a standardized, mechanical response to a given stimulus or set of stimuli. Instead, they stress the open and malleable quality of habits which provide agents with the power to 'respond with a certain type of solution to situations of a certain general form' (Merleau-Ponty, 1996: 142). In fact, since the defining criterion of this type of understanding is *practical efficacy* (and not logical coherence or theoretical systematicity), habits, dispositions or know-how are capable of being refined, revised and if necessary, *transformed* through practice.

Third, they invoke this type of understanding to account for the fact that everyday actions, choices and expressions are very often coherent, concerted and systematic *without* therefore being the product of the conscious adherence to explicitly defined rules, norms and maxims in the intentional execution of a pre-conceived plan. Just as the learning of the mother tongue enables children to produce (more or less) grammatically correct sentences long before they start to grasp the theoretical principles of grammar, large sections of everyday social practice consists of the application of *practical* principles of action and thought, which often remain thoroughly opaque to those who apply them or, as Sapir phrased it, take place 'in accordance with an elaborate and secret code that is written nowhere, known by none and understood by all' (1949 [1927]: 556).

Finally and crucially, all of these authors (to varying extents), allocate a central role to the *body* as the primary carrier of this form of practico-habitual understanding. In fact, because the starting point of their analysis is not the *thinking* subject who relates to the world through a process of pure *intellection*, but an *agent* who is actively engaged in the practical realization of her particular projects, the relationship between subject and object is not primarily one of theoretical understanding, but rather of embodied skill and practical competence. 'Consciousness', writes Merleau-Ponty, 'is in the first place not a matter of "I think that" but of "I can".' (1962: 137). To "know" or "understand" one's everyday lifeworld is not the same as being capable of providing a discursive account of its constituent elements or producing an explicit representation of the way in which they all hang together. While such accounts are undeniably part of everyday social life, they are by no means crucial to competent social practice and are themselves subtended by a different type of understanding. A type of understanding that is often quite difficult to capture in theoretical propositions, since it exists mainly in the form of practical procedures.

What is true for a skill like typing, applies to all the embodied skills which enable social agents to relate to an entire world of objects in a manner that is both systematic *and* intelligent *without* requiring the intervention of discourse or deliberation. As Merleau-Ponty put it: 'My body has its world, or understands its world, without having to make use of my "symbolic" or "objectifying" function.' (1996: 141). It is through their embodied abilities that the world "makes sense" to social agents, spontaneously discloses itself as a range of possibilities to be and to do, not (to borrow phenomenological terminology) as a set of *noemata*, the objects of a conscious intentionality, but rather as an assembly of *manipulanda*, the instruments of a corporeal knowledge. This knowledge comprises both 'techniques of the body' (Mauss, 1974) itself – i.e. ways of sitting, walking, eating, breathing and skills like swimming, rock-climbing or tying a shoelace – but also the skilful use of instruments and tools that transform, extend and enhance the body's innate potential. In fact, by learning how to drive a car, fly a plane, use a microscope or a telephone the social agent is capable of overcoming the physical limitations of his body making him, in Freud's words, into 'a kind of prosthetic God' (1961 [1929]: 44).

It is this insistence on the role of the body as a source of habitual skill and practical knowledge that also leads these authors to question some of the cardinal oppositions that haunt philosophical and sociological reflections on human subjectivity and practice such as "voluntarism" vs. "determinism", "freedom" vs. "constraint", "agency" vs. "structure" or "creativity" vs. "habit". In fact, the way in which such binary opposites construct the problem of the conditions for creative action very often prevents the fact from being realized that the capacity to be creative, to improvise and freely "choose" between different lines of action tends to be *strengthened*, rather than curtailed through habitual, embodied learning. Dewey captured this quite well:

> By a seeming paradox, increased power of forming habits, means increased susceptibility, sensitiveness, responsiveness. Thus, even if we think of habits as so many grooves, the power to acquire many and varied grooves denotes high sensitivity, explosiveness.
> (Dewey, quoted in Ostrow, 1981: 288)

Compared to the professional football-player who spends every waking hour on the pitch, honing his shots, refining his passes, perfecting his dribbles, who is obsessed by the game that keeps him up at night, the amateur who plays every other week is undoubtedly less "determined" by the written and unwritten rules of the game. However, few would assert that the latter actually has more "freedom" in the game. In fact, where the amateur often has to consciously look for the ball at his feet, to stop and scan his surroundings before making a pass and to guess where his shot is likely to end up, the professional instinctively "grasps" how much kinetic energy to put into his kick, "understands" the right angle to place his shot, "knows" the correct position in which his foot needs to hit the ball and the time it takes to travel the distance to his team-mate. Furthermore, where the amateur simply sees a space between two opponents or a lone team-mate, the professional immediately spots an "opening", an opportunity or a threat, is capable of perceiving a dynamic pattern of possibilities and impossibilities, is able to anticipate, improvise and create "chances" precisely *because* his practical, embodied mastery of the game allows him to commit to the habitual, what for the amateur are consciously controlled actions and hence to perceive a "meaning", where the layman only sees a random whirl of bodies.

As Berger and Luckmann already pointed out, 'the background of habitualized activity opens up a foreground for deliberation and innovation' (1967: 53). Put differently, the more social agents are controlled by the game, the more they are in turn capable of controlling it, taking advantage of it and turning the game "to their hand". This leads us to a central paradox, namely that the more "culture" has gone into the production of a particular aspect of everyday practice – i.e. the earlier and the more intensely it has been subjected to social regulation – the more likely it is to appear as the most spontaneous manifestation of an innermost "nature", not only to those who perform a given act, but also to those who bear witness to it.

History-in-bodies

If Bourdieu is hence far from the first to point out the importance of a pre-reflexive and pre-discursive mode of cognition to the understanding of everyday social practice, let alone use the term 'habitus' to designate the foundation of this type of cognition, he does expand this concept in at least three important directions. First, he aims to give practical knowledge a more firmly historical mooring by treating it as a *doubly* historical product. The practical skills that agents invest in their everyday social practice are themselves the product of the labour of previous generations as deposited in language, tools, objects, institutions, etc. (i.e. *fylogenesis*) which each agent internalizes, partly or wholly, within the course of a situated and dated social trajectory (i.e. *ontogenesis*). Second, he expands traditional conceptions of embodiment to not only include sensori-motor skills, postural schemes and speech patterns, but also the visceral dimension of the body as expressed in such somatic sensations as attraction and repulsion, taste and distaste, desire and disgust (see further down). Finally and most importantly for inquiry, he explicitly ties the concept to a developed notion of social differentiation and class-division:

> Because the social is also instituted in biological individuals, there is, in each biological individual, something of the collective, and therefore properties valid for a whole class of agents – which statistics can bring to light. Habitus understood as an individual or a socialized biological body, or as the social, biologically individuated through incarnation in a body, is collective, or transindividual – so it is possible to construct *classes of habitus, which can be statistically characterized.*
>
> (Bourdieu, 2000b: 157, *my emphasis*)

To say that social agents are endowed with 'habitus' (or perhaps better, *are* habitus) is first of all to underline the fact that they are *not* gifted with what Karl Mannheim called 'perfectly universal minds' that are capable of 'experiencing all that there was to experience and of knowing all there was to know, and enjoying an elasticity such as to make it possible at any time to start afresh' (1972 [1928]: 294). Instead, it serves to highlight the deceivingly trivial fact that social practice is always the product of skills and competences that are acquired in the course of a *situated* and *dated* social experience and is hence per definition partial, discrete and differentiated in nature.

Formulated in a less negative manner, it is because of their habitus that social agents are not condemned to a 'radical empiricism' (Lahire, 2011: 16) which forces them to re-invent social life at each and every turn and to constantly re-establish the basic parameters for meaningful social interaction. Instead of being reduced to the state of a *mens momentanea*, a "momentary mind", helplessly caught up in the fleeting conjunctures of face-to-face interaction, the habitus invests in each new situation the accumulated experiences of all past situations and hence make it possible to define and interpret this situation as meaningful. Being the product of the protracted exposure to the immanent tendencies of a particular socio-cultural environment, the habitus enables a practical anticipation of these tendencies. Crucially, because each new situation is defined and interpreted in terms of previous experiences, the habitus is also the basis for a relative autonomy vis-à-vis this situation, selecting from among the manifold determinations and incitations it offers, those to which its history predispose it. As Bourdieu puts it:

> In fact, because each new situation is defined and interpreted in terms of previously constituted experiences, habitus tend to be marked by a bias or selectivity towards the familiar, especially when it operates in situations that present itself with a certain degree of regularity and constancy. The result is that 'the informative efficiency of every new experience tends to decline as the number of experiences already integrated into the structure of the habitus increases'.
>
> (Bourdieu, 1977b)

This effect of closure imposes a relative degree of *irreversibility* on any type of learning-process. Just as agents who have acquired the ability to read and write in a particular language (often at a great expense of time and effort) cannot willingly return to their initial state of illiteracy and are henceforth "forced" to perceive a meaning where previously they only saw incomprehensible signs, the incorporation of new sensori-motor skills into the habitus durably transforms all *subsequent* incorporations. The difficulty that the average Anglophone speaker has in reproducing the speech pattern associated with the French "r" or that a French person has in pronouncing the English "h" provide a good example of the ways in which the early social conditioning of the body sets effective limits to its capacity to fully integrate *new* sensori-motor-habits. That this does not only apply to the incorporation of new body-techniques (ways of speaking, walking, etc.), but also (and perhaps *a fortiori*) to the conditioning of the body's visceral compulsions will be shown by the case of culinary tastes discussed in Chapter 5.

It is this durability and relative irreversibility of dispositions which also endows the habitus with an important *mnemotechnical* function. Because bodily knowledge is largely *dispositional* and *procedural* in nature, it is often enough to place the body in a particular physical state in order to evoke the corresponding mental state. Everyday examples of this 'evocative power of bodily mimesis' (Bourdieu, 1984: 474) are the manner in which, in order to recall the individual digits that make up my pin-code or a friend's phone number, I first trace their corresponding movements across the keypad or the way in which a pianist, after years of neglecting his art, often only needs to place himself in front of his instrument, put his body in the appropriate position and roam over the keys in order to re-activate his musical skill. It is through such forms of bodily rehearsal – what Merleau-Ponty called 'consecratory gestures' (1996: 146) – that the body places the agent in the right "frame of mind".

If this illustrates the impressive capacity of the body to function as a "memory pad", capable of durably storing and re-activating the lessons it has learned long ago, it again highlights how, once learned or incorporated, dispositions are often exceedingly difficult to *un*-learn. Unlike theoretical knowledge or explicitly held "values", which can be held up to conscious scrutiny, inspected for their veracity and logical consistency and, if need be, revised, modified and even abandoned through explicit instruction and rational debate, embodied dispositions – as embedded in postural schemes, speech patterns and quasi-visceral inclinations – often prove considerably more impervious to conscious introspection and deliberate transformation. If, as every aspiring *petit-bourgeois* knows all too well (see Chapter 8), it is often much easier to change the *grammaticality* of one's speech acts than it is to change one's accent, this is because '[w]hat is "learned by body" is not something that one has, like knowledge that can be brandished, but something that one is.' (Bourdieu, 1990b: 73).

A *sense* of place

It is precisely this role of the habitus to make virtue out of necessity, to transform a "having" into a "being", a particular set of social conditions into a more or less durable mode of perceiving, judging and acting that lend it such a crucial role in the naturalization and hence legitimation of class-differences. More specifically, the conception of social practice that is contained in the formula *conditions → dispositions → practices* offers a means of accounting for the fact that the latter are at once socially constructed, while presenting themselves with all the semblance of being innate. The differentiation of social conditions – rooted in the unequal distribution of capital (as described in the previous chapter) – leads to a differentiation of the type of condition*ings* to which agents are exposed – i.e. to the type and range of experiences that are available to them at a given moment in time – which in turn produces durable distinctions in the "point-of-view" of social agents who find themselves to be different without any conscious assertion of difference. Furthermore, while the existence of an "elastic" habitus that retains a constant flexibility in the face of ever-changing circumstances can be asserted as a *theoretical* possibility, this elasticity is itself a function of the possibilities inscribed in social conditions. It is here that the abovementioned analogy with a game again becomes useful. In fact, games are not just the "training grounds" in which social agents acquire, develop and deploy their practical skills, but they also function as "markets" in which they gain a sense of the *value* of these skills, that is, of their degree of prowess in playing the game at hand. It is the realization of this value that in turn determines their propensity to invest in the game. Just as a given degree of success tends to lead agents to invest more time and effort in playing the game (which in turn tends to increase success, etc.), failure or under-achievement in turn tends to produce withdrawal and even self-exclusion from the game (since very few people like to play the games in which they systematically lose). It is through their continuous engagement in various "games" or "fields" and the incessant verdicts they exert – those of the family, the peer-group, the educational system or the labour market – that social agents gradually construct a practical awareness of the value of their own abilities (including the value of their own body, see Chapter 4). By internalizing the value attributed to their actions, words, gestures and appearance, their world gradually acquires its distinct morphology, presenting itself as a series of probabilities, possibilities and impossibilities (*"that's not for the likes of us"*).

According to Bourdieu, it is precisely this practical adjustment of aspirations and preferences to their objective chances of realization which, more than any explicit ideology or legitimizing discourse, contributes to the reproduction of the social order. One of the most elaborate accounts of how this practical sense of social structure and social place functions in everyday life is provided in his analytic of taste and aesthetics, condensed into the now seminal *Distinction* (1984). In his magnum opus, Bourdieu attempted to demonstrate that Kant's illusive 'faculty of discriminating and judging', far from being a universal a priori, is instead an 'historical transcendental' produced under quite particular social conditions (i.e. those of artists and intellectuals). However, he also aimed to show that this faculty cannot be reduced to the ranking, classifying and evaluating operations of the mind, but is instead rooted in the visceral proclivities and aversions of the socially informed body. It is the latter which helps to transform the arbitrary nature of class-tastes into the ineluctable necessity of bodily affect, which can take the form of a quasi-mystical communion (of which love and especially the "love of art" provide the paradigm) or, instead, of an unbridgeable difference born of physical revolt. Class-tastes hence play a crucial role in ensuring that agents' preferences, practices and aspirations are "reasonable" – i.e. commensurate with their means of realization – *without* therefore being "rational", in the sense of being the product of a strategic, calculated adjustment of goals and means as advocates of Rational Action Theory would have it. If social practice undeniably exhibits a *ratio*, it is not that of a pre-conceived plan or project, drawn up after careful consideration of all possible lines of action, but it is rather a form of rationality that, in the words of Merleau-Ponty, 'is precisely proportioned to the experiences in which it is disclosed' (1996: xix).

From this it follows that agents' practices and beliefs, including their particular relationship to the body, are always circumscribed by class in a twofold manner. First, by the objective limits that characterize their social position, which define the *type* and *range* of experiences to which any given agent is exposed. Secondly, by the practical classifications of the class-habitus which, being the incorporation of these limits, tend to recognize them as "natural", "normal" or "self-evident", in short, *mis*recognize their existence as "limits". If this seemingly renders the structuring role of the habitus – and indeed the analytic utility of the concept itself – as redundant with the determinations inscribed in a given social position, Bourdieu insists that it is only in situations of quasi-perfect coincidence between positions and dispositions – i.e. when habitus operate in conditions that are identical or highly similar to those in which they were produced – that one could act "as if" practices were the direct product of the conditions in which they unfold.

However, when there is a discrepancy between agents' *present* and *past* position in the social structure – as in situations of crisis or those of (upward or downward) mobility – and dispositions hence come to function in situations that differ from those in which they were produced, it becomes possible to isolate the specific efficacy of the habitus. In fact, since agents' positions can change more rapidly than their dispositions, the analysis often registers this efficacy as a "lag" or "gap" in their practices and opinions. The latter are, as it were, suspended halfway between those characteristic of their social origins and those that are most typical of their current social position. This lag tends to be all the more pronounced, the more the dispositions that organize a given area of practice are (1) linked to the earliest (and hence most formative) social experiences; are (2) the product of a largely *practical* inculcation (rather than explicit theoretical instruction) and (3) evade subsequent restructuration by a systematic, comprehensive pedagogy of the type provided by the educational system. As the analyses presented in the following chapters will aim to show, the dispositions that structure the ways in which different classes use their bodies often partake of all these three characteristics. Not only are they the product of a social conditioning that – like the development of tastes in food – largely circumvents discourse and representation and speaks *directly* to the body (and this from day one), but they also largely escape the transformative scope of the educational system which – with the exception of everything related to speech and pronunciation – does not officially scrutinize and sanction this particular dimension of the class-habitus. The reason for highlighting these three characteristics is that, in my view, they define the conditions under which one can productively use the concept of habitus. If the concept will come to play such a crucial role in the analyses to follow, this is because it provides a means of accounting for (1) the relative intransigence of the body to conscious, intentional strategies of self-transformation *without* thereby having to regress to a biological reductionism that attributes this intransigence to genetic hardwiring or innate physiological functions (as will be illustrated by the case of "dieting" discussed in Chapter 4) and (2) for the regularity and systematicity of a domain of practice which, like the relationship to the body, is characterized by the relative absence of explicit rules or norms of conduct.

A 'class unconscious'

The recognition that 'we can know more than we can tell' (Polanyi, 2009 [1967]: 4) also has important consequences for the manner in which one conceptualizes what are generally referred to as the "norms" or "values" of a given social group. In fact, explaining social *regularities* – which the analysis can grasp in the form of a statistical association between a particular set of practices or beliefs and a given social category – in terms of the conscious adherence to a system of ethical *rules* or an explicit moral *code* tends to become all the more problematic, the less a given area of practice is subjected to systematic codification, as is the case with the relationship to the body.

If the different aspects of this relationship are marked by a clear stylistic affinity and present themselves to everyday perception as relatively *systematic* configurations of practices and properties – often to the extent that each individual element comes to function as a practical metonym capable of evoking the entire "character" of a person or "lifestyle" of a group (*"They eat fast-food"*, *"He wears a track-suit"*) – fact remains that these particular ways of relating to the body are rarely acquired through a rational, systematic pedagogy aimed at inculcating an explicit body of ethical principles or at consciously instilling a particular "world-view". In fact, as Boltanski (1971: 217ff.) already pointed out, the "rules" that govern the uses of the body within a particular group rarely ever present themselves as such, that is to say, as a coherent system of explicit guidelines and imperatives for social action. In fact, the few times that these rules do become explicit, is when they are transgressed and even then they most often present themselves in a *negative* form (*"Don't eat like a pig!"*, *"Don't lean on the table!"*, etc.) or in the mode of *tautology* (*"Sit like a girl!"*, *"Stand like a man!"*, etc.).

To help account for this systematic and coherent nature of practices in the absence of any explicit mechanisms that ensure their internal coherence and concertation, Bourdieu points to another characteristic of habitus, namely its tendency to transfer dispositions from one domain of practice to another. In fact, the incorporation of particular ways of perceiving, judging and acting into the habitus does not only enable them to persist well beyond their original conditions of learning, but also to be transposed *from* these conditions onto other areas of practice. In this manner, everyday uses of the body, such as those entailed in the performance of heavy manual labour, have a tendency to "spill over" onto other domains of practice, such as ways of walking, talking or eating (also see Crossley, 2001: 125ff.). For instance, the instrumentalist ethos that favours a free and uninhibited use of the body and shuns any type of formality or restriction is not only expressed in a preference for clothing that is "practical" and enables freedom of wear or a taste for dishes that are simple, solid, straightforward and "go down well" (as opposed to everything that is too fidgety and finicky), but even subtends the apparently most "natural" uses of the body such as ways of laughing, sneezing or blowing one's nose. More than any conscious striving for logical or stylistic coherence, it is this transfer of dispositional schemes – of which the transfer of motor-habits is a crucial dimension – that endow the practices of a given class with their distinctive "fingerprint". If the body can hence be said to "determine" our practices, it is not by way of some innate biological template, but through a socially acquired *articulatory style*. As Merleau-Ponty notes: 'Although our body does not impose definite instincts upon us from birth, as it does upon animals, it does at least give to our life *the form of generality*, and develops our personal acts into stable dispositional tendencies' (1996: 146, *my emphasis*).

Crucially, these 'dispositional tendencies' transcend the plain of the purely stylistic and encompass a distinct *moral* dimension. Few of the most everyday uses of the body are in fact strictly speaking "neutral" and each social group tends to wield its own criteria of "good" or "bad", "right" or "wrong" ways of speaking, walking, standing, sitting, eating, laughing, etc. This sense of right and wrong is, furthermore, differentiated in accordance with the cardinal divisions of social space so that there are "manly" and "feminine", "refined" or "vulgar", "professorial" or "working-class" ways of accomplishing the most mundane acts. Again, because these morally qualified uses of the body are acquired in a practical manner, they do not need to rise to the level of an explicit ethical code. What endows the relationship to the body with its logic and structure is *not* the intentional coherence of an *ethics*, but rather the practical systematicity of a class *ethos*, a 'generative formula not constituted as such which enables objectively coherent responses, compatible with the practical premises of a practical relationship to the world, to be generated for all the problems of everyday existence' (Bourdieu, 1984: 418).

As the product of the incorporation of the regularities that characterize a given social universe – i.e. of the events, interactions, problems, etc. that repeatedly arise within this universe – the ethos provides agents with a practical sense of what "ought" to be done, what "can" be done or what is "not done" in any given situation. Acquired *in* and *for* practice, the principles of the class ethos assert themselves *practically*, that is to say, in the actions and comportment of those whose conduct they regulate. It is precisely this practical dimension which, as Foucault points out, was at the heart of the original Greek conception of *ethos*:

> *Ethos* was the deportment and the way to behave. It was the subject's mode of being and a certain manner of acting visible to others. One's *ethos* was seen by his dress, by his bearing, by his gait, by the poise with which he reacts to events, etc.
>
> (Foucault in Bernauer and Rasmussen, 1988: 6)

As such, an ethos functions as an embodied morality, an ethics made flesh, in which a group's most deep-seated values and convictions become deposited at the level of bodily *hexis* and condensed into such indices as the pressure that goes into a handshake, the pitch of one's voice, the space one occupies with one's body and one's bearing, the distance one keeps from others, the pace of one's actions and words, in short, in all the gestures that constitute the 'ceremonial idiom' (Goffman, 1967: 56) of a particular group. While the term *ethos* will hence be used to refer to the *moral* dimension of the class-habitus, it is a sense of morality that, as Charles Taylor points out:

> is not, or is only imperfectly, captured in our representations... It is carried in patterns of appropriate action: that is, action which conforms to a sense of what is fitting and right. An agent with this kind of understanding recognizes when he or she or others 'have put a foot wrong'. His or her actions are responsive throughout to this sense of rightness, but the 'norms' may be quite unformulated, or formulated only in fragmentary fashion.
> (Taylor, 1993: 51)

In fact, while agents are often hard-pressed to fully explicate the principles that inform their sense of "right" or "wrong", they are nevertheless quick to spot any transgressions of this moral sense. So whereas men may not be able to consciously enumerate all the features that define the norms of accomplished masculinity, they are nonetheless quite capable of identifying certain manners of walking, standing, sitting or speaking, as "effeminate" or "queer". More importantly, because this sense of morality is largely carried in bodily postures and gestures, any departures from the tacit norms of appropriate conduct are not just excluded as "un-*think*-able", but are often quite literally "un-*do*-able".

For instance, feminist scholars like Henley (1977) or Young (2005) have shown how the dominant norms of feminine propriety are expressed in postural schemes – like sitting cross-legged for extended periods of time, keeping the knees together while running or bending down, pulling in the stomach and thrusting out the chest while walking, etc. – which women tend to perform unthinkingly, but which are a veritable acrobatics for men, who often find themselves incapable of adopting such "unnatural" uses of the body. Conversely, when women attempt to consciously resist such norms by adopting the postures that convey the sense of power and freedom typical of masculine kinesics, they not only face grave social injunctions (especially the risk of being branded as "loose"), but are also confronted with the resilience of their own body scheme. The latter often responds to such "unfamiliar" movements with all the physical calls to order through which the body signals that it is operating "out of line" or "out of place" (blushing, stuttering, sweating, etc.). This again illustrates how the effective transformation of relationships of domination entails a lot more than a simple intellectual conversion or an "awakening of consciousness". Indeed, instead of speaking of a 'class consciousness', as an explicit representation of the shared interests of a given class, its boundaries and its relationships

52   Social order, body order

vis-à-vis other classes, it is perhaps more apt to speak of a 'class unconscious', as a communal mode of comportment, carried in the most minute postures and gestures of the body and expressed in its apparently most spontaneous of reactions.

'Modus operandi' and 'opus operatum'

While the notions of *habitus* and *ethos* help underline the centrality of the socially informed body as the primary means through which agents "in-*habit*" the social world, the discussion so far has still not exhausted the full meaning of the proposition that 'class is a phenomenon of the flesh' (Charlesworth, 2000: 65). There is in fact a second, more *literal* sense in which social agents can be said to "embody" their particular position in social space. The particular point-of-view that is engendered in a given class of social condition(ing)s is not just durably rooted "in" the body, in the form of *hexis* and quasi-visceral dispositions, but also effectively *transforms* the body in its apparently most natural and "objective" of features. Bourdieu points to this inherently reflexive dimension of tastes when he observes that 'taste, a class culture turned into nature, that is, *embodied*, helps to shape the class body' (1984: 190, *original emphasis*).

This is already evident in all the deliberate modifications of appearance through cosmetic and sartorial indices that come to function as 'social markers deriving their meaning and value from their position in the system of distinctive signs which they constitute and which is itself homologous with the system of social positions' (1984: 192), such as the oppositions between "heavy" and "light" make-up, tanned vs. pale skin, dyed vs. "natural" hair or, in another register, "heavy" vs. "subtle" perfumes. Such conscious manipulations of its surface are, however, not the only manner in which class-taste helps to fashion the body. In fact, the tastes that are engendered in a particular class of social conditions also play a crucial role in shaping the body's *physicality*. Bourdieu even goes as far as defining the body as:

> the most indisputable materialization of class taste ... which it manifests in several ways. It does this first in the seemingly most natural features of the body, the dimensions (volume, height, weight) and shapes (round or square, stiff or supple, straight or curved) of its visible forms, which express in countless ways a whole relationship to the body, i.e., a way of treating it, caring for it, feeding it, maintaining it which reveals the deepest dispositions of the habitus.
>
> (1984: 190)

In this sense, the socially informed body or habitus is not only, to borrow Bourdieu's own terminology, a 'modus operandi' – a practical matrix of actions, perceptions and evaluations durably somatized into bodily states of attraction and repulsion, desire and disgust – but also an 'opus operatum', a material object that is marked by the necessity that is inscribed in a particular social position and trajectory. The following chapters will in fact try to show, that there is a quite literal twist to Bourdieu's proposition that social agents are 'classified by their classifications' (1984: 6). More specifically, they will aim to demonstrate that it is largely through the relatively coherent system of practical classifications, commonly referred to as "taste", that bodies gradually acquire their distinctive and distinguished social morphology, in short, become '*class*-ified'. As the 'only tangible manifestation of the "person"' (Bourdieu, 1984: 192) and hence the material foundation of an accomplished social and (socially defined) sexual identity, the body is in a sense predisposed to become the object of particularly intense and affectively charged symbolic investments.

It would, however, be somewhat naïve to reduce the manner in which social conditions physically "condition" the body solely to the conscious, intentional ways in which social agents aim to mould their physical appearance in accordance with the templates provided by their particular class or class fraction (working out to become "bigger", dieting to become "thinner", etc.). Important as such deliberate forms of "body-work" are to understanding the social differentiation in physical properties, they should not blind the analysis to the more mundane and subtle manners in which class-differences contribute to shaping the physical body. The particular conditioning of musculature and posture through physical work, the habituation to certain types of food and their long-term effects on the body's size and shape or even the more complex pathways that link psychosocial stress to the physiology of organic development, auto-immunity and ageing (see Wilkinson, 1996: esp. 175ff.) are but a few examples of the ways in which the body is materially fashioned by the "inert violence" of day-to-day existence. The main reason for highlighting this distinction between conscious, deliberate forms of body-management and -modification and the more habitual, pre-reflective manners in which class-tastes shape the body, is that while the former very often tend to reinforce the latter (of which they are often only a more systematic expression), the opposite does not always hold true. In fact, as will be shown by the case of dieting discussed in Chapter 4, deliberate attempts to alter one's physique can run counter to the opaque logic of class-taste which, being durably inscribed in the body, often proves particularly difficult to subject to conscious control and hence has all the appearance of an "innate" resistance.

Being and seeming

In a sense, there is nothing new about the proposition that the body plays a central role in the process whereby "class" as a *relational* property, becomes transformed into "class" as an innate, *substantialist* trait. In fact, Erving Goffman already formulated a similar insight in the early fifties. As a sociologist who, perhaps more than any other, was keenly aware of the social strategies of the *parvenu*, namely he or she who appropriated or emulated symbols of upper-class status (in the area of speech, clothing or demeanour, for instance) in order to project a more favourable image of self, Goffman clearly recognized the importance of *physical* attributes as durable and reliable indices of social status. Indeed, in his very first published paper Goffman observed:

> Evidence concerning previous activity is crucial because class status is based not only on social qualifications, but also on the length of time a person has possessed them. Owing to the nature of biological growth and development, acquired patterns of behaviour typically provide a much less reliable view of a person's past than is provided by *acquired changes in his physical structure*.
>
> (1951: 301, *my emphasis*)

This fundamentally *embodied* character of class-taste sets effective limits to all strategies of symbolic emulation or "bluff". More specifically, attempts to exploit the relative autonomy of the symbolic – i.e. to change one's position in the objective social hierarchies (defined by the different types of capital) by modifying one's position in the hierarchy of symbolic forms (ways of speaking, dressing, etc.) – are always limited by the body in a twofold manner. First, because the essence of "class" – in the double sense of the term – is inherently defined by its *mode of acquisition*, that is to say, by an early and diffuse inculcation of forms of comportment, which can only be acquired through the prolonged immersion in a particular set of social conditions and can never be fully transmitted through conscious, explicit training, let alone through deliberate imitation. Second, because the body *itself* comes to bear the traces of the social condition(ing)s of which it is the product in its physical, perceptible features and hence conveys a meaning that is, quite literally, incarnated.

The first point has already been discussed in the preceding sections. Put briefly, the intentional emulation of a lifestyle is to its practical incorporation, what the learning of a foreign language is to the acquisition of a mother tongue. Whereas in the former case, learning is often based on the deliberate imitation of an explicitly constituted *model* that is defined according to clearly specified *rules* (as found in etiquette-books or fashion-, beauty- or lifestyle-magazines) in the latter, it takes the form of a practical *mimesis*, in which agents "learn" the central aspects of class-identity by following the embodied examples of others. Like our professional football-player, dominant groups can play the cultural game with such "class", because of their early and prolonged familiarization with a universe of refined objects, properties and persons (something which will be elaborated in Chapter 7). This fundamentally distinguishes Bourdieu's '*sense* of distinction' from the Veblenian explanatory scheme to which his critics have repeatedly tried to reduce it (see for instance Elster, 1983; Alexander, 1995). A considerable part of his analytic of taste is in fact devoted to showing that precisely *because* dominant groups acquire their "culture" under conditions that tend to exclude its very awareness as such – i.e. as an arbitrary set of practices and representations rooted in particular historical circumstances – and instead promote its incorporation as "second-nature", that they have no need for deliberate strategies of conspicuous distinction and are, in a very real sense, distinguished *despite* themselves.[2] One of the supreme manifestations of such a cultivated nature is undoubtedly the capacity for "relaxation in tension", the ability to act and be "natural" in even the most formal and highly ritualized of situations. It is the type of *certitudo sui* that is bred of familiarity, through the early and sustained inculcation of forms of deportment and etiquette, that can only be displayed with such and grace precisely *because* they operate at the level of the habitual.

Indeed, the difficulties entailed in trying to subject the minutiae of behaviour to reflexive scrutiny are perhaps felt most acutely by those who are situated close enough to the dominant to accept their definition of the legitimate body, while at the same time lacking the means to fully realize this definition, namely members of the middle-class or *petit-bourgeoisie*. The gap between acknowledgment and knowledge which defines their relationship to the dominant lifestyle, forms the basis for a constant self-consciousness and self-monitoring, which not only finds its expression in all forms of verbal and non-verbal "hyper-correction", but also infuses their actions with an often paralyzing reflexivity, that aims to correct gestures and words in the very act of producing them. As such, it is the exact opposite of bourgeois "ease" which is always quick to spot such attempts as "snobbish", "pretentious" or "pedantic". Because their own social aspirations constantly incline them to perceive and judge their own appearance and comportment through dominant taxonomies, the relationship to the body of those who occupy *intermediate* positions in the social structure (both in the sense of "in between" or "in the middle", but also of "transitional" or "liminal"), could perhaps be best described as marked by a "tension in relaxation" (as will be discussed more fully in Chapter 8).

However, it is not just through its overall bearing that the body betrays its own social conditions of production and constrains strategies of symbolic bluff. The lifestyle associated with a particular position in social space also leaves its durable traces in what Veblen called 'the conformation of the person'. The necessity inscribed in a particular social position and trajectory is in fact not only registered at the level of bodily automatisms or *hexis*, but also becomes materialized in the body's physical attributes, which come to function as embodied cues of social location. Goffman mentions the condition of a man's hands or physical height as examples of such 'symbols of status based ultimately on the long-range physical effects of diet, work and environment' (1951: 301) and Chapter 4 will aim to show that the same applies to the body's size and shape. The symbolic value that is attributed to such physical indices of "class" is no less crucial in shaping agents' sense of worth, and hence the ease or discomfort with which they negotiate everyday social life, than that which is ascribed to their particular manner of using or "carrying" the body.

There is nevertheless a crucial difference between the two. In fact, whereas the potential for embarrassment that is contained in all forms of symbolic pretension often already *presupposes* face-to-face interaction and verbal exchange, it is through such corporeal emblems of class that social agents very often find themselves to be "de facto" distinguished, that is to say, outside of any direct social contact or any explicit status-claims. As embodied subjects, who bear the marks of their origins and trajectory in their bodies social agents tend to signify *despite* themselves. Stronger still, because the physical body is perceived as the most tangible evidence of a person's "essence", there is little need for explicit confirmation or contradiction of this essence, because the body says more than enough. In this sense, there is also a more literal meaning to Merleau-Ponty's aforementioned assertion that our being-in-the-world "condemns us" to meaning.

From the above it follows that the body can be treated as the site of a *twofold naturalization* of social categories of perception and evaluation. First, because it provides the basis for a mode of "learning" in which these categories are largely acquired in a *practical* manner, that is, below the level of explicit discourse and representation, which endows them with all the appearance "innateness" or "second-nature". Second, because these embodied categories (i.e. "taste") in turn engender a preference for practices, products and goods that contribute to reflexively shaping the body and hence helps to further strengthen their appearance as being rooted in "nature", that is, in an innate biological essence. The remainder of this chapter will be devoted to exploring the third and final manner in which the logic of embodiment and class-domination intersect.

'I can', 'it can', 'I must'

In fact, up to this point the discussion has mainly focused on the dual sense in which social agents can be said to "embody" their social conditions of existence. Throughout this discussion, the body has simultaneously figured as the generative principle *behind* 'class-ified' practices and beliefs (the 'body-subject'), as well as the physical realization and expression *of* such practices and beliefs (the 'body-object'). In doing so however, it has largely neglected an aspect of embodiment that is no less crucial in understanding the manner in which class-divisions affect and are in turn affected by the body. In fact, to say that we "are" and "have" bodies does not just mean that our intentionality is always subtended by a pre-reflective grasp on the social world, nor does it merely serve to highlight the fact that we are endowed with visible properties that are subjected to social scrutiny and prone to function as distinctive signs of social and moral value. It also means that embodiment ineluctably subjects us to the rhythms, cycles, and imperatives of physico-organic being. To be and to have a body is also to be subjugated to the vegetative cycles of nutrition, excretion and sleep, to be exposed to the forces, frictions and inertias of the physical world and hence to the risk of illness and injury, to be caught up in the irreversible process of ageing and hence to be confronted with the realities of growth, development, decay and, ultimately, death.

It is precisely this visceral dimension of embodiment that often proves remarkably absent from sociological commentaries on the body. Several authors have in fact noted how the numerous tomes that have sociology's "turn to the body" often wield curiously ethereal and "disembowelled" conceptions of embodiment (see Freund, 1988 or Wacquant, 1995). Instead of tackling the sensuous realities of the hungry, sweaty, aching, and mortal body, these commentaries often remain wedded to old intellectual habits which construe the body as just another "text" to be read, a "sign" to be deconstructed or a "discourse" to be subverted. This criticism not only applies to the various semiotic, post-modern or post-structuralist readings of the body, but also characterizes theoretical approaches that are otherwise keenly aware of the body's role in human cognition and action. Existential phenomenology, and the work of Merleau-Ponty in particular, proves to be a case in point. In fact, in as much as his work places the "lived body" squarely in the centre of the analysis of perception, his definition of embodiment remains restricted to those aspects that are most directly involved in human motility and cognition, namely the *exteroceptive* capacities provided by the five senses as well as the *proprioceptive* sense of one's own body in physical space.[3] Drew Leder (1990), who has produced one of the most systematic accounts of the phenomenology of everyday embodiment already pointed out this Platonic bias in the work of Merleau-Ponty:

> [Merleau-Ponty] treats the person as essentially embodied, not a pure consciousness contingently encased. Yet the lived body he describes is never complete. There is little discussion of metabolism, sleep, visceral processes, birth and death ... [B]y virtue of this emphasis on the 'higher' and ecstatic regions of the body, the Merleau-Pontian subject still bears a distant resemblance to its Cartesian predecessor, never fully fleshed out with bones and guts.
>
> (Leder, 1990: 36)

While he fundamentally agrees with Merleau-Ponty that 'intentionality' is rooted in the constitutive capacities of the body – an "I can", rather than an "I think" – Leder insists that this is not the only manner in which embodiment subtends perception. In fact, those aspects of embodiment that are most directly involved in our 'being-in-the-world' are themselves supported by a host of physiological processes that operate according to a logic that is often as *anonymous*, as it is *autonomous*. Central to his argument is that this vegetative dimension of embodiment has a phenomenological structure that differs considerably from that of the 'ecstatic body'. In fact, instead of being lived as an assembly of active, constitutive capacities, the visceral body presents itself as an array of autonomous processes, which not only operate outside of the scope of individual volition, but also function in a manner that largely eludes conscious introspection and comprehension. Cells divide, regenerate or die off, oxygen and nutrients are absorbed in the bloodstream, synaptic connections are formed or dissolved, hormones are secreted and all of this in a manner that is profoundly obscure to lay understanding (as it is still is, to a considerable extent, to the life sciences). According to Leder, it is this corporeal *autonomy* and *anonymity* which means that the body not only presents itself in the aspect of an 'I can', but also in the form of an 'it can' and an 'I cannot'. In fact, the visceral dimension of embodiment does not just limit individuals' control and understanding of their own bodies, but also impinges on their existence with its own set of ineluctable *demands*. In fact, the visceral body sets effective limits to individual action by forcing agents to regularly interrupt their plans and project in order to satisfy such vegetative demands as nutrition, excretion and rest. It is precisely this imperative nature that also endows vegetative being with the character of an 'I must' (eat, drink, breathe, defecate, sleep, etc.).

Together, the autonomous and opaque nature of vegetative being means that the body often presents itself in the ambivalent aspect of being 'foreign-mine' (Buytendijk, 1974: 295). While it is indisputably *my* heart that beats in *my* chest, *my* hairs and nails that grow, *my* stomach that growls, *my* limbs that feel tired or *my* joints that ache, this sense of "mine" is not one of personal ownership and control. While there is some degree of latitude in the manner in which agents choose to respond to the demands that are dictated by their bodies, they cannot choose to ignore them or do so at the potential risk of self-injury and, ultimately, self-destruction. The most dramatic sense of the body as an "alien" presence – a "some-*thing*" which controls, rather than is under control – is undoubtedly provided by the experience of injury or illness. It is here that each agent is fully confronted by the experiential rift in the 'unity of bodily and personal subjectivity' (Buytendijk, 1974), an experience of disjunction which was so admirably captured by Marcel Proust:

> It is in moments of illness that we are compelled to recognize that we live not alone but chained to a creature of a different kingdom, whole worlds apart, who has no knowledge of us, and by whom it is impossible to make ourselves understood: our body.
>
> (Quoted in Burwood, 2008: 263)

It is in fact not only through the injunctions and verdicts of *social* life that agents come to take 'a statistical and objective view on themselves' (Merleau-Ponty, 1996: 434). The experience of one's own body as objectified and foreign is not just something that imposes itself on social agents from "outside", through the incessant judgments of others, but also originates from "within". It is through experiences such as hunger, fatigue, pain and illness that we are reminded of the fact that our bodies, for lack of a less Cartesian expression, have "a mind of their own".

This recognition by no means implies an essentialist conception of human physiology as fully autonomous vis-à-vis its social environment. Social epidemiologists have in fact produced ample evidence that shows how the apparently most autonomous, self-regulating aspects of human physiology like skeletal development, blood-pressure or hormonal secretion are fundamentally affected by individuals' position in the class-structure (for a review see Freund and McGuire, 1995 or Wilkinson, 1996). Nor does it somehow invite a regression towards biological reductionism. The fact that vegetative existence imposes its inescapable demands does not preclude the (equally important) fact that social agents still have considerable leeway in the *manner* in which they meet these demands. As the following chapters will aim to show, the ways in which social agents accommodate biological imperatives are no less variable in terms of social position and can hence by no means be simply deduced from their biological make-up. However, it *does* imply that this variability is ultimately one of style and form, *not* of absolute choice.

The two bodies

To be and *to have* a body is therefore to be doubly "in-corporated", to be at once part of a social *and* a biological order, each with its own irreducible logic and its own distinct set of demands. This makes the body into a site where two types of objectivity intersect and intertwine. While it should be stressed, again, that these two 'objectivities' do not constitute fully autonomous dimensions, it is equally true that their respective logics never fully coincide and quite often prove to be at odds with one another. The *phenomenological* implications of our corporeal autonomy and anonymity have already been explored at length by authors such as Buytendijk (1974), Plessner (1975) and Leder (1990). Less attention has however been devoted to its properly *sociological* significance and especially its role in the (re)production of social- and class-*boundaries*. In fact, what makes this vegetative aspect of embodiment so relevant for sociological analysis – especially when it tackles the realities of *class* – is not just its autonomy and anonymity, but above all its *universality*. A considerable part of this study will in fact be devoted to drawing out the full implications of the deceivingly trivial observation that *all* social agents are and have bodies. One of the more important of these implications is that all agents, *without a single exception*, are fundamentally united in their shared submission to the cycles, rhythms, and imperatives of vegetative existence. While there is nothing inherently problematic about this "common" corporeality, this study will attempt to show that it does tend to become a problem in social systems that are fundamentally characterized by the existence of hierarchy, rank and status and especially for those groups – i.e. the dominant – who can only maintain their position through the symbolic assertion of difference, distance and distinction. It is within such social systems that the logic of the "two bodies" – the body politic and the biological body – often become antithetical. In fact, whereas the former operates according to a logic that particularizes, ranks, excludes and differentiates, the latter functions in a manner that is universal, inclusive and levelling, rendering each and every one as radically equal in their "common" submission to the imperatives and liabilities of physical, vegetative being. More generally, the view of the body as one of the primary sources of egotistical drives and a-social tendencies – a common sociological theme ever since Durkheim's ruminations on the social agent as 'homo duplex' (2005 [1914]) – all too easily overlooks the fact that the body is not only an important principle of *individuation*, but also functions as a powerful principle of *equalization*.[4] In fact, underneath all the lasting and often subtle *differences* that social life inscribes in bodies by virtue of their position in the hierarchies of capital, gender, age-group or race, *all* social agents are positioned as radically *equivalent* in their submission to and dependence on the demands of physical, vegetative existence which constitutes, in Georg Simmel's opening words, 'the level on which everyone meets'.

Mary Douglas (1970), who approached the problem of these "two bodies" from the perspective of comparative ethnology, was one of the first to address these tensions between the collective demands of the social body and the universal imperatives of the biological body. According to Douglas, one can observe a clear correspondence between, on the one hand, the strength of the external boundaries and the internal divisions of any given social system and, on the other, the degree in which the body and elementary bodily processes like eating, drinking, urination, defecation or perspiration – all of which constitute a *transgression* of boundaries – are considered to be problematic, that is, become subjected to an elaborate system of social regulations. In fact, the stronger the internal and external divisions of any social system, the more these bodily processes become subjected to censorship, modulation or stylization. Douglas even argues that this strong correspondence between social and bodily control can be observed across such a wide array of societies, that it takes the form of a law or a rule, which she coined 'the rule of distance from physiological origin', better known as the 'purity rule'. According to this rule:

> The distance between the two bodies is the range of pressure and classification in the society. A complex social system devises for itself ways of behaving that suggest that human intercourse is disembodied compared with that of animal creation. It uses different degrees of disembodiment to express the social hierarchy. The more refinement, the less smacking of the lips when eating, the less mastication, the less the sound of breathing and walking, the more carefully modulated the laughter, the more controlled the signs of anger, the clearer comes the priestly-aristocratic image.
>
> (Douglas, 1970: 80)

If one abstracts from the more functionalist undertones of her argument ('A complex social system devises...'), Douglas at least has the merit of raising the problems that universal embodiment poses for the (re)production of social boundaries. In fact, by rendering *all* social agents as radically equal in their submission to the universal demands of vegetative being and by forcing each and every one to engage in acts (eating, drinking, defecating, etc.) that visibly attest to their "common" nature, the autonomous dimension of embodiment challenges the differences that – otherwise and everywhere separate – social agents.

As mentioned, this challenge presents itself most acutely for those whose status depends on the assertion of distance and difference, namely among those who are situated at the top of the social hierarchy. For instance, in his seminal *The King's Two Bodies* (1957), Ernst Kantorowicz dissected the intricate legal contraptions that medieval jurists had to develop in order to reconcile the official image of the monarch as an omnipotent, omniscient and transcendental ruler, who embodied the integrity and continuity of the body politic, with the biological reality of the king as 'a Body mortal, subject to all Infirmities that come by

Nature or Accident, to the Imbecility of Infancy or old Age, and to *the like Defects that happen to the Bodies of other People*' (Plowden, quoted in Kantorowicz, 1957: 7, *my emphasis*). However, it is in the aforementioned work of Norbert Elias (2000) that one finds the best illustration of how the tension between the "two bodies" tends to be greatest among dominant social groups. He has shown how the need to maintain difference and distinction, itself inscribed in the struggle for social domination, is one of the most powerful motors behind the "civilization" of the relationship to the body. By censoring, repressing or modulating what is most "common" in themselves, the dominant also negate everything that positions them as radically equal to others, especially those occupying inferior social positions.

Faced with this symbolic denial of their "common" characteristics, dominated groups can often only respond with strategies of inversion, countering intellectual sublimation with bodily degradation and accentuating rather than repressing the body's "vulgar" features. In his study of the literary universe of Rabelais, Bakhtin (1965) already showed how the visceral realities of the 'material bodily lower stratum' provided a popular idiom to subvert the dominant hierarchies. Through obscenity, scatology and grotesque exaggeration, the rituals of 'Carnival' celebrated the manifold ways in which the body transgresses its own boundaries – through processes like urination, defecation, flatulence, eating, drinking and sex – and hence helped to symbolically undermine the official differences inscribed in the dominant social order by *inverting* the sacred principles on which it was founded (the dominance of the immortal Soul over the mortal Body, abstinence over gluttony, wisdom over folly, etc.). However, the grotesque representations of the body in Carnival not only served as a means of social critique, but also as a ritual affirmation of solidarity in which 'the bodily element is deeply positive. It is presented not in private, egotistic form, severed from the other spheres of life, but as something universal, representing all the people' (Bakhtin, 1965: 19). While this carnivalesque spirit has lost much of its ritual character, remnants of it still persist in the expressive explosiveness of working-class language (as analysed by Charlesworth, 2000: 203ff.), itself a crucial dimension of the popular relationship to the body. Flaunting censorship and euphemization, popular language draws heavily on the idiom of the body ("slag", "cunt", "fucker", "shit-head", etc.) as both a means of subverting dominant values – especially clear in all the calls to order directed at anyone who develops "airs" and "pretensions" (*"He thinks his shit doesn't stink!"* as the popular saying goes) – while at the same time expressing solidarity with those with whom one is so close that ritualized insults become a form of mutual recognition and affection.

This grotesque exaggeration of bodily processes is, however, only one of the ways in which the commonality of the body is used as a means of challenging social differences. To pick a somewhat more cultivated example from literary history, the recognition of the body's equalizing potential even subtends one of Shakespeare's most famous monologues. In fact, when in the *The Merchant of Venice*, the Jew Shylock pleads for equal treatment with his Christian protagonists, he bases his claims *not* on the universality of moral, theological or legal principle, but instead appeals to their shared corporeality:

> I am a Jew. Hath not a Jew eyes? Hath not a Jew hands, organs, dimensions, senses, affections, passions, fed with the same food, hurt with the same weapons, subject to the same diseases, healed by the same means, warmed and cooled by the same winter and summer as a Christian is? If you prick us, do we not bleed? If you tickle us, do we not laugh? If you poison us, do we not die? And if you wrong us, shall we not revenge? If we are like you in the rest, we will resemble you in that.
>
> (2006 [1596–1598]: 78)

If those who are situated at the *dominant* end of power-relationships (of class, gender, age, etc.) place themselves on the side of Culture, Mind and Rationality by censoring everything that refers to Nature and common corporeality, the interests of the dominated are often tied up with the body, which serves as a constant reminder of the fundamental equality that all agents share in their status as vegetative, biological, but also frail and mortal beings. Indeed, in her comparative study of French and American workers, Lamont showed how her North African interviewees explicitly countered the logic of (class) racism by pointing to 'the universality of our physiological characteristics ("we are all nine-month babies"; "we all have ten fingers") and to the universality of human needs' (2000: 204). A similar logic could help explain the enduring popularity of the 'material bodily lower stratum' among comedians, political satirists and cartoonists who continue to make grateful use of the body's subversive potential, whether through *caricature* – that 'distortion of the bodily image intended to break the charm and hold up to ridicule one of the principles of the effect of authority imposition' (Bourdieu, 1984: 208) – or any other type of bodily imagery that brings the "high and mighty" down to the physical realities of gustation, procreation and defecation.

Transcendence and negation

We can now return to a point that was made earlier in this chapter. In fact, if the body is the object of such affectively laden forms of investment, this is not only because it is the most tangible manifestation of social *identity*, but also because its own autonomous logic threatens the very *differences* that are needed to sustain this identity. This not only makes the body into an ideal case to study the principles on which this identity is founded – i.e. those of the class *ethos* – but also to analyse the strategies of distinction that social groups, especially those who are situated at the top of the class-structure, deploy to symbolize their distance from those who occupy inferior social positions. It is this logic which fundamentally implicates the body in the process of 'transcendence' and 'negation' as originally outlined by gender-theorist Raewyn Connell (see Connell, 1987: 65ff.). According to Connell, the reproduction of structures of masculine domination hinges on two, closely intertwined processes. First of all, it requires the symbolic 'negation' of all the *similarities* that necessarily exist between men and women. She argues in fact that the social production of gendered identities does not operate solely, or even primarily, through the accentuation of physical *difference*, but rather consists of the early and sustained negation of all the aspects in which men and women physically *resemble* one another. This is because physical differences (and especially those that are most closely tied to the logic of sexual reproduction) cannot, by themselves, sustain the existence of sexual inequalities in the broad array of social situations in which they manifest themselves. This is most obvious in the case of small children who 'have gender forms vehemently imposed on them long before they are capable of reproducing, or even have much understanding of the business of reproduction' (Connell, 1987: 81). If sexual differences were indeed so "natural", then they would hardly require the impressive amount of social labour that goes into their continued (re)production. In fact, this reproduction not only requires existing sexual similarities are negated and differences are highlighted. It is also crucial that sexual differences are *created* which have no direct or only a weak basis in human physiology, a process that Connell dubs as 'transcendence'. Crucial to her argument is that 'transcendence' does not simply imply the inculcation of gendered categories of thought or distinct sexual "world-views", but also comprises the *physical* transformation of male and female bodies in accordance with socially defined templates:

> The social definition of men as holders of power is translated not only into mental body-images and fantasies, but into muscle tensions, posture, the feel and texture of the body. This is one of the main ways in which the power of men becomes 'naturalized', i.e. seen as part of the order of nature.
> (Connell, 1987: 85)

Contra feminist theories that perpetuate the dualism of Culture vs. Nature by reducing patriarchy to a set of cultural meanings that are simply "draped" onto otherwise immutable physical differences, Connell argues that patriarchal structures help produce the very physical reality – i.e. the strong, large masculine body and the frail feminine physique that signals the "natural" superiority of men over women – they merely purport to express.

What this study will attempt to show, is that a similar logic underpins the ways in which the body is implicated in the reproduction and legitimization of *class*-domination. Just as the assertion of masculine dominance presupposes the systematic denial of everything that positions men and women as equal, the legitimization of *class*-differences hinges on the symbolic negation or censorship of all the "vulgar" characteristics that the dominant – in their capacity as visceral, vegetative beings – ineluctably share with the dominated. This means both to repress or censor the different manifestations of the body's vegetative autonomy, while at the same time cultivating a relationship to the body that testifies to agents' ability to control visceral imperatives and hence to "transcend" common animality. This can be done, as Elias (2000) showed, by removing vegetative processes from the public eye and hence "privatizing" them (urination or defecation), by hedging them with feelings of shame (flatulation) or, when this proves impossible or impractical, by strongly modulating or stylizing them (table manners).

Moreover, this logic not only applies to these vegetative processes themselves, but also to any physical properties that are deemed indicative of the way in which people accommodate such processes. These properties are subjected to a *physiognomic* perception which reads them as an index of an "active" or "passive", "attentive" or "careless", "controlled" or "resigned" relationship towards the body's visceral autonomy and hence towards Nature. Unkempt hair, bad teeth, a corpulent physique, untrimmed fingernails or body odour are all seen as signs of a facile surrender to Nature and hence of a "lazy" character or "passive" personality. In this manner the relationship to the body and bodily autonomy – what Berger and Luckmann called the 'continuing internal dialectic between identity and its biological substratum' (1967: 182–183) – comes to function as a practical metaphor for the relationship to the social world. If the "natural" relationship to the body of those who occupy the most precarious social positions is read as 'an index of *laisser-aller* ("letting oneself go"), a culpable surrender to facility' (Bourdieu, 1984: 193), then it is through their visible 'capacity to dominate their own biological nature', that the dominant affirm 'their legitimate claim to dominate social nature' (1984: 491). That this capacity for self-control and self-denial does not only manifest itself in the relationship to the body, but also expresses itself in that other fundamental dimension of existence, namely the relationship towards *time*, will be discussed in the following chapter.

Notes

1 For a more elaborate review of the differences and similarities between Bourdieu's concept of habitus and the notion of 'habit' as it figures in the work of Dewey and Merleau-Ponty, see Ostrow (1981). Crossley (2001) also provides an extensive review of the intellectual parallels in the thinking of Dewey, Ryle, Merleau-Ponty and Bourdieu.
2 This was to some extent even acknowledged by Veblen himself, whose Pragmatist sympathies made him a lot more aware of the pre-reflective foundations of the lifestyle of the "leisure class" than he is generally credited for. Not only did he insist that 'a standard of living is of the nature of habit' and should be understood as 'an habitual scale and method of responding to given stimuli' (1953 [1899]: 82), but he also recognized the role of habitually acquired, *embodied* cues of social status: 'Especially does it seem to be true that a life of leisure in this way persisted in through several generations will leave a *persistent, ascertainable effect* in the *conformation of the person*, and still more in his *habitual bearing and demeanor*' (ibid.: 49–50, *my emphasis*). Fact remains however, that he was quick to subsume such forms of practical inculcation under the category of 'passive habituation' and spends most of the *Theory of the Leisure Class* discussing those types of status display that involve 'taking thought and assiduously acquiring the marks of honourable leisure' (ibid.). In doing so, he failed to recognize the truly distinguishing hallmark of the dominant habitus and the *double* symbolic

profits that accrue to those who are endowed with it, namely the privilege of being "naturally" cultivated or having innate "class".

3 A similar critique has been formulated by feminist scholars. The work of Iris M. Young (2005: esp. 46ff. and 97ff.) in particular has been instrumental in showing how phenomenology's neglect of the physiological, visceral dimension of embodiment has resulted in a highly androcentric account of the "lived body". In fact, by failing to address the role of autonomous bodily processes – like menstruation and pregnancy – she argues that traditional phenomenology has ignored a considerable part of feminine embodiment and therefore of women's everyday experience of the social world.

4 In an essay entitled 'The Dualism of Human Nature and its Social Conditions' (2005 [1914]) Durkheim explicitly takes up the Kantian (and Cartesian) position which equates the body with the site of egoistic and asocial inclinations, while treating mental faculties as the ultimate source of reason and social order:

> Our intellect like our activity takes two very different forms: there are sensations and sensuous inclinations on the one hand, conceptual thinking and moral action on the other. [...] Our sensuous appetites are necessarily egoistic, they have as their aim our individuality and it alone. When we satisfy our hunger, our thirst, etc., without any other inclination coming into play, it is ourselves and ourselves alone that we satisfy. On the other hand, moral action is distinguished by the fact that the rules to which it conforms are susceptible to universalization; it strives, per definition, towards impersonal ends. Morality only begins with disinterest, the attachment to something other than ourselves.
>
> (1914: 5)

3 The body in social time

> The innermost structure of the mentality of a group can never be as clearly grasped as when we attempt to understand its conception of time in the light of its hopes, yearnings, and purposes. On the basis of these purposes and expectations, a given mentality orders not merely future events, but also the past.
> (Mannheim, 1968 [1936]: 188)

Before we will turn to look at the concrete ways in which class relationships shape the manner in which social agents use, perceive and invest in their bodies, there is one more thread that needs to be stitched into the theoretical argument. The core of this chapter hinges on a simple proposition, namely that the relationship to the body is inextricably bound up with that other fundamental dimension of social existence, namely the relationship to *time*. I will argue that differences in the manner in which social agents relate to their bodies can only become fully intelligible, when they are re-inserted in the temporal horizon that characterizes their particular class and which defines the 'purposes and expectations' towards the future, that Mannheim saw as particularly indicative of the mentality of a social class. By bringing out the implicit temporal dimension of bodily practice, this chapter will aim to show that what is at stake in both the everyday disputes over the "correct" manner of treating and presenting one's body, as well as in the semi-official struggles over the definition of "legitimate" physical care, is often an entire way of relating to *time* in general and to the *future* in particular. This implies that an adequate sociological understanding of the body, of its social uses and socially produced properties cannot dispense with a sociology of time and temporal dispositions.

Time for pain

One of the first to point out the significance of the 'time orientation' of a given group in understanding the ways in which its members come to experience their bodies was Mark Zborowski (1952/1969), a pioneer in the cultural study of the perception of pain. Zborowski's work starts from the fundamental assumption that human agents rarely submit or passively undergo the signals and sensations emitted by their bodies, but always perceive and evaluate these signals within the cultural framework provided by their group. In order to grasp this cultural dimension, he compared the manner in which the experience of 'being-in-pain' was verbalized and rationalized by male patients from four 'ethnocultural' groups – Italian and Irish immigrants, Jewish patients and so-called 'Old Americans' – treated in a New York veterans' hospital. Far from provoking a mechanical and standardized response, as physiological explanations assumed, he found the experience of pain to differ drastically between the members of these four groups. For Zborowski, the only way to account for these differences was to trace them back to the shared cultural heritage of the patients. He argued that one of the crucial ways in which their culture helped to shape the significance attributed to morbid sensations was by imposing a particular *temporal perspective* and especially by fostering a 'future-' or 'present-oriented' conception of time:

> [I]ndividuals reared in cultures that can be qualified as 'future-oriented' may tend to evaluate the meaning of their pain according to its implications for their future. Such patients will be most concerned with such questions as how their present experience may affect their health, earning capacities, or family life in days or years to come. They will be inclined to think in terms of the *effects* of the sensation, rather than in terms of the sensation itself. The future-oriented emphasis of the culture may foster anxieties directed toward the future.
>
> (Zborowski, 1969: 46)

Members of 'future-oriented cultures', like the Jewish patients or the 'Old Americans' he interviewed, tended to foreground the symptomatic significance of pain, perceiving it as an indicator of an underlying, potentially more threatening condition and focalizing their anxieties accordingly. The experience of pain itself could be made bearable and even be mastered, *only if* agents were capable of inscribing it in a particular sequence of events, that is, were able to understand its causes, its evolution and above all its long-term consequences. This not only characterized their specific way of coping with pain itself, but also informed their more general conceptions of health and illness. The latter was perceived as an ever-present possibility, lurking at the edges of good health and hence requiring constant vigilance and active measures of self-protection aimed at enhancing the body's natural defences. This attitude is almost diametrically opposed to the cultural conceptions of pain that characterize 'present-oriented' cultures:

> On the other hand, in 'present-oriented' societies, when people are most concerned with the immediacy of their life experiences, the patients may be more affected by the actual sensation of pain rather than by its possible implications for the future. They may be more preoccupied with its relief rather than with the cure of the condition of which the pain is a symptom.
>
> (Zborowski, 1969: 46–47)

In this manner, Zborowski showed how the concerns and anxieties of patients from Irish and Italian descent centred mainly on the manner in which pain interfered with the practical routines of their daily lives. As an impediment to normal action, pain not only deprived the body of its capacity for labour, but, more generally, of its physical force and hence not only threatened economic survival, but also affected one of the central pillars of masculine identity, namely its valorizing self-assertion in work (see Chapter 1). Within such a *functional* perspective on pain, there was little or no concern with the symptomatic significance of morbid sensations. Instead, pain and illness were very often conflated and when the former ceased to exist, the latter was also thought to have disappeared. While Zborowski hence has the distinct merit of drawing out the implicit connection between the experience of the body and the experience of time, he nonetheless fails to inquire into the particular conditions that produce such differences in temporal outlook. Instead, these differences are largely treated as the attributes of a largely homogenous and immutable "culture". More generally, his analyses are steeped in a culturalist essentialism that quite often regresses to the outright stereotypical in its descriptions of differences in "national character", such as the fighting strength of the Irish, the emotionality of the Italians, the foresight of the Jew or the entrepreneurial spirit of the Old Americans (for a similar critique see Kleinman *et al.*, 1994: 2ff.).[1] What is perhaps most puzzling about his work is the way in which it systematically overlooks one of the central factors that determines both the *manner* and *degree* in which agents have to use their bodies and hence both the general level of physical "wear and tear" and the particular type of risk to which they are exposed, namely their social and especially *class-*position. While some allowance is made for the role of occupational factors in determining the significance that is attributed to particular *types* of pain (manual workers more often worry about functional impediments like herniated joints, while those performing intellectual work more often worry about headaches), the importance of class in circumscribing the everyday uses of the body is largely swept away under the rug of a fixed cultural type.

Pain and prevention

A considerably more nuanced and complex understanding of the relationships between social position, temporality and bodily experience can be found in the early work of Luc Boltanski.[2] Like Zborowski, Boltanski also pursues the question of the social perception, evaluation and expression of somatic sensations, but places it squarely within the dynamic of class relationships and the logic inscribed in the social division of labour. One of the most pertinent features of this division, at least from the perspective of a sociology of the body, is that it defines the degree to which social agents have to "rely" on their body, its physical performance and especially its physical *force*, in order to secure their basic means of existence. By defining the level of physical intensity with which social agents *use* their bodies, class-differences – which in their crudest form are articulated along the distinction between "manual" and "mental" work – fundamentally contribute to the manner in which agents perceive, evaluate and respond to the signals emitted by their bodies and, more generally, influence the *level of attention* that they are both capable and willing to pay to such signals.

It is especially among those who have to make the most intensive use of their body, namely the members of the working-class, that one finds the most instrumental relationship toward its particular needs and demands. The reason for this is twofold. The first is the very nature of manual work as a sustained and unmediated relationship to the objects, frictions and inertias of the physical world. Not only does the prolonged experience of such work tend to habituate agents to heightened levels of physical discomfort and hence already raises the threshold of attention they pay to the body, but it also increases the general 'flux of physical sensations' – both in *acute* (muscle fatigue, bruises, sprains, scratches, burns, etc.) and *chronic* (arthritis, muscular inflammation, deformations, etc.) form – which in turn 'introduces noise in the communication between the subject and his body' (Boltanski, 1971: 222). Put differently, by increasing the *general* level of physical sensations emitted by the body, the experience of manual labour hampers the ability to discern and identify *particular* morbid signals. Second, and perhaps more importantly, the very *intention* of deciphering and identifying such signals already presupposes an attentive and reflexive relationship to the body, which is fundamentally at odds with the economic imperative of maximizing its physical potential. This necessity in fact constrains agents to work as much *with* as *against* their bodies, that is to say, to not only exploit the body's capacity for intensive and sustained effort, but also to resist and overcome spontaneous physical reactions like pain or fatigue. As such, the development of a caring, attentive attitude 'can have no other effect than to diminish the resistance which [manual workers] are able to oppose to their body and hence to reduce, both in quality and quantity, the labour it furnishes' (Boltanski, 1971: 222).

Conversely, as one rises in the social hierarchy and the direct importance of the body as a source of labour power decreases, social agents are increasingly able of adopting a more reflexive and attentive, that is to say, *autonomous* relationship towards their body. Such a relationship is not only possible because agents make less intensive use of their bodies, but also because the objective degree of security that characterizes their position in social space systematically increases. In fact, apart from the unequal physical demands that their conditions of existence place on members of different social classes, Boltanski identifies another, more fundamental reason why differences in social position unequally favour the inculcation of an attentive and therapeutic relationship to the body. What underlies the propensity to pay active attention to the signals and sensations emitted by the body, to interpret such signals as potential "symptoms" of an underlying condition, to proactively pursue knowledge about the body's hidden states (through self-examination or regular medical check-ups) and to systematically engage in certain acts or refrain from others because they are deemed to be "good" or "bad" for one's health, is a more 'global attitude towards life and towards time in particular' (Boltanski, 1969: 111). This attitude consists in the more general disposition to orient and evaluate current actions in terms of their future consequences, to renounce immediate gratifications in favour of gains that are situated in a more or less distant point in the future, to trade in the probable for the possible, in short, to adopt a strategic attitude of "prevision" towards time and the future. It is precisely the durable inculcation of such an attitude which Boltanski argues, is unequally probable for members of the different social classes.

He demonstrated this in his own study on the diffusion of modern techniques of childcare (*puériculture*), especially those inspired by Pasteurian medical theory (Boltanski, 1969). Looking for the principle that could account for the unequal rate at which different social classes adopted these techniques – rapidly among the upper classes and especially among the *petit bourgeoisie*, slowly and often piecemeal among the working-classes – he attributed it to the affinities that exist between, on the one hand, the particular *ethos* of the different classes and, on the other, the implicit philosophy that animated these techniques:

> Boiling a pacifier constitutes an infinitely more complex sanitary act than, for instance, dressing a wound or putting a cold compress on the forehead of a child that has a headache; it means engaging in an *act of prevision* whose *results are random* and whose *efficacy is indirect* [...] By demanding this particular type of attitude towards time which consists in engaging in long and cumbersome actions, to 'go through the trouble', to renounce an immediate satisfaction in view of a larger good that *is situated in the future*, the Pasteurian rules of childcare necessarily have an *ascetic character*.
>
> (Boltanski, 1969: 111–112, *my emphasis*)

He argues, furthermore, that such an ascetic philosophy is not only typical for modern techniques of childcare, but is characteristic of the entire ensemble of techniques, practices and know-how that can be subsumed under the heading of "preventive medicine". By defining illness not as something that should be negotiated *if* and *when* it presents itself, but as an *eventuality* that should be constantly anticipated and actively avoided by engaging in (or refraining from) actions whose very outcome will only manifest itself in a more or less distant point in the future, these techniques objectively demand both a long-term perspective on the body and its needs, as well as a certain degree of self-denial (on this point also see Turner, 1996: 96). In this sense, the conception of the "responsible" medical subject which is tacitly implied or explicitly demanded by modern preventive medicine is not unlike that of the "rational" agent envisioned by economic science and advocates of "rational action theory" in particular. In both cases, agents are deemed to adopt a strategic, calculating relationship towards existence which is geared to the minimization of individual costs and the maximization of individual gains, whether in monetary (i.e. income, interest, etc.) or non-monetary form (i.e. health, longevity, etc.). Just as the *homo economicus* is deemed to adopt a long-term perspective on his earnings and spending, to defer current consumption in favour of future gains through strategies like saving or investment; the *homo medicus* is supposed to take up a long-term view of the body and its needs and, especially, 'to adopt a rational attitude towards illness which, reinserted into a life-plan in the form of a possible eventuality, can hence be mastered and overcome by long-term prevision' (Boltanski, 1971: 221). More importantly, like economic theory, medical science tends to largely take such a strategic disposition towards long-term prevision for granted and fails to inquire into the social conditions that enable such a disposition to be durably inculcated and meaningfully deployed. Boltanski contends however, that it is precisely these conditions that are themselves unequally distributed across social space. More specifically, he argues that the very intention of anticipating and *a fortiori* of mastering the future, of orienting one's current actions in terms of future outcomes and, more generally, the willingness to sacrifice the present and present gratification to the future is itself dependent on the degree in which this future presents itself as manageable and foreseeable, that is, on the objective degree of security and hence the subjective sense of control that social agents have over their *present*. It is precisely among those who are situated at the bottom of the social hierarchy and hence occupy the most precarious social positions, that such objective security and subjective control are rarely given and that the conditions for the meaningful development of an *ethos* of foresight and calculation often prove least favourable.

The particular relationship between social position, social power and temporal experience will be discussed in more detail in the following sections. For now it is important to point out that their conditions of existence tend to lock members of dominated groups in a particularly tight double bind. On the one hand, their basic means of existence depend, more than for any other class, on the physical performance of their bodies, which are therefore exposed to the highest degree of "wear and tear" and hence to potential injury and illness. On the other hand, the economic insecurity that marks their conditions of existence, also more than for any other class, tends to obstruct the very development of an attentive and preventive relationship to the body, which would allow them to identify and act upon the potential signs of pathology or dysfunction. As Boltanski notes:

> Members of the working class cannot reinsert illness within a temporality, because illness is for them precisely that which interrupts time, that which breaks up the normal run-of-things and obliterates the future entirely, that over which one has no hold, in short an economic and familial catastrophe of which one dare not even think.
>
> (Boltanski, 1971: 222)

Without therefore having to rise to the level of a conscious representation of the body, its needs and desires, the working-class relationship to the body seems to hinge on a particularly sharp distinction between the state of health and illness. Because their conditions of existence tend to prevent them from paying *proactive* attention to their somatic sensations and even encourage them to ignore and repress such sensations (the capacity to withstand pain and fatigue being a fundamental dimension of a valorized identity, not just among working-class men), illness often tends to present itself as a wholly random and unannounced event which abruptly interrupts the experience of health. This conception of illness as an unforeseeable "accident" also informs the definition of the preferred type of treatment that members of the working-class come to expect from medical professionals. Like Zborowski, Boltanski argues that the popular concern with illness tends to be restricted to its most external and in a sense most "superficial" manifestations, namely to the manner in which it obstructs the body's capacity to function *normally* and especially to the painful sensations it produces. The ideal cure or remedy is therefore that which swiftly restores the body to its "healthy" state, that is, to its capacity to function and perform without physical impediments or pain. Because illness is treated as synonymous with pain and discomfort, any treatment that manages to remove the latter is also thought to have successfully removed the former.

It is this entire conception of health and illness, as well as the experience of the body in general, which tends to change as one moves up the social hierarchy. While the body's direct importance as a source of labour power decreases, the objective degree of security that characterizes social positions tends to simultaneously increase. It is precisely this security that provides agents with the necessary hold over the present that enables them to actively confront and plan for the future and hence to meaningfully adopt a long-term perspective on social existence. Boltanski argues that this shift in temporal experience and the concomitant transformations in the relationship to the body can already be observed as one moves from the working to the middle-classes. In fact, the same principle that obstructs the meaningful appropriation of the different techniques of preventive medicine among members of the working-class, namely their intrinsically *ascetic* and *long-term* character, is as the basis of their particularly rapid diffusion among those social groups whom everything inclines to adopt both an *ethos* of self-denial towards the social world and a particularly *future*-oriented conception of time, namely the *petit bourgeoisie* and especially its upwardly aspiring fractions (see Chapter 8). The attitude of constant self-monitoring and self-discipline, of self-imposed austerity and the willingness to renounce current gratifications in favour of future gains, objectively demanded by these techniques, in fact resonates most strongly with the ethos of those who occupy an *intermediate* position in the social structure.

This ethos is also at the basis of a qualitatively different conception of health and illness. Instead of being experienced and expressed as radically different somatic states which tend to alter in an abrupt and accidental manner (one "falls" ill), health and illness are seen as strongly interwoven and separated from each other only by gradations. Within this perspective, illness no longer presents itself as an unforeseeable event, but as a constant possibility which, when left unattended, will gradually erode and eventually undermine the state of health. Rather than being experienced as something which abruptly interrupts the experience of time, illness *itself* is seen as having 'a history, an often invisible start, an evolution, an ending, consequences', in short, 'it is inscribed in time' (Boltanski,

1971: 221). While Boltanski's propositions on the relationship between class position, temporality and the experience of the body have an obvious relevance from the point-of-view of medical sociology, this study will aim to show that their significance extends well beyond the issue of health and illness. The following chapters will in fact aim to demonstrate that a number of ways in which social agents "invest" in their bodies derive their logic from the temporal perspective that is engendered by their particular position *in* and trajectory *through* social space. Before sketching out the manner in which this socially constituted 'sense of time' informs the more broader relationship to the body, I will first turn to the more general principles that underlie Boltanski's propositions on temporality, tracing their origins in the work of Bourdieu, in order to show how they are tied in with the conceptions of social structure and social action that have been outlined in the previous chapter.

The causality of the probable

In fact, one of the most constant (yet constantly overlooked) themes throughout Bourdieu's intellectual trajectory is his quasi-Heideggerian concern with the *temporal* dimension of social practice, and especially the socio-historical conditions that underlie the genesis of a strategic and "rational" outlook towards the future. As a topic that was originally forced upon him by his own experiences in colonial Algeria, where he personally witnessed the conflicts – indissolubly social and mental – that ensued, when agents who were attuned to the collective rhythms and cycles of a subsistence-economy were thrust into a capitalistic universe that demanded rational calculation and long-term investment (see Bourdieu, 1979 [1963]: 64ff.; Bourdieu, 1990d; also Bourdieu, 2000a), it would surface time and time again throughout his later work.[3] At the core of his propositions on the social experience of time is a critique of the model of social action propounded by economic theory. Bourdieu criticized this model, first, because it fails to grasp the distinction between the *theoretical* and *reflexive* knowledge of the social (and economic) world produced by the analyst in his capacity as detached and disinterested observer and the *indigenous* and *practical* understanding of the immanent structures and tendencies of this world by agents who are exposed to them from day one. Instead, it tends to simply project the experience of the former in the heads of the latter and ends up creating 'a sort of a monster with the head of the thinker thinking his practice in reflexive and logical fashion mounted on the body of a man of action engaged in action' (Bourdieu and Wacquant, 1992: 123). A second point of criticism centres on the fact that economic theory tends to treat the basic attitudes that define "rational" economic conduct – like the propensity to maximize personal gain, to save or to invest, to defer current gratifications for future gains, to act with foresight and prevision and, more generally, to adopt a "strategic" attitude towards time and the future – as innate attributes of *all* social agents. By doing so, it circumvents the double question of both the historical genesis of that particular social universe in which "economic rationality" becomes the dominant mode of conduct – i.e. the capitalist economy – as well as the social conditions, (both economic *and* cultural) that need to be met, *within* contemporary societies, in order for such strategic dispositions to be durably constituted and meaningfully deployed. Drawing on his own ethnographic observations of the time-perspective of Kabyle peasants and the newly formed Algerian sub-proletariat, Bourdieu argues that the very intention of actively mastering the future and adopting an attitude of foresight towards it, already presupposes a minimum hold over the present:

> The art of estimating and seizing chances, the capacity to anticipate the future by a kind of practical induction or even to take a calculated gamble on the possible against the probable, are dispositions that can only be acquired under certain social conditions, that is, certain social conditions.
>
> (Bourdieu, 1990b: 64)

Below a given threshold of minimal security and *certainty*, of the type provided by stable employment for instance, the very capacity to develop a coherent vision of the future, let alone the ambition to actively control it, often tends to disappear altogether. In fact, the prolonged exposure to precarious social conditions marked by a high degree of uncertainty leads to 'a kind of generalized and lasting disorganization of behaviour and thought' (Bourdieu, 2000b: 221), which (often) manifests itself in a fatalistic (if realistic) resignation to the given or (sometimes) in the development of quasi-millenarian hopes or dream-like plans that often lack any real basis for success. It is only when social and especially *economic* conditions allow for a suspension of the necessities of day-to-day survival, that the ambition to actively confront, plan for and invest in the future can develop. Several studies have in fact shown that agents' temporal horizon not only tends to extend further into the future, but also becomes internally more differentiated, the higher they are situated in the social. This is shown, amongst others, by the fact that, as one rises in the social hierarchy, agents' "subjective" representations of their own future tend to become increasingly more developed and elaborate (see for instance O'Rand and Ellis, 1974; Lamm *et al.*, 1976).

The particular experience of time that is engendered in the relationship between a (class of) habitus and the possibilities inscribed in a given set of social conditions can itself be understood as the form *par excéllence* of the dialectic of positions and dispositions outlined in the last chapter. In fact, agents' position in the distribution of the different types of capital does not only inform their 'sense of place', as a practical, *embodied* "feel" for social structure and their current position in it, but is also at the basis of their 'sense of time'. The latter can be defined as the practical anticipation of the future, experienced as a more or less closed or open 'field of possibilities', and the concomitant propensity to orient current actions in terms of goals or gains that are situated in a more or less distant point in time. Again, the process through which temporal aspirations become adjusted to their objective chances of success has little to do with the conscious, rational deliberation over the probabilities of success of different lines of action, which are themselves explicitly constituted as "projects". Instead, it most often takes the form of a 'practical induction' which can be defined as 'a shared modal understanding of eventualities as possible or impossible, normal or exceptional, probable or improbable, and hence as a shared evaluation of certain expectations and aspirations as "reasonable" and others as "unreasonable".' (Brubaker, 2004: 44). Far from being the product of a universal, abstract capacity for foresight and calculation, this practical anticipation of the future or 'protention' is itself the product of agents' *past* experiences with the immanent regularities and tendencies of the social world (or the different fields), which are carried over into the present by the temporal dispositions inscribed in their habitus.

This enduring presence of the past inside the present is also at the basis of another fundamental property of temporal dispositions, pointed out by Mary Douglas and Baron Isherwood, namely that when 'discussing time, then, we have to take account of the self-fulfilling character of a short- or long-term view' (1996 [1979]: 147). In fact, because they are the *incorporated* form of the possibilities inscribed in a particular set of social conditions, temporal dispositions and the aspirations they engender, have a tendency to perpetuate the very conditions of which they are the product. As such, the practical adjustment of aspirations to chances is *in itself* – that is, apart from the explicit sanctions of the family, the educational system, job counsellors, etc. – a crucial element in the reproduction of social inequality and even counts as 'one of the most powerful factors of conservation of the established order' (Bourdieu, 2000b: 231). This is particularly clear in the case of dominated groups, like the sub-proletariat, whose prolonged exposure to uncertainty tends to foreclose the development of a coherent, long-term vision of the future that is itself the very precondition to escape uncertainty – either through *individual* strategies of accumulation or through *collective*, revolutionary transformations of their conditions – and instead leads to a resigned, even fatalistic acceptance of domination. Bourdieu stresses however, that this quasi-circular adaptation to the given, even if it is more common than populist narratives of "resistance" would have it, is only one manner in which the temporal outlook of a social group contributes to its own self-exploitation and, sometimes, to its own demise. In fact, contrary to some of the more superficial criticisms of Bourdieu's theses on social reproduction (see for instance Jenkins, 1992; Alexander, 1995), the inherent tendency of (temporal) dispositions to perpetuate themselves *beyond* the conditions in which they are produced, can result in maladaptation and transformation, as much as adjustment and reproduction.

In the ever-shifting tectonics of social space, positions often tend to change at a more rapid pace than their associated dispositions, as is shown quite clearly by the fate of *declining* social groups. Here, such a 'hysteresis effect' (Bourdieu, 1984: 109; Bourdieu, 1990: 62) tends to introduce a *lag* between, on the one hand, changed circumstances and changed opportunities and, on the other, the dispositions that are required to *recognize* these changes and hence adapt to them (through reconversions of one's capital-structure, for instance). This often leads to continued investments in a future that is no longer objectively possible which often precipitates a downward trajectory. Historical examples are the fate of large fractions of the aristocracy and the rural peasantry and, more recently, that of small shopkeepers and fractions of the industrial workforce. Alternatively, a considerable portion of *Distinction* (1984: esp. 125ff.) is devoted to showing how the devaluation of educational titles (produced by the expansion of higher-education) and the associated frustration of aspirations, which increasingly assigned agents to inferior social positions than those promised to previous generations was (and is) itself one of the most important motors of social change. Not only did it lead those who were relegated to less prestigious social positions to redefine these positions (often producing conflicts with its traditional occupants), but it also led to the creation of entirely new occupational fields of which those professions that are devoted to the management and presentation of the body (dieticians, fitness-instructors, chiropractors, etc.) are also an outcome.

The self-fulfilling character of a group's temporal outlook is perhaps nowhere as clear as in the case of those who occupy intermediate positions in social space, and especially the *upwardly* aspiring fractions of the middle-classes. Just as a number of their properties, not in the least those pertaining to the body, can only become fully intelligible when one takes into account their *synchronic* position vis-à-vis other groups, and especially their position *between* the working and the dominant class, their particular relationship to the social world and hence to the body cannot solely be defined in terms of their *current* social conditions, but also needs to take into account the effects of their orientation towards a *potential* (or *past*) social position, that is, their individual or collective *trajectory*. Being situated closer to dominant social positions and hence having considerably higher chances of access to such positions (at least relative to members of the working-class), their "pretension" to attain them nonetheless tends to exceed their actual resources to do so, especially within the span of a single generation. Bourdieu argues that this discrepancy between aspirations and chances, ambitions and possibilities, is compensated by the development of a rigorously ascetic ethos of self-imposed prohibitions and renunciations in which *present* gratifications become systematically subordinated to *future* rewards:

> The whole existence of the rising petit bourgeois is the anticipation of a future which he will, in most cases, only know by proxy, through his children, on whom he projects his ambitions. The future he 'dreams of for his son' eats up his present. Because he is committed to strategies extending over several generations, he is the man [*sic*] of the deferred pleasure, the deferred present that will be taken later, 'when there is time', 'when we've paid off the mortgage', 'when the children are older' or 'when we're retired', in other words, very often when it is too late, when, having given credit on his life, he has no time to collect his 'due' and must 'cut his coat according to his cloth'.
>
> (Bourdieu, 1984: 352–353)

It is this particular orientation towards the future that distinguishes, both objectively and subjectively, the *petit-bourgeois asceticism* from the strategies of self-denial imposed on members of the working-class. In the case of the former, their upwardly oriented aspirations lead to the adoption of a series of *self-imposed* renunciations which often 'develop in such a way as to become the foundation for a genuine system of life' (Durkheim, 1995 [1912]: 316). This inherently separates them from the *forced* austerity of members of the working-class where, through the necessity that is imposed by their social conditions and especially the ever-present threat of social precarization, the desire for social advancement (and the accumulation of resources it requires) is often eclipsed by the necessity of constructing a "floor" under their conditions of existence, that is, to safeguard against a downward career into the sub-proletariat, a concern which is 'as important to understanding the dispositions of the skilled workers as the potentiality of promotion for clerical workers and junior-executives' (Bourdieu, 1984: 589, n. 21). To the "defensive" asceticism of the former, the latter oppose an "offensive" asceticism whose investments are inherently oriented toward attaining positions higher than the ones they currently occupy. The specific *modality* that these investments will take, in turn depends on the particular composition of agents' capital-structure, that is, on the particular *fraction* of the middle-classes to which they belong. These will generally take the form of educational investments for those fractions richest in cultural capital, while more often cantering on economic and financial investments (loans, stocks, etc.) for those who are (relatively) most well-endowed with economic capital. In both cases, members of the *petit-bourgeoisie* 'invest in their economic and educational strategies, ascetic dispositions that make them the ideal clientele of the bank and the school

> cultural goodwill and the spirit of economy, seriousness and dedication to work – so many guarantees that the petit-bourgeoisie offer to these institutions, while simultaneously placing themselves completely at their mercy (contrary to the possessor of a *real* capital, economic or cultural), because it is only through them that they can obtain the profits of a fundamentally negative capital.
>
> (Bourdieu, 1984: 22)

Furthermore, our analyses (especially Chapter 8) will aim to show that the same ascetic and voluntaristic dispositions which are manifested in the relationship to culture or the economy are also at the basis of a cosmetic voluntarism that makes men and women from the *petit-bourgeoisie* into the ideal consumers of the products and services offered by the contemporary diet- and fitness-industry.

Investment

If I have somewhat belaboured the question of the conditions that underlie the development of a strategic, proactive and long-term perspective on time, existence and the body, this is largely because this question often proves remarkably absent from sociological narratives on 'body consciousness' and bodily 'reflexivity'. In fact, the sociological literature on the topic not only proves particularly sweeping in its propositions on the contemporary status of the body as a source of quasi-universal anxiety, but also tacitly credits *all* social agents with the temporal dispositions that enable it to be perceived as a flexible and malleable "project". A few examples:

> In the post-traditional environments of high modernity, neither appearance nor demeanour can be organized as a given; the body participates in a very direct way in the principle that the self has to be constructed.
> (Giddens, 1991: 99–100)

> In modern societies, consumer culture has made the project of the body a general activity [...] The Protestant Ethic is turned inside out and the body becomes a project alongside, or inextricably bound up with, the self as a project.
> (Turner, 1995: 260)

> The body, one may say, has become the last shelter and sanctuary of continuity and duration; whatever 'long-term' may mean, it can hardly exceed the limits drawn by bodily mortality. [...] Hence the rabid, obsessive, feverish and overwrought concern with the defence of the body. The boundary between the body and the world outside is among the most vigilantly policed of contemporary frontiers.
> (Bauman, 2000: 183–184)

> In the affluent West, there is a tendency for the body to be seen as an entity which is in the process of becoming; a *project* which should be worked at and accomplished as part of an *individual*'s self-identity.
> (Shilling, 2003: 4, *original emphasis*)

While there are undeniably differences in the manner in which these authors conceptualize the causes and consequences of this contemporary fascination with the body, they nonetheless converge in treating such fascination as all but endemic to life in high, reflexive, liquid or post-modernity.[4] This is not to deny the blatantly obvious fact that the past decades have indeed witnessed a veritable explosion in the offer of techniques, products and services devoted to the management, maintenance and modification of the body. Still less, that this has resulted in entirely novel categories of needs, as well as the emergence of new concerns and anxieties. This fact alone, however, does not warrant the crucial question of the *socially constituted principles* that both help to produce such needs, as well as render agents susceptible to such concerns and anxieties in the first place, to be simply swept away under the most broad-stroked assertions on the contemporary relationship between body, society and self-identity.

Following Bourdieu and Boltanski, I will argue that one of these principles should be located in the particular *temporal horizon* that defines a particular class or class fraction. How this socially constituted 'sense of time' informs agents' practical conceptions of health and illness, and especially the degree in which they are capable (and hence willing) to adopt a "preventive" attitude towards their bodies, has already been discussed at length. Such a focus on the practical conceptions of health and illness is itself not unimportant. In fact, as one rises in social space, the concern with the body's long-term welfare tends to increasingly inform the manner in which social agents come to perceive, use and treat their bodies. However, investments in health constitute only a portion of the different ways in which agents relate to their bodies and are, at any rate, not always clearly distinguished from other types of bodily investment. It is indeed not in the name of health alone (and perhaps not even primarily), that agents willingly engage in the type of self-denial and the "long and cumbersome actions" that Boltanski defined as characteristic of techniques of preventive medicine.

In fact, if one abstracts from the particular *results* they envision, there is an inherent similarity between such rituals as sterilizing a pacifier to avoid the future risk of infection and meticulously applying creams and lotions that promise to "*defy the effects of ageing*", to "*protect against the future production of melanin, blemishes and prevent freckles*" or provide an "*insurance policy for the skin's healthy future*".[5] The same logic can also be observed in the various forms and formulas of "fitness" or "exercising", where agents engage in a type of physical activity that is itself reduced to a series of highly ritualized, decomposed and abstract movements, often completely divorced from any direct finality (scoring a goal, landing a punch, etc.) and instead oriented towards long-term, abstract and often wholly "negative" gains such as "cardiovascular health" or protection against the process of ageing. Similarly, the taste for "light" or "organic" foods also implies a semi-learned conception of the *long-term* effects of specific qualities and quantities of food on the body, be it through the slow accumulation of toxins or the progressive build-up of fat. In fact, the case of organic food even combines a concern with the impact of food-consumption on the body, with worries over "sustainability", that is, the long-term effects of food-production on the environment

However, it is especially in the domain of weight-concern and dieting that one can most clearly observe the tacit or explicit demands for a long-term perspective. In fact, the wide range of products and services devoted to the management of body-size and shape not only tend to demand a constant state of self-monitoring and self-control, but often require agents to frame their entire perception of temporal divisions in terms of a bodily referent. In this manner, fitness- and lifestyle-magazines abound with advice on how to "*keep the winter kilos away*" or to "*get rid of those holiday pounds*", provide tips on how to "*spring clean your body*" or how to "*get your best summer figure*". This logic, which incites agents (and above all women) to organize their entire conception of time around its relevance for the body's form and appearance, does not only apply to short-term, seasonal cycles, but effectively extends to the perception and judgment of the entire *life-course*. In this way, the same magazines that remind their readers that "*it's the time of year to get into shape!*" also offer advice on "*how to keep off post-wedding pudge*", provide them with tips on how to "*get rid of baby flab*" or help them to "*combat the middle-age spread*".

What unites the various types of advice, guidelines or "tips and tricks" provided by the beauty- and fitness-industry is the way in which they demand that individuals adopt a long-term perspective on existence and their bodies. In a modern-day version of Pascal's wager, they all hinge on the belief that present actions will generate future rewards that are, strictly speaking, uncertain and can never be fully verified, but which are nevertheless thought to be unobtainable, if one did not engage in such actions in the first place. For instance, no one knows with full certainty that the creams and lotions that are diligently applied today will actually produce "younger-looking skin" in 30 years from now or that the regular trips to the gym will effectively result in better circulation, lower blood-pressure and limber joints at old age (better yet, even if this does turn out to be the case, one could never be fully certain that the same results would not have been obtained *without* such investments). However, the potential benefits such investments are thought to procure are largely considered to outweigh the uncertainty of their outcome. Without therefore suggesting that an understanding of the temporal horizon of a particular group or class is, in itself, a *sufficient* condition for explaining the way in which its members use, perceive and care for their bodies, it becomes clear that such investments draw a considerable part of their "sense" from a practical conception of the future as open and amenable to personal control and hence worthy of investment. From this it does not follow that the capacity to adopt such a temporal perspective will automatically lead agents to engage in such long-term investments, since these investments also depend, in both form and content, on the practical value that each class assigns to properties as strength, endurance, beauty or health. However, the opposite does seem to hold true, namely that in the absence of the conditions that enable agents to "pro-ject" themselves beyond the immediate present, to see themselves as "having a future", investments that are oriented towards long-term, invisible and often wholly negative gains will increasingly appear as abstract and "non-sensical". In this sense, grasping the temporal horizon that accompanies a given location in social space can be said to be a *necessary* condition for understanding the ways in which its occupants invest in their bodies.

This question of investment is, furthermore, not one of absolutes, of investment vs. non-investment (or disinvestment). What distinguishes the different classes or class-fractions is not so much whether or not they invest in their bodies – complete disinvestment from the body being rare, even among the most dispossessed – but rather the specific "return-on-investment" that their particular type of body-work envisions. In this sense, one of the main oppositions that define class-differences in bodily management and modification is a preference for practices that produce short-term, visible and tangible results, predominantly found among dominated social groups, and those that are instead oriented towards the pursuit of long-term, abstract and invisible benefits, characteristic of those who occupy dominant social positions. For instance, in their study on the role of class-differences in shaping women's perception of appearance and ageing, Dumas *et al.* (2006) distinguished between a working-class preference for so-called 'alloplastic' practices – i.e. those that are largely restricted to the short-term manipulation of appearance through clothing, cosmetics and jewellery – and a bourgeois proclivity for more encompassing, 'autoplastic' investments, namely those concerned with the long-term management of *physique*, that is, with the visible properties of the physical body (size, shape, skin-tone, etc.) as well as its more "hidden", organismic functions. In fact, as our own analyses will aim to show, the *temporal* opposition between short-term and long-term investments often translates into a *spatial* opposition that distinguishes between practices that are directed at the cultivation of the visible and the invisible, "outer" and "inner" beauty, between an interest in the body's *surface*, often associated with superficiality and shallowness, and a concern with the management of its *depths*, often deemed synonymous with the development of inner being, character and personality. More importantly, the *sense* of time that is inculcated within a given social position/trajectory is not only central to grasping the way in which the relationship to the body is structured *within* a given class or class fraction, but it also crucial to understanding how each class perceives the ways in which those who occupy *different* positions in social space treat and manage their bodies.

Time-perspective and self-control

The question of the temporal dimension of social and bodily practice is in fact not a purely analytical one, but is also raised within social space itself. This is captured well in a classical formulation by the Cosers:

> The inability to understand a group's time perspective not only makes it more difficult *for the observer* to comprehend the general orientation of the group, but it will also lead to gaps in social communication *between the different constituent groups of a society.*
> (Coser and Coser, 1963: 640, *my emphasis*)

In fact, the different relationships towards time and the future, which correspond to different positions *in* and trajectories *through* social space, hardly ever present themselves as neutral, equally valid alternatives. Instead, the definition of the "correct" temporal outlook, and hence of "time" in general, is itself the object of social conflict and, more specifically, a key stake in the struggles to impose the legitimate vision of the social world. Several authors have in fact shown how, historically, disputes over the proper definition of time – a "classification struggle" *par excéllence* – constitute an essential dimension of the struggle for social domination. Jacques Le Goff (1980), for instance, demonstrated how in the thirteenth and fourteenth century, conflicts over the official definition and uses of time constituted a fundamental dimension of the struggles between ecclesiastic authorities and an increasingly powerful merchant class. He even goes as far as defining this conflict between the *'temps de l'Église'*, the infinite and indivisible time belonging to God and therefore forbidden to human appropriation, calculation and prediction, and the *'temps du marchand'* which hinged on a conception of time as inherently predictable, oriented and amenable to quantitative measurement, as 'one of the major events in the mental history of these centuries in the heart of the Middle Ages' (1980: 30).

Similarly, Norbert Elias' (2002 [1969]) seminal study of the court society under Louis XIV also revealed how a number of conflicts between the ruling aristocracy and the ascending bourgeoisie can be traced back to differences in their respective temporal *ethos*. Whereas the latter were characterized by a 'saving-for-future-profit ethos' in which consumption and expenditure were systematically geared to *expected* income and hence to the future, the aristocracy distinguished itself by a "status-consumption ethos" that sacrificed the long-term accumulation of capital, and hence the rational management of incomes, to the conspicuous consumption of luxuries that determined the struggle for status within the courtly figuration. The following chapters will aim to show that such conflicts over the appropriate temporal outlook are no less important in understanding the classification struggles within *contemporary* social space. More importantly, they will try to demonstrate that it is precisely in the disputes over the correct manner of perceiving, using and treating the body that the temporal dimension of such struggles finds its clearest and, quite often, most violent expression. In fact, what the Cosers somewhat euphemistically referred to as 'gaps in social communication' very often prove to be quite explicit forms of class ethnocentrism. Because each class spontaneously projects its own relationship to the social world and to time onto others, that is to say, misrecognizes the social conditions underlying the differences in their respective "points-of-view", these differences often end up being interpreted and described in wholly *essentialist* terms. Inverting cause and effect, the everyday perception of class-differences tends to treat social position as the *outcome* of agents' temporal outlook – making status a function of the capacity for foresight, self-discipline and strategic action that is deemed crucial for social success – rather than one of its preconditions. It hence helps to transform a product of social necessity into a matter of individual choice, a personality-trait or the attribute of some other essentialist "nature". In this manner, the '"being-in-the-present" that characterizes dominated social groups and often takes the form of a 'realistic hedonism' (Bourdieu, 1984: 394) that refuses to "cut corners" and takes advantage of the "good times" as they come, is perceived by those who occupy more elevated social positions as an inherent failure to transcend primal needs and desires, an intrinsic lack of self-control or self-respect and an abdication of personal responsibility, in short, as a culpable surrender to "nature".

Lack of self-control, passivity, capitulation to bodily impulse and desire, there is nothing inherently new about the themes that populate such social commentary. From their inherent idleness, their gargantuan appetites (both culinary *and* sexual), their predilection to violence, addiction and obscenity to other forms of degeneracy, working-class bodies have always provided the grotesque mirror-image of dominant and *petit-bourgeois* morality (see Valverde, 1998; Jordan, 2001). What does seem relatively new is that with the expansion of the market in consumer goods and services (especially those aimed at the presentation and management of the body), the focus of such commentary seems to have gradually shifted from individuals' capacity as *producers* to their status as *consumers*. As the abovementioned example shows, dominated groups are no longer solely castigated for their economic idleness and lack of discipline in labour (although such themes are still very much alive), but are increasingly singled out for their "non-control" in matters of consumption, their inability to cope with the 'challenge of affluence' (Offer, 2006) or, in the language of the new therapeutic morality, their failure to provide their body with the care and attention it deserves. In the conditions of generalized affluence and material abundance that modern "consumer culture" is thought to provide, rationality is no longer defined solely in terms of the capacity for thrift and accumulation, but also by the ability to "make the right choices", to resist the various temptations and "cheap thrills" that consumer capitalism puts on offer, to indulge and to enjoy, but to do so with restraint and moderation. One of the most striking manifestations of such 'calculating hedonism' (Turner, 1996) is the contemporary fascination with dieting and weight-control which forms the topic of the next chapter.

Notes

1 One example helps to illustrate this "cardboard"-conception of culture. For instance, when trying to account for the self-monitoring, non-verbal and defensive dispositions of the Old Americans, Zborowski does not hesitate to reach back to the original mentality of the early "Frontiersmen":

> Historically, [this attitude] can be traced to the unfamiliar and alien environment encountered by the early settlers in the New World, who found strange fruits, animals and people whose unfamiliar tastes, looks or comportment could mean destruction or death [...] In dealing with native tribes, whether in peace or war, much was based on a correct interpretation of signs and symbols rather than on verbal communication. [...] The same traditions of the early frontiersmen also give rise to the apprehension with regard to the environment that is expressed in the notion that pain and illness are caused by external agents. [...] In the old country nature was an ally; in the new it was an enemy to be conquered. [...] As many other traits of American national character, such as self-reliance, spirit of freedom, or action-mindedness, are traced to the origin of American society, so attitudes towards illness and pain could stem from these times.
>
> (1969: 90–91)

2 "Early" here refers to the period that Boltanski was still a close collaborator of Bourdieu and which predates his turn towards a more "pragmatic" conception of sociology (see Boltanski and Thévenot, 2006 [1991]). One of his main interests in this period was the relationship between scientific, "learned" taxonomies and practical, "lay" forms of classification and especially the manner in which the former are diffused and assimilated within hierarchical social systems (see Boltanski, 1969; also Boltanski, 1970).

84 *Social order, body order*

3 It is already of central interest in his (unpublished) study of the relationship between French banks and their clientele (Bourdieu *et al.*, 1963), informs a crucial part of his analysis of class-differences in reproductive strategies and attitudes towards fertility (Bourdieu and Darbel, 1966: 143ff.), is at the heart of his conception of the "causality of the probable" as a structuring factor in educational strategies and academic investments (Bourdieu, 1974) and is elaborated more extensively in his later reflections on social being and time (Bourdieu, 2000b [1997]: 206ff.).

4 For instance, while Giddens stresses that 'it would be a major error to suppose that the phenomena analysed in the book *Modernity and Self-Identity* are confined in their impact to those in more privileged material circumstances' (1991: 6), Shilling acknowledges that 'the notions of the body as project/option/regime [...] do not provide us with a general theory of bodily experience' (2003: 192) and seems well aware that '[t]he idea that the body is positively central to people's identities has obvious limitations when dealing with the bodies of the poor, the starving and the homeless' (ibid.). However, such limitations do not lead him to develop a more systematic account of the relationship between social class, social power and embodiment.

5 All these phrases have been taken from popular fitness- and lifestyle-magazines, as well as the websites from some of the largest producers of beauty-products.

Part II
Modes of embodiment

4 The perceptible body*

> If it is true that the human body is in one sense a product of social activity, it is not absurd to assume that the constancy of certain traits, revealed by an average, depends on the conscious or unconscious fidelity to certain norms of life. Consequently, in the human species, statistical frequency expresses not only vital but also social normativity. A human trait would not be normal because frequent, but frequent because normal, that is, normative in one given kind of life.
>
> (Canguilhem, 1978 [1966]: 91)

'If I would have been a qualified physician, I would have first written a good monograph on obesity. I would have then established my domain in this remote corner of science, and would have had the double satisfaction of having as patients, persons who were perfectly well, as well of being besieged daily by the fairer half of mankind' (Brillat-Savarin, 1975 [1826]: 122–123). This is how the famous French epicurean and founding father of modern gastronomy, Jean-Anthelme Brillat-Savarin, opens what is perhaps one of the earliest treatises on the topic of "obesity". While hardly a diet-faddist and a strong advocate of that 'classical plumpness [*embonpoint*] that constitutes a charm to the eyes' (1975: 133), he nonetheless felt compelled to outline the key causes and formulate potential remedies for that affliction by which 'without the individual being ill, the limbs gradually gain in size and lose their form and primitive harmonies' (1975: 123). Basing his reflections on the topic on the 'more than five-hundred conversations I have had with fellow-diners threatened or afflicted by obesity' (1975: 123), he proceeds to outline the key factors that contribute to this excessive expansion of girth. Apart from a natural predisposition for corpulence and a diet rich in 'starches and flours', he mentions the lengthening of sleep, a lack of exercise as well as an excess in eating and drinking as the prime culprits. Given the particular lifestyle in which these factors combined, he confidently asserts that 'obesity is never found among the savages, nor among those classes of society that have to work to eat and eat only to survive' (1975: 125). Instead, he draws his prime examples of '*obésité monstrueuse*' from among the foremost members of the French and European nobility of the time with one character in particular, a certain Mr. Rameau 'mayor of La Chaleur in Burgundy', standing at a mere 5 feet 2 inches, but weighing an impressive 500 pounds.

That Brillat-Savarin's observations on the girth of Europe's elites are not entirely impressionistic is shown half a century later, when Sir Francis Galton published the first anthropometric record of the English aristocracy in the then still fledgling journal *Nature* (also see Mennell, 1991). In *The Weights of British Noblemen during the Last Three Generations* (1884), Galton traces the evolution of average weight throughout the life-course of three consecutive generations of aristocrats born between 1740 and 1829. Regardless of the conclusion he reaches (the oldest generation attains their heaviest weight much earlier than the youngest), it is the actual weights reported by Galton that are of true interest. In fact, his sample of '109 peers, 39 baronets ... and 1 eldest son of a peer' (1844: 266) does not only prove to be considerably heavier than the average weight of men at the time, but had a body-mass that, by contemporary medical standards, would be considered as severely overweight and this at a time of which Friedrich Engels would later write that 'every working-man, even the best, is constantly exposed to loss of work and food, that is to death by starvation' (2009 [1845]: 67).[1]

Little could these authors therefore suspect that this 'irritating minor ailment' (*indisposition fâcheuse*), as Brillat-Savarin called obesity, would in a matter of generations become elevated to the status of an "epidemic" by the World Health Organization, which estimates that at least 400 million people worldwide fit the medical category of "obese". Still less could they envision that a corpulent physique would cease to be the distinguishing hallmark of those who are situated at the top of the social hierarchy and would instead come to characterize those who occupy the most precarious social positions. In fact, one of the most consistent findings to emerge from the rapidly expanding literature on to the 'obesity epidemic' is the existence of a strong *inverse* relationship between social position and body-weight, particularly marked among women, but increasingly observed among men as well. An impressive number of studies now attest to the fact that weight-differences are far from randomly distributed across social space, but are instead clearly aligned with the boundaries inscribed in the social and sexual division of labour (see the reviews by Sobal and Stunkard, 1984 and McLaren, 2007). While relatively rare among those who occupy dominant social positions, obesity proves to be disproportionately prevalent among those who are situated at the bottom of the class-structure. The frequency with which this inverse relationship has been observed for the majority of post-industrial societies warrants body-weight to be treated as a 'social fact' whose distribution and evolution cannot be adequately explained by leaning exclusively on genetic hardwiring or individual psychology. This makes it all the more puzzling to observe that sociologists have thus far paid only scant attention to the manner in which class-inequalities become, quite *literally*, inscribed in the physical dimensions of the body. Even though the discipline's notorious "turn to the body" has generated an impressive literature on the topics of weight-concern, dieting and eating disorders, the dynamics of *class*-relationships in producing both the physicality of bodies *and* the manner in which they are perceived and evaluated often prove remarkably absent from such accounts.

Sociology's fear of fat

Even though the current study of obesity and weight-differences remains largely dominated by biomedical heuristics, attempts to develop a properly *sociological* perspective on the subject got off to a promising early start. In the late 1960s – when the 'medicalization' of corpulence was only just gaining momentum (see Sobal, 1995) – Cahnman (1968) already advocated a 'sociogenic' perspective on obesity that moved beyond concerns with individual pathology and instead treated corpulence as a source of *social* stigmatization. Drawing on Goffman's (1963) seminal study of stigmatized identities (which, quite tellingly, makes little mention of the plight of the corpulent), he argued that the obese are subjected to a particularly pernicious type of ostracization.[2] While bearing a stigmatized trait that is equally visible as that of ethnic minorities or the physically disabled, they differ from the latter in the degree to which they are held *personally* responsible for their own deviant identity (also see DeJong, 1980). In fact, more than any other 'abomination of the body' (Goffman, 1963: 14), corpulence is read through a moralizing lens in which neither faulty genetics nor brute misfortune, but individual choice and (lack of) personal responsibility are seen as the prime culprits. To be fat is first and foremost a sign of not *wanting* to be thin, of an innate lack of self-respect and a failure to take proper care of one's own body and (hence) oneself. Unlike stigmatization on the basis of relatively "fixed" traits like ethnicity or gender, the obese "choose" their own deviant identity and are hence fully deserving of the scorn they bring upon themselves. According to Cahnman, the obese themselves come to internalize such widespread stereotypes which in turn produces quite profound feelings of shame and self-loathing.

Despite this early attempt at "socializing" obesity and weight-differences, body-weight would remain at the margins of sociological interest for almost two more decades. It would not be until the end of the 1980s, when the body and all things bodily erupted onto the sociological stage, that issues like weight-concern, dieting and would come to occupy a more secure place on the sociological agenda. Curiously however, most key texts associated with this "turn to the body" choose to broach the issue of weight and physical appearance through a discussion of the increased prevalence of eating disorders (and *anorexia nervosa* in particular), rather than through a discussion of rapidly rising obesity-figures.

> A content analysis of the words "anorexia", "anorexic" and "bulimia" as opposed to "obesity", "obese" or "overweight" in some of the key works associated with this turn to the body proves highly illustrative of this bias: Turner's seminal *The Body and Society* (2008 edition) has 139 entries for the former and 19 for the latter, Bordo's *Unbearable Weight* (1993) mentions eating disorders 319 times, while showing only 44 entries for obesity, Shilling's *The Body and Social Theory* (2003) mentions anorexia 9 times and has no entries for obesity (but one for 'overweight'), Giddens' *Modernity and Self-Identity* (2003), which would be highly influential for so much theorizing on the body, shows 11 entries for eating disorders and only

1 for obesity, Featherstone et al.'s *The Body: Social Process and Cultural Theory* (1991) proves slightly more balanced with 13 entries for eating disorders and 11 for corpulence, while O'Neill's *Five Bodies* (2004) has 2 entries for obesity and none for eating disorders.

One of the reasons for this bias might be that a focus on extreme forms of bodily and self-control, rather than on a phenomenon like the "obesity epidemic", proves considerably more compatible with social theories that postulate both a universalized body-consciousness in societies of 'late', 'high', 'reflexive' or 'post'-modernity in which the body supposedly becomes the malleable object of increasingly reflexive and individualized 'lifestyle-choices' (a point well-noted by Crossley, 2004). The latter is the view of Giddens who boldly asserts that: '*Everyone* today in the developed countries, apart from the very poor, is "on a diet"' (1992: 32, *original emphasis*). In fact, under conditions of 'high modernity', individuals are increasingly pressured into forging their own distinctive self-identity and the cultivation of the body plays a crucial role in 'reflexively influencing this project of the self' (Giddens, 1991: 105). However, this constant pressure to uphold a distinctive and coherent self can quite easily regress into a 'pathology of reflexive self-control' (Giddens, 1991: 105) of which anorexia is but one symptom. Little mention is made of the fact that eating disorders still have a quite distinct class-etiology (Darmon, 2009) and instead we learn that they are only the 'extreme forms of the control of bodily regimes which has now become generic to the circumstances of everyday life' (Giddens, 1991: 105). Giddens' propositions in turn provide the intellectual backdrop for Shilling's concepts of 'body project', 'body options' and 'body regimes' (Shilling, 2003). Shilling's reflections on the contemporary status of the body starts from a central paradox: while social agents (arguably) possess an unprecedented degree of knowledge and control over their bodies, the same technico-scientific advances that have enabled this knowledge/control have also undermined the traditional certainties about what the body is and how it should be perceived. This not only produces considerable anxiety about appearance and self-presentation, but also engenders 'a tendency for the body to be seen as an entity in the process of becoming; a *project* to be worked at and accomplished as part of an individual's self-identity' (Shilling, 2003: 4, *original emphasis*).

Susan Bordo adopts a similar view, but for her the 'instability of the contemporary personality construction' (1993: 201) reflects the "structural" contradictions inherent in modern consumer capitalism. In her view, the twin extremes of anorexia nervosa and obesity are born out of the incompatible demands that this economic system places on individuals, namely the *ascetic* work ethic imposed in the sphere of production and the *hedonistic* indulgence promoted in the area of consumption. The existence of pathological overweight and underweight should hence be understood as the over-development of one of the opposing tendencies that economic life instils in every individual, while *bulimia* is in its turn considered as the ultimate embodiment of the 'unstable double bind' (ibid.) that holds the two together. Apart from briefly mentioning the role of corpulence in hindering class *mobility* (ibid.: 195), little is said about the fact that the obese and the anorexic tend to be disproportionately located at quite opposite ends of social space. Instead, Bordo argues that the role of physical size and shape in symbolizing class position has 'eroded considerably since the 1970s' and weight increasingly comes to function as 'a symbol for the emotional, moral or spiritual state of the individual' (1993: 193).

At this point it should become clear that when browsing through the literature for clues into the *class*-differentiation in bodies one cannot help but feel a bit "unsatiated". While most authors concede that contemporary investments in one's physique are themselves rooted in 'certain material preconditions which economically struggling [people] lack' (Bordo, 1993: 62), have 'obvious limitations when dealing with the bodies of the poor, the homeless and the starving' (Shilling, 2003: 192) or are hampered by 'the realities of poverty and unemployment' (Featherstone, 1991: 177), this has not led to a more systematic reflection on the relationship between social status, physical size and weight-concern. Instead, one is often confronted with the most sweeping propositions on the status of bodies in 'high', 'liquid', 'post-' or 'reflexive' modernity, which are not only rarely substantiated with empirical evidence, but which also curiously manage to overlook an impressive body of epidemiological research that tends to paint a quite different picture of the relation between social class and body-mass.

Deconstructing the "obesity epidemic"

It is a sad testament to the 'benign neglect' (Trostle and Somerfeld, 1996) that still typifies the relationship between epidemiology and the social sciences, that so much theorizing on the body hovers well above the empirical realities uncovered by social epidemiologist and health scientists. Somewhat ironically, it is these disciplines that can be credited, more so than sociology, for demonstrating how the apparently most "natural" traits (height, weight, blood-pressure, hormonal cycles, etc.) are governed by *social* as much as biological principles of distribution. If sociologists have largely ignored the social foundations of human morphology and physiology, this has not prevented the latter from eagerly staking out the field. In fact, prior to 2004, more than 360 published studies had already tackled the relationship between human body-mass and a wide variety of indices of social position such as income, level of education, occupation (see Sobal and Stunkard, 1984 and McLaren, 2007). One of the most frequent and consistent findings to emerge from this expansive and expanding body of research is the existence of a strong, *inverse* relationship between body-weight and social position, particularly clear among women, but increasingly observed among men as well. Far from being randomly distributed across social space, weight-differences prove (increasingly) aligned with the boundaries inscribed in the social and sexual division of labour. While still relatively rare among those who occupy dominant social positions, obesity proves disproportionately prevalent among those who are confined to the most precarious regions of social space.

Body-mass is conventionally measured using the "body mass index" or BMI (weight in kg/[height in m]^2). Since the analyses presented throughout this chapter are based on *self-reported* height and weight and given the tendency of respondents to *over*-state their height and *under*-state their weight (resulting in a lower BMI), these analyses offer a rather *conservative* estimate of actual class-differences in body-size. Table 4.1 provides an illustration of the class-gradient in body-mass. It shows how average BMI systematically increases as one moves from those who hold a master's or a postgraduate degree to those with little or no formal education. This means that, for persons of the same height, the average weight difference between those at the top and the bottom of the educational hierarchy is 3.0 kg for men and 7.7 kg for women (even after adjusting for age-differences between these groups).[3] In addition, the percentage of respondents who would be classified as "obese" rises from 1 out of 10 women from the highest income-categories and 1 out of 20 women with a master's or postgraduate degree to almost 1 out of 5 of housewives, women with a minimum income (17 per cent) and those with little or no formal education (19 per cent). A similar inverse relationship between body-size and social position is found among men, although here differences prove less marked. Whereas men who did not finish secondary education are twice as likely to be classified as medically "obese" than those who obtained a university degree, differences in terms of income and employment status prove less considerable (with income even showing a slightly *positive* relationship, a point to which the analysis will return). It is especially among women that the opposition between public and private, paid employment and domestic labour (or unemployment), translates into considerable differences in physical size, with housewives being on average 5.9 kg heavier than women who are employed full-time (height being equal).

That contemporary weight-differences are governed by *social* as much as biological principles of distribution, becomes even more apparent when they are studied within a comparative perspective. Whereas the probability of being labelled as "obese" is inversely related to social status in the majority of "post-industrial" social formations, the opposite holds true for "developing" societies where body-weight systematically *increases* as one rises in the social hierarchy (Molarius *et al.*, 2000; Monteiro *et al.*, 2004). Furthermore, when the general level of affluence rises among the latter – to the point where the majority of the population no longer faces the threat of malnutrition and starvation – the prevalence of obesity gradually shifts from the top to the bottom of the social structure (Monteiro *et al.*, 2004). Such findings already offer an indication that the body's size and shape are not strictly speaking "neutral" properties, but are invested with a symbolic value which, like any other symbolic property, is determined by its relative rarity or "commonness". As long as the majority of the population faces the existential threat of starvation and bears the visible marks of hunger and malnutrition, a corpulent physique is valued as a distinctive and distinguished marker of a dominant social status. However, when the level of material

Table 4.1 Body-size characteristics by gender, level of education, income and professional status

	Avg. BMI[a]		% BMI < 18.5		% BMI [25–30]		% BMI > 30		Avg. height (cm)		N	
	♂	♀	♂	♀	♂	♀	♂	♀	♂	♀	♂	♀
Educational capital	***	***							***	***		
Less than HS	26.2[b]	25.7	1.8	5.2	37.8	28.3	17.2	19.3	173.7	162.0	1,698	2,339
HS (technical/vocational)	25.8	25.2	0.9	5.8	42.3	31.0	13.0	13.0	175.4	162.7	921	750
HS (academic)	25.3	24.2	1.2	5.0	40.5	24.2	8.6	10.5	175.7	163.5	492	597
Bachelor	25.5	23.6	0.6	6.4	39.5	21.0	9.9	7.6	176.9	164.1	731	1,028
Master[c]	25.2	22.8	1.5	6.0	39.1	16.2	7.9	5.3	177.3	164.5	621	411
Economic capital	*	***							***	***		
<750€[d]	25.1	25.0	1.5	6.7	28.7	26.3	12.7	17.2	174.0	162.2	232	339
750–1,000€	25.1	25.0	3.7	8.2	31.9	25.8	12.4	14.0	174.2	161.9	404	679
1,000–1,500€	25.6	24.9	1.5	6.1	39.0	26.5	12.6	15.7	174.8	162.8	985	1,131
1,500–2,500€	25.8	24.9	1.3	5.6	40.5	25.6	13.1	14.6	174.9	162.7	1,264	1,347
>2,500€	25.6	24.0	1.5	4.7	40.9	23.6	10.8	9.2	177.0	164.2	1,238	1,186
Professional status	***	***							***	***		
Paid work	26.0	23.8	0.8	4.3	35.8	21.9	12.4	7.5	176.1	163.3	2,401	1,921
Housework	n.a.	26.0	n.a.	2.5	n.a.	31.8	n.a.	18.6	n.a.	162.3	19	635
Unemployed	25.9	25.4	0.4	6.3	38.7	26.1	16.2	15.2	174.7	161.7	276	320
Retired/unable to work	25.3	25.3	2.1	7.4	43.9	28.0	12.0	18.0	172.2	162.9	1,658	1,964
Total	25.6	24.7	1.5	6.0	39.0	24.8	12.5	13.3	175.4	163.2	4,836	5,482

Source: BNHS '04

Notes

a All scores are adjusted for age-differences.
b This number reads as follows: *"Men with less than a high school degree have an average BMI of 26.2."*
c Including postgraduates.
d Refers to the net monthly income of the family.
n.s. = non-significant, *** p < .005, ** p < .010, * p < .05, n.a. = number of observations too low to make meaningful inferences.

security rises to the point where the majority can physically sustain itself, corpulence gradually loses this distinctive character. As the possibility of a large body becomes increasingly available to all, the socially dominant instead turn to a slender, "toned" physique as a means of asserting their distance from material necessity. More importantly, contrary to what the notion of an "epidemic" might suggest, there is very little indication that weight-differences between the classes are somehow attenuating. In fact, studies that tackle the long-term evolution of the social gradient in body are quite unisonous in concluding that the "weight gap" between those at the top and the bottom of the social hierarchy is in fact widening (Molarius et al. 2000; Kark and Rasmussen, 2005; de Saint-Pol, 2007). Whereas the average weight of men and women who occupy dominant social positions has often remained remarkably stable, it is precisely among dominated social groups, and especially the most disadvantaged fringes of the working-class, that the most "epidemic" increase in obesity figures has been observed.

What gives these findings a paradoxical quality, is that the very results produced by epidemiologists tend to call into question the widespread use of the term "epidemic" to describe current trends in body-weight. In fact, the rather indiscriminate manner in which the media, public health officials and scientists alike wield the language of infectious pathology often obscures the fact that little in the current distribution and evolution of corpulence warrants the image of a viral pattern. While it may provide a seemingly apt metaphor for the pace at which *average* body-weight has increased, under closer scrutiny the notion of an "epidemic" appears as one of those metaphors that are 'generally borrowed from the language of physics or biology' and are hence 'liable to smuggle in an inadequate philosophy of social life and, above all, to discourage the search for specific explanation by supplying to easily the appearance of explanation.' (Bourdieu et al., 1991: 22). There are in fact several ways in which the image of a disease (and an infectious disease in particular) skews a proper *sociological* understanding of contemporary weight-differences. First, by implying that corpulence is something that is equally (and increasingly) probable for all, it tends to brush over the unequal distribution of material and cultural resources which enable or obstruct the cultivation of the 'legitimate body' and hence from the social relationships of domination and exclusion that undergird it. The frequency with which obesity is still referred to as a "disease of affluence" only further detracts from the fact that it disproportionately affects the most precarious strata of affluent societies. Secondly, by reifying obesity as an active, autonomous "force" that affects largely passive organisms or "hosts", the model of a disease tends to impose a *mechanistic* understanding of the manner in which socialized bodies are shaped by their environments. Even if the circumstances of everyday life can be said to have become increasingly more "obesogenic", this fact alone does not explain *how* or *why* the conditions that favour the development of a corpulent physique have such a differential impact across social space. If the increased availability of high-calorie foods, the mechanization of work and transportation or decreasing labour-times are indeed key causes of obesity, this still does not explain why they affect those who are situated at the bottom of the

The perceptible body 95

social hierarchy disproportionately more than those at the top. Such a mechanistic view overlooks the fact that environmental changes always operate through the mediation of class-specific schemes of perception and judgment (*habitus*) which define, amongst others, the legitimate size and shape of the body and hence play a key role in shaping its physicality. Finally, the discourse of an 'epidemic' tends to construct obesity almost exclusively as an indicator of *organic* pathology. In doing so, it tends to overlook the fact that corpulence does not only affect individual well-being through its "direct", physiological pathways (diabetes, hypertension, etc.), but also in a more "indirect" and symbolic manner, that is to say, through agents' practical awareness of the value of their own bodies as a source of recognition or, inversely, as an object of stigmatization. Indeed, whereas social epidemiologists have been instrumental in uncovering the social *causes* of contemporary weight-differences, they tend to pay less attention to their social *effects*, that is, to the ways in which corpulence or slimness affect the self-understanding of social agents and the manner in which this, in turn, shapes their everyday practice. The remainder of this chapter will be devoted to tackling this simultaneously *structured* and *structuring* character of weight-differences.

Social class and body-mass

That body-weight varies as a function of agents' position within the different hierarchies of capital (i.e. as a function of capital-*volume*) has already been illustrated (see Table 4.1). Hence, as one moves from members of the working-class, through the *petit-bourgeoisie* to those who occupy dominant social positions, average body-mass declines in an almost linear fashion. This proves particularly the case among women. For instance, female professionals (lawyers, doctors, etc.) are on average 7.7 pounds lighter than female unskilled workers (height being equal) and where more than one out of three of the latter qualify as "overweight" (of which 15 per cent are labelled as medically "obese"), this drops to less than one out of five of the former (4 per cent of which qualify as "obese").[4] At the same time, female professionals are three times more likely to be classified as medically "underweight" than female workers. Similar differences in body-mass are found among men, although these prove considerably more attenuated. Even though working-class men have a higher average BMI and are somewhat more likely to be labelled as "obese" than those who occupy dominant social positions, differences between the classes are far less articulated (with junior-executives even having a higher *average* weight than farmers, for instance).

> Interestingly, the analysis not only uncovers a class-gradient in body-weight, but also reveals a clear differentiation in terms of men and women's *height*. Not only do those who occupy the most elevated social positions have the highest probability of being endowed with the most slender physique, but they are also, on average, *taller* than those who are situated at the bottom of the class-structure. Compared to those with little or no formal education, men and women who obtained a Master's or postgraduate degree are 3.6 cm

and 2.4 cm taller, respectively, while male and female senior-executives are, on average, 3.3 cm and 2.3 cm taller than unskilled workers. While such differences again highlight the inherent conditionability of the physical body vis-à-vis the social conditions in which it is inserted, the relationship between class-position and height is of a qualitatively different nature, than that between class and weight. In fact, while the latter retains its "open" character and remains responsive to changes in social conditions throughout the individual life-course (Cfr. *infra*), the social conditioning of height possesses a fundamentally irreversible quality. Reflecting the effects of early social condition(ing)s on morphological development, class-differences in height are permanently ingrained in the body and hence constitute what Najman and Smith (2000: 4) call 'frozen social relations'.

However, if physical characteristics prove clearly differentiated along the "vertical" axis of social space, this should not blind the analysis to the secondary differentiation of such characteristics in terms of the particular *type* of capital that defines agents' position in social space. As Chapter 1 has argued, this second dimension differentiates class-fractions on the basis of their relative possession of economic and cultural capital. To this opposition between the dominant and the dominated fractions of the dominant class correspond two different lifestyles and two distinct manners of relating to the body, that is, 'two contrasting ways of defying nature, need, appetite, desire' (Bourdieu, 1984: 254). On the one hand, there is the 'hedonistic aesthetic of ease and facility' (1984: 176) of the economically dominant pole which expresses itself in the 'ostentatious freedom of gratuitous expense' (1984: 254–255) and uses the display of 'luxury, as the manifestation of distance from necessity' (1984: 255). On the other, the culturally dominant fractions are marked by a more purist ethos which has 'affinity with the ascetic aspect of aesthetics' (1984: 176) and distinguishes itself through 'asceticism, a self-imposed constraint' (1984: 255) which forms the basis of a lifestyle that is 'as remote from concupiscence as it is from conspicuous consumption' (1984: 497).

If the body is indeed the 'most indisputable materialization of class taste' (1984: 190), one should expect such oppositions to also be reflected in agents' physical dimensions with the culturally dominant pole of social space being most conducive to the leanest body-types. Interestingly enough, class-differences in BMI provide some evidence for this. For instance, the fact that the average BMI of men appears to vary only slightly *between* social classes, conceals the differences rooted in capital-structure *within* the dominant and middle-classes (Table 4.2). As one moves from the commercial employers and senior-executives through the professions to the higher-education teachers and the cultural producers, average body-mass decreases in an almost linear fashion (the average difference between the employers and the cultural producers, *ceteris paribus*, is 11 pounds). Whereas three-quarters of the commercial employers and two thirds of the senior-executives have a body-mass that qualifies them as "overweight", this drops to half of the academics and 40 per cent of the artists and cultural producers. A similar opposition is found among men in the upper fringe of the middle-classes, between those

Table 4.2 Body-size characteristics by gender and class fraction

	Avg. BMI[a]		% BMI < 18.5 ('underweight')		% BMI [25–30] ('overweight')		% BMI > 30 ('obese')		Avg. height (cm)[a]		N	
	♂	♀	♂	♀	♂	♀	♂	♀	♂	♀	♂	♀
	**	**							**	**		
Dominant class	**25.0**	**22.9**	**0.8**	**7.6**	**39.1**	**16.4**	**9.0**	**5.3**	**178.6**	**165.4**	**319**	**233**
Commercial employers	25.9[b]	n.a.[c]	0.0	n.a.	58.7	n.a.	15.2	n.a.	179.3	n.a.	46	10
Senior-executives	25.2	23.1	1.9	7.8	55.3	25.5	9.3	11.8	179.5	165.7	109	52
Professions	24.6	22.1	0.0	11.8	43.0	14.7	6.9	4.4	177.8	166.2	69	69
Higher ed. and scientific occup.	24.8	23.4	0.0	4.5	43.1	21.2	7.8	7.6	179.1	166.2	51	66
Cultural producers and artists	23.9	21.9	2.3	11.1	29.6	11.1	9.1	0.0	178.4	164.3	44	36
Upper-middle-classes	**25.1**	**23.7**	**1.1**	**3.8**	**36.2**	**19.8**	**10.7**	**7.7**	**177.9**	**164.9**	**789**	**1,105**
Financial services	26.2	24.2	1.2	5.7	37.0	31.4	16.0	8.6	177.9	164.9	81	35
Junior-executives	26.1	23.6	1.1	4.7	36.4	15.6	6.3	7.0	177.9	164.7	176	128
Socio-medical services	24.8	23.8	0.0	3.7	35.0	25.7	5.0	8.7	177.8	165.0	41	218
Teachers secondary	24.3	23.3	1.4	2.1	36.2	20.8	5.0	7.3	176.6	165.0	69	96
Lower-middle-classes	**25.3**	**23.4**	**0.5**	**5.0**	**33.9**	**18.8**	**12.0**	**8.9**	**177.9**	**164.8**	**555**	**870**
Shopkeepers	25.4	23.4	0.0	4.4	33.0	16.5	18.8	9.9	178.0	163.5	112	91
Office-workers (admin.)	25.1	23.7	0.7	4.4	36.3	19.4	11.2	8.3	176.4	165.0	267	360
Office-workers (pres.)	n.a.	22.9	n.a.	6.7	n.a.	16	n.a.	2.7	n.a.	165.0	15	75
Teachers primary	25.4	23.4	0.0	6.9	42.9	11.8	7.1	9.8	177.1	165.2	28	102
Working-classes	**25.7**	**24.4**	**1.4**	**3.3**	**41.0**	**20.3**	**12.5**	**13.2**	**176.6**	**163.8**	**656**	**431**
Skilled manual (incl. foremen)	25.7	n.a.	0.9	n.a.	42.4	n.a.	11.5	n.a.	177.6	n.a.	56	16
Semi-skilled manual	25.8	24.3	1.6	2.7	44.5	24.5	13.4	10.0	176.8	164.2	291	112
Unskilled manual	26.0	24.5	2.1	3.5	35.8	20.3	12.4	15.4	176.2	163.4	309	303
Farm workers	25.5	n.a.	0.0	n.a.	39.6	n.a.	10.4	n.a.	176.5	n.a.	48	15
Total	**25.3**	**23.4**	**1.6**	**5.9**	**38.6**	**25.2**	**12.3**	**13.5**	**175.4**	**163.0**	**4,881**	**5,615**

Source: BNHS '04

Notes
a Both BMI and height have been adjusted for age-differences.
b Figures in italic denote the strongest tendency in a column.
c Number of observations too low, to make meaningful inferences.
n.s. = non-significant, *** $p < .005$, ** $p < .010$, * $p < .05$, n.a. = number of observations too low to make meaningful inferences

98 *Modes of embodiment*

employed in the financial services (insurance, real-estate, etc.) and the secondary education-teachers, which on average are 13 pounds lighter than the former (height being equal). Among women, differences between class-fractions prove less marked, although it is again among the culturally dominant fractions that one finds both the leanest body-types, as well as the highest percentage of women who qualify as medically "underweight" (something to which we shall return in Chapter 7). Because most measures of class or social position used in epidemiological research on weight-differences remain wedded to a *one-dimensional* conception of social structure, they tend to ignore these *secondary* differences in tastes and lifestyles rooted in capital-*composition*, rather than capital-*volume*. In doing so, they tend to conflate two quite distinct relationships to the body which, as far as men seem concerned, are materialized into quite different physiognomies. This opposition within the dominant and middle-class could help to account for the repeated observation made within the epidemiological literature, that the (statistical) relationship between social position and body-mass, especially among men, tends to be *non-significant* or *positive* when measured through income-differences, while it is more likely to be *negative* when measured through differences in educational capital (McLaren, 2007).

The social perception of body-weight

Even if the epidemiological literature on obesity tends to impose a rather partial understanding of the social production of contemporary weight-differences, it at least has the merit of challenging some of the key assumptions that pervade so much sociological theorizing on the body. More specifically, its results tend to question the existence of a quasi-universal anxiety concerning the body's size and shape that so many theorists of the body tend to view as endemic to life in 'consumer culture' or 'late modernity' (on this point, see Crossley, 2004). In fact, on the basis of the literature one is often led to believe that most, if not *all* social agents are engaged in one form of weight-loss or another (see the above-mentioned quote by Giddens). A closer look at how weight-concern is actually distributed across social space tends to paint a somewhat more complex picture of the contemporary "diet-craze" (Table 4.3 and 4.4). While the impact of the dominant norms of appearance can already be seen in the fact that virtually *no one*, regardless of gender, occupation, education or income, wants to *gain* weight, this fact alone does not warrant the conclusion of a generalized anxiety about body-size and shape. In fact, less than one out of five men and a quarter of women actually claimed they were trying to *lose* weight, while a quarter of all women and a third of all men indicated they were quite unconcerned about their physical size and roughly 30 per cent of both sexes reported they would like to maintain their current weight (Bennett *et al*.'s [2009: esp. 152ff.] study of class and lifestyle in the UK similarly reported a remarkably low number of people who claimed they were on a diet). More important for the case at hand, this "subjective" degree of weight-concern clearly varies in terms of agents' position in social space. In fact, the results of the analysis suggest that the desire to control

Table 4.3 Weight-concern and body-mass by gender, educational capital, economic capital and professional status

	Men										Women									
	Unconcerned		Maintain		Lose		Gain				Unconcerned		Maintain		Lose		Gain			
	%	(BMI)	%	(BMI)	%	(BMI)	%	(BMI)	N		%	(BMI)	%	(BMI)	%	(BMI)	%	(BMI)	N
Educational capital																				
Less than HS	52.7[a]	25.5[b]	29.6	26.5	13.6	30.4	4.1	20.6	1,685		45.1	24.9	30.4	26.0	21.7	30.8	2.8	20.0	2,292
HS (technical/vocational)	41.5	25.5	36.9	26.5	18.8	29.5	2.7	21.7	912		33.3	24.0	35.4	24.6	28.7	29.0	2.6	18.6	729
HS (academic)	41.1	24.4	33.3	25.5	22.0	28.6	3.7	21.1	491		26.7	23.3	37.7	23.7	33.3	27.3	2.3	18.7	586
Bachelor	33.2	24.0	37.3	25.0	27.0	28.3	2.9	20.3	725		22.4	22.2	42.3	22.9	32.9	25.8	2.3	18.8	1,001
Master	29.6	23.8	41.5	24.8	26.3	27.1	2.5	20.1	610		24.7	21.3	41.2	22.0	33.0	24.8	1.1	20.1	399
Economic capital																				
<750€	53.8	25.1	21.7	25.1	19.6	28.0	4.9	21.7	232		42.3	24.3	27.7	24.4	28.0	28.4	2.0	18.7	338
750–1,000€	49.3	24.7	29.5	25.8	14.7	29.2	6.5	20.4	404		42.7	24.0	30.3	24.6	23.4	29.5	3.6	20.2	678
1,000–1,500€	45.4	24.9	31.9	25.7	18.7	28.7	4.0	21.7	984		34.5	24.0	34.7	24.2	28.1	28.4	2.6	18.8	1,130
1,500–2,500€	39.1	24.7	36.2	26.1	21.1	28.5	3.6	21.0	1,264		25.6	23.3	36.8	24.1	34.6	27.6	3.0	18.6	1,347
>2,500€	33.6	24.0	37.5	25.1	26.0	28.4	3.1	19.9	1,238		22.6	22.7	43.3	22.9	32.8	25.8	1.4	18.9	1,185
Professional status																				
Paid work	38.3	24.4	35.6	25.4	23.0	28.3	3.0	20.7	2,399		24.9	22.3	39.3	23.0	33.9	25.8	1.9	18.4	1,921
Housework	n.a.	n.a.	n.a.	n.a.	n.a.	n.a.	n.a.	n.a.	19		29.4	25.3	38.7	24.2	29.4	29.5	2.5	21.2	635
Unemployed	48.9	24.3	27.0	25.5	18.1	28.8	5.9	22.6	276		28.2	23.1	30.9	24.3	37.2	29.0	3.7	18.5	320
Retired/unable to work	41.3	25.3	36.9	26.0	18.7	29.3	3.1	20.6	1,658		39.1	24.3	35.0	24.9	23.3	29.6	2.6	19.1	1,963
Total	32.9	24.7	27.8	25.7	16.4	28.6	2.9	20.9	5,202		24.5	23.6	29.4	23.9	24.3	27.7	2.0	19.1	6,095

Source: BNHS '04

Notes
a Figures in italic indicate the strongest tendency in a column.
b This number reads as follows: "Men who did not finish higher secondary education and are unconcerned about their weight have an average BMI of 25.5."

Table 4.4 Weight-concern and body-mass by gender and class fraction

	Men										Women									
	Unconcerned		Maintain		Lose		Gain				Unconcerned		Maintain		Lose		Gain			
	%	(BMI)	%	(BMI)	%	(BMI)	%	(BMI)	N		%	(BMI)	%	(BMI)	%	(BMI)	%	(BMI)	N
Dominant class	27.7	23.3	41.0	24.7	25.9	27.6	1.2	n.a.	230		27.7	21.0	39.7	22.0	30.0	25.3	1.7	n.a.	199
Commercial employers	36.6[a]	25.7[b]	36.6	25.7	24.4	29.1	2.4	n.a.	40		n.a.	n.a.	n.a.	n.a.	n.a.	n.a.	n.a.	n.a.	8
Senior-executives	22.1	22.9	50.0	25.5	28.0	28.7	0.0	n.a.	52		25.5	21.5	38.3	22.7	30.6	26.9	2.1	n.a.	46
Professions	34.5	24.0	34.5	24.0	29.1	26.4	1.8	n.a.	52		25.9	19.5	37.0	21.4	35.2	24.9	1.9	n.a.	53
Higher ed. and scientific occup.	17.4	24.2	52.2	24.9	26.1	26.3	4.0	n.a.	46		24.1	22.9	36.2	22.2	39.7	24.5	0.0	n.a.	58
Cultural producers and artists	46.3[c]	22.1	31.7	23.4	22.0	27.7	0.2	n.a.	40		35.3	20.2	47.1	21.8	14.7	25.0	2.9	n.a.	34
Upper-middle-classes	32.2	24.3	37.7	25.2	27.5	28.2	2.6	n.a.	721		23.3	22.4	40.1	22.7	34.6	25.6	2.3	n.a.	1,026
Financial services	29.2	25.6	37.5	26.8	30.6	28.0	2.8	n.a.	72		18.2	23.4	36.4	21.1	39.4	28.1	6.1	n.a.	33
Junior-executives	33.5	23.4	34.1	24.8	28.7	28.5	3.7	n.a.	162		23.8	22.8	39.3	22.6	35.2	25.0	1.6	n.a.	120
Socio-medical services	31.6	24.0	42.1	24.1	26.3	27.1	0.0	n.a.	45		19.4	21.5	49.5	22.3	29.1	26.6	1.9	n.a.	205
Teachers secondary	38.7	23.8	33.9	25.0	25.8	27.6	1.6	n.a.	62		22.2	22.6	49.5	23.8	28.3	24.1	0.0	n.a.	93
Lower-middle classes	37.7	24.4	34.9	25.1	24.7	28.8	3.2	n.a.	507		23.6	22.3	37.0	22.9	37.5	25.2	2.0	n.a.	806
Shopkeepers	36.6	25.7	36.6	25.8	22.6	29.7	4.3	n.a.	92		34.1	22.2	29.3	22.9	35.4	25.8	1.2	n.a.	81
Office-workers (admin.)	36.5	24.1	37.3	25.1	23.9	27.9	2.4	n.a.	249		21.1	22.0	37.8	23.1	39.9	25.3	1.2	n.a.	326
Office-workers (pres.)	n.a.	n.a.	n.a.	n.a.	n.a.	n.a.	n.a.	n.a.	13		22.4	22.4	42.1	22.8	32.9	24.4	2.6	n.a.	72
Teachers primary	19.2	23.4	42.3	24.5	34.6	28.8	3.8	n.a.	26		25.0	22.5	37.0	22.6	37.0	25.2	1.0	n.a.	96
Working-classes	45.2	24.8	32.0	25.8	19.1	29.4	4.2	n.a.	831		33.5	22.7	35.2	24.0	29.0	27.3	2.3	n.a	380
Skilled manual	43.7	24.7	36.6	26.0	17.8	28.5	1.9	n.a.	302		n.a.	n.a.	n.a.	n.a.	n.a.	n.a.	n.a.	n.a.	15
Semi-skilled manual	40.1	25.1	35.2	26.3	21.1	28.6	3.7	n.a.	322		36.4	22.1	33.6	23.7	29.0	27.0	0.9	n.a.	105
Unskilled manual	48.1	25.0	26.6	25.9	18.2	29.0	7.0	n.a.	207		30.5	23.3	36.8	24.3	29.0	27.7	3.7	n.a.	260
Farm workers	48.9	24.2	29.8	25.1	19.1	31.5	2.7	n.a.	23		n.a.	n.a.	n.a.	n.a.	n.a.	n.a.	n.a.	n.a.	6
Total	32.9	(24.6)	27.8	(25.5)	16.4	(28.6)	2.9	(21.1)	5,202		24.5	(23.3)	29.4	(23.9)	24.3	(27.7)	2.0	(19.1)	6,095

Source: BNHS '04

Notes
a This number reads as follows: "37 per cent of male commercial employers are unconcerned about their weight."
b This number reads as follows: "Male commercial employers who are unconcerned about their weight have an average BMI of 25.7."
c Figures in italic indicate the strongest tendency in a column.

The perceptible body 101

or change weight can itself be understood as a particular case of the more general dialectic of aspirations and chances as outlined in the preceding chapters. More specifically, the propensity to invest in body-size and shape not only appears to vary with the possession of the actual means to do so, but also with the chances of material and symbolic profit that social agents can reasonably expect from such investments, that is to say, with their degree of access to the symbolic markets in which appearance can function as a form of capital.

> In this manner, those who have the most intimate experience of their bodies as *instruments* of labour, rather than as objects which generate symbolic value through their "form", namely members of the working-class and especially working-class men, also report the lowest levels of weight-concern. A third of working-class women and nearly half of working-class men state they are unconcerned about their current body-weight, while 30 per cent and 20 per cent, respectively, indicate they would actually like to lose weight. Interestingly, it is among women (and to a lesser extent among men) of the middle-classes or *petit-bourgeoisie* that one finds the strongest desire to *lose* weight. Situated closer to those who occupy dominant social positions, they tend to share their interest in the body's "form" and more readily accept the dominant definition of the legitimate masculine and feminine physique. However, the discrepancy between the recognition of this definition and the possession of the capital to fully realize it, which (here as elsewhere) defines the *petit-bourgeois* relationship to the dominant lifestyle, appears to be at the basis of a more anxious and "proactive" relationship to the body. Not only did nearly 40 per cent of women from the lower and a third of women from the upper fringes of the middle-class indicate they were trying to lose weight, but nearly half of them stated they had already been on *several* diets (compared to little over a third of women who occupy dominant social positions). This simultaneously distinguishes them from members of the working-class, who don't share their concern with appearance, but also from upper-class women, who prove to have a somewhat less anxious relationship to their physical size. Not only do they tend to have the highest levels of satisfaction with their weight (see Table 4.5), but half of them claim they have *never* been on a diet (see Table A4.1 in appendix), a quarter state they rarely ever weight themselves, while 40 per cent indicate they would like to maintain their current weight.

More importantly, the analysis does not only show that weight-concern proves far from *universal*, but also that such concern is by no means *mechanically* linked to actual physical size. In fact, the desire to lose weight is itself a function of the practical norms that govern the perception of the "legitimate" body within a given class or class fraction defining what its members come to view as a "fat", "slender" or "normal" body. A number of indices in fact show that as one rises in the social hierarchy, these norms become increasingly more restrictive. As the pressure to maintain a distinctive and distinguished physique increases, the limits within which body-weight is allowed to vary tend to become increasingly narrower. Not only do men and women who occupy dominant social positions indicate they would have to gain *less* weight before they would start noticing, but they also report a lower amount of weight-gain before they deem it necessary to go on a diet (see Table A4.1). Furthermore, women (but not men) who occupy dominant social positions also report an "ideal weight" that is lower than that of working- and middle-class women, while the gap between this ideal and their *current* weight also proves to be smallest. One could be tempted to simply attribute such findings to the perceptible logic of weight-change. According to this logic, a 5 kg increase in weight does not produce the same, immediately visible results for someone who weighs 100 kg, than it does for someone who weighs 60 kg and given that those who are situated in the most precarious regions of social space are, on average, heavier than those who are positioned at the top, weight-gain (especially when it is gradual) is more likely to pass unnoticed. While tempting, such an explanation ignores the fact that the apperception of the "objective", physical body is always mediated by the evaluative categories proper to a given class. This is shown by the fact that the *same* body-mass, especially among those who have the largest physical size, is associated with quite different levels of subjective weight-concern.

> Differences in reported weight-concern only receive their full meaning, when they are related to the actual weight distributions of the different social classes and class-fractions (see figures in Table 4.3 and 4.4). For instance, while almost half of the men and women with little or no formal education state that they are "*unconcerned*" about their weight, as opposed to less than a third of men and women with a university degree, they do so at an average body-weight which is considerably higher than the latter (25.5 and 24.9, respectively, compared to 23.8 and 21.3). Similarly, while the desire to "*maintain*" one's current weight becomes stronger as one moves from working-class men and women to those in the dominant classes, the average body-weight decreases from 25.8 and 24.0 for the former to 24.8 and 22.1 among the latter. The relationship between body-mass and the degree of weight-control seems especially important in understanding differences the perception of weight among women. For instance, while the desire to lose weight seems to vary on slightly between housewives, the unemployed and women who are engaged in the labour force (and among the latter between unskilled manual workers and female executives), this conceals the fact that these groups differ considerably in terms of their actual weight, with those housewives (29.5) and unemployed women (29.0) who indicate they want to lose weight having an average body-mass which almost ranks them as medically "obese", while women who are employed full-time have an average BMI of 25.8 (the respective BMI of manual workers and executives being 27.3 and 26.6).

Although one could argue that such differences in weight-concern are partly due to the inclination to provide socially desirable responses, the fact that those who are situated at the top of the class-structure systematically report *lower* thresholds of appropriate weight-gain is in and of itself significant. More importantly, there is some evidence to suggest that the classificatory schemes which inform the perception and judgment of the body among dominant social groups not only produce a more fine-graded perception of weight-change, but effectively manage to set limits to the variation of body-size among these groups. To illustrate this, the analysis needs to move beyond the discussion of physical differences *between* classes, to the distribution of bodies *within* each class.

Average and norm

While suggestive, the results presented thus far in fact quickly become mystifying, if one forgets that they are based on differences in *average* body-mass. If statistical averages always require a good deal of circumspection when gauging inter-group-differences, this holds even more true when one tries to argue that such differences should be understood, at least partly, as the product of processes of social distinction. In fact, even if anthropometric averages are not only expressive of *biological* variation, but also reveal a 'social normativity' – as noted by Canguilhem in the opening remarks to this chapter and by Halbwachs (1912) before him – and are hence indicative of the collective norms that govern the ways in which the body is perceived, judged and managed within a given class or class fraction, such averages offer preciously little information on how *strongly* such norms are imposed within a given group. However, it is precisely the degree of conformity to such norms which is of key interest here. In fact, if the central role of restraint and moderation in the dominant relationship to the body owes a considerable part of its logic to the dialectic of distinction and pretension and especially to the pressure it exerts on the dominant to maintain their distinctive physique, this ascetic-*cum*-aesthetic relationship to the body should impose itself more *uniformly* among those who occupy dominant social positions. This means that one should expect the latter to not only have the lowest *average* weight, but also to be clustered more strongly around this average. As a relational principle of explanation, the logic of distinction hence forces the analysis to not only look at weight-differences *between* social classes, but also to examine the distribution of weight-differences *within* each class or, put differently, to treat the *intra*-class variation in body-weight as a function of its *inter*-class variation.

This is what is shown by an analysis of the overall *distribution* of body-mass by educational capital and class (Figures 4.1 and 4.2). In fact, as one moves up the social hierarchy, it is not just the average body-weight which systematically decreases, but it is the distribution of weight *as a whole* which shifts towards a leaner body-size, and this for both women *and* men. For men, the fact that *average* body-weight varies only slightly between levels of educational capital and class-positions not only obscures the fact that the most stigmatized (i.e. corpulent) physique becomes increasingly more rare as one moves from dominated to dominant social position, but also that the variation of weight itself becomes contained within increasingly more narrow boundaries. This proves even more

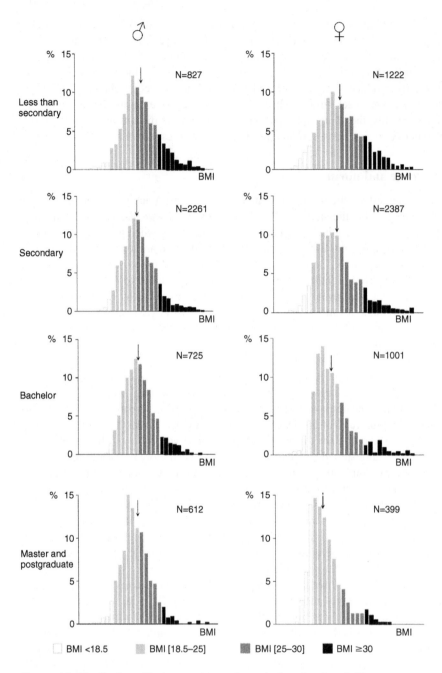

Figure 4.1 Distribution of body-mass by gender and educational capital*

Source: BNHS '04

Note
* The arrow denotes the average BMI for that specific category.

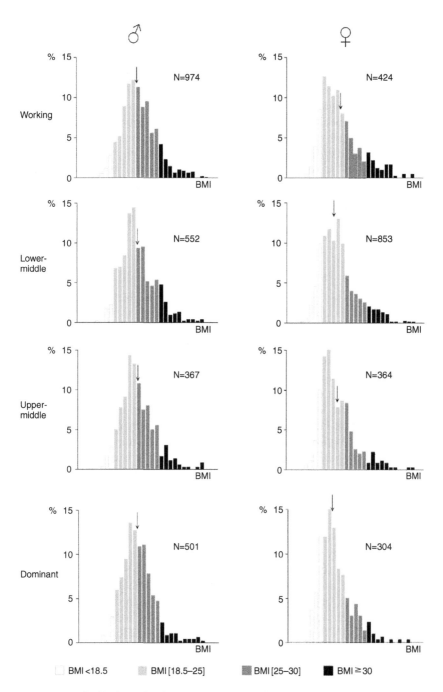

Figure 4.2 Distribution of body-mass by gender and social class*

Source: BNHS '04

Note
* The arrow denotes the average BMI for that specific category.

clear among women, where weight-differences become systematically concentrated in the lowest categories as one rises in the social hierarchy. In accordance with the logic of distinction, dominant tastes not only tend to produce the lowest *average* body-weight, but also impose more restrictive boundaries on the range within which body-weight is allowed to legitimately vary. The distribution of weight-differences among men and women who occupy dominant social positions therefore suggests that they not only *perceive* their bodies using particularly stringent criteria of judgment, as the preceding sections have attempted to show, but that these criteria also effectively translate into physical sizes that are concentrated more strongly around the dominant norm. Without therefore denying that differences in body-size and -shape are subjected to biological variation (which would simply be trading in one type of reductionism for another), the analysis does suggest that *social* mechanisms, in this case the logic of distinction, manage to set effective limits to such variation.

Diet and *diaita*

Thus far, the analysis has mainly looked at the ways in which class-differences subtend the social *production* and social *perception* of weight-differences, as well as their mutual relationship in defining the degree of weight-concern that defines different social groups. In doing so, it has said little about the factors that determine the propensity to actually engage in strategies of weight-loss and, more importantly, their overall success. However, one of the reasons the focus on weight-*differences* not only serves to call into question the supposed *universality* of contemporary body-consciousness, but also the purported increase in the *plasticity* of the body. In fact, the voluntarism that is implied by concepts like 'body projects' or 'body-options' inevitably runs up against an impressive amount of studies that demonstrate the recalcitrance of body-weight to intentional, deliberate change (see for instance, Kramer *et al.*, 1989; Miller, 1999; Jeffery *et al.*, 2000). While the human body proves capable of remarkable *short-term* transformations in body-mass (a good example are the impressive weight changes achieved by athletes), these studies underline the relative ineffectiveness of dieting – both clinically supported as well as individual "lifestyle-diets" – in securing *permanent* weight-loss. Not only does weight *regain* appear to occur in the majority of observed cases (with some estimates judging that more than 90 per cent of dieters revert back to their original weight within 5 years of initiating weight-loss, see Kramer *et al.*, 1989), but the probability of regaining weight also proves positively related to the initial weight before dieting, which makes weight-loss strategies even less effective for those struggling with the most extreme forms of corpulence.

Such findings are frequently invoked as clinical evidence for the fact that body-mass is in fact *genetically* predetermined and hence largely impervious to intentional modification. This view is defended by the so-called 'set-point'-theory of obesity (Nisbett, 1972; Leibel, 1990), which holds that an individual's amount of body fat is genetically fixed at a predetermined level and that the obese are simply endowed with naturally high 'set-points'. More importantly, the theory postulates that the amount of fatty tissue is regulated homeostatically, so that to any decrease in caloric intake and/or increase in energy-expenditure will trigger physiological responses (decreased energy-expenditure, increased fat-storage, etc.) aimed at restoring weight to its original level or actually raising the 'set-point' as a built-in defence against such forms of self-imposed "starvation". The notion of predetermined 'set-points' is compelling for several reasons. Not only could it help to account for the difficulties involved in weight-loss (especially the renowned "yoyo-effect" in dieting), but the theory is also potentially liberating in that it could provide a scientific defence against the often unrealistic expectations fostered by the dieting industry, which explains its popularity among feminist scholars and diet-sceptics (see Orbach, 1978; Schwartz, 1986; Rothblum, 1994). It proves less adequate, however, when asked to account for the historical evolution and social distribution of contemporary weight-patterns. If the rapid pace at which *average* body-weight (and hence the average 'set-point') has increased over the past decades already renders evolutionary changes in the population highly implausible (Speakman, 2007), than genetic explanations are even more hard-pressed to account for the fact that differences in body-weight (and hence the variation in 'set-points') prove so clearly aligned with positions in the social structure. More importantly, an appeal to genetic hard-wiring becomes even more unconvincing when trying to explain how the prevalence of a corpulent physique has managed – within a matter of generations – to shift from the top of the social hierarchy to its bottom, as the recent history of most "post-industrial" social formations has shown and as can be observed in "developing" societies today. If body-size were indeed attributable to genetic predisposition, then this inversion of its social gradient would require a degree of *inter-* or *intra*-generational mobility that seems to defy the laws of social physics.

Existing research into the logic of weight-differences hence presents us with somewhat of a paradox. If explanations that lean exclusively on genetic hardwiring are hard-pressed to account for the clear *social* and *historical* variations in body-weight, than the cosmetic voluntarism preached by the contemporary cult of dieting or the finalism implied in concepts such as 'body-projects' proves equally inadequate to explain why body-weight, as a *social* product, nevertheless proves so intractable to intentional change. One clue to solving this paradox is provided by the etymology of the word "diet" which derives from the Greek *diaita* meaning "way of life" or "mode of living". In fact, contrary to what the commercial dieting-industry and public health-campaigns all too often suggest, the factors that shape body-weight cannot be reduced to eating habits and/or physical exercise alone. While undoubtedly highly salient elements in determining the size and shape of the body (which is why they form the topic of the following two chapters), they are themselves part of an entire constellation of solidary and mutually reinforcing practices and beliefs that together constitute the lifestyle of a particular class or class fraction. From this it follows, that the success of *durable* transformations in any *single* dimension of practice depends on the degree to which such changes can themselves be 'integrated into the total system of attitudes and customs which alone can give [them] a foundation and a meaning' (Bourdieu, 1990c: 104). Far from being abstract, interchangeable elements, the particular ways of relating to the body that are expressed in eating habits or sporting activities draw a considerable part of their *practical* significance from their integration into this system of practices and beliefs. Practices and beliefs which, when themselves considered in isolation, will often appear as wholly tangential to the problematic of weight and physical appearance, such as conceptions of the sexual and domestic division of labour, occupational aspirations, the social and temporal organization of family-life and leisure or attitudes towards child-rearing. That is why the adoption of changes in *one* particular dimension of practice, like eating habits, tend to give rise to a host of novel problems and contradictions, *if* such changes are not accompanied by a more encompassing transformation of lifestyle and, especially, by changes (i.e. improvements) in the material and cultural conditions of existence that such a transformation objectively demands.

These contradictions are experienced in particularly acute manner by working-class women who endeavour weight-loss. Not only do they have to engage in practices of self-denial that often only further compound the strictures of an existence that is already marked by necessity and privation, but which are also at odds with the dietary needs of their families (and especially its male members) whose proclivities for the filling and substantial often prove quite incompatible with such an ascetic stance (Charles and Kerr, 1988; Lupton, 1996). If, furthermore, they are unable to escape the dominant norms of femininity they encounter in magazines and television-programmes, the intrinsic motivation to attain such norms tends to become all the more abstract and unreal, the less they can reasonably expect – in terms of symbolic recognition or material rewards – from investing in their appearance. Finally, given that the durable inculcation of such ascetic dispositions often hinges on little more than the *individual* appropriation – outside of any systematic and sustained pedagogic action – of an abstract set of dietary principles and guidelines encountered in such magazines and programmes which have themselves been stripped of their practical reference to any concrete and particular lifestyle – which is the precondition for their commercialization, which is precisely predicated on the idea that the "ideal body" is very much within the reach of *everyone* – then the practices to which they give rise, are bound to remain superficial, fragmentary and discontinuous, in short, will fail to produce lasting results.

Hysteresis-effects

It is, however, not just the *systematic* character of lifestyle that tends to make comprehensive and lasting changes in any of its specific dimensions particularly difficult. To show that the concept of habitus can provide a way of accounting for 'the recalcitrance of embodied existence to self-fashioning' (McNay, 1999: 97) and can do so, moreover, *without* having to invoke the (largely unproven) existence of innate, biological mechanisms of weight-regulation, we need to return to an argument made in the second chapter. There I argued that is precisely because the relationship to the body is acquired in manner that not only largely eludes reflexive scrutiny, but also escapes the transformative scope of the educational system – where "physical education" (in the broadest possible sense of the term) still occupies a marginal position at best – it remains durably marked by the primary conditions in which it was inculcated (see Chapter 2). As the following chapter will aim to show, this is especially true of the relationship to *food*, which plays a crucial role in fashioning the physicality of the class body. That this 'hysteris' of dispositions also affects changes in human morphology, can be most clearly observed in those cases in which social agents' *current* position in the social structure differs, more or less drastically, from their social origins.

In fact, epidemiological studies that have analysed the evolution of individual body-mass among socially *mobile* agents (Langenberg *et al.*, 2003; Ball and Mishra, 2006) have consistently revealed such a 'hysteresis-effect'. While upwardly mobile individuals prove to have a BMI that is *lower* than those in their position of origin, it nonetheless remain *higher* than that of those in their current social position (a similar intermediate position marks the downwardly mobile). More importantly, the extent of this weight difference appears to hinge on both the "moment" and the "momentum" of their social ascent (or descent). First, those who shift social position early on in life (through parental mobility) tend to come closer to the average weight that is characteristic of their *new* social position, than those who are exposed to their condition(ing)s of origin for a longer period of time (Ball and Mishra, 2006). Secondly, those who traverse a larger section of social space (i.e. have a "steeper" social trajectory) prove to be further removed from the average weight of their position of origin, than those who shift into "neighbouring" social positions.

Such results are interesting for two reasons. First, because they help to show that body-weight is a lot more amenable to durable change (i.e. weight-loss) than the theory of predetermined set-points (or genetic explanations in general) would lead one to believe, but also because they demonstrate that such change hinges less on *individual* determination and self-discipline, than on a real transformation (i.e. improvement) in the material and cultural arrangements of existence. Secondly, they also show that even *despite* such an improvement, the upwardly mobile never fully attain the body-size that is characteristic of their new social position and hence lend support to the enduring importance of primary dispositions in shaping the class body. The latter seems particularly important in understanding the *dual* barriers to attaining the legitimate body for those who are situated at the bottom of the class-structure. Not only are they confronted with the *objective* necessity of conditions of existence that provide neither the real means, nor the real incentives to realize the dominant physique, but, more importantly, they also face the intransigence of their own *tastes* which, being the *embodied* form of this necessity and hence functioning at the level of the pre-discursive and the pre-reflexive, prove particularly resistant to intentional modification. No wonder then, that when they do decide to engage in intentional weight-loss strategies, they tend to have the lowest average success-rates.

> Our analyses tend to confirm the overall low success-rate of dieting as a means of securing durable weight-loss (Appendix, Table A4.1). Only 30 per

cent of men and a third of women who went on a diet, indicate they had managed to maintain their weight-loss, while nearly 40 per cent and a third, respectively, reported they were back at their original weight before their previous diet or were even heavier than before. Crucially, these success-rates are themselves further differentiated in accordance with social position. So whereas almost 40 per cent of women with a Master's or a postgraduate degree and nearly half of upper-class women (47 per cent) claim to have lost weight during their previous diet *and* have managed to maintain their weight-loss, this drops to a quarter of women with little or no formal education and one out of five women from a working-class background. The latter in turn most often indicated they had regained all the weight they had lost or were actually heavier than before (this is the case for 54 per cent of working-class women and more than a third of those who did not finish secondary education)

This 'hysteresis' of the class-tastes does not only seem relevant to understanding the internal logic of weight-change, but also seems crucial to grasping the "lived" experience of the body and especially its perceived "plasticity". In fact, since these tastes impose themselves with all the necessity of an ineluctable nature, the high rates of diet-failure – produced by the inherent mismatch between the lifestyle (and dispositions) *objectively* demanded for the cultivation of the legitimate body and the dispositions constituted in conditions of material and cultural necessity – have every chance of being lived in the wholly *individualized* mode of self-incrimination and personal failure (*"It's stronger than me"* or *"I can't help myself"*). While the remainder of this chapter will explore how this fundamentally affects social agents' self-identity and self-understanding, one should add that there is also a quasi-political dimension to the perceived malleability of one's own body. The case of dieting and weight-concern does in fact provide some support for Mary Douglas' proposition that the 'physical experience of the body, always modified by the social categories through which it is known, sustains a particular view of society' (1973: 93). In fact, it is in the apparent immutability of their own bodies, that those who occupy the most precarious social positions (and especially working-class *women*) find another confirmation of the inertia and sense of powerlessness that marks their experience of the social world and the ethos of resignation before the given that this experience engenders. Conversely, members of the dominant class – for whom restraint and moderation have become durably inculcated as "second nature" and are a constitutive element of their "diet" (in the original sense of the term) – can rely most strongly on the "natural" inclinations, and especially aversions, of their bodies in order to secure the most valorizing physique. They hence reap the double symbolic rewards of at once having the legitimate body, which at the same time owes nothing to conscious effort, let alone a cynical strive for distinction. This not only separates them from the vulgar physique of the working-class, but also distinguishes them from the "superficiality" of the *petit-bourgeoisie* who are not only marked by a more anxious concern with appearance (see Chapter 8), but who also quite explicitly flaunt their investments in physical capital (see Featherstone, 1987).

Current body, dream body

Thus far, the analysis has attempted to establish several things: First, that weight-differences are strongly aligned with the divisions inscribed in the social and sexual division of labour. Second, that concern with the body's size and shape tends to increase as one rises in the social hierarchy. Third, that body-weight becomes perceived through increasingly more fine-grained and restrictive schemes of evaluation as one moves from dominated to dominant social positions and that, consequently, the variation in physical size becomes contained between increasingly more narrow boundaries. Finally, that the conditions to effectively transform the size and shape of the body are themselves *social* in nature and become more favourable as one rises in social space. However, in analysing these various aspects of the relationship between social class and physical size, we have been forced to rely on a quite blunt indicator, namely the "body mass index". While it might provide a practical estimate of differences in body-mass, the BMI has some important limitations. Apart from the relatively arbitrary nature its divisions into "normal" and "pathological" weight (which is not so much a problem of the index itself, rather than of its particular social uses), one of its most important drawbacks is that it makes no distinction in terms of actual body-*type* and is completely oblivious to differences in muscle and body fat. In this manner, a nominally identical BMI can be associated with quite distinct morphologies and hence with quite different relationships to the body (see Monaghan, 2007).

Furthermore, while analyses of the social differentiation in BMI help reveal how physical properties are distributed across social space, they provide little insight into how members of different social classes perceive and evaluate such properties and, more specifically, into their particular definition of the "ideal" or most "disliked" physique. Such elements are nevertheless crucial in aiming to understand the practical value that social agents assign to their own physical capital and hence of the "subjective" degree of satisfaction and confidence they derive from their own bodies. In fact, as Bourdieu asserts:

> The chances of experiencing one's own body as a vessel of grace, a continuous miracle, are that much greater when bodily capacity is commensurate with recognition; and, conversely, the probability of experiencing the body with unease, embarrassment, timidity grows with the disparity between the ideal body and the real body, the dream body and the 'looking-glass self' reflected in the reactions of others.
>
> (1984: 207)

In order to avoid the problems inherent in the use of BMI and to gauge the value that the different social classes attribute to differences in body-size and -shape, a

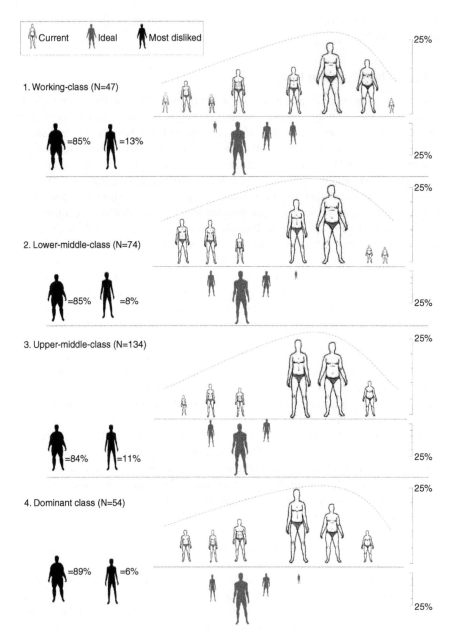

Figure 4.3 Current, ideal and most disliked body by social class (*men*)*

Source: BoS '10

Note
* The size of the figures is proportionate to their observed frequency. The full table that went into the production of this graph can be found in the appendix. For reasons of presentation, figures for current and ideal body are represented on a different scale.

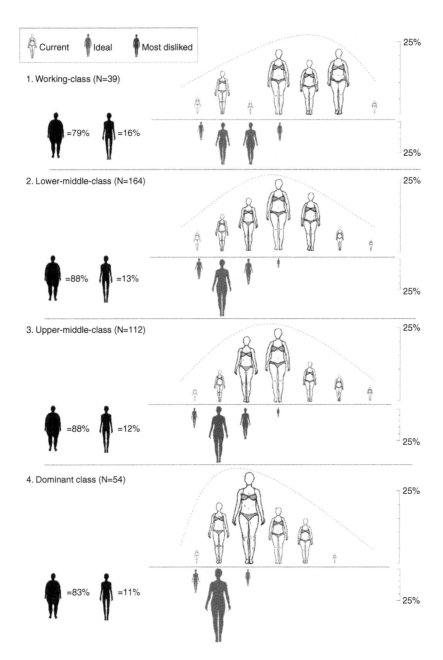

Figure 4.4 Current, ideal and most disliked body by social class (*women*)*

Source: BoS '10

Note
* The size of the figures is proportionate to their observed frequency. The full table that went into the production of this graph can be found in the appendix. For reasons of presentation, figures for current and ideal body are represented on a different scale.

114 *Modes of embodiment*

smaller survey of respondents (N=891) was presented with a diagram representing different types of male and female bodies (see Appendix 3). They were then asked to choose the figure that was closest to their own body at the time of the survey, as well as the figures they would like to have and most definitely did *not* want to have.

> Analysis of their judgments reveals that the extent of the disparity between ideal and current body is itself closely related to one's position in social space. One of the first striking results (Figures 4.3 and 4.4), is the existence of a considerable degree of consensus among both male *and* female respondents as to what exactly constitutes the "ideal" or, *a fortiori*, the most "disliked" body and this largely *regardless* of social position. When asked to identify the body-type they found *least* desirable, more than 80 per cent of both male and female respondents chose the most corpulent figure (Type 11). Similarly, more than 40 per cent of men from both working-class (41 per cent) and dominant (46 per cent) backgrounds chose a muscular, "toned" physique (Type 5) as the type of body which they preferred to look like most. For women, the situation proves somewhat different. Whereas virtually *all* women chose a slender silhouette as their personal ideal, the preference for a lean body-type (such as Type 4) becomes considerable more explicit as one moves from working-class women (31 per cent) through those in the lower- (45 per cent) and upper-middle-class (46 per cent) to women who occupy dominant social positions (61 per cent). Again, given that the logic of distinction would exert the strongest pressure on dominant groups to maintain the most distinguished appearance, one would indeed expect them to most strongly agree over the definition of what constitutes the ideal appearance.

That such pressure *is* quite effective in realizing the most valued physique becomes clear when one looks at the actual distribution of physical capital between the social classes. Like the analyses of the BMI, the results show that the different social classes have a highly unequal probability of embodying the dominant definition of the ideal male or female physique. As one rises in the social hierarchy, the *overall* distribution of body-types tends to shift from the most devalued (i.e. corpulent) to the most valorized silhouettes and this, again, more explicitly among women than men. While for the latter, a large body-size appears to be more pronounced among those who are situated at the bottom of the class-structure, there are no significant differences in the degree to which men at opposite ends of the social hierarchy are able to realize the most valued physique (in this case Type 5). Such differences prove considerably more marked among women. The probability of being endowed with the most stigmatized physique decreases considerably as one rises in the social hierarchy, with the percentage of women who claimed to have Type 8 as their current body decreasing from 23 per cent of working-class women, over 10 per cent of those in the upper-middle-class to 3 per cent of women from dominant social backgrounds. Inversely, the chances of attaining those body-types deemed most attractive (Type 4 and 5) increase from 20 per cent among working-class women,

29 per cent and 34 per cent of those in the lower- and upper-middle-classes to 58 per cent among women who are situated at the top of the social hierarchy. Quite tellingly, one third of working-class women (31 per cent) choose as their personal ideal, the type of body (Type 5) that more than a third (36 per cent) of those in the dominant class actually claim to have. The overall result is that the gap between the type of body respondents claim to have and the physical appearance to which they aspire, becomes systematically smaller as one rises in social space.

Hexis and cathexis

This discrepancy between the body that "is" and the body that "ought to be" has, as Bourdieu argues, quite serious consequences for the manner in which social agents experience their bodies and especially for their ability to project a confident and contented self-image. In fact, the analysis indicates that members of dominated groups, and especially *women* who are situated at the bottom of the class-structure, have durably internalized the dominant perception of their own physique. Even if they prove least inclined to perceive their bodies and their perceptible features as a source of value that requires constant maintenance and investment (as indicated by their level of weight-concern discussed in the previous sections), this by no means implies that they are somehow oblivious to the value that the dominant norms of physical beauty assign to their bodies. For instance, when asked to rate their personal satisfaction with their weight on a scale from 0 to 10 (Table 4.5), working-class women and those with little or no formal education (including unemployed women and housewives) consistently rate themselves lowest in weight-satisfaction. Similar results were found for men, although here differences in average weight-satisfaction between the classes again proved somewhat more attenuated. That weight-satisfaction is an integral element of agents' satisfaction with appearance in general, is also shown by the fact that respondents' ratings of their own physical appearance varied in a highly similar manner. Again, it is among those who are situated at the bottom of the social hierarchy that the average scores proved lowest. That the dominant definition of the 'legitimate' and 'illegitimate' body even affects those that tend to be most shielded from the *direct* scrutiny of their physical capital, is shown by the fact that unemployed women and housewives tend rate themselves lowest both in terms of appearance- and weight-satisfaction.

Conversely, while the objective pressure to maintain the most distinguished appearance is undoubtedly highest among those who occupy dominant social positions, they also prove to draw the highest level of personal satisfaction from their bodies. Not only do upper-class men and women have the highest scores in terms of satisfaction with weight and appearance, but they are also less likely to describe themselves as "overweight", more often indicate that they consider themselves as attractive and less often define themselves as "below average" in beauty. Conversely, whereas more than half of respondents who obtained a Master's or a postgraduate degree (men *and* women) and from a dominant social background viewed themselves as attractive, this drops to roughly a third of working-class men and women. Similarly, working-class women (22 per cent)

Table 4.5 Satisfaction with weight and appearance by gender, educational capital, professional status and social class[a]

	Satisfaction with weight (0–10)[b,c]		Satisfaction with appearance (0–10)		N		% describe themselves as 'overweight' or 'obese' (%)		'I find myself an attractive person' (% agree)		'I find myself below average in beauty' (% agree)		N	
	♂	♀	♂	♀	♂	♀	♂	♀	♂	♀	♂	♀	♂	♀
Educational capital	***	***	*	**										
Less than HS	6.3	5.6	6.9	6.5	909	968	32	44	38	41	30	37	56	81
HS (technical/vocational)	6.5	6.0	7.0	6.9	376	293	47	39	35	37	8	19	45	77
HS (general)	6.8	6.3	7.1	6.8	270	324	29	34	31	36	19	28	34	41
Bachelor	6.6	6.2	7.1	6.9	255	331	31	36	35	37	13	23	108	144
Master and postgraduate	7.1	6.8	7.3	7.2	299	114	29	22	55	55	18	15	108	151
Occupational category	*	*	***	**										
Unemployed	6.3	5.7	6.9	6.6	160	185	n.a.	n.a.	n.a.	n.a.	n.a.	n.a.	6	17
Housework	n.a.	5.8	n.a.	6.7	4	250	n.a.	29	n.a.	43	n.a.	23	0	22
Unskilled workers	6.0	5.7	6.4	6.4	257	325	n.a.	53	n.a.	30	n.a.	42	14	36
Skilled workers	6.6	6.1	7.1	6.9	536	198	29	43	45	42	*19*	25	45	21
Craftsmen and shopkeepers	6.4	6.1	6.9	7.0	150	134	n.a.	n.a.	n.a.	n.a.	n.a.	n.a.	14	17
Office-workers	6.4	5.9	7.0	6.7	570	914	30	33	40	44	13	19	170	298
Junior-executives	6.6	6.6	7.2	7.2	100	244	38	39	47	52	15	34	68	33
Professions	6.9	(6.4)	7.6	(6.4)	38	19	n.a.	n.a.	n.a.	n.a.	n.a.	n.a.	9	12
Commercial employers	7.0	n.a.	7.7	n.a.	26	4	n.a.	n.a.	n.a.	n.a.	n.a.	n.a.	4	0
Total	6.5	5.9	7.0	6.7	2,116	2,172	32	34	42	43	17	23	356	510

Notes

a Satisfaction-scores on weight and appearance are drawn from SHW '06. Statements on weight and appearance come from BoS '10. Given the relatively small sample-size (N=892) of the latter, it was not possible to provide meaningful results for all occupational categories.
b All scores have been adjusted for age-differences.
c Numbers in italic denote the highest score for that particular indicator.
n.s. = non-significant, *** $p < .005$, ** $p < .010$, * $p < .05$, n.a. = number of observations too low to make meaningful inferences.

proved almost three times as likely as women who occupy dominant social positions (8 per cent) to consider themselves below average in beauty.

Such results show how the "subjective" or "lived" experience of the body can neither be reduced to the type of generic alienation implied by the Sartrean 'body-for-others' – which simply treats the self-awareness caused by the objectifying gaze of others as a *universal* condition of "being-in-the-world" and especially of "being-with-others" – nor to the type of corporeal "absence" or "transparency" that often subtends phenomenological descriptions of the "lived body". What unites these apparently opposed perspectives is the silence with which they brush over the *social* conditions that are at the root of bodily self-consciousness or, inversely, of the body being experienced as self-evident or "forgotten". They tend to ignore, first, that the power to *objectify*, that is, to impose a particular definition of the legitimate body and the value of its traits, is far from universal but is itself commensurate with social power. Secondly, they tend to overlook the fact that those physical properties which elicit stigmatization or valorization (like corpulence or slimness) are themselves *social* products which are not randomly distributed across social space.

In fact, even if the relative autonomy of biological heredity vis-à-vis the logic of social reproduction effectively prevents *any* class or class fraction from establishing an absolute monopoly over the most valued physical traits (or being fully condemned to the most devalued ones), fact remains that the different social classes *are* unequally armed to impose their particular definition of physical value. That this autonomy 'sometimes endows those least endowed in all other respects with the rarest bodily properties, such as beauty' (Bourdieu, 1984: 193) and hence enables them to partially circumvent the hierarchies of class privilege (as a form of symbolic capital in the marriage mobility of women for example, see Elder, 1969; Offer, 2001), should not detract from analysing how dominant conceptions of the 'legitimate body' serve to uphold such hierarchies.

Hence, far from being an inevitable consequence of "being-in-the-world" or "being-for-others", the experience of the body as haunted by the objectifying gaze of others is the particular plight of those who are unable to ignore the dominant definition of the legitimate physique, while at the same time being deprived of the means to meaningfully realize this definition. It is this gap between recognition and ownership, between ideal and current physique which leads to 'a fascinated awareness of oneself and one's body, to a consciousness fascinated by its corporality' (Bourdieu, 2008: 86). Conversely, the ability to experience one's own body as "absent", that is, as self-evident, valorized and fully justified in being is not a gift of nature, but is itself the social privilege of those who, quite literally, embody the norm. It is the rare freedom granted to those for whom bodily *hexis*, that socially informed way of carrying and presenting the body, is synonymous with bodily *cathexis*, the libidinal investment in one's own body which flows from the capacity to impose one's own criteria of apperception and forms the basis for its self-assured and contented projection towards others (and hence, quite paradoxically, for it being experienced as "absent" in everyday practice).

A moral physiognomy of class

'The human figure', writes Georg Simmel, 'is the scene in which psychophysiological impulses struggle with physical gravity. The manner of fighting and resolving this battle repeatedly in each succeeding moment determines the style in which individuals and types present themselves to us' (1965 [1901]: 278). When discussing these physiognomic properties of the body (and the face in particular) he noted how 'closed eyes, head dropping to the chest, slack lips, lax musculature merely obeying gravity' are all treated as 'evidences of reduced spiritual life' (1965 [1901]: 278). From the above it become clear that Simmel's observations can equally be extended to the size and shape of the body, where the oppositions between the straight and the curved, the square and the round, the toned and the bulging are 'immediately read as indices of a "moral" physiognomy, socially characterized, i.e., of a "vulgar" or "distinguished" mind, naturally "natural" or naturally "cultivated"' (Bourdieu, 1984: 193). While the preceding analyses have aimed to show that social agents have a highly unequal probability of being endowed with such morally qualified physical attributes, they have left one crucial element of this equation unexplored. If socially produced physical differences do indeed contribute to the naturalization of class-divisions (by transforming them into innate differences of "character" and "personality"), then physical size should not only be invested with a particular aesthetic or moral value, but would also need to signal *social* identity. It is precisely this homology between morally qualified physical traits and positions in the social structure that makes the body into more than just a "symbol" of class-status, but effectively transforms it into 'an embodied *theory* of the division of labour' (Martin 2000: 202, *original emphasis*). In fact, far from being a simple "expression" of social status, the shape of the body effectively provides an "explanation" for that status of the type: "Fat people are lazy and unmotivated. The poor and the unemployed are fat. *Ergo*: They are poor and unemployed because they are passive and lack ambition."

To gauge whether social agents did not only attribute a differential value to specific types of bodies, but were also capable of divining indices of social position from differences in body-size and -shape, the survey also asked respondents to choose which silhouette they thought was most "typical" of four distinct social categories. These categories were chosen to reflect different locations in social space, ranging from those who occupy the most precarious social positions (an unemployed man or woman) over those who are situated in a more "stable", but still dominated position (a male or female worker) to those who are situated at the top of the social structure. Among the latter, the questionnaire also distinguished between those whose status derived mainly from an *economically* dominant position (a businessman or -woman) and those who mainly wielded *cultural* authority (a male or female artist) in order to gauge whether the social perception of bodies also discriminated between differences based on the particular *type* of social status.

The results of respondents' classifications are summarized in Figures 4.5 and 4.6. These figures present the three most commonly attributed silhouettes for each of the four social categories in terms of the social background of the

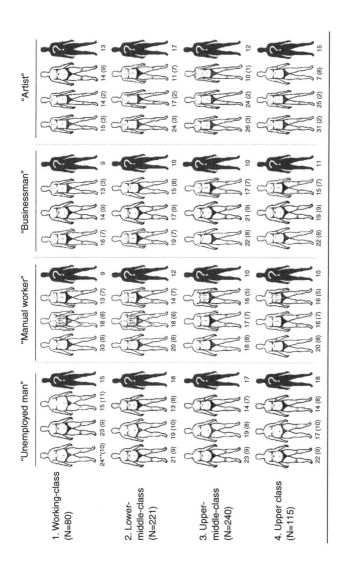

Figure 4.5 Classification of male silhouettes by social class* (% and type)

Source: BoS'10

Notes

* This figure presents the three most commonly attributed silhouettes for a particular social category, as well as the percentage of respondents who claimed they didn't know which silhouette to choose. The number in brackets corresponds to the body types presented on the figure found in the appendix. A full overview of responses can also be found in the appendix.
** This number reads as follows: *"24 percent of working-class respondents chose Type 10 as the most typical silhouette for an unemployed man."*

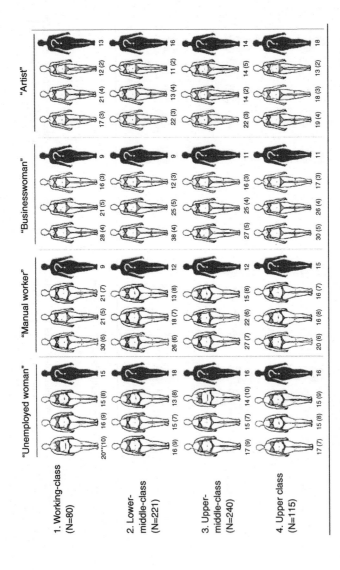

Figure 4.6 Classification of female silhouettes by social class* *(% and type)*

Source: BoS'10

Notes

* This figure presents the three most commonly attributed silhouettes for a particular social category, as well as the percentage of respondents who claimed they didn't know which silhouette to choose. The number in brackets corresponds to the body types presented on the figure found in the appendix.

** This number reads as follows: *"20% of working-class respondents chose Type 10 as the most typical silhouette for an unemployed woman."*

respondents. In addition, they also show the percentage of respondents who proved unable (or unwilling) to select a particular figure. These figures already reveal that while such a classificatory exercise is admittedly somewhat artificial (not only for reducing body-shape to a *two-dimensional* representation, but also for abstracting it from the entire system of pertinent features that agents draw upon to classify and evaluate others, which also includes sartorial and cosmetic indices, not to mention bodily hexis), it does not prove to be completely meaningless for respondents. For the majority of responses, only one out of ten respondents indicated they did not know which body-type to attribute to a particular social category, while for others the proportion of 'don't know'-answers never exceeds 20 per cent. Furthermore, the fact that the three most commonly chosen silhouettes manage to group between half and three quarters of the responses for a particular category further suggests that agents prove quite capable of equating physical and social characteristics.

A comparison of the classifications of respondents from different social classes again reveals a considerable consensus as to which silhouette gets attributed to a particular social category. With the exception of one category (the male artist), *none* of the selected body-types revealed statistically significant differences in terms of respondents' social class. One thing that respondents clearly agreed upon is that those who dwell in the most precarious regions of social space – in this case the "unemployed" (both men and women) – are most likely to have the most devalued (i.e. corpulent) physique. Not only did more than half of the respondents from each class associate unemployment with the most corpulent silhouettes (Types 8 to 11), but in addition, almost *none* of them attributed the ideal male and female physique (Type 5 and 4, respectively) to an unemployed man or woman. The same seems to hold true for the category of "manual workers", although here significant differences again emerge between men and women. Especially in the case of "female workers", respondents again proved more likely to attribute larger body-types to this category (Types 6 to 8) and less inclined to equate working-class women with the most desirable physique (less than 4 per cent of respondents from each social class chose Type 4 as a typical female working-class physique).

> This classificatory exercise also brings out one of the distinguishing features of the evaluative schemes involved in 'class-ification', as opposed to those that are used to classify objects in the natural or physical world (e.g. the division of animals into mammals, amphibians, etc. or the divisions of shapes in circles, squares, triangles, etc.), namely that '[b]ecause they are used to classify the native social world, the categories refer to a universe that also belongs to the person who makes use of them and who, when organizing a set of exterior objects, simultaneously determines his own social position in relation to them' (Boltanski and Thévenot, 1983: 651). This not only means that the categories that are applied to the perception of the social world are rarely endowed with the affective neutrality that characterizes "natural" taxonomies (and hence come closest to their etymological origins in the Greek *kategorein* meaning "to accuse publicly" or "speak against"), but also that agents'

particular positions *on* the social world, and its internal divisions, always betray their own position *in* that world. This can be illustrated by the manner in which respondents classified the body of a female "manual worker" (Figure 4.6). While almost *all* respondents tend to attribute a heavy physique to this particular category – which indicates a fairly widespread recognition of the dominant taxonomies – their classifications do appear to vary with their own particular position in the social structure and especially their relative distance from the working-classes. For instance, while the classifications of *working-class* respondents indicate that they recognize the dominant definition of the physique of a "female worker", as shown by the fact that they rank them as being heavier than both "businesswomen" or "artists", they nonetheless appear to defend a somewhat more favourable representation of this category. Not only did they more often choose a slimmer silhouette as being emblematic for women of their own group (one out of five working-class respondents still chose Type 5 as a typical working-class silhouette, compared to 13 per cent of upper-class respondents), but their responses also most clearly differentiated between the physique of a "female worker" and that of an "unemployed woman", which working-class respondents, and especially working-class *women*, tend to rank as being heavier than respondents from other social categories. It is as if their responses betray a fear of being confounded, by the dominant taxonomies, with those who are situated at the very bottom of the social hierarchy (i.e. the unemployed and the sub-proletariat) and hence as an effort to distinguish themselves from those whose lifestyle deviates from the "respectability" that is so fundamental to working-class identity (Skeggs, 1996). That such fear is not entirely unfounded, is illustrated by the classifications of those who are situated higher-up in the class-structure. As their objective distance to the working-classes increases, respondents not only tend to more readily attribute a larger silhouette as being typical for a "female worker" (24 per cent of upper-middle-class respondents and 28 per cent of upper-class respondents chose Type 8, 9 or 10 as opposed to 13 per cent of working-class respondents), but also appear to differentiate less strongly between this category and that of the "unemployed woman".

The classification of male "workers" proved somewhat less straightforward. The first thing to note, is that the traditional association between working-class masculinity and muscularity does not emerge particularly strongly from respondents' judgments. Less than one out five respondents, from each social class, chose a muscular physique as the most common body-type for "male workers", with respondents from the working-class and lower-middle-class being somewhat more inclined to select the most muscular physique (Type 6) as most emblematic of this category. At any rate, the clear association between 'working-class' and a less desirable physique, as was the case for women, proved less strong for the category of male workers with members of the dominant class (16 per cent) even being somewhat more inclined to associate them with the ideal male physique (Type 5) than working-class respondents themselves (9 per cent).

More generally, the equation of the most desirable body-shape with dominant and the most stigmatized physique with dominated social groups does not seem to fully apply to the social perception of the male body. This is further underlined by the classifications of the third social type, namely the "businessman". Respondents appear much more likely to attribute a corpulent physique to this category than to that of the 'male workers' (even though they are still considered to have a leaner body type than the 'unemployed'). There is, however, some variation between social classes in the degree to which respondents subscribe to the equation of corpulence and the world of business. Interestingly, working-class respondents prove most divided on what the most common body for a 'businessman' actually is, with 10 per cent of respondents still attributing them with the 'ideal' male physique (as opposed to 4 per cent of respondents from a dominant background) and one out of three respondents (34 per cent) attributing them with the leanest body types (Types 3 to 5) as opposed to one out of five of respondents from the upper-middle and dominant classes.

That the perception of class bodies operates along strongly *gendered* lines becomes even clearer when one looks at the manner in which respondents classified the most common figure for a "businesswoman". Close to 30 per cent of respondents from both working-class (28 per cent) and dominant social backgrounds (30 per cent) attributed them with the most desirable body type (Type 4), while two thirds of working-class respondents (65 per cent) and almost three quarters of those at the top of the social hierarchy (73 per cent) chose a lean physique (Types 3 to 5) as being most typical for a "businesswoman". These results further underline how the *social* classification of bodies and bodily properties is intrinsically tied to their *sexual* classification. It is especially among those who occupy a dominated position in the *sexual* division of labour (i.e. women), that one finds the closest correspondence, both in terms of the actual distribution of physical size *and* its symbolic evaluation, between social and physical value. While this correspondence shows that women, as a whole, are confronted with a much more pervasive scrutiny of their physique than men, it also reveals that it is women who are situated at the *bottom* of the class-hierarchy that tend to find themselves in the most contradictory position. While the logic of sexual domination leads them to place considerably more value on the visible, physical signs of social identity than men, they are simultaneously excluded from the social conditions in which the most valued physique can be effectively realized.

The inherent *over*-determination of social and (socially defined) sexual characteristics is, however, not restricted to the perception of women's bodies. There is another manner in which the classificatory schemes that organize the perception of physical differences tend to establish equivalences between positions in the social and sexual division of labour as was already discussed in Chapter 1. This is shown particularly clearly by the manner in which respondents differentiated between the bodies of men who mainly wield *economic* power (the "businessman") and those who are associated with *cultural* authority (the male "artist"). Their classifications suggest that this opposition between "temporal" and "spiritual" authority is perceived as a particular form of the opposition between the masculine and the feminine. Whereas most respondents attributed the former with a large, heavy and hence masculine physique, they tend to disproportionately associate men who are engaged in *cultural* production with a slender, frail and effeminate body (Type 2 and 3) and this increasingly so as one rises in the social hierarchy. More importantly, the fact that this opposition between the "heavy" and the "light" is not without its basis in the actual distribution of weight-differences between the economically and culturally dominant fractions of the upper and middle-classes (as shown in Table 4.2), in turn contributes to the legitimization of this opposition (rooted in capital-*composition* rather than *volume*) as being seemingly rooted in nature, and *sexual* nature in particular.

A "disease of the will"

There is, however, an even more fundamental reason why *weight*-differences in particular contribute in such an effective manner to the naturalization of class-divisions. In fact, most contemporary social systems are characterized by the fact that *bodily* characteristics – especially those related to relatively "ascribed" traits like biological sex, ethnicity, age or physical disability – can no longer be invoked as a legitimate justification for differences in social status. Stronger still, excluding agents from social positions on the basis of such ascribed traits is often subjected to legal sanctions. That is why Goffman, after pointing out the significance of physical attributes as signs of social status (see Chapter 2), quickly rushed to add that 'the use of inherited characteristics as symbols of status is typically found, of course, in a society of castes not of classes' (1951: 301, n. 1). While a reference to such characteristics might function as a means of legitimizing status-differences in a feudal social order, such a reference clashes with the dominant sociodicy in social systems where status, especially through the legitimizing action of the educational system, is deemed to be the product of individual *merit*. It is precisely in this respect, however, that the significance of body-*weight* stands out. In fact, as discussed in the beginning of this chapter, a person's weight is distinguished from other, equally visible aspects of his or her appearance in that it is deemed to be largely under individual control and hence seen as a matter of personal responsibility (see Cahnman, 1968 or DeJong, 1980). As DeJong observed: 'the obese have much more in common with those who possess a characterological stigma than those who are physically handicapped' (1980: 85). To be fat is above all seen as a sign of not *wanting* to be thin and hence to wilfully choose one's own stigmatization. If obesity is indeed a disease then it belongs to that same category of afflictions that nineteenth century medical theorists referred to as 'diseases of the will' (see Valverde, 1998).

I will argue that it is precisely this "hybrid" character of weight-differences – suspended halfway between nature and culture, a "being" and a "having", a gift and an achievement – that makes them into such an effective vehicle for the legitimization of class-differences. While undeniably "of the flesh" and therefore partaking of the charm and charisma of a natural gift, a person's weight is simultaneously read as the most tangible index of his or her degree of willpower and self-control. In this sense, a well-managed figure is not unlike the skilful display of cultural and linguistic competence in providing proof of a 'cultivated nature' which has 'all the appearances of grace or a gift and yet acquired, so therefore "deserved".' (Bourdieu, 1993: 235). Conversely, a corpulent physique provides the ultimate 'visual representation of non-control' (Ritenbaugh, 1982) attesting to its owner's inability to transcend primary and primal drives, to harness "vulgar" appetites and hence to overcome "nature". More importantly, while the display of cultivated tastes can to some extent become subjected to strategies of symbolic pretension or bluff (in the domain of clothing, speech or demeanour, for instance), the physical body tends to provide the most indisputable evidence of "class" (or the lack thereof).

The contemporary celebration of slimness and the concomitant stigmatization of corpulence hence delivers a crucial contribution to the process whereby 'the social conditions necessary for the acquisition of form of bodily hexis are misperceived as natural, individual, moral dispositions instead of socially mediated forms that relate directly to cultural relations of domination and exclusion' (Charlesworth, 2000: 158). Rooted in the physiognomic premise that 'the human body is the best picture of the human soul' (Wittgenstein, 2001 [1949]: 152), it helps to transform a product of social necessity into a matter of individual "personality" or "character". In doing so, it contributes to representing the social order as an inherently ethical order in which individuals are not separated by their unequal access to the different sources of capital, but ranked according to their degree of personal ambition and moral fibre. It has been the main goal of this chapter to show how class-relationships contribute to physical shaping the body and how, in turn, such physical differences help to naturalize class-divisions. However, by choosing body-weight as a starting point, our analysis has in a sense started at the end, that is, with the body as the final *product* of the conditionings associated with a given social position or trajectory. In the following chapters we will look at some of the factors that actually contribute to producing the particular morphology of a class, starting with the key contribution made by tastes in food.

Notes

* The author retains full copyright over the diagrams of body-types.
1 A highly abridged version of this chapter was published in the *Routledge Companion to Bourdieu's Distinction* (Vandebroeck, 2014).
2 Although anthropometric data for this period always require a considerable degree of circumspection, the heaviest weight reached by the oldest generation reported in Galton's study (those born between 1740 and 1769), namely 83 kg (184 pounds) is still considerably higher than the *average* body-weight of adult British males of the period which Fogel (1994: 373) estimates to be around 61 kg (134 pounds). When one relates this to the average height of men at the time, which Fogel judges to be around 167 cm (ibid.: 372), this results in a Body Mass Index of 29.7, which is just below the contemporary cut-off point for obesity.
3 In fact, *Stigma* mentions the obese once in a list that includes 'the divorced, the aged, the physically handicapped, the ileostomied and the colostomied.' (Goffman, 1963: 34).
4 This difference is calculated by multiplying the respective values of BMI for these two categories with the *average* length for women (1 m 63 cm), that is, without taking into account that length is itself closely related to social position.

5   The hungry body

> It is a falsification of significant features of human existence to say that people are omnivores.
>
> (Levins and Lewontin, 1985: 260)

In an essay entitled *Psycho-Analysis and the History of Art* (1953), the art historian Ernst Gombrich commits the somewhat sacrilegious act of likening the aesthetic experience to the one type of enjoyment from which modern aesthetics (ever since Kant) had vehemently tried to separate it, namely to the sensuous and visceral pleasures provided by food and eating:

> Botticelli's Venus, or a self-portrait by Rembrandt, clearly have other dimensions of meaning and embody different values – but when we speak of the problem of correct balance between too much and too little we do well to remember cookery. For it is here that we learn first that too much of a good thing is repellent. Too much fat, too much sweetness, too much softness – all the qualities, that is, that have an immediate biological appeal – also produce these counter-reactions which originally serve as a warning signal to the human animal not to over-indulge [...] I mean that we also develop it as a defence mechanism against attempts to seduce us. We find repellent what offers too obvious, too childish, gratification. It invites regression and we do not feel secure enough to yield [...] The child is proverbially fond of sweets and toffees, and so is the primitive, with his Turkish delight and an amount of fat that turns a European stomach. We prefer something less obvious, less yielding. My guess is, for instance, that small children and unsophisticated grown-ups will be likely to enjoy a soft milk-chocolate, while townified highbrows will find it cloying and seek escape in the more bitter tang or in an admixture of coffee or, preferably, of crunchy nuts.
>
> (Gombrich, 1985 [1953]: 39)

Whatever one is to make of his speculations on the existence of innate 'warning-signals' or psychological 'defence-mechanisms' (let alone his rather indiscriminate use of the first-person-plural), Gombrich's argument is compelling for two reasons. First, because it draws attention to what one could call the 'physiognomic' properties of food, namely to the manner in which its apparently most objective characteristics, such as flavours (sweet, bitter, etc.) and textures (cloying, crunchy, etc.) are always invested with an indissolubly social, psychological and moral meaning (highbrow, childish, unsophisticated, etc.). Secondly, and perhaps more importantly, because it shows that "good taste", whether it applies to works of art or the domain of cooking, is always defined *negatively*, that is, as rooted in a negation of cheap thrills and facile pleasures and hence of everything that provides 'too obvious, too childish, gratification'.

In fact, by drawing analogies between "taste" as the capacity to discern in aesthetic matters and taste as the elementary proclivity for particular qualities and quantities of food, Gombrich's argument in a sense anticipates Bourdieu's analytic of the 'aesthetic disposition'. The latter argues in fact that the same disinterested concern with form and formality that defines the aesthetic outlook is not just limited to the domain of legitimate culture, but is at the basis of a more general 'stylization of life', which encompasses the entire range of practices, properties and beliefs that constitute the dominant lifestyle, including those pertaining to food and drink. Like Gombrich, he argues that the central features of this lifestyle can only be understood *relationally*, as inherently defined *against* the vulgar tastes of those who reduce everything to its immediate function, who are only interested in substance and the substantial and know no other enjoyment than the primal, unmediated pleasure of the senses. It is in fact in the domain of food that we perhaps find the best illustration of the fact that the cultivation of "taste" is inseparably tied to the cultivation of distaste, which is first and foremost a distaste for everything that is "vulgar" and "common":

> Disgust is the ambivalent experience of the horrible seduction of the disgusting and of enjoyment, which performs a sort of reduction to animality, corporeality, the belly and sex, that is, to what is common and therefore vulgar, removing any difference between those who resist with all their might and those who wallow in pleasure, who enjoy enjoyment [...] Nature understood as sense equalizes, but at the lowest level.
>
> (Bourdieu, 1984: 489)

This equal*izing* dependence on Nature is nowhere demonstrated as dramatically as in the acts of eating and drinking, which provide the most visible manifestation of our universal subjection to vegetative, organic being. In many ways, eating and drinking constitute the transgressive acts *par excéllence*. Not only do they efface the boundaries between subject and object, interior and exterior, but they also blur *social* boundaries and threaten to remove the distance that otherwise (and everywhere) separates dominant and dominated. Consequently, as this chapter will aim to show, there is nothing that tends to polarize the different classes and class-fractions more than their relationship towards food as manifested both in their "choices" for particular types of food, as well as their distinctive *manner* of consuming them.

The (social) sense of the senses

The Kantian bias against the 'taste of the tongue, the palate and the throat' (Kant, 2000 [1781]: 97) which can only be the basis of a 'pathologically conditioned satisfaction' (ibid.: 94) and is hence opposed to the free, disinterested disposition that defines the aesthetic outlook, tends to detract from the fact that eating constitutes a quite complex sensori-motor experience, whose different aspects are themselves unequally amenable to stylization or aestheticization. In fact, if one abstracts from the strictly convivial pleasures of "dining together", the act of eating can be said to provide three distinct forms of sensuous pleasure which can themselves be ranked according to the relative degree of contact between the embodied subject and "food-as-object" they presuppose. First of all, there is the pleasure linked to the most distant, disembodied and hence most "spiritual" of the senses, namely that of hearing, but above all of *sight*. This is the type of pleasure that is directly associated with the *appearance* of food, its formal properties and its overall presentation, all of which are known to have a direct impact on appetite and digestion (see Buytendijk, 1974: 133ff.). Given its distanced and highly differentiated character, it is also the type of enjoyment that provides the most room for stylistic judgment, coming closest to the pure, disinterested play of forms and colours that defines the aesthetic experience.

Secondly, there is the pleasure provided by the more "materialistic" senses of smell, taste and touch which tends to be considered as inferior in that it already presupposes proximity, contact and above all *incorporation* and hence abolishes the distance between subject and object that forms the basis for the disinterested aesthetic judgment. Nevertheless, it still allows for the demonstration of one of the central traits of the aesthetic disposition, namely the capacity to discern and judge subtle differences, to detect nuances and trace "distinctions" (of which the ability to discriminate and judge between different types of wine provides the most elaborate example). The ability to draw such fine-graded distinctions cannot, as Barlösius (1999: 71ff.) has shown, simply be deduced from the *physiological* structure of the sense of taste itself – which is remarkably undifferentiated, recognizing only the broad categories of sweet, sour, bitter and salty – but is instead the product of its particular *social* conditioning.

This conditioning not only determines the degree of differentiation of the system of culinary categories (its "refinement" and "breadth"), but also, as Gombrich points out, invests the most elementary flavours with a moral *meaning*, such as the opposition between everything that is sweet and hence facile, seductive, providing the basis for 'too obvious, too childish gratification' and that which is bitter, which does not please "naturally", but which requires "learning" to be fully appreciated (see Lupton, 1996). This second type of enjoyment also includes all the tactile, kinaesthetic pleasures provided by different types of food such as the "crunch" of raw vegetables, the "succulence" of steak or the "cloying feeling" of caramel. Like flavours, such tactile sensations also help express the logic of social oppositions such as the "firmness" of red meat with its masculine connotations or the "softness" of fish with its feminine undertones.

Furthermore, since it is a type of pleasure that is still primarily related to the *formal* rather than the *substantial* properties of food – its density, texture and structure – it also provides the basis for stylization, as is shown by the extensive gastronomic vocabulary that is devoted to expressing these tactile qualities (silken, *moelleux*, *craquant*, fibrous, creamy, etc.).

Together, these two forms of sensuous pleasure form the basis of legitimate culinary tastes, the domain of *haute cuisine* which aims to strike the perfect balance between the visual, the gustatory and the tactile properties of a meal. This conception of the act of eating as a free play of the senses of sight, taste and touch finds its temporary culmination in the so-called "molecular" or "deconstructive" cuisine of chefs like Blumenthal and Adrià. In fact, by decomposing and recomposing the organic links between the appearance, taste and texture of food ("bacon and egg ice-cream", "snail porridge", "frozen parmesan air with cereals", etc.), such cuisine aims to produce a type of sensory "defamiliarization" that is not unlike the *ostranenie* that the Russian formalists defined as the distinguishing hallmark of all true art and literature.

Crucially, this gastronomic relationship to food is itself purged from any reference to the third and final type of pleasure that food can be said to provide. This is the elementary pleasure associated with the visceral sensation of repletion or "fullness". Indissolubly physical and psychological, it is the type of enjoyment that provides the most tangible feeling of comfort and security, often hearkening back to the most archetypical social relationships, namely those of the familial and above all maternal universe. At the same time, it is also the most diffuse and undifferentiated type of pleasure. Compared to the quasi-infinite range of culinary discriminations enabled by the senses of sight, taste, smell and touch, the visceral sensation of fullness is, quite literally, a "gut feeling" providing few perceptible gradations between the state of extreme hunger and that of extreme repletion. This lack of sensory differentiation combined with the fact that hunger or repletion are, like any other type of somatic sensation, highly affectively charged, makes this type of pleasure particularly ill-suited for any form of dispassionate aestheticization.

The reason for distinguishing between these types of sensuous pleasure is that their relative importance in defining the relationship to food varies significantly in terms of agents' position in social space. It is in fact in the domain of food that we find a privileged case for studying how the social division of labour translates into what Simmel called 'the division of labour between the senses' (1997 [1907]: 115). In fact, the fundamental opposition between function and form, necessity and luxury, constraint and freedom finds its sensuous expression in two different conceptions of culinary pleasure and two opposed modes of perceiving and judging food. On the one hand, there is the 'taste of necessity' which claims food 'as a material reality, a nourishing substance which sustains the body and gives strength' (Bourdieu, 1984: 197) and hence judges it in terms of its substance and content, that is, its capacity to nourish and sustain and, above all, to provide physical and visceral gratification. On the other, there is the 'taste of luxury' in which the proclivity (and aversion) for particular types of food is

130 *Modes of embodiment*

increasingly determined by the concern with "form", that is to say, with their presentation and symbolic properties, but also with their effects on the body's appearance and well-being. Crucially, this concern with the formal aspects of food and eating is itself based on a denial of their most "common" aspects. By comparing the ways in which the different classes and class-fractions perceive and judge food, this chapter will aim to show that there is considerable truth to Marx's famous proposition that 'the *forming* of the five senses is a labour of the entire history of the world down to the present' (2007 [1844]: 108, *original emphasis*), that is to say, a history of class-struggle.

Substance and function

It was in fact Marx who argued that the experience of necessity and privation produces an 'abstract' relationship to food and prevents it from being appropriated in a properly 'human' (i.e. non-animalistic) mode:

> The *sense* caught up in crude practical need has only a *restricted* sense. For the starving man, it is not the human form of food that exists, but only its abstract being as food; it could just as well be there in its crudest form, and it would be impossible to say wherein this feeding-activity differs from that of animals.
>
> (2007 [1844]: 109, *original emphasis*)

Reducing products, practices and properties to their bare function, the taste of necessity tends to reveal itself in a functionalist attitude towards food, which not only treats the quality of a meal as a function of its quantity, but also expresses itself as a taste for "heavy" dishes, "solid" foods, "strong" flavours and "firm" textures. This insistence on substance and function also implies a rejection of any form of formalization or stylization of meals or the act of eating, which is not only seen as obtrusive and unnecessary (i.e. the "frills and fusses" that only "get in the way" of a good meal), but also (correctly) perceived as a way of introducing restrictions and censorships into the one dimension of lifestyle, where privations are ill-tolerated and where freedom and abundance are meant to reign.

> The number of respondents who agreed with the proposition that "*Eating well means, first of all, getting more than enough to eat*" decreases sharply from 66 per cent of unskilled and farm-workers to 33 per cent of clerical workers, 22 per cent of teachers and 24 per cent of those in the professions and from 66 per cent of those with little or no formal education to 18 per cent of those with a Master or a postgraduate degree. Similarly, the number who consider "steak and chips" (combining meat and potatoes and hence the filling, substantial dish *par excéllence*) to be "*among the best things there is*" goes from 55 per cent of unskilled workers to 34 per cent of office-workers and members of the professions and reaches its low among the junior-executives (27 per cent) and especially among the ascetic taste of the teachers (Cfr. *infra*), only a quarter of which agree with this statement

(while 63 per cent *dis*agree). At the same time, over half of unskilled workers and farmers indicated they did not care about the looks of a meal, as long it tasted good (compared to a third of the office-workers). Similarly, when asked to choose their favourite from a list of ten different dishes, half of working-class men chose the most substantial, abundant dishes such as the "*steak with pepper cream sauce and hash browns*" (28 per cent) or the "*beef stew with chips*" (22 per cent), while least often choosing dishes like the "*vegetable quiche with salad*" (6 per cent) or the "*steamed cod with leeks and mashed potatoes*" (3 per cent). The analysis of the food-expenditure of manual workers also reveals some pertinent indices (see Table A4.6 in appendix). In fact, members of the working-class tend to have the highest expenditure, in both relative *and* absolute terms, on the most substantial types of food, especially meat and meat-products (particularly beef, pork, bacon, minced meat, sausages and prepared meats [*charcutérie*]) which account for over a fifth of their total food-expenditure, but also on bread, potatoes (an enduring staple of the working-class diet) and fats, especially butter and margarine.

The taste of necessity not only manifests itself in the primacy attributed to substance and content over form and manner(s), but also reveals itself as a taste for the familiar and the traditional. Being the embodiment of the necessity that circumscribes the quantity/quality of products available to those who occupy the most precarious positions, the taste of (or *for*) necessity transforms these objective constraints into an elective affinity for that which is known and given and, more importantly, a distrust and distaste for that from which they are at any rate excluded. A number of indices in fact suggest that members of the working-class rarely look upon food as a site for experimentation and innovation, in short, as the domain of freedom and choice generally implied by the notion of "taste". For instance, unskilled workers and farmers (and especially the men) proved almost three times more likely than teachers and five times more likely than members of the professions to agree with the statement "*I like familiar food the best*", whilst least often agreeing with propositions like "*I love to explore new recipes and new flavours*" or "*I'm interested in the manner in which food is prepared in other cultures*". Similarly, the number of respondents who claimed they had "never eaten" four or more out of the ten dishes that they were asked to judge, increases sharply as one moves from the senior-executives and professionals (7 per cent) through the junior-executives (9 per cent) and office clerks (13 per cent) to the unskilled workers and farmers (26 per cent).

This taste for the familiar is also, and perhaps above all, a taste for the *familial*. In fact, the refusal of form and formality in favour of a relationship to food that is free and unrestrained – both in the *type* and *quantity* of food consumed, as well as in their *manner* of consumption – also defines the appropriate *setting* for its consumption, namely among the primary group of family and (close) friends and above all within the privacy of the home, the domain of absolute freedom, where one can "be oneself" because one is "among equals". In fact, despite the dramatic expansion in the possibilities for outdoor food-consumption and especially the lowering of the cost to do so, the working-classes still largely treat eating as a private affair and in this respect are clearly distinguished from the middle- and dominant classes, for whom it often serves as a "ritual" for the display of cultural competence or the maintenance and accumulation of social capital.

> Unskilled workers not only most often agreed with the statements "*Eating at home is still the best*" (77 per cent compared to 49 per cent of clerical workers, 39 per cent of the teachers and 38 per cent for members of the professions) and "*I'd rather not spend too much money on going to a restaurant*" (41 per cent as opposed to 34 per cent of office-workers and 31 per cent of the professions), but also spend the lowest amount – in both absolute and relative terms – on *outdoor* food-consumption and especially on restaurants (see Table A4.6): 256 euros or 6.2 per cent among farm-workers, 493 euros or 10.4 per cent among unskilled workers, compared to 1,135 euros or 17.3 per cent among members of the professions and 1,564 euros or 22.1 per cent among the commercial employers. This is also reflected in their *frequency* of restaurant-visits with a fifth of unskilled workers claiming they did not go to a restaurant in the six months preceding the survey (while only 12 per cent claimed they went to a restaurant at least twice a month or more).

In order to fully grasp the meaning behind the different responses to these statements one also needs to relate them to the oppositions inscribed in the *sexual* division of labour and the particular form they take within each class. In fact, one of the reasons why class-differences in the responses to such statements as "*Eating at home is still the best*" or "*I like familiar food the best*" prove much more pronounced among women than men, undoubtedly lies in the traditional image of femininity (and through it, of the female body) that is tacitly implied by such statements. In fact, as one rises in the social hierarchy and women increasingly have access to forms of social valorization that lie *outside* of the domestic sphere – in the form of educational credentials, occupational status or social capital (through the involvement in voluntary work, charities, associations, etc.) – this image tends to clash more strongly with their practical sense of social and personal value. In this respect, the attitudes of middle- and upper-class women are not only strongly opposed to those of *working-class* women – who draw a much larger part of their social value from their status as "good" wives and mothers, especially as it pertains to their skills as cooks – but also to those of middle- and upper-class *men*. This shows how the oppositions inscribed in the social division of labour can exacerbate or attenuate those inscribed in the *sexual* division of labour by defining areas of potential conflict or relative agreement between men and women *within* a given class or class fraction.

The taste for the familiar is the direct antithesis of the aesthetic relationship to food which transforms culinary taste into an instrument of permanent discovery and a means of both demonstrating and accumulating cultural capital, a disposition that is often inculcated in middle- and upper-class families from a very early age

The hungry body 133

onwards (see Lupton, 1997 or more recently Wills *et al.,* 2011). It is perhaps one of the most striking aspects of the popular relationship to food that it manages to perpetuate an ethos of indulgence and functionality in the face of an ever-expanding industry that glorifies the "art" of cooking and dining, as shown by the proliferation of culinary-magazines, books, TV-shows (if not entire TV-channels), not to mention all the forms of commercial and public campaigns aimed at promoting a "healthy diet" which, each in their own way, have contributed to diffusing the dominant culinary aesthetic (and the conception of the body that it is inextricably bound up with). Even within the legitimacy-imposing context of a survey on cultural practices and preferences (it is important to point out that the opinions on food and dining presented in Table 5.1 were collected within a survey that was largely devoted to legitimate culture), the responses of farmers and manual workers, and especially the *men* of this class, still betray a quite strong opposition to the dominant lifestyle which in matters of culture or politics they would more often conceal.

> There is in fact little or no indication that the youngest fractions of the working-class are somehow more receptive to the dominant culinary aesthetic. When comparing the responses of the youngest group of working-class respondents (18 to 35 years, $N=203$) with those of the oldest (45 to 65, $N=137$) to the different statements on food and dining, they either showed *no* significant differences in their agreement or these differences actually revealed the youngest group to have the most functional attitudes towards food. For instance, the proportion who agreed with the statement "*I'm interested in the way in which food is prepared in other cultures*" varied from 46 per cent of the former to 57 per cent of the latter, from 60 per cent to 64 per cent, for the proposition "*I love to try out new recipes and new flavours*", while 66 per cent and 58 per cent, respectively agreed with the statement "*I like familiar food the best*". Similarly, those who agreed with the statement "*Steak and chips, that's one of the best things there is*" went from 56 per cent among the youngest to 48 per cent among the oldest respondents.
>
> (source: GCPS '03–04)

Without therefore minimizing the effects of symbolic domination in this particular aspect of their lifestyle, the results of our analysis provide some support for the proposition that 'the art of eating and drinking remains one of the few areas in which the working-classes explicitly challenge the legitimate art of living' (Bourdieu, 1984: 179). However, before branding such heterodoxy as a form of cultural "resistance", the confident assertion of a culture "for itself" or, even worse, as the product of cultural "lag" that will simply disappear when the culinary habit(u)s of the dominant finally "trickle down" to the dominated, it should not be forgotten that the working-class relationship to food remains fundamentally marked by the necessity inscribed in their living conditions.

There are several ways in which necessity impinges on the structure of the popular diet. First and foremost, is the manner in which the working-class relationship to food is fundamentally shaped by *economic* imperatives. As a class who by their very social definition have little more to offer than their labour

Table 5.1 Attitudes towards food and dining by gender, educational capital and class fraction (% agree)

	"I'd rather not spend too much money on going to a restaurant."		"Eating well is among the most important things in my life."		"I like familiar food the best."		"I love to try out new recipes or flavours."		"Eating well means, first of all, getting more than enough to eat."	
	♂	♀	♂	♀	♂	♀	♂	♀	♂	♀
Educational capital										
Less than HS	48[a]	59[b]	63	61	69	67	50	58	66	63
HS (technical/vocational)	39	39	52	56	54	47	63	64	51	41
HS (general)	37	37	63	53	40	26	61	70	32	37
Bachelor	33	32	57	50	28	19	71	70	29	21
Master and postgraduate	33	29	59	56	27	16	72	67	18	16
Class fraction										
Unskilled workers and farmers	35	49	60	72	74	56	45	65	68	62
Skilled workers	40	42	58	61	55	44	63	73	55	59
Shopkeepers and craftsmen	33	50	55	59	38	38	69	78	53	46
Clerical workers	34	33	60	55	42	30	69	70	34	32
Teachers (prim./sec./higher)	*41*	40	54	47	26	16	71	63	39	12
Junior-executives	26	21	58	63	22	15	67	82	27	18
Professions	32	(30)[c]	67	(40)	14	(9)	76	(60)	14	(40)
Commercial employers	27	24	59	38	35	32	64	54	37	36
Unemployed	*64*	51	64	56	56	62	61	63	54	50
Housework	(100)	51	(100)	61	(100)	53	(0)	57	(100)	54
Total	42	46	59	57	53	49	59	63	50	46

Notes
a This number reads as follows: "48 per cent of men who did not finish high school agree with the statement 'I'd rather not spend too much money on going to a restaurant'."
b Figures in italic denote the strongest tendency for that particular indicator.
c The number of observations is too low to make meaningful inferences.

Table 5.1 (continued) Attitudes towards food and dining by gender, educational capital and class fraction (% agree).

	"Steak and chips, that's still one of the best things there is."		"I'm interested in the way in which food is prepared in other cultures."		"Eating at home is still the best."		"It's not important that a dish looks good, as long as it tastes good."		N	
	♂	♀	♂	♀	♂	♀	♂	♀	♂	♀
Educational capital										
Less than HS	58[a]	*51*	41	43	77	76	*51*	38	546	620
HS (technical/vocational)	52	36	47	54	68	52	37	29	334	305
HS (general)	44	28	53	65	62	39	40	19	105	80
Bachelor	34	23	53	60	55	30	30	12	182	215
Master	26	12	55	*70*	43	27	25	21	103	57
Class fraction										
Unskilled workers and farmers	59	*51*	40	53	77	59	50	*42*	93	66
Skilled workers	55	36	54	57	66	64	41	26	273	70
Shopkeepers and craftsmen	45	40	56	46	54	51	26	40	50	41
Clerical workers	43	27	50	61	60	40	35	20	222	286
Teachers (prim./sec./higher)	30	21	50	67	59	26	37	12	27	43
Higher clerks/junior-exec.	33	15	50	*79*	53	23	32	9	94	34
Professions	33	(36)	*68*	(55)	32	(50)	36	(27)	22	11
Commercial employers	36	18	44	54	50	11	37	7	63	28
Unemployed	*60*	50	46	54	69	62	*42*	30	45	96
Housework	(0)	43	(0)	49	(100)	*70*	(0)	35	1	227
Total	50	39	46	52	66	58	41	29	1,321	1,362

Source: GCPS '03–04

Note
a Figures in italic denote the strongest tendency in a column.

power – both in the form of physical dexterity, but above all of physical *strength* – and whose social reproduction hence depends most strongly on the physical performance of their bodies, working-class tastes remain inherently defined by 'the necessity of reproducing labour power at the lowest cost' (Bourdieu, 1984: 177). Rooted in a quasi-mechanistic experience of the body as an instrument that is valued primarily for its skill and force, the taste of necessity transforms economic imperatives into an elective affinity for foods that are both strong and strengthening, fatty and filling, cheap in cost and rich in calories. As the Grignons already noted, the taste of necessity tends to transform economic constraints into a moral imperative:

> [F]rom faintness to accidents on the job, from a reduction in performance to a reduction in salary or even unemployment [...] popular language never ceases to recall that one needs to eat to 'hold out', [...] to 'maintain morale', in short, one needs to eat at the risk of sub-proletarizing.
>
> (Grignon and Grignon, 1980: 548)

In addition to this strictly *economic* imperative of maintaining the body's capacity for labour, the popular hedonism in matters of food is also explained by the fact that food is often 'the only affordable and authorized type of consumption and, within given limits, the only "luxury" that is not completely inaccessible' (Grignon and Grignon, 1980: 548). In fact, as long as the absence of capital prohibits other goods and services from meaningfully competing with food in the overall system of needs – because they are either too costly in economic terms or require a minimal degree of cultural capital for their meaningful appropriation – the space of possible pleasures is often restricted to what Charlesworth called 'the search for pleasures in the rudiments of those given in the body' (2000: 279), that is, to the primary and sensuous gratifications provided by eating and drinking. This conception of food as the basis of a circumscribed "luxury" is perhaps most evident in the central role it occupies in the emotional economy of working-class families and especially in the relationship between mothers and children. Schwartz aptly summarizes this centrality of food in the working-class conception of child-rearing:

> Point of honour, element of parental valorisation, traditional status of food as the site of working-class scarcity or the primary source of abundance, all these elements contribute to polarizing collective attention onto one primordial concern: that the children may eat.
>
> (1990: 144)

The desire to feed children and feed them well, itself often rooted in personal memories of childhood-privation (see Warrin *et al.*, 2008 or Bruch, 1973), remains an integral element of parental and social valorization. Given that scarcity often imposes strict limits on the types of pleasure that parents can provide children (in the form of gifts, outings, etc.), food is often one of the last domains in which restrictions are tolerated, since the pleasures it provides, constitute an elementary physical and psychological buffer against the hardships that define their social conditions. This is undoubtedly also one of the reasons for the popular indulgence towards children's consumption of sweets and snacks, an indulgence which the dominant vision is often quick to disqualify as a reckless and irresponsible gamble with children's health. However, the importance of being able to provide children with a modicum of tangible pleasure, in a social universe that is otherwise pervaded by necessity, often overrides concerns over the long-term and often quite "abstract" effects that particular qualities and quantities of food might have for their well-being. Stronger still, for children a strong, sturdy and even plump body is not only seen as a sign of health and physical robustness, but also visibly testifies to the maternal ability to feed children and feed them well. Even if such views are increasingly problematized, through the growing awareness of the dangers of childhood-obesity for instance, potential concerns are often shrugged off by invoking the body's innate resilience and the conviction that childhood plumpness is merely a temporary state and children will eventually "grow out of it" (see Chapter 9).

To these conceptions of "food-as-fuel" (Lupton, 1996) as well as the basis for a primary and circumscribed hedonism needs to be added a third way in which the taste of necessity manifests itself in food-preferences. In fact, the same functional ethos that relates to food as a source of *physical* compensation is also revealed in the uses of food as a source of *psychological* compensation and emotional solace. This relationship to food – which could perhaps be best qualified as "anaesthetic" rather than "aesthetic" – seems particularly important in understanding the dietary preferences of working-class *women*. The centrality of food and eating as a primary form of coping with emotional disturbance, psychological distress and depression, especially in understanding the etiology of eating disorders and obesity, has been extensively documented in the work of authors like Bruch (1974), Orbach (1988) or Lupton (1996). In fact, the obvious reference to the *orality* of the act of eating and its origins in the universe of primary relationships (especially that between mother and child), has given rise to much psycho-analytical theorizing on the relationship between food and emotion. However, less attention has been devoted to the properly *social* conditions that lead individuals to turn to food (rather than more capital-laden forms of "therapy") as a means of alleviating stress, depression and anxiety.

Without claiming that such "anaesthetic" uses of food are somehow exclusive to working-class women (or even the working-class as a whole), there is some evidence to suggest that their particular situation, and especially their status as being *doubly* dominated (both in the social *and* sexual division of labour) is particularly conducive to the development of such uses. In fact, if in matters of food, the men of their class clearly challenge the dominant lifestyle, than working-class women display an even more remarkable heterodoxy with regards to the dominant ethos of health and slimness, especially since (as the preceding chapter has aimed to show) the dominant definition of the legitimate physique imposes itself more strongly on women as a whole. Not only do they seem to grant a particularly central place to food and eating (almost three quarters of female unskilled workers and farmers and 60 per cent of skilled workers agree with the statement that *"Eating well is among the most important things in my life"* and in this respect they already differ sharply from middle- and upper-class women, especially when one takes into account the particular meaning they attribute to this proposition) but they also prove most eager to equate the quality of a meal with its quantity (62 per cent of unskilled and 60 per cent of skilled workers agree with the proposition that *"Eating well means getting more than enough to eat"*, while only 27 per cent and 29 per cent *dis*agree) and half of the unskilled workers and farmers even consider a heavy, substantial dish like steak and chips to be *"one of the best things there is"* (which they also ranked among their favourite dishes, see Table 5.2).

This shows that the realistic hedonism which defines food as the site of a primary abundance and circumscribed luxury is by no means restricted to working-class men. However, if the experience of necessity seems to exert a similar effect on the ways in which men and women come to relate to food, for the latter, the effects of social domination are further compounded by those of *sexual* domination. In fact, in addition to the instrumentalization of their bodies through manual labour and all the privations and renunciations of the self this implies, working-class women are also assigned the quasi-monopoly over domestic labour and all the responsibilities, not to mention drudgeries, it imposes. It is their domestic role which defines them as the legitimate *providers* of pleasure, responsible for the physical and psychological needs of their families (often at the cost of a considerable amount of *self*-denial and *self*-renunciation), of which the ability to provide culinary pleasure is a particularly central dimension. Given its centrality in the act of pleasure-*giving* and its more general importance within working-class cosmology, food is also one of the few 'legitimate' sources of pleasure, that is, one which is at once accessible and does not wholly contradict their social and sexual identity.

Schwartz (1990: 474ff.) already drew attention to this role of food as a 'substitutive pleasure' in the emotional economy of working-class women which provides them with a source of 'solitary, auto-erotic, captivating and unrestrained pleasure, that hosts and displaces onto orality an otherwise inhibited sexuality' (ibid.: 483). That the experience of occupying a doubly dominated position often makes it particularly difficult for working-class women to perceive their bodies as an autonomous source of pleasure – most notably *sexual* pleasure – is something which will be discussed more fully in Chapter 9. Here, I merely want to highlight that their social and sexual position is particularly conducive to the social uses of a food as a source of compensation. In fact, given that the sexual oppositions between the private and the public, the inside and the outside, the home and the café tend to be most pronounced among those who are situated at the bottom of the social hierarchy (as Chapter 1 has aimed to show), one could argue that for working-class women, food and eating are often invested with an escapist, compensatory and "analgesic" quality that is entirely homologous to that of alcohol and drinking among the men of their class (on this point also see Lhuissier and Régnier, 2005).

Crucially, the realistic hedonism of those who are 'condemned to finding pleasure in the pure, unmediated pleasures of the body' (Charlesworth, 2000: 257) is itself inseparable from an entire philosophy of time and the future which is engendered in conditions of economic insecurity. In fact, the propensity to sacrifice the immediate, tangible pleasures provided by eating and drinking to the long-term benefits of health and appearance is itself a function of the *perceived* chances of reasonably obtaining such benefits. Hence, the more these benefits are themselves viewed as abstract and unreal, the less inclined agents will be to *willingly* suffer what, in conditions that are already marked by necessity and privation, can only be viewed as *additional* forms of abstinence and self-denial. Stronger still, this 'being-in-the-present which is affirmed in the readiness to take advantage of the good times and take time as it comes' (Bourdieu, 1984: 183), which the dominant vision is often quick to reduce to a facile surrender to visceral desires – a form of "gastro-anomie" to misquote Fischler (2001) – is also an 'affirmation of solidarity with others, inasmuch as this temporal immanentism is a recognition of the limits which define the condition' (Bourdieu, 1984: 183). Hence, far from being the expression of an anomic, unregulated relation to the body, this culinary hedonism is itself an integral element of the popular ethos. As such, it can function as a powerful principle of conformity and any form of abstention – especially in the name of values like beauty and health that are associated with those who occupy more elevated positions in social space – risks being perceived as an attempt to distinguish oneself from the primary group.

Style and form

Whether one looks at the different attitudes towards food and dining (Table 5.1), the specific structure of their food-expenditure (Tables A4.4 to A4.6 in appendix) or their judgment of particular types of dishes (Table 5.2), the analysis consistently reveals a boundary separating the manual from the non-manual occupations, the skilled workers from the office clerks. This boundary not only marks a change in food-habits, but also points to a more general transformation of the relationship to the body. As economic pressures relax and the body no longer serves as the primary source of labour power, the conditions for the development of both an aesthetic and therapeutic, that is to say, an *autonomous* relationship to the body, prove increasingly met. In fact, as one moves from the working to the middle-class, one can observe a clear shift from what Roland Barthes (1961: 986) called the 'nutritional' (*nutritive*) to the 'protocolary' (*protocolaire*) value of food, that is, from food as a nourishing substance to food as a *symbol* for the expression of social occasion with all the form and formalities this implies. Compared to the farmers and the (un)skilled workers, the dietary practices and preferences of the office-workers, the teachers and the small business-owners not only betray a more explicit concern with "form" – in the threefold sense of the *appearance* and *presentation* of food, its appropriate *manner* of consumption, as well as its effects on the *physical form* and shape of the body – but are also marked by a growing negation of the most functional aspects of eating.

Table 5.2 Ranking of favourite dishes by social class, *men*

	Working	*Lower-middle*	*Upper-middle*	*Dominant*
1	Steak with pepper sauce and hash browns (28%)	Steak with pepper sauce and hash browns (31%)	Steak with pepper sauce and hash browns (31%)	Steak with pepper sauce and hash browns (19%)
2	Beef stew with chips (22%)	Beef stew with chips (14%)	Stir-fried shrimp with rice and vegetables (17%)	Stir-fried shrimp with rice and vegetables (17%)
3	Grilled salmon with asparagus and rice (17%)	Stir-fried shrimp with rice and vegetables (13%)	Grilled salmon with asparagus and rice (12%)	Grilled salmon with asparagus and rice (17%)
4	Stir-fried shrimp with rice and vegetables (11%)	Grilled salmon with asparagus and rice (10%)	Beef stew with chips (11%)	Steamed cod with leeks and mash (10%)
5	Spaghetti Bolognese (6%)	Steamed cod with leeks and mash (7%)	Ham and endives with Béchamel sauce (9%)	Beef stew with chips (10%)
6	Ham and endives with Béchamel sauce (6%)	Bangers and mash (7%)	Spaghetti Bolognese (8%)	Ham and endives with Béchamel sauce (8%)
7	Vegetable quiche with salad (6%)	Ham and endives with Béchamel sauce (6%)	Bangers and mash (5%)	Bangers and mash (8%)
8	Steamed cod with leeks and mash (3%)	Spaghetti Bolognese (6%)	Steamed cod with leeks and mash (5%)	Vegetable quiche with salad (6%)
9	Bangers and mash (3%)	Vegetable quiche with salad (6%)	Vegetable quiche with salad (2%)	Spaghetti Bolognese (6%)
N	**36**	**70**	**123**	**52**

Source: BoS '10

Table 5.2 (continued) Ranking of favourite dishes by social class, women

	Working	Lower-middle	Upper-middle	Dominant
1	Steamed cod with leeks and mash (23%)	Stir-fried shrimp with rice and vegetables (27%)	Stir-fried shrimp with rice and vegetables (26%)	Stir-fried shrimp with rice and vegetables (24%)
2	Steak with pepper sauce and hash browns (19%)	Grilled salmon with asparagus and rice (16%)	Grilled salmon with asparagus and rice (16%)	Vegetable quiche with salad (19%)
3	Grilled salmon with asparagus and rice (16%)	Spaghetti Bolognese (13%)	Vegetable quiche with salad (15%)	Beef stew with chips (19%)
4	Spaghetti Bolognese (13%)	Steamed cod with leeks and mash (11%)	Steamed cod with leeks and mash (11%)	Grilled salmon with asparagus and rice (13%)
5	Stir-fried shrimp with rice and vegetables (13%)	Vegetable quiche with salad (9%)	Spaghetti Bolognese (9%)	Spaghetti Bolognese (9%)
6	Beef stew with chips (10%)	Steak with pepper sauce and hash browns (9%)	Steak with pepper sauce and hash browns (9%)	Steamed cod with leeks and mash (5%)
7	Ham and endives with Béchamel sauce (3%)	Ham and endives with Béchamel sauce (9%)	Beef stew with chips (6%)	Ham and endives with Béchamel sauce (5%)
8	Vegetable quiche with salad (3%)	Beef stew with chips (5%)	Ham and endives with Béchamel sauce (5%)	Bangers and mash (5%)
9	Bangers and mash (0%)	Bangers and mash (1%)	Bangers and mash (3%)	Steak with pepper sauce and hash browns (3%)
N	31	151	107	63

Source: BoS '10

For instance, as one moves from the skilled workers to the office clerks, the number of people who judge the quality of a meal as a function of its *quantity* (and hence by its capacity to nourish) drops from almost 60 per cent of the former to a third of the latter. Similarly, the proportion that indicates they find a filling dish like the steak and chips to be "*one of the best things there is*" varies from more than half (55 per cent) of the skilled workers to 34 per cent of the office-workers and a quarter of the teachers. That the latter – rich in cultural, but (relatively) poor in economic capital – prove particularly sensitive to the *aesthetics* of a meal is shown by the fact that they least often agree with the proposition that the taste of a dish is more important than its appearance (21 per cent agree while 64 per cent disagree). This tendency to adopt an ascetic and restrictive relationship towards food in the name of values like health and appearance is also shown by their judgment of particular types of dishes. Whereas one fifth of working-class women still chose the steak as their favourite dish, this drops to less than one out of ten for the female office-workers and the teachers, who instead more often opted for "lean" and "light" dishes like the "*stir-fried shrimp with vegetables and rice*" (chosen by a quarter of the office clerks and a third of the teachers) or the "*grilled salmon with asparagus and rice*" (chosen by 16 per cent and 23 per cent of these categories, respectively).

This growing concern with the long-term effects of food on the body's "form" can also be gathered from a more specific analysis of the structure of their food-expenditure. In fact, as one moves from the working- to the middle-class, the average amount of the food-budget that is spent on meat (and especially the cheapest and most fattening types of meat such as pork, bacon, minced meat, hamburgers, sausages, etc.) decreases considerably from more than a fifth among the farmers and the manual workers to 17 per cent of the office-workers, 16 per cent of the teachers and 15 per cent of the junior-executives. The same applies to the consumption of the most "filling" types of food (i.e. those rich in carbohydrates) such as bread and potatoes, as well as particularly high-calorie foods such as soft-drinks. At the same time, the consumption of light and healthy foods such as (fresh) fish, fruit and vegetables tends to increase. A final indicator that members of the middle-class prove more receptive to the dominant concern with form and manner is provided by the time and money they devote to *outdoor* food-consumption and especially to restaurant-visits. If 20 per cent of the unskilled workers and farmers and 14 per cent of the skilled workers claimed they had not been to a restaurant in the six months preceding the survey, this drops to 7 per cent of the office-workers and 2 per cent of the small business-owners and only 1 per cent of the teachers. Similarly, as one moves from the unskilled and skilled workers to office clerks, the average amount spent on food for *domestic* consumption decreases (in both relative and absolute terms), while the amount spent on restaurants increases considerably, with office-workers already spending more than twice as much on restaurant-visits than farmers.

Matter and manner

While the preceding pages tend to support Levins' and Lewontin's observation that, *socio*-logically speaking, human beings are no true omnivores, they have only grasped part of the intricate relation between class-condition and dietary habit(u)s. In fact, in order to fully grasp the logic behind the "choices" for particular types of food – of which the analysis of household-expenditure can provide only the most stenographic impression – the analysis also needs to take into account the fact that eating is not just a visceral necessity, but also a *physical act*, a specific constellation of 'body techniques' (Mauss, 1973 [1934]), which engage the entire *corporeal schema* and especially the socially structured uses of the hands and mouth. In fact, as an 'incorporated principle of classification which governs all forms of incorporation' (Bourdieu, 1984: 190), the class habitus not only determines the choices for particular flavours, textures and quantities of food, but also informs the socially (*and* sexually) approved ways of manipulating and assimilating them. A full understanding of the ways in which class circumscribes the relationship to food therefore needs to look beyond the most obvious (and easily quantifiable) characteristics of food – like economic cost or caloric content – and also include differences in their particular *mode of consumption*.

> One of the most important limitations of working with surveys on household-expenditure is that they are often entirely oblivious to the distinctions that stem from differences in the *mode of production and consumption* of different types of food (see Bourdieu, 1984; Boltanski, 1970). In fact, while the different social uses that can be made of a particular product are never entirely independent of its intrinsic properties (e.g. "fast-food"), it is equally true that one can rarely ever deduce such uses from these properties alone. In fact, the entire social meaning that is invested in the consumption of particular types of food can shift or even invert depending on its particular mode of preparation, such as fish that is steamed or baked in butter, chicken that is boiled or grilled, or beans that are used raw in a salad or cooked in a cream sauce. More generally, the categories of goods and products delineated by surveys on household-consumption, however detailed they may be, rarely ever coincide with what Barthes (1961: 981) coined the 'signifying units' (*unités signifiantes*) of the 'food system', namely the specific set of practical taxonomies that agents deploy in their perception and appropriation of different types of food. By lumping together items that these taxonomies would distinguish (white or wholegrain bread, skimmed or full milk, milk-chocolate or *fondant*, etc.) and separating items that they treat as equivalent (beef, bread and bananas), these categories often effectively blur the practical logic that structures the relationship to food of a specific class (fraction). Apart from ignoring all the meaningful distinctions that stem from differences in the mode of production and consumption, they also tend to overlook differences related to the *quality* and *variety* of specific types of food. Being oblivious to the distinction between "quality-brands"

and cheaper, "generic" substitutes or overlooking everything that is implied by the consumption of specific varieties which – like the choice for "organic" or "light" – are themselves highly indicative of the relationship to the body, these categories have the effect of artificially minimizing social differences in food-consumption. These factors combine to make the statistical shopping-basket (as presented in Tables A4.4 to A4.6) into a rather conservative estimate of actual class-differences in food-consumption.

In this manner, the popular primacy attribute to substance over form is not only expressed in a taste for foods and dishes that are solid, substantial and filling, but also translates into a particular *mode* of appropriation and incorporation, a specific *style* of eating of which Charlesworth again provides an apt description:

> It is not only that the basics of life are constituted as *pleasures* but that the articulation also denotes a *way* of eating, a modality of pleasure, an involved, un-stylized eating in which the mouth is filled and messes made: 'a good trough', has its own aesthetic sensuousness which is neither aesthetic in a formal sense nor sensuous in the usual sense of the word.
> (2000: 279–280, *original emphasis*)

It is through the mediation of such socially (and sexually) defined *styles* of eating that class-differences in food are fully realized. For instance, if members of the working-class, and working-class *men* in particular, most often choose the steak as their favourite dish and if they have the highest average expenditure (in both absolute and relative terms) on *beef*, this is not only because it is considered to be the most substantial and nourishing type of meat and hence most capable of *providing* strength, but also because it is the type of meat that in a sense *requires* strength to eat (Roland Barthes speaks of that 'heavy substance which dwindles under one's teeth in such a way as to make one keenly aware at the same time of its original strength and of its aptitude to flow into the very blood of man' [1957: 62]). It hence allows for the assertion of an ethos of virility, which equates masculinity with mastication and the kinaesthetic pleasures of cutting, rending and chewing, all of which are expressive of a 'practical philosophy of the male body as a sort of power, big and strong, with enormous, imperative, brutal needs' (Bourdieu, 1984: 192).

> The same logic no doubt also explains their relative *under*-consumption of fish (21 per cent of male manual workers claim they rarely or never eat fish, while 11 per cent claim to eat it several times a week, compared to 8 per cent and 21 per cent of the office clerks, 4 per cent and 38 per cent of the junior-executives and 5 per cent and 44 per cent of the academics, respectively). Not only is it perceived as a food that is too soft and bland, literally lacking in substance and content, but it also requires a mode of consumption which 'totally contradicts the masculine way of eating, that is, with restraint, in small mouthfuls, chewed gently, with the front of the mouth, on the tips of the teeth (because of the bones)' (ibid.: 190). The enduring popularity of

a fruit like bananas among the working-class, which has the highest relative spending on this particular type of fruit (16 per cent of the total amount spent on fruit among unskilled workers compared to 13 per cent among office clerks, 12 per cent among senior-executives and 10 per cent among the academics) also obeys a similar principle. Not only is it the type of fruit that conforms closest to the popular demand for substance and nourishment, but it also requires little in terms of manipulation and preparation such as peeling, plucking, cutting, in short, of all the actions that are too fidgety and fiddly for male hands and hence require a "feminine touch".

Finally, a similar set of oppositions can be found in the area of drinks, where the differences in the patterns of expenditure between beer – and especially *lager*, invested with both masculine and popular connotations – and wine – perceived as both a bourgeois and feminine drink, especially outside France – draws a considerable part of its logic from differences in their dominant mode of consumption. The former, served in a large, sturdy glass clasped firmly with open palm, raised to the mouth with the elbow extended outward, drunken in large swigs with mouth opened wide and head thrown back is almost diametrically opposed to the latter, which is served in a slender, fragile glass that is grasped lightly, between the tips of the fingers, drunken in small sips with closed lips and without moving arm and elbow too far out and away from the body. To these different *techniques* of drinking also correspond two distinct *rhythms*, with lager generally being consumed quickly and in quantity (the capacity of "keeping up with the rounds" being a particularly important point of masculine honour), while the legitimate manner of consuming wine instead requires that one "takes one's time" (often accompanied by all the rituals of "airing" and "decanting").

More generally, the case of table manners shows how bodily discipline is itself inseparably tied to *temporal* discipline. In fact, the symbolic censorship of the most functional, animalistic and hence most "common" aspects of the acts of eating and drinking is not only achieved through a high degree of *stylization*, but also by extending these acts in time, subjecting them to a particular sequence and pace in order to negate haste and urgency and hence to demonstrate one's capacity to control and defer visceral imperatives by "taking one's time". A child that is told not to eat "like it's your last meal" or "as if your life depends on it", is not only instructed in a more disciplined, restrictive use of the body and especially the mouth – taking smaller bites, not opening the mouth too wide when ingesting food, keeping it closed while chewing, chewing longer on each bite, producing less noise when chewing and swallowing, etc. – but also acquires a practical sense for the appropriate *tempo* in which the act of eating needs to unfold, neither too fast (which would imply gluttony), nor too slow (which would betray dawdling or a lack of purpose). It is precisely this importance attributed to "restraint" (in the dual sense of the term) in the dominant way of eating and the dominant relationship to the body, which led Le Wita to define the bourgeois meal as 'one prolonged rule of politeness in which each party apologizes for holding everyone else up' (1994: 77).

Time budget-surveys provide a tentative indication of such class-differences in the time spent on dining (see Appendix, Table A4.7). Whereas the *total* amount of time that is devoted to food and eating seems to vary only slightly between the social classes – with unskilled workers spending just two minutes more than clerical workers and roughly the same as junior-executives on an average working-day – more significant differences emerge when the analysis distinguishes between the time that is devoted to the *preparation* (and cleaning up) of meals and the actual time spent on their *consumption*. In fact, while the former decreases sharply as one rises in the social hierarchy, the latter tends to vary in an opposite manner. On average, unskilled workers spend 15 minutes more than clerical workers, 23 minutes more than junior-executives, 34 minutes more than members of the professions and 38 minutes more than the employers on the preparation of meals. However, when one looks at the time devoted to food-*consumption*, this relationship with social position tends to invert. On a work-day, unskilled workers spend 13 minutes less on dining than office clerks, 23 minutes less than junior-executives, 16 minutes less than the professions and one hour less than the employers. Based on these results, one could venture to say that the basic opposition between function and form not only underlies social differences in the consumption of particular types (and quantities) of food, but also seems to govern the social uses of *time* devoted to meals. In fact, whereas the taste for substantial dishes dictates that members of the working-class rarely economize on time (and especially *women*'s time) when it comes to the preparation of meals, their lack of concern with dining as a ritual act leads them to devote considerably less time to it than middle- and upper-class families (on this point also see Charles and Kerr, 1988). The latter, in turn, not only have a taste for dishes that are lighter and healthier, but also take less time to prepare (another indication that middle- and upper-class women place more value on their own time than their working-class counterparts). This economizing of time and effort in the domain of food-production is matched by an increasing ritualization of food-*consumption* in which the "family meal" not only serves as a site for social integration, but also comes to function as a socializing matrix in which children acquire the techniques that are necessary for the future accumulation of cultural and social capital (see Wills *et al.*, 2011).

Such social differences in the *manner* of appropriating and incorporating food seem increasingly important in understanding the relationship between social class and taste. In fact, with changes in the mode of food-production and the corresponding decline in prices leading to the gradual extension of formerly distinguished products (salmon, veal, beef, etc.) to groups that were previously excluded from their consumption, some of the most pertinent differences between the classes are no longer situated solely at the level of the actual goods that are consumed, but are increasingly determined by their *manner* or *style* of consumption. However, it is precisely these differences in the *mode* of appropri-

The hungry body 147

ation, that tend to be particularly elusive to survey-analysis, which can often only grasp such differences partially and indirectly (through, for instance, the *time* that is devoted to certain practices).

While the homogenous and homogenizing character of the categories employed by survey-questionnaires hence has the effect of artificially attenuating class-differences *in general* – the 'choice' for the same practice or product often concealing different, even opposed social uses – it tends to most strongly obscure the oppositions between the tastes of the middle-class and the lifestyle of the dominant class. In fact, if members of the working-class are often de facto distinguished by their exclusion from particular categories of goods and services, it is the infinitely more subtle differences between the established and the outsiders, those whose mode of consumption betrays early exposure and prolonged familiarization and those whose "vulgar" uses of distinguished products betray a discrepancy between (cultural) manners and (economic) means that are quite often effaced through the blunt mechanics of the survey. Hence, if the analyses presented in the last two chapters still provide ample support for Feuerbach's famous proposition that "man is *what* he eats", it seems to be equally true that "man is *how* he eats."

Elective austerity and conspicuous consumption

The preceding analyses have aimed to show that in their relationship to food the cardinal opposition between the classes is defined by, on the one hand, the popular taste of necessity which is expressed in a preference for foods that are cheap, filling and substantial (such as bread, potatoes, meat and fats) *and*, on the other, its negation in the dominant taste of luxury which manifests itself in a proclivity for foods that are both light, more costly in price and less costly in time. However, the symbolic denial of biological need and visceral desire that, in matters of food as elsewhere, defines the lifestyle of the dominant class, itself takes a different form depending on the particular *type* of capital – economic power or cultural authority – that defines their distance from necessity:

> It is clearly no accident that the dominant art and the dominant art of living agree on the same fundamental distinctions, which are all based on the opposition between the brutish necessity which forces itself on the vulgar, and luxury, as the manifestation of distance from necessity, or asceticism, as self-imposed constraint, two contrasting ways of defying nature, need, appetite, desire; between the unbridled squandering which only highlights the privations of ordinary existence, and the ostentatious freedom of gratuitous expense or the austerity of elective restriction; between surrender to immediate, easy satisfactions and economy of means, bespeaking a possession of means commensurate with the means possessed.
>
> (Bourdieu, 1984: 254–255)

In this manner, the same opposition between substance and form, quantity and quality, matter and manner re-emerges in a different form, in both the middle and the dominant classes, between their *dominant* fractions, richest in economic capital (shopkeepers, small business-owners, senior-executives, commercial employers, etc.) and their *dominated* fractions who are most well-endowed with cultural capital (teachers, cultural producers, academics, etc.). While both share a position of dominance vis-à-vis members of the working-class and are hence united in a number of dietary preferences, most notably a concern with restriction and form, these fractions are nevertheless clearly opposed in the specific *manner* in which they symbolically assert this dominance, both in the domain of food as well as in their relationship to the body in general.

The analysis of their attitudes towards food and dining as well as their household-expenditure on food tends to reveal two distinct taste-patterns. On the one hand, there is the ascetic, health-oriented taste of the intellectual fractions of the dominant and middle-classes, represented in this case by the teachers in primary and secondary education, the artists and cultural producers and those in academic occupations. These fractions are distinguished by the strongest refusal of the most "material" and materialistic of foods, that is to say, those who are at once the most substantial, filling and fattening, but also the most expensive in cost. This can perhaps be illustrated best by looking at the differences in consumption of the type of food which is most often associated with both these qualities and has often come to stand as the ultimate symbol of gluttony and decadence, namely *meat*. In fact, as one moves from the commercial employers, through the senior-executives and professions to the academics and the cultural producers, the relative amount spent on meat and meat-products tends to systematically decrease (see Table A4.4). At the same time, the proportion of the food-budget that is spent on lighter, healthier foods such as vegetables and fish varies in an inverse manner, with artists and cultural producers spending almost as much or more on fresh vegetables and fresh fish than senior-executives and commercial employers, but out of a considerably smaller total expenditure. In fact, the culinary asceticism of the dominated fractions of the *petit-bourgeoisie* and the dominant class (which quite often takes the form of vegetarianism) also reveals itself in the fact that the proportion of their food-budget that is devoted to fruit and vegetables often equals or exceeds the amount spent on meat and meat-products.

> Teachers are amongst those fractions of the middle and upper classes who least often agree and most strongly *dis*agree with statements like "*Steak and chips, that's still one of the best things there is*" (63 per cent disagree compared to 31 per cent of unskilled workers, 53 per cent of the junior-executives and 50 per cent of those in the professions), "*Eating well means, first of all, getting more than enough to eat*" (64 per cent disagree compared to 22 per cent, 58 per cent and 64 per cent for the other categories, respectively) or "*Eating well is among the most important things in my life*" (31 per cent disagree as opposed to 24 per cent of unskilled workers and the junior-executives and 25 per cent of the professions). In addition, the proportion of respondents who claimed they *"never eat meat"* also proved systematically highest among those fractions of the *petit-bourgeoisie* and the

dominant class that are most well-endowed with *cultural* as opposed to *economic* capital, in the case of our survey the teachers in primary and secondary education (14 per cent), the artists and the cultural producers (9 per cent) and those in academic or scientific occupations (16 per cent), compared to 3 per cent of the office clerks, 2 per cent of the junior-executives and 7 per cent of those in the professions (source: BoS '10). This observation cannot be solely attributed to the fact that these fractions are among the most "feminized", since (as Chapter 1 has argued) the sex-ratio of a class fraction is itself one of the key properties that define a social position (and hence as much an *explanans* than an *explanandum*), but also because other fractions with highly similar gender-ratio's, although lower and higher possession of economic capital (respectively), such as the clerical occupations centred on presentation and representation (secretaries, hostesses, etc.) and those in the socio-medical services (therapists, counsellors, etc.) show clearly different patterns (3 per cent and 7 per cent claim to never eat meat, respectively). An analysis of the household-expenditure on food reveals a similar picture. In fact, whereas the average proportion of the food-budget that is spent on meat and meat-products systematically declines as one rises in the social hierarchy, it does so much more strongly when one moves from the farmers (22.1 per cent) and the unskilled workers (20.1 per cent) through the teachers (15.9 per cent) to the academics (12.2 per cent) and cultural producers (13.2 per cent), than from the former through the shopkeepers (18.0 per cent) to the senior-executives (15.7 per cent) and, to a lesser extent, the commercial employers (13.9 per cent).

On the other hand, the relationship to food of the *dominant* fractions of the dominant class is also characterized by the symbolic negation of the crude, practical hedonism of working-class tastes, but rather than denying necessity and visceral pleasure through an ascetic ethos of elective austerity, as is done by those who are rich in cultural, but (relatively) poor in economic capital, they express their distance from necessity through a refined hedonism that substitutes quality for quantity, rarity for substance. This is shown quite clearly by the tastes of the commercial employers (and to a lesser extent the senior-executives) who not only have the highest average expenditure on food (in absolute terms), but also spend the largest amount on *outdoor* food-consumption and especially on restaurant-visits, which take up nearly a quarter of their overall food-budget, compared to less than a fifth for the professions and the academics, 10 per cent of the manual workers and 6 per cent of the farmers. In fact, more than half of the commercial employers (53 per cent) reported they visited a restaurant at least twice a month (while only 3 per cent claimed they had not gone to a restaurant at all), compared to 40 per cent of the professions and the junior-executives, 26 per cent of the office-workers and the teachers and 12 per cent of the unskilled workers and farmers. In addition, more than half the employers (54 per cent) *dis*agreed with the proposition "*I'd rather not spend too much money on going to a restaurant*" and in this respect

150 *Modes of embodiment*

differed strongly from members of the professions (44 per cent) and *a fortiori* from the teachers (38 per cent).

> The teachers are in fact distinguished from the rest of the middle-class, and especially from the office clerks, not so much by the frequency with which they visit a restaurant (1 per cent and 7 per cent, respectively, claim they have not been to a restaurant in the past six months, while 26 per cent of both categories claim they have done so 12 times or more), but rather by their willingness to spend money on the occasion. Compared to the latter, they agree more strongly with the statement that they would rather not spend too much money on going to a restaurant (Table 5.1) and in this respect appear closer to members of the working-class, and skilled workers in particular, from whom they are nonetheless distinguished by a considerably higher frequency of restaurant-visits (with only 12 per cent and 17 per cent of unskilled and skilled workers stating they have been to a restaurant 12 times or more). The analysis of their food-expenditure also shows that teachers spend slightly less of their overall budget on *outdoor* food-consumption (2.8 per cent compared to 3.1 per cent of office-workers) and despite having a higher average food-expenditure, they only spend slightly more (13.7 per cent) of their food-budget on restaurant-visits than the office clerks (13.2 per cent).
>
> (source: EU-HBS '05)

More generally, whereas the culturally dominant fractions appear marked by an attitude of ambivalence towards an act which, regardless of its degree of symbolic refinement, remains "materialistic" – in the sense of being directly linked to physical gratification, the appropriation of material objects, but also as a symbol for the flaunting of economic wealth – the economic fractions of the dominant and middle-classes display an ethos of hedonistic, yet refined indulgence which favours "haute cuisine" over "haute culture", sensuous pleasure over intellectual enjoyment. Instead of negating biological necessity through sobriety and elective restriction, they assert their distance from nature by their capacity for gratuitous expense (*potlatch*) on acts of consumption that not only provide a primary, but also a fleeting type of pleasure. The analysis of the consumption of drinks, and alcoholic drinks in particular, reveals a similar opposition. Compared to the academics and the cultural producers, the employers spend considerably more, in both absolute and relative terms, on the consumption of the most rare and expensive types of alcohol, especially champagne and spirits (whiskey, brandy, etc.) and relatively less on the consumption of beer (especially lager). The artists and the academics are in turn distinguished by the highest average expenditure on the traditional, artisanal beers (Trappists, Tripels, etc.) which partake of the popular aura associated with beer, but unlike lager – the archetypical working-class drink, consumed quickly and in quantity – are linked to a more stylized and ritualized mode of consumption, which actually brings them closer to wine (being similarly amenable to descriptions in terms of colour, aroma and "bouquet", which could also explain their increasing popularity in *haute cuisine*).

The social inertia of food-tastes

The analysis of the relationship to food also helps to shed light on one of the central aspects of the broader relationship to the body, namely the tendency of practically acquired ways of perceiving, using and treating the body to perpetuate themselves *beyond* their original conditions of production. In the previous chapter, this inertia of 'hysteresis' class-tastes was used to account for the fact that even if the *objective* conditions for the cultivation of a valorized physique become available, as in situations of upward mobility, their direct effect on practices and beliefs (and hence on the physical body) is always refracted through the *previously* constituted dispositions of the habitus, which themselves take time to adjust to these new conditions. Stronger still, it is precisely because these dispositions become durably inscribed in the body, in the form of bodily automatisms and quasi-visceral proclivities, and hence largely operate *below* the level of reflection and discourse, they often prove particularly resistant to intentional transformation and therefore set effective limits to the degree in which a particular habitus can fully adjust to *new* social conditions.

This is shown particularly well in the case of tastes in food. The latter provide a quasi-paradigmatic example of the lasting effects of primary social condition(ing)s on agents' practices and preferences. Being the product of a *direct* social conditioning of the body and bodily desire, which itself takes place within one of the most archetypical and affectively charged of social relationships (that between mother and child), tastes in food tend to bear 'the strongest and most indelible mark of infant learning, the lessons which longest withstand the distancing or collapse of the native world and most durably maintain nostalgia for it' (Bourdieu, 1984: 79). The extra-ordinary capacity of taste to trigger long-forgotten memories and emotions, often associated with a regression to the earliest social experiences (see Lupton, 1994), has already been the subject of much lyrical commentary (not to mention a grateful topic of much food-advertising). What concerns us here are its properly *sociological* implications and especially the ways in which this 'hysteresis' of culinary dispositions is itself one of the key conduits through which early social condition(ing)s continue to exert an influence on the relationship to the body.

> In fact, whereas the synchronic point-of-view, which only takes into account agents' *current* position in the social structure, already revealed considerable class-differences in the attitudes towards food and dining (as shown in Table 5.1), it tends to obscure the secondary differences linked to social trajectory that separate agents *within* a particular social position. The analysis of such differences reveals a clear differentiation in the attitudes towards food and dining of those who occupy a relatively "stable" position within their class (i.e. whose social origins correspond to the modal origin of that class) and those who are characterized by an *upward* or *downward* social trajectory (i.e. whose social origin lies below or above the modal origin of

Table 5.3 Attitudes towards food and dining by gender, social class and social origin (% agree)

	"I'd rather not spend too much money on going to a restaurant."		"Eating well is among the most important things in my life."		"I like familiar food the best."		"I love to try out new recipes or flavours."		"Eating well means, first of all, getting more than enough to eat."	
	♂	♀	♂	♀	♂	♀	♂	♀	♂	♀
Working-classes[a]	**39**	**46**	**59**	**70**	**57**	**48**	**62**	**71**	**56**	**65**
Mother less than HS	39[d]	48	60	72	58	49	59	72	58	65
Mother HS or higher ed.	34	(46)	56	(59)	59	(39)	85	(67)	43	(41)
Middle-classes[b]	**29**	**35**	**58**	**56**	**32**	**26**	**69**	**72**	**34**	**29**
Mother less than HS	37	39	57	55	35	30	69	67	37	35
Mother high school	26	28	63	57	31	19	70	83	35	17
Mother higher ed.	31	22	56	57	19	19	66	80	14	14
Upper classes[c]	**28**	**29**	**59**	**44**	**30**	**26**	**65**	**64**	**31**	**34**
Mother less than HS	25	35	65	50	42	50	63	56	39	41
Mother HS or higher ed.	33	24	53	38	20	12	68	67	23	28
Total	**42**	**46**	**59**	**58**	**53**	**49**	**59**	**63**	**50**	**46**

Notes
a This category includes farm workers, unskilled and skilled manual workers.
b This category includes teachers in primary and secondary education, clerical workers, shopkeepers and craftsmen.
c This category includes members of the professions and employers.
d This number reads as follows: "39% of members of working-class men whose mother did not complete high school agree with the statement 'I'd rather not spend too much…'."

Table 5.3 (continued) Attitudes towards food and dining by gender, social class and social origin (% agree)

	"Steak and chips, that's still one of the best things there is."		"I'm interested in the way in which food is prepared in other cultures."		"Eating at home is still the best."		"It's not important that a dish looks good, as long as it tastes good."		N	
	♂	♀	♂	♀	♂	♀	♂	♀	♂	♀
Working-classes	**55**	**47**	**53**	**55**	**69**	**59**	**44**	**33**	**289**	**118**
Mother less than HS	55	44	53	54	71	59	43	36	255	100
Mother HS or higher ed.	56	(61)	54	(53)	60	(56)	57	(17)	34	18
Middle-classes	**38**	**25**	**54**	**62**	**59**	**38**	**35**	**20**	**337**	**368**
Mother less than HS	41	27	53	59	66	42	37	22	209	241
Mother high school	35	24	55	67	48	33	29	13	92	91
Mother higher ed.	30	19	58	75	41	23	35	19	36	36
Upper classes	**37**	**27**	**48**	**62**	**47**	**27**	**35**	**13**	**81**	**34**
Mother less than HS	42	38	39	53	54	29	37	12	41	17
Mother HS or higher ed.	33	18	58	71	40	24	33	24	40	17
Total	**50**	**39**	**46**	**52**	**66**	**58**	**41**	**29**	**1,321**	**1,362**

Source: GCPS '03–04

their class). To demonstrate this 'hysteresis-effect', the analysis took the responses of different social categories to the statements on food and dining, but further differentiated them according to the social origin of the respondents (see Table 5.3), represented in this case by the educational capital of the mother (given the centrality of the maternal role in the transmission of class-tastes, especially in the domain of food, see Charles and Kerr, 1988; Lupton, 1996). In order to avoid comparisons between groups that were too small, the different occupational categories were aggregated into three larger classes (working-, middle- and upper-class). Whereas the overall responses of these classes largely confirm the results of the earlier analysis, they still conceal quite important differences between agents endowed with different volumes of *inherited* cultural capital. These differences prove most clearly marked for those statements that probed the importance of substance and quantity in the choice of food, as well as those that gauged respondents' degree of culinary traditionalism. For instance, the proportion of middle- or upper-class respondents who agreed with statements like "*Eating well means, first of all, getting more than enough to eat*" or "*Steak and chips, that's still one of the best things there is*" was often more than twice as high among those with little or no inherited cultural capital (i.e. from working-class origins) as compared to those whose mother obtained a degree in higher-education. At the same time however, the number of upwardly mobile individuals who agreed with these statements remained *below* that of working-class respondents, which indicates a partial adaption to the dietary habit(u)s of their new social position. Similarly, those members of the middle- and upper-classes who are marked by an upwardly mobile trajectory tend to agree more with propositions such as "*I like familiar food the best*" or "*Eating at home is still the best*" and are in this respect closer to members of the working-class, than those who share their *current* position in the social structure, but are endowed with higher levels of inherited cultural capital. A similar intermediate position is observed among respondents who are characterized by a *downward* social trajectory, especially members of the working- and middle-classes whose mothers obtained a degree in secondary or higher-education. Whereas their culinary opinions largely prove in line with those who share their current social position, their responses nevertheless still tend towards those of their social position of origin.

(source: GCPS '03–04)

This "inertia" of the attitudes towards food and dining also helps to clarify precisely what Bourdieu meant when he stated that 'it is taste – the taste of necessity or the taste of luxury – and not high or low income which commands the practices adjusted to these resources' (1984: 175). Contra mechanistic explanations which *directly* relate practices and preferences to the social conditions in which they unfold and which tend to treat the relationship to food as a simple function of income or education (i.e. as an income- or education-"effect"), the notion of habitus serves as a reminder that the necessity inscribed in a given class-condition can *only* determine practices, *if* agents have already incorporated this necessity – as a "taste" for the possible and the given – and are hence *predisposed* to accept the limits it imposes as "self-evident", "natural" and even "desirable".

As already discussed in Chapter 2, this structuring role of the habitus only becomes apparent when there is a discrepancy between agents' current and past positions in social space. It is here that analysis clearly registers the "lag" that results when class-tastes function in conditions that differ from those in which they were originally produced. Put differently, knowledge of the objective conditions that define a given position in social space is in itself not sufficient to account for practices and preferences *without* knowledge of the dispositions that agents bring to such a position, which can themselves lead to more or less divergent practices depending on the "fit" between positions and dispositions. If, against deterministic interpretations of the concept, the analysis clearly demonstrates habitus' capacity for transformation and adaptation to changed social circumstances, it also shows how such adaptation is rarely ever complete and how primary tastes manage to perpetuate themselves *even if* the objective conditions for their transformation have become available. Given the centrality of culinary tastes in shaping the *physicality* of the body (as discussed in the previous chapter), their relative inertia is crucial to account for what McNay called the 'recalcitrance of embodied existence to self-fashioning' (1999: 97). Crucially, this recalcitrance is not that of an innate biological resistance, but is instead rooted in the opaque logic of *socially* produced bodily dispositions. However, because these dispositions have all the appearance of "innateness" and because everyday language inclines social agents to perceived and judge their bodies in wholly Cartesian terms, this intransigence of class-tastes has all the likelihood of being interpreted as the innate power of biological drives and desires over mental discipline and self-control, a culpable surrender of the self in the face of the overwhelming force of appetite (*"It's stronger than me"*, *"I can't help myself"*, etc.).

6   The playful body

> The social body constrains the way the physical body is perceived. The physical experience of the body, always modified by the social categories through which it is known, sustains a particular view of society [...] As a result of this interaction the body itself is a highly restricted medium of expression. The forms it adopts in movement and repose express social pressures in manifold ways.
>
> (Douglas, 1970: 72)

Where Chapter 4 has focused on the social logic that structures the "outer body" – its size, shape and perceptible features – while Chapter 5 has tackled the social norms governing the "inner body" – its needs, compulsions and repulsions – then this chapter will aim to trace the social rules that govern the particular *uses* of the body, its movements, postures and gestures. It will do so by examining the way in which differences in social position and trajectory structure the more playful uses of the body as expressed in this particular case by the preferences for different types of sports. In fact, unlike other forms of leisure, such as reading a novel, attending a play or watching a movie, in which individuals largely participate in what Defrance calls a 'mimetic reality', sports are a special type of pastime in that they 'situate the practitioner (*amateur*) in a physical action which engages the body in its entirety and exposes it to the forces, frictions and inertia of the physical world' (2003: 49). Instead of providing the type of detached, Platonic enjoyment that accompanies the appropriation of symbolic goods, sports imply a total engagement of the body with all the risks, pleasures and pains this implies. By studying how sports transform the body into a 'highly restricted medium of expression', it should be possible, as Mary Douglas suggests, to shed further light on the social pressures that it undergoes.

Semantic elasticity

If the preceding chapters have repeatedly highlighted the difficulty of adequately grasping the social *meaning* that agents invest in responses to survey-questionnaires, then this applies *a fortiori* to the study of sporting-preferences. In fact, such preferences very often present themselves to the analyst as little more than words which – despite their nominal identity – often lump together quite different *modalities* of engaging in a particular physical activity. Just as the consumption-categories of surveys on household-expenditure often conceal the *dispersion* that flows from the fact that social agents can make "distinguished" uses of the most "common" products (and vice versa), so do statistical taxonomies of sporting-practices often obscure the fact that there are "vulgar" ways of practising "elevated" sports (e.g. tennis in jeans and sneakers on a municipal court) and "refined" ways of practising "vulgar" sports (*futsal* instead of football).

The tacit homogenization of a sporting-practice that results from subsuming it under the same heading ("football", "tennis", etc.) tends to be further compounded by the technical necessities of statistical analysis and especially the logic of aggregation, which often force the analysis to combine practices that have little more in common than a similar instrument (e.g. ball, racket, bicycle, etc.), a shared location (e.g. the "gym") or a common timeframe (e.g. "winter-sports"). Moreover, this degree of 'semantic elasticity' (Bourdieu, 1990a: 164) itself tends to vary from one sport to the next. Unlike *golf*, for instance, which can only be played using specialized equipment, at specific times, in reserved locations, whose access is in turn dependent on a host of official (fees, clothing, etc.) and more hidden (invitations, social capital, etc.) entry-requirements, an activity like *jogging*, which demands no specialized infrastructure or equipment, can be practiced individually and virtually anywhere at any time, allows for a wider range of social uses and is hence considerably more "polysemic". However, the elasticity of a particular sport is never infinite and the possible range of different social uses of a given sport can never be fully detached from the particular relationship to the body it tacitly or explicitly demands:

> We can hypothesize as a general law that a sport is more likely to be adopted by a social class if it does not contradict that class's relation to the body at its deepest and most unconscious level, i.e. the body schema, which is the depository of a whole world view and a whole philosophy of the person and the body.
>
> (Bourdieu, 1984: 217–218)

In fact, the common-sense view of sports as a conduit for "escape" or "release", an arena for the temporary suspension of the restrictions that are imposed on bodily expression in everyday life (most notably those pertaining to aggression and violence, see Elias and Dunning, 1986: 222ff.), should not detract from the fact that even in the situations of relative 'corporeal anomie' provided by sports, social agents never fully abandon the principles of their class *ethos*. Functioning as a *proprioceptive sense of propriety*, it is this *ethos* that defines which movements and gestures are deemed "appropriate" or "vulgar", "distinguished" or "common" in both the *social* and *sexual* meaning of these terms.

Inverting the logic of Bourdieu's hypothesis, one can therefore analyse the specific set of physical requirements and "body-techniques" that define a given sport, in order to gain a better understanding of the "norms" that structure the social uses of the body within a particular class (fraction). In fact, even though sporting-practices are always marked by a degree of indeterminacy, they are nevertheless comprised of a relatively stable set of organizing principles, which always constrain the potential uses that can be made of it. For instance, while the social history of sports like boxing or rugby (see Elias and Dunning, 1986) certainly reveals differences in the "gentlemanly" and "proletarian" uses that have been made of these sports, fact remains that those who enter the ring or step onto the pitch can expect to incur punches, blows, blocks and collisions and hence need to be willing and able to expose their bodies to these potential threats to its integrity.

In this manner, each sport constitutes a specific programme of bodily action that distinguishes it from others and which defines such aspects as the body's *position in physical space* (on the ground as in wrestling or judo, upright and elevated as in tennis), the particular *type of bodily movements* (smooth and gradual as in yoga or tai chi, abrupt and explosive as in boxing), the *rhythm* and *pace* of physical action (slow and self-imposed as in golf, rapid and sustained as in ice-hockey), the *finality* of the performed gestures (abstract and extrinsic as in aerobics, concrete and intrinsic as in badminton) and whether or not physical actions are performed individually (e.g. swimming) or are part of a concerted "team-effort" (e.g. basketball) with all the collective obligations this imposes. In addition to the rules concerning the appropriate bodily *hexis*, there are also the (tacit or explicit) requirements with regards to the body's *physical potential*. These include, first and foremost, the *degree* and *type* of physical strength it presupposes and, more specifically, whether or not it demands the capacity to generate explosive, kinetic energy (e.g. kick-boxing), favours endurance as the capacity for sustained physical exertion (e.g. triathlon), privileges technique and "form" over physical force (e.g. golf) or substitutes a high energy input for a high investment of cultural competence (e.g. sailing, diving, etc.). These rules also include the *degree of physical contact*, both with other players as well as the material world and hence the potential for friction, collision and injury. Such contact can be inscribed at the heart of the sport ("knocking out" or "flooring" one's opponent as in kick-boxing), be incidental or accidental and heavily circumscribed by regulations (e.g. futsal), take place through the intermediary of specific instruments (e.g. fencing) or can be excluded from the practice altogether (e.g. golf). Finally, sports not only tend to differ in the particular *uses* of the body they presuppose, but also in the manner in which they contribute to physically *transforming* the body, either temporarily (bruises, black eyes, sprains, etc.) or durably (increased musculature, weight-loss, "boxer's nose", etc.). As specific assemblies of body-techniques which are characterized by 'the possibilities and impossibilities for the expression of bodily dispositions which they provide' (Bourdieu, 1990a: 162), sporting-practices hence provide a type of "prism" which help to illuminate the more general principles that structure the relationship to the body of different classes and class-fractions. However, before looking at the ways in which class-differences shape the proclivity for *particular* types of sports, it seems important to discuss the factors that influence the probability of practising *any* type of sports.

The need for sports

In fact, analysing the role of class-differences in shaping the "choices" for particular sporting-practices means first of all examining the social conditions of possibility for the development of the free, playful and autonomous relationship to the body that *any* type of sport implies. In fact, as Table 6.1 illustrates, the "need" for sports as a quasi-visceral desire for gratuitous physical exertion and expression proves far from natural and is itself unequally distributed across social space. While a host of factors contribute to generating the demand for sports, one of the central ways in which social necessity helps to shape such demand is through the particular definition of physical force and effort that characterizes the different classes and class-fractions.

In fact, in order to adequately understand the expenditure of effort within the specific context of sporting activities, it seems necessary to address the more general conceptions of physical force – its uses, its value and its aims – that are engendered in different locations in social space. Among working-class men and women and especially among the most precarious fractions of the working-class (i.e. the unskilled workers) who are marked by the lowest rates of sports-involvement, this conception is inseparably tied to the *instrumentalization* of the body through manual or domestic labour which foster a practical conception of the body as 'a tool of labouring intent rather than the body as an end of pleasure-in-itself' (Charlesworth, 2000: 261). In social universes that are marked by the profound scarcity of other forms of capital, the body and its capacity for labour remains one of the most precious resources. Not only is it the central means of social reproduction, but it also constitutes one of the few means to procure any of the precious few "extras" that other classes can simply procure through capital.

However, as will be discussed more fully in Chapter 9, economic constraints alone cannot account for the particularly central role that physical strength and prowess occupy among working-class men and women. In fact, if their conditions of existence force them to make the most intensive uses of their bodies, this economic imperative tends to generalize into a more global '*ethos* of devotion to effort' (Schwartz, 1990: 291) which extends well beyond the sphere of paid labour. The capacity for sustained physical effort and the ability to confront the most degrading effects of labour with self-denial and self-determination is not only a material necessity, but is also a fundamental means of popular self-valorization and an integral element of an accomplished social and sexual identity. In fact, if working-class men and women display such a strong desire for self-assertion through work and effort, this is also because their labour is one of the few resources they *can* spend and spend in quantity. As Schwartz observes, 'giving and deploying one's force without restraint is also proving that one has force in abundance:

Table 6.1 Participation in sporting activities by gender, educational capital and class fraction

	♂				♀			
	% practices regular sports…		% father sports when R between 12–14 yrs.[a]	N	% practices regular sports…		% father sports when R between 12–14 yrs.	N
	…between 12–14 yrs.	…now (>35 yrs.)			…between 12–14 yrs.	…now (>35 yrs.)		
Educational capital								
Less than HS	59[b]	41	10	408	25	35	13	488
HS (technical/vocational)	70	54	12	284	46	47	16	223
HS (general)	65	54	17	70	54	50	15	103
Bachelor	56	67	17	167	56	55	23	188
Master and postgraduate	70[c]	54	21	92	70	61	22	51
Class fraction								
Unskilled workers	64	19	10	73	40	46	21	91
Skilled workers	71	50	22	300	47	37	20	85
Shopkeepers and craftsmen	73	61	27	44	58	50	26	26
Clerical workers	77	60	24	266	56	50	29	393
Teachers	73	72	30	34	68	63	22	57
Higher clerks/junior-executives	80	76	26	109	62	62	23	37
Professions	(82)	(60)	(29)	17	70	65	35	20
Entrepreneurs	69	37	27	48	(53)	(47)	(23)	15
Unemployed	72	58	13	26	40	52	13	40
Housework	(50)	(50)	(0)	2	32	43	12	189
Total	67	51	19	1,386	42	61	20	1,397

Source: GCPS '03–04

Notes
a This heading reads as follows: "The percentage of respondents whose father practiced sports when they themselves were between the age of 12 and 14 is…"
b This numbers reads as follows: "Of men who did not complete high school, 59% practiced regular sports when they were between the age of 12 and 14."
c Numbers in italic denote the strongest tendency for that particular indicator.

The playful body 161

[this] agonistic generosity also symbolizes a wealth of physical resources, and reminds us that we are in a social universe where the body remains one of the most precious goods and reserves and the basis for a mode of self-assertion.

(1990: 293–294)

This often frenetic desire for self-achievement through work and effort (i.e. to "keep busy") is perhaps most evident in all those forms of *over*-investment of time and energy which far surpass their explicitly stated goals, like meticulously tidying an interior that is rarely ever used for social functions or keeping a vegetable-garden even if cheaper and easier ways to procure food have long become available.

> When asked how much time they spent during the week on "heavy household-duties", male unskilled workers (only a quarter of whom indicate they practice sports on a regular basis, see Table 6.1), indicate they spent at least 3 hours (180 minutes) on intense household-activities (gardening, DIY, etc.), compared to 1 hour and 25 minutes among the office clerks, 56 minutes among the teachers, 1 hour and 11 minutes among the junior-executives and members of the professions and 1 hour and 3 minutes among the employers. Among women, such differences are even more pronounced with female unskilled workers spending an average of 2 hours and 15 minutes and skilled workers 1 hour and 40 minutes on "heavy" household-chores, compared to 59 minutes for female office clerks, 48 minutes for the teachers, 33 minutes for junior-executives and 26 minutes for female professionals.
>
> (source: PaS '09)

We will return to this 'ethos of devotion to effort' more fully in Chapter 9. What is important for our current argument, is that this instrumental ethos is itself a key factor in inhibiting the development of a free and disinterested relationship to the body. Contrary to dominant narratives on the "passivity" of the working-class, the low rate of sports-involvement among members of the working-class is explained by the expenditure of physical effort per se, but rather the *gratuitous* and *autotelic* nature of such expenditure. If physical effort is spent, it is always in view of a particular goal and oriented toward practical aims. This makes that any type of exertion that does not serve a clear purpose or produces direct results is quickly perceived as an unwarranted "luxury" and this all the more so, the more the particular actions and aims that define a given sport are themselves seen as abstract and unreal (jogging, aerobics, etc.), that is, purged from any reference to an immediate and tangible outcome.

This conception of sports as a gratuitous and somewhat "irresponsible" pastime also helps to explain why an exception tends to made for those who are largely freed from the responsibilities of adulthood, namely the youngest age-groups (on this point also see Featherstone, 1987). In fact, among members of the working-class and working-class men in particular, involvement in sports appears primarily as the prerogative of *youth* which – being on the side of

162 Modes of embodiment

"nature" and the body – is 'spontaneously and implicitly credited with a sort of *provisional license* expressed, among other ways, in the squandering of an excess of physical (and sexual) energy' (Bourdieu, 1978: 837, *original emphasis*). The simple observation that class-inequalities in the demand for sports tend to widen with age (see Table 6.1) again tends to problematize mechanical explanations in terms of biological ageing or those that invoke a standardized and overly homogenizing conception of the life-course.

> Even though sports are practiced more intensely by those who are situated at the top of the social hierarchy *at any given age*, class-differences among men become considerably more pronounced as respondents get older. Asked if they practiced any sports *between the ages of 12 years old and 14 years old*, almost two thirds (64 per cent) of the male unskilled workers answered affirmatively compared to roughly three quarters (73 per cent) of the office-workers, teachers (77 per cent) and junior-executives (80 per cent). However, when asked if they *currently* practice sports on a regular basis, this figure drops to a quarter of unskilled workers and, if one further restricts the analysis to those respondents that are over the age of 35 years old, it decreases to less than a fifth (19 per cent). Compared to the latter, male office-workers (older than 35 years old) are three times more likely to actively engage in sports, while the teachers and the junior-executives are nearly four times as likely to do so. Furthermore, when questioned on the reasons why they did *not* practice any sports, 21 per cent of male unskilled workers agreed with the proposition "*I'm too old for it*" compared to 6 per cent of shopkeepers, 9 per cent of clerical workers and 13 per cent of the teachers and members of the professions and this despite the fact that they were actually *younger* than the other social categories who provided age as a reason (the average age of unskilled workers being 40 years old, compared to 56 years old for shopkeepers and craftsmen, 57 years old for office clerks, 54 years old for teachers and 55 years old for members of the professions). Similar differences emerge when looking at women's engagement with sports. Again, regardless of age, those who are situated at the top of the class-structure tend to have systematically higher rates of involvement than working-class women, less than half (46 per cent) of which claim to practice sports on a regular basis compared to nearly two-thirds of the female junior-executives (62 per cent) and women from the professions (65 per cent). However, instead of widening with age, class-differences among women tend to become increasingly more attenuated. In addition, working-class women rarely invoke "age" as an important reason for not practising sports (only 2 per cent of unskilled and none of the unskilled workers agreed with the proposition "*I'm too old for it*") and instead they more often indicate factors like a "*lack of time*" (63 per cent and 60 per cent, respectively), "*inconvenient hours*" (38 per cent and 37 per cent) or economic cost (17 per cent and 24 per cent), which is another indication of the fact that they often do not value their own bodies enough to invest in their physical capital.
>
> (source: PaS '09)

It is this entire conception of physical force, of its social functions and the value it procures, that tends to change as one moves from the working to the middle- and dominant classes. As social reproduction becomes less dependent on the performance of the body and instead depends on professional activity that is considerably more "disembodied", both in terms of its physical demands, but also of the risks to which the body is exposed, the meaning of physical effort and exertion shifts dramatically. Instead of being forced upon agents by their conditions of existence, effort tends to take on an *elective* character and in doing so becomes imbued with a radically different set of meanings. If those who are situated at the bottom of the class-structure tend to view their bodies as a means to an end, then among those who occupy more favourable social positions, physical effort becomes increasingly severed from its direct utility.

Instead, it tends to take on a more "autonomous" quality either by transforming the body itself into the object of labour (*"going to the gym"*) or by foregrounding the importance of effort in and of itself. The latter is particularly clear in all the form of aestheticization of pain and suffering (discussed in the second half of this chapter) in which physical discomfort and the risk associated with intense physical action become a means of self-transformation, not to mention a way of 'exciting significance' (Atkinson, 2007) by infusing a modicum of exhilaration in an otherwise highly predictable, "disembodied" and "civilized" everyday life (on this point also see Elias and Dunning, 1986). Such autonomous uses of are also evident in the ways in which effort and exertion are used as a means of alleviating mental stress and anxiety, especially as it pertains to everyday professional life, which prove to be an increasing motivation to practice sports as one rises in the social hierarchy.

> If the conception of sports as a form of "release" or "compensation" from the stress of occupational life is not alien to members of the working-class, it does become considerably more marked as one rises in the social hierarchy. In fact, when presented with several reasons for practising a sport, only a third (34 per cent) of men *and* women who did not finish secondary education indicated they did so "*as a compensation for all the work I have*", compared to 76 per cent of women and 56 per cent of men with a Master's or postgraduate degree. Similar differences are found in terms of class-fraction with the percentage who reported they viewed sports as a psychological outlet or source of compensation going from 58 per cent of unskilled workers (42 per cent among men, 66 per cent among women), 44 per cent of skilled workers, 61 per cent of the office clerks, 60 per cent of the teachers, 79 per cent of the junior-executives to 74 per cent of those in the professions.
>
> (source: PaS '09)

A social morphology of sporting-preferences

While the distribution of the overall probability of practising sports provides some insights into the ways in which class circumscribes the relationship to the

164   Modes of embodiment

body, it still obscure the social oppositions that are expressed in the preference for different *types* of sports or, equally important, different *ways* of practising the same sport. In fact, the very social definition of the term "sports", as understood by respondents, tends to encompass everything from the occasional stroll or bike-ride through town ("doing the rounds"), the weekly ritual of "going to the gym", the collective discipline of training twice a week and playing a match on Sundays to the quasi-professional devotion to practices which – like triathlon – can become the focal point of an entire lifestyle. Needless to say, such a broad conception of "practising a sport" tends to efface a host of pertinent differences between the social classes. To get a sense of these differences, the analysis compared the preference of different social groups across a wide range of sporting-preferences (Table 6.2).

The analysis of these preferences shows how they are first of all expressive of the logic of the *sexual* division of labour and the system of oppositions it inscribes in bodies of the type open/closed, centrifugal/centripetal, active/passive, free/restrained, fast/slow, extroverted/introverted etc. In fact, different sports are unequally suited for the expression of sexual dispositions such as the *masculine* proclivity for physical competition and confrontation, for activities that allow for the display of physical prowess, strength and endurance or, inversely, the *feminine* interest in appearance and bodily "form", that is, for physical activity that is aimed at the cultivation of the body itself or which transforms the body into a means of expression (e.g. dancing, yoga). If one hence ranks sports in terms of their gender-ratio a series of systematic oppositions emerge. On end of the spectrum, one finds male-dominated sports like football (only 8 per cent of those who chose it as their favourite sport are women), which is played *outdoors*, in full exposure to the "elements" (heat, cold, rain, etc.), in which physical performance is oriented *towards* and measured *against* a concrete and clearly defined objective, which provides ample opportunity for physical *confrontation* ("duels", tackling, sliding, etc.) and values both explosive strength as well as physical endurance. On the other extreme, one finds strongly "feminized" activities like aerobics or yoga (97 per cent and 93 per cent, respectively are women) which are purged from any type of direct competition, confrontation or even contact between their practitioners, which privilege form, technique and execution over strength, endurance and exertion and which often reduce physical action to a system of abstract movements – i.e. divorced from any immediate aim or practical purpose – oriented towards often equally abstract goals ("stronger abs", "inner calm", etc.) that tend to be wholly *extrinsic* to the activity itself.

To these two extremes correspond two diametrically opposed relations to the body, rooted in two contrasting experiences of social power. On the one hand, an *agonistic* conception, in which the body functions as both "instrument" and "obstacle", as that which is simultaneously valued for its capacity to *generate* physical force, as well as its ability to *withstand* physical forces (blows, kicks, fatigue, friction, etc.) and hence something that one works as much *with* as *against*. This is particularly clear in the masculine proclivity for "risky" sports

Table 6.2 Sports-preferences by educational capital, class fraction and social trajectory (%)

	Mountain-biking	Football	"Outdoor"-sports*	Golf	Squash, badminton	Martial arts, boxing	Cycling	Tennis	Jogging
Gender-ratio (♂/♀)	100/0	92/8[a]	84/16	82/18	78/22	72/28	62/38	57/43	52/48
N	22	105	25	11	27	28	319	58	177
Educational capital									
Less than HS	1[b]	4	2	1	0	1	37	3	5
HS (technical/vocational)	4	9[c]	2	0	2	2	22	2	12
HS (academic)	0	6	2	1	3	2	24	5	13
Bachelor	2	7	2	1	3	1	16	5	*21*
Master or postgraduate	0	7	2	4	2	2	15	*11*	19
Class fraction									
Unskilled workers and farmers	2	7	0	0	0	0	15	0	13
Skilled workers	6	*18*	3	0	3	2	21	5	13
Shopkeepers and craftsmen	3	3	*10*	0	0	0	15	3	18
Clerical workers	1	9	2	1	3	1	17	3	20
Teachers (prim./sec./higher)	3	12	2	0	0	5	9	5	*22*
Junior-executives	3	4	1	2	4	1	27	7	20
Professions	0	9	0	9	5	0	9	9	18
Commercial employers	0	13	4	0	0	0	33	4	13
Social trajectory									
Upward	1	7	1	2	2	2	16	5	*19*
Stable	2	7	2	1	2	1	26	4	12
Downward	2	*14*	4	2	6	4	22	6	8
Total	2	8	2	1	2	1	23	4	13

Notes
* Includes sailing, rock-climbing, windsurfing, kiteboarding, etc.
a This figure reads as follows: "Of those who indicated football as their favourite sport, 92% are men and 8% are women."
b This figure reads as follows: "1% of those who did not finish secondary education indicated mountain-biking as their favourite sport."
c Figures in italic indicate the strongest tendency in a column.

Table 6.2 (continued) Sports-preferences by educational capital, class fraction and social trajectory (%)

	Volleyball	Basket-, net- and handball	Walking, hiking	Fitness, gym*	Swimming	Equestrianism	Gymnastics	Aerobics	N
Gender-ratio (♂/♀)	52/48	50/50	47/53	41/58	38/62	33/67	8/92	8/92	
N	21	23	151	120	101	25	37	75	1,388
Educational capital									
Less than HS	1	1	17	6	8	1	5	4	362
HS (technical/vocational)	1	2	12	9	7	3	1	5	393
HS (academic)	2	1	13	8	9	1	5	5	112
Bachelor	3	1	8	9	5	2	3	8	302
Master or postgraduate	4	3	4	13	5	1	0	8	130
Class fraction									
Unskilled workers and farmers	2	6	15	7	17	0	7	7	54
Skilled workers	0	1	7	7	5	2	3	2	173
Shopkeepers and craftsmen	0	0	13	10	13	8	0	3	39
Clerical workers	3	1	4	13	6	2	1	8	345
Teachers (prim./sec./higher)	*10*	2	2	7	7	0	2	*10*	59
Junior-executives	2	3	6	7	4	4	1	3	102
Professions	0	0	5	9	5	5	5	9	22
Commercial employers	0	0	4	*19*	8	4	0	0	24
Social trajectory									
Upward	4	2	*12*	8	4	1	2	9	166
Stable	1	1	11	8	7	2	3	5	961
Downward	0	0	6	2	8	4	*4*	4	50
Total	2	2	11	9	7	2	3	5	100

Source: PaS '09

Note
* Also includes weight-lifting and bodybuilding.

(motorsports, skydiving, mountain-biking, etc.) in which bodily integrity is itself at stake. On the other hand, one finds an *aesthetic* or *therapeutic* conception which is rooted in the experience of the body as a perceptible "form", an object for the scrutiny and enjoyment of others which defines feminine being as a "being-perceived". Instead of being used as a means to an end, projecting outwards towards the completion of clearly defined goals, the body is treated as an end in itself, judged in terms of its perceptible qualities or by its ability to "signify" through it gestures and postures (as in ballet or other forms of dance).

More importantly, this opposition does not only structure the appropriate *uses* of the body, but also helps to define the type of *visible* profits that men and women come to expect from practising a particular sport. In fact, the system of oppositions that defines movement as open or closed, extraverted or introverted is itself derived from the more basic oppositions between the large and the small, the heavy and the light, the expansive and the introverted which inform the masculine demand for sports that produce a big, muscular body and the feminine desire for a slender and lean physique. Moreover, such differences do not only lead to a preference for different *types* of sporting-practices, but also inform the different *meanings* that men and women invest in the same practice such as "*going to the gym*".

> If women already have a higher probability of visiting a gym (only a quarter of our sample claimed to have never set foot in a gym, compared to almost half of the men) and have a slightly higher frequency of visits than men (more than three quarters claim to visit or have visited the gym at least once a week, compared to two thirds of the men), the most striking differences between the sexes are revealed by their actual reasons for attending. For women, weight-*loss* is by far the most important motivation with nearly 40 per cent of women indicating they went to the gym in order to "*lose weight*" (38 per cent), which increases to nearly half of women if one also includes those respondents who indicated they wanted to "*maintain my figure*" (10 per cent). This stands in shrill contrast to men, who most often invoked weight- and especially muscle-*gain* as their most important reason for visiting a gym. Nearly a third of male respondents indicated they went to a gym to "*become more muscular*" (32 per cent), followed by "*health*" (23 per cent) and "*improving physical fitness*" (15 per cent), while "*losing weight*" or "*maintaining my figure*" were among the reasons that were least often chosen.
>
> (source: BoS '10)

Form and force

However, in order to avoid regressing to essentialist definitions of Masculinity and Femininity, it should be stressed that the manner in which sexual dispositions inform sporting (or other) practices, is itself further specified according to social position. For instance, while women in general are much more likely than men to engage in physical activity that explicitly centres on the cultivation of the body itself and more often invoke weight-loss or the improvement of appearance

168 *Modes of embodiment*

as reasons for practising a sport, this "typically" feminine concern with physical form is itself unevenly distributed between the social classes. Like the social distribution of weight-concern and dietary preferences discussed in the last two chapters, the degree in which sports-preferences are defined by the explicit search for extrinsic profits like beauty and slimness, strongly depends on the material and symbolic rewards that women can reasonably expect from such properties, that is, on their access to occupational markets in which appearance can function as a form of capital.

> Queried about their most important reasons for practising a sport, housewives less often agreed with the proposition "*In order to lose weight*" (25 per cent) and "*It makes my body more attractive*" (36 per cent), than women who were employed (37 per cent and 51 per cent, respectively). The latter are themselves further differentiated according to occupational category with 37 per cent of female unskilled workers, 29 per cent of skilled workers, 47 per cent of office-workers and 46 per cent of junior-executives providing weight-loss as a reason, while 48 per cent of unskilled and 36 per cent of skilled workers invoked a more attractive physique, compared to 53 per cent and 57 per cent of clerical workers and junior-executives (source: PaS '09). In addition, our own survey revealed that while more than two thirds of the housewives (70 per cent) and female unskilled workers (65 per cent) claimed they had *never* been to a gym, this figure drops to a fifth of office clerks (21 per cent), a third of the teachers (33 per cent) and junior-executives (31 per cent) and less than one out of five (15 per cent) of the professionals and senior-executives (although the low number of observations for this category [N = 17] make generalization tentative). The analysis of women's motives for going to the gym also confirm the observations made in Chapter 4, namely that it is especially among *middle-class* women that one finds the strongest desire for weight-loss. More than half of women from the *lower* middle-classes (office clerks, sales clerks, etc.) and 46 per cent of those from the upper fringes of the middle-class indicate they went to the gym to either "lose weight" or to "maintain my figure", making it by far their dominant motive for gym-attendance (if this also applies to half of working-class women, it should not be forgotten that they already constitute a highly over-selected group, given their overall low gym-attendance).

Similarly, the "typically" masculine proclivity to treat sports as an arena for (regulated) physical confrontation and an occasion to demonstrate physical strength and prowess tends to take on a more or less sublimated form depending on men's class-position. This can already be seen in the unequal propensity with which men who occupy different social positions equate masculinity with muscularity. In fact, two quite different conceptions of masculinity, of the relationship to the social world, to the body and to time are condensed into the opposition between so-called "anaerobic" exercises like weight-lifting – specifically aimed at building muscle *mass* and increasing the capacity for short-term, explosive

The playful body 169

strength – and "aerobic" activities like jogging or swimming aimed at increasing overall "fitness" and physical endurance. The former centres on physical activity that consists of short bouts of intense, high-resistance exercises (*"high weights, low reps"*) whose logic most closely emulates the movements and postures of the labouring body (lifting, pulling, pushing, etc.), not to mention the agonistic relationship to the world and to the self it implies (as exemplified by the body-building jargon of *"attacking the weights"* or *"bombing the muscle"*, see Fussell, 1991). The latter, like jogging for instance, tends to consist of longer periods of physical exertion which are often accompanied by a far-reaching rationalization of the relationship to the body. This rationalization applies to the activity itself, which is often minutely organized according to pre-constructed schemes and schedules – gradually building up effort over time, strictly timing periods of exertion and relaxation, alternating between high- and low-intensity exertion ("interval-training"), etc. – but also to elementary bodily functions like respiration and heart-rate. These become subjected to strict regulation in order to achieve quite abstract goals that are themselves often couched in the language of scientificity (optimizing oxygenation, increase the burning of fat, building up stamina, etc.).

> When asked about their most important reason for going to the gym, 46 per cent of manual workers, 47 per cent of those in the lowest income-categories and 44 per cent of those with a secondary degree in technical or vocational training indicated they wanted 'to become bigger and more muscular', compared to 27 per cent of the office clerks, 30 per cent of the junior-executives, 25 per cent of those in the highest income brackets (i.e. a family income of more than 4,000 euros a month) and a third of those with a master's or postgraduate degree (34 per cent). At the same time, the number of men who indicated they go to the gym for reasons of health or *"to increase stamina"* varied in an almost inverse manner. While only 6 per cent of manual workers, none of those with no formal education or a degree in technical or vocational training or those in the lowest income-brackets selected this as their most important reason, this increases to 15 per cent of the office clerks, a third of the junior-executives (33 per cent) and 30 per cent of those with a Bachelor's degree (but only 6 per cent of those with a Master's or postgraduate degree). At this point it might also be pertinent to recall the classification of body-types presented in Chapter 4, where working-class men not only most often chose the most muscular physique as their personal ideal, but also most often indicated the most slender silhouette as their *least* preferred body type. Similarly, they also proved to be among those groups who indicated they wanted to *gain* weight.

Again, these different manners of investing in the body are rooted in two contrasting philosophies of time and the future (see Chapter 3). In fact, while the various fitness-programmes and "work out"-formulas are often equally abstract in the *type* of physical action they presuppose – i.e. a series of discontinuous, repetitive and mechanical movements often directed at isolated parts of the body (*"working the abs"*, *"toning the calves"*, etc.) and hence 'entirely opposed to the

Table 6.3 Gym-attendance by gender, educational capital and class fraction (%)

	Attended/attends gym...				Most important reason for going to gym						
	...never	...in the past	...now	N	Lose weight	Gain muscle	Health	Improve fitness	Relaxing	Maintain figure	N
1 Men											
Less than HS	75[a]	21	4	57	(13)[b]	(13)	(53)	(0)	(13)	(7)	15
HS (technical/vocational)	34	51	15	41	7	44	15	15	15	4	27
HS (academic)	56	41	3	32	(7)	(21)	(29)	(14)	(21)	(0)	14
Bachelor	37	51	13	101	8	30	14	30	3	8	63
Master or postgraduate	30	52	18	104	11	34	26	6	14	1	70
Working-class	58	33	9	43	(6)	(35)	(18)	(6)	(18)	(6)	17
Lower-middle-class	43	43	14	72	10	34	24	12	12	2	41
Upper-middle-class	41	52	7	128	11	24	22	27	8	3	74
Upper class	31	48	21	52	6	33	31	17	14	6	35
Total	43	45	12	335	10	32	23	15	11	4	167
2 Women											
Less than HS	69	24	7	70	(32)	(0)	(21)	(11)	(32)	(5)	19
HS (technical/vocational)	24	66	11	75	40	4	11	11	15	13	53
HS (academic)	41	48	12	42	17	0	17	22	17	22	23
Bachelor	21	65	14	142	44	1	19	14	10	7	111
Master or postgraduate	20	61	19	149	36	1	19	20	8	9	118
Working-class	62	30	8	37	(43)	(0)	(7)	(14)	(29)	(7)	14
Lower-middle-class	24	62	14	161	42	3	17	12	10	11	116
Upper-middle-class	24	61	15	111	39	0	21	18	10	7	84
Upper class	17	69	14	65	28	2	17	25	11	11	53
Total	27	60	16	521	38	1	18	16	12	10	267

Source: BoS '10

Notes
a This number reads as follows: "75% of men who did not finish high school never went to a gym."
b Figures in brackets indicate that the number of observations was too low to make meaningful inferences.

total, practically oriented movements of everyday life' (Bourdieu, 1984: 214) – they are unequally abstract in the specific *outcome* or "return-on-investment" they envision. In the former case, these take the form of the short-term, tangible and visible profits of increased size and musculature (often aided by the use of supplements or steroids to enhance "growth" and produce "quick results"). In the latter, it is oriented towards the long-term, immaterial and invisible benefits of physical "well-being", a highly abstract notion which often takes the form of a purely "negative gain", such as a delay in the effects of ageing and bodily decay.

Hard and soft

The above mentioned examples illustrate that the class-related properties associated with different types of sports are, here as elsewhere, inseparably tied to their sexual properties. In fact, the same sets of oppositions that structure *sexual* differences in sporting-preferences (i.e. function vs. form, intrinsic vs. extrinsic profits, strength vs. style, etc. – also inform social and especially *class-*differences in the perception and judgment of different types of sports. Whereas popular sports such as weight-lifting, boxing or even football are often branded as "vulgar" and "violent" in their glorification of the typically masculine values of confrontation, strength and risk-taking, the sports that are more often practiced by those who are situated at the top of the social hierarchy – characterized by their high degree of euphemization of physical violence and physical exertion – are often labelled as "dull", or "effeminate", especially when perceived from the bottom of social space. These dual properties of sports allow us to raise a more general point about the qualification of practices and properties pertaining to the body. In fact, as the previous chapters have aimed to show, the sexual and social characteristics of sporting (or other) practices can be said to be the product of two quite *distinct* logics. On the one hand, the logic of *sexual* domination, which equates the masculine with the assertive, the competitive and the confrontational, in short, with the display of physical force and hence with the "body-as-subject", while instead orienting women towards practices that are introverted, non-competitive and centred on the management of physical form, that is, of the "body-as-object". On the other, the logic of *social* domination which induces dominant groups to assert their distance from necessity through a concern with style and manner, while forcing dominated groups to adopt an instrumental attitude towards their body and leads them to judge it in terms of its skills and force, that is, its functionality. However, if the social and sexual characteristics of given practices are rooted in quite different logics – i.e. the concern with physical form as a means of enhancing sexual desirability *or* as an instrument of social distinction – in everyday practice and perception, these characteristics very often converge. This convergence is in no small part due to the fact that the perceptual schemata that are used to qualify properties, practices and persons – as embedded in the everyday words used to express these oppositions (i.e. high/low, large/small, heavy/light, hard/soft, fast/slow, etc.), but also in the type of bodily movements and postures that define them (expanding/contracting, rising/falling, upright/bent, etc.) – are themselves marked by a degree of indeterminacy that enables them to shift between the semantic registers of class and gender. It is hence no coincidence that as one rises from the working to the middle and dominant classes that sports become increasingly more "feminized" (as indicated, amongst others, by their gender-ratio). As Bourdieu notes:

> [T]he most distinctive practices are those which ensure the most distanced relation to the adversary; they are also the most aestheticized, in so far as violence is more euphemized in them, and form and formalities win out over force and function.
>
> (Bourdieu, 1990a: 157)

Another way of looking at this is that sporting-practices tend to become more "disembodied", the higher one rises in social space. This means first and foremost that the actual degree of physical contact between the players – whether it be intentional (tackling, striking, flooring, etc.) or unintentional (touching, stroking, colliding, etc.) – tends to systematically decrease as one moves from sports that are popular among members of the working-class (and especially working-class *men*) to those that are more often practiced by the middle and dominant classes. The same applies to the type of effort and strength they require with popular sports often calling for a more sustained, high-paced type of physical exertion, while those that are practiced higher-up in the social hierarchy often impose a stricter regulation of effort and an overall slower pace of physical action.

This can be illustrated by the case of the so-called "ball-sports" which methodological necessity (or convenience?) often lumps together into one category. In fact, within this quite heterogeneous ensemble, the analysis suggests a distinction between on the one hand, sports such as football, basketball or handball and, on the other, those like volleyball and, *a fortiori*, tennis. While the former, which prove slightly more popular among members of the working-class, provide ample room for the "rough and tumble" of direct physical confrontation (always liable of bursting into open conflict) with players using their bodies to tackle, pass or block their opponents; the latter, which are more often played by members of the middle and dominant classes, effectively prevent any physical contact between adversaries. Incidentally, these different types of ball-sports are also marked by their own distinct *tempo*. Compared to football or basketball, which are marked by a quicker pace and (hence) a more continuous expenditure of energy, volleyball or tennis are subjected to a more strict sequencing (i.e. the ritual of "game-set-match") in which bouts of intense action alternate with periods of rest and preparation.

> Ball-sports also illustrate the importance of class-differences in the *modality* of practice. This is particularly important when trying to account for the differences in social recruitment between sports that often appear highly similar in nature, such as football and "futsal" (or indoor-football). Whereas the

former is played outdoors, in most weather conditions (hence fully exposing players to the "elements"), on a large pitch and provides ample opportunity for direct, physical confrontation (tackling, sliding, etc.), the latter is played indoors, on a smaller field, for a shorter period of time and imposes strict prohibitions on physical contact between the players. In addition, the use of a smaller ball and harder surface requires more "ball-control" and favours shorter passes and tighter turns. Overall, futsal is hence marked by a stronger euphemization of violence and physical confrontation, places less emphasis on strength and endurance and instead foregrounds skill, technique and form, which is in turn reflected in the social characteristics of its practitioners: 41 per cent have a degree in higher-education (18 per cent of which have a master's degree), compared to 33 per cent of those who name football as their favourite (only 8 per cent at the master- or postgraduate-level) and while it is still very popular among working-class men (47 per cent of its practitioners are unskilled or skilled workers, compared to 43 per cent of football-players), it is played more often than football among members of the professions and the employers (12 per cent compared to 3 per cent of football-players) and especially among the teachers (18 per cent as opposed to 6 per cent of football-players), a category that is otherwise marked by a fairly low proclivity for any type of competitive "team-sports". The fact that the average age of football-players is 28 years old, while that of futsal-players is 31 years old shows that differences in the preference for these sports cannot be attributed to generational or age-differences alone.

(source: PaS '09)

The sexualized properties of sports not only determine the distribution of sports between the classes, but also shape their differential preference among class-fractions. It is hence no coincidence that as one moves from the farmers and manual workers to the *petit-bourgeoisie* and the dominant class and, within the latter, from the commercial employers and members of the professions through the junior-executives to the teachers, that sports tend to become both more balanced in terms of their ratio of female to male participants *and* more strongly euphemized the element of competition and aggression. Again, the analysis suggests an opposition between the more ascetic relationship to the body of the culturally dominant fractions of the middle- and upper-classes and the more hedonistic ethos of their wealthiest fractions. The dispositions of the former find their clearest realization in an activity like running or jogging which is by far the most popular sport among teachers (more than one out of five claim it as their favourite). Not only is it a type of physical activity that is "austere" and "ascetic" in that it requires relatively little in terms of specialized and expensive equipment (like scuba-diving or sailing) or access to reserved and exclusive locations or clubs (like tennis or golf), but also in the importance it attributes to self-denial and effort for effort's sake. Privileging stamina over strength, it replaces the proclivity for physical confrontation and competition – often associated with working-class machismo or the competitiveness of the world of business – with the values of *self*-control and *self*-discipline.

> While there proves little variation between the teachers and the office clerks or junior-executives (the other two groups who are among the most avid runners) in terms of the *frequency* with which they go running (47 per cent of the teachers and office-workers claim to go at least 3 times a week, compared to 50 per cent of the junior-executives), their actual *reasons* for doing so prove more clearly distinguished. Overall, the teachers appear to be less concerned with the *extrinsic* and above all *visible* profits that running is thought to provide. Only a quarter (24 per cent) indicated *"weight-loss"* as an important reason, compared to 43 per cent of the office clerks and 55 per cent of the junior-executives, while roughly a third (36 per cent) invoked *"a nicer figure"* compared to 46 per cent and 42 per cent of the latter, respectively. The proportion of respondents who indicated they most often went running *"with friends"* similarly goes from 39 per cent of the office clerks, 32 per cent of the junior-executives to 29 per cent of the teachers, while the number who reported they tended to run *"alone"* varies almost inversely from 47 per cent of the office clerks to 57 per cent of the teachers to 70 per cent of the junior-executives.
>
> (source: PaS '09)

The distance from material necessity that characterizes economically dominant social positions in turn finds its expression in an activity like golf which – even more than tennis, which has been more affected by symbolic "devaluation-through-popularization" – still retains much its exclusive character. It is after all an activity which everywhere aims to maximize *distance*. Distance first of all between players and non-players, which are separated by barriers that are at once social and physical. Social, since practice is marked by a host of explicit and hidden entry-requirements, themselves dependent on the possession of the appropriate amount of capital (especially economic and social). Physical, since the sport itself takes place in reserved, exclusive spaces that tend to be the perfect realization of the bourgeois vision of nature as an orderly and harmonious "landscape", purged from any references to the social world. Distance also between the players themselves with any form of direct physical contact being strictly forbidden. Finally, distance also in the relationship of the player to his or her own body which is purged from any visible references to physical effort, haste and exertion (sweating, panting, etc.) and instead takes the form of a casual and detached attitude, both in its rhythms and execution (gauging wind and distance, contemplating the appropriate club, etc.). Overall, golf constitutes a form of physical activity in which force and function tend to give away fully to style and form (i.e. perfecting one's "stroke") and in which the cultivation of physical capital tends to be overshadowed by the accumulation and maintenance of other resources, most notably *social* capital, especially in professional relationships.

> Those who claimed golf as their favourite sport were also those who most often indicated they practiced it with *"colleagues"* (18 per cent, compared to 8 per cent of those who chose football, 5 per cent of those who practice running and 1 per cent of those who chose swimming) and most often

reported they practiced the sport "*in order to meet new people*" (68 per cent, compared to 62 per cent of footballers, 38 per cent of runners and 30 per cent of those who indicated swimming as their favourite sport). At the same time, they prove considerable less concerned with its presumed effects on the body with only 8 per cent reporting they practiced golf in order to "*lose weight*" (compared to 44 per cent of the footballers and the runners and 35 per cent of the swimmers) and only a quarter indicated they practiced golf to "*obtain a more attractive physique*" (compared to a third of the footballers, 45 per cent of the runners and 41 per cent of the swimmers).

(source: PaS '09)

The sacred and the profane

For a full understanding of the manner in which class-tastes shape the preference for particular types of sports, it is once again important to move beyond a purely synchronic perspective and also include the structuring effects of social *trajectory*. This can be illustrated by examining the sporting-preferences of *upwardly* mobile agents. In fact, the same belief in individual effort and personal merit as foundations of social success, the asceticist faith in self-denial and the propensity to defer immediate gratifications in favour of future gains, which colour such diverse domains of practice as marital and reproductive strategies, educational choices, monetary investments or dietary preferences can also be found in their more playful uses of the body. It is in fact no coincidence that those who are marked by an upward social trajectory also show a strong proclivity for those types of sports, like jogging and especially long-distance running or triathlon, that could be qualified as "ascetic" in that they tend to foreground stamina and endurance, that is, "effort for effort's sake", over brute strength or pure technique. In fact, contrary to sports like football or tennis, in which the body is primarily evaluated in its capacity as an "instrument" honed toward skilfully completing particular goals or negotiating specific obstacles, these sports are distinguished by the degree to which they constitute the body *itself* as the main "goal" or "obstacle". More specifically, their stress on *endurance*, as the ability to rationally manage energy-expenditure over prolonged periods of exertion (instead of releasing it in short, explosive bursts), shifts the focus away from bodily effort as a means to an end and instead constitutes the body itself as a "limit" or a "boundary" that needs to be pushed or overcome (the infamous "breaking through the wall"). In addition, these sports are also determined by their highly *individualistic* character. Rather than being the product of a collective and concerted effort (with all the dependencies and sharing out of responsibility this implies), success is often measured according to purely personal and often quite abstract standards (improving one's own time, controlling one's heart-rate, etc.).

> Compared to those who occupy a "stable" position (i.e. one that corresponds to the modal trajectory of their class), the upwardly mobile not only tend to have a higher probability of practising any given sport (only 41 per cent

indicated they practice no sports whatsoever, compared to half of those who occupy a stable position or are caught in a downward trajectory), but they also tend to practice a larger number of different sports (35 per cent indicated they regularly practiced two sports or more, compared to 25 per cent of those who are marked by a stable position and 23 per cent of those who have "negative" slope). More importantly, the ascetic dispositions of the upwardly mobile manifest themselves in the preference for particular *types* of sports. For instance, nearly one out of five (19 per cent) of the *upwardly* mobile respondents picked "*jogging*" as their favourite sport, which is more than double the number of the *downwardly* mobile (8 per cent) and still considerably above the proportion of respondents who are marked by a "*stable*" position (12 per cent). This asceticism also colours the *modality* of practice of a given sport. For instance, when one isolates those respondents that indicated jogging as their most frequent type of sporting activity (N=154), nearly three quarters (72 per cent) of those who qualify as "*upwardly mobile*" indicated they most often practiced this sport "*alone*", compared to half (52 per cent) of those who are marked by a "s*table*" social position, while only 10 per cent of the former and 17 per cent of the latter indicated to ran as part of a "*club*". At the same time, those who are upwardly mobile also appear as more devout practitioners with 58 per cent indicating they run at least three times a week or more, compared to 47 per cent of those who occupy a stable position. Similar differences are found among those who indicated "*cycling*" as their favourite sport (N=286), where 59 per cent and 7 per cent of the upwardly mobile reported to cycle alone or as a member of a club, respectively, compared to 49 per cent and 17 per cent of those occupying a stable social position.

(source: PaS '09)

As Atkinson's (2007) sociography of Canadian triathletes has shown, it is no wonder that these sports provide a privileged mode of expression for the asceticist dispositions of the *aspiring* fractions of the middle-classes. He argues that triathlon in particular, with its combination of activities that most strongly favour endurance over strength or technique (i.e. running, swimming or cycling), its celebration of "training" (*askesis*) and effort for effort's sake and its demand for a high degree of rationalization of everyday life (diet, exercise, etc.) resonates most strongly with the "active" lifestyle and achievement-oriented ethos of these groups. If these groups prove so clearly drawn to these types of sports, it is perhaps because they enable them to re-enact (and perhaps resolve) the tensions and dramas that mark their broader social careers. It is the latter which incline them to constantly push themselves beyond their limits, to place their future aspirations above their current means and, above all, to rely on *individual* effort in attaining such aspirations. This could explain their proclivity for sporting-practices that instead of favouring an agonistic attitude towards others (i.e. out-manoeuvring and defeating an opponent) or towards the barriers and obstacles of the physical world, displace this attitude primarily onto the relationship between the agent and his or her body. It is the ability to, more than anything else, master and overcome the resistance of one's *own* body which becomes central. This quasi-Cartesian conception of sports as a site for the exertion of Mind over Matter, of individual willpower and self-determination over the inherent inertia and recalcitrance of the body is particularly evident in the manner in which triathlon (like long distance-running or "fell-running") hinges on an aestheticization of pain and suffering. In fact, instead of being something that needs to be avoided at all costs (e.g. yoga) or simply be accepted and endured as inevitable to the practice itself (e.g. boxing), pain and discomfort are sensations that are often actively sought out. This attitude is aptly summarized by Haruki Murakami: 'Pain is inevitable. Suffering is optional' (2008: 5). It is precisely in the ability to push on *despite* the warning-signals of a body that indicates it has reached its limits, that its practitioners often find a source of personal pride and achievement. When confronted with such contemporary forms of "mortification of the flesh", one is reminded of Durkheim who famously wrote that 'the way in which he braves pain is the best indication of the greatness of man.

> Never does he rise more brilliantly above himself than when he subdues his nature and makes it follow a path contrary to its inclinations. By so doing, he singles himself out from among all other creatures who blindly go where pleasure calls, and he gives himself a special place in the world. Pain is the sign that certain ties that bind him to the profane world are broken; because it is proof that he has partially freed himself from this world, it is considered an instrument of deliverance.
> (2001 [1912]: 234)

The "profane" can here be understood (in Durkheim's sense) as referring to everything that is "natural" in the individual and hence forms the basis of her a-social, egoistic drives and tendencies which are antithetical to the very notion of Society which, in Durkheim's view, always implies a given degree of individual sacrifice and suffering ('So that we may fulfil our duties towards society, we must be prepared to violate our instincts at times – to go against the grain of our natural inclinations' [2001: 235]). However, it can also be taken, as Chapter 2 has argued, as that which all individuals have in "common", namely that which unites them on the same biological level. According to this interpretation, going against one's "nature" and subduing the "profane" is also a means of distinguishing oneself from others.[1] In fact, Atkinson shows how triathletes' narratives are often suffused with the logic of distinction. Not only do they define their own lifestyle against those whose physical passivity betrays an inherent lack of self-discipline and an inability to resist the manifold temptations offered by "consumer culture" (the "couch potatoes" who *"blindly go where pleasure calls"*), but they also stress the "intelligent" and "civilized" aspects of their own sport against those types of physical activity which, like football or ice-hockey, are seen as a vulgar display of brute force and a blind squandering of strength and energy.

To conclude...

Needless to say, a full understanding of the often intricate ways in which class-dynamics shape the playful uses of the body would need to go well beyond the stenographic description provided in the preceding pages. Given the limitations in both the quantity and quality of the data that were available, this chapter has offered little more than an outline of an analysis to would demand a more in-depth examination of the homologies between the space of sporting-practices, or, more precisely, 'the space of the different finely analysed modalities of the practice of different sports, and the space of social positions' (Bourdieu, 1990a: 158). Having said that, the last three chapters have hopefully provided the reader with an emerging sense of how the different divisions and oppositions that the analysis has uncovered in each of these different aspects of the relationship to the body fit together. The third and final part of this study will be devoted to drawing out these inter-relationships in a more systematic fashion. In fact, if the last three chapters have in a sense "decomposed" the relationship to the body as it manifests itself in some of its most pertinent dimensions, then the following three chapters will aim to "recompose" it, by showing how the concern with the body's size and shape, the preference for particular qualities and quantities of food and the more playful uses of the body are themselves part of a relatively coherent system of practices and beliefs, a 'somatic culture' (Boltanski, 1971), which is itself intelligibly linked to the more general ethos that characterizes the different social classes.

Note

1 Durkheim actually seems to play on the indeterminacy of these two senses of the "profane" in his description of the role of ascetic figures: 'Such is the historical role of the great ascetics. When their acts and deeds are analysed in detail, we wonder what useful end they serve. It is striking how extreme they are in their professed contempt for all that usually excites men's passions. But these extremes are necessary to sustain in the faithful a *sufficient disgust for easy living and ordinary pleasures*. An elite must set the goal too high so that the masses should not set it too low. Some must go to extremes so that the average man should stay at an appropriate level' (2001 [1912]: 235, *my emphasis*).

Part III
Class bodies

7 Relaxation in tension

What is noble?

- Care for the most external things, in so far as is this care forms a boundary, keeps distant, guards against confusion.
- Apparent frivolity in word, dress, bearing, through which a stoic severity and self-constraint protects itself against all immodest inquisitiveness.
- Slowness of gesture and of glance...
- Pleasure in forms; taking under protection everything formal, the conviction that politeness is one of the great virtues; mistrust for letting oneself go in any way...

(Nietzsche, 1968 [1885]: 496–497)

The preceding chapters have aimed to show that a focus on *embodiment* is often indispensable in trying to account for the central paradox that the various ways of using, perceiving and judging the body clearly reveal a *social* logic and structure, while at the same time presenting themselves with all the ineluctable necessity of an immutable nature. More importantly, they have tried to demonstrate that because class-differences become inscribed in the body, that is, are at once individualized and naturalized, that there is often no need for the conscious, intentional assertion of social distance and that social agents very often prove to be distinguished *despite* themselves. While this applies to *all* social groups, it seems particularly important to underline when dealing with dominant tastes and the dominant relationship to the body. If the logic and language of exposition often force one to describe dominant tastes "as if" they were the product of a conspicuous attempt at signalling difference, then the very notion of a '*sense* of distinction' – that 'acquired disposition which functions with the obscure necessity of instinct' (Bourdieu, 1984: 499) – serves to highlight the fact that dominant tastes are objectively distinguished without any conscious effort at distinction. In fact, the embodied character of class-tastes already tends to preclude the question of whether distinction is "sincere" or "contrived", "authentic" or "cynical", "natural" or "conspicuous". As long as the generative principle behind the most everyday lifestyle-choices is located at the level of explicit choice and conscious deliberation, the very idea of practices that are guided by an objective intention without implying subjective strategizing is in fact bound to appear as 'the oxymoron of unconscious strategy' (Alexander, 1995: 152ff.; also Elster, 1985).

However, as already discussed in Chapter 2, one of the main reasons why the dominant do not have to resort to strategies of conscious distinction is because they assimilate their "culture" under conditions that tend to exclude its very awareness as such. That is why Bourdieu insists that 'the search for distinction has no need to see itself for what it is, and all the intolerances – of noise, crowds etc. – inculcated by a bourgeois upbringing are generally sufficient to provoke the changes of terrain or object which, in work as in leisure, lead towards the object, places or activities rarest at a given moment' (1984: 249). From this it follows that one of the surest indicators of "taste" is, somewhat paradoxically, the capacity for distaste. 'The discourse about dislike and ugliness', writes Mary Douglas, 'is more revealing than the discourse about aesthetic beauty' (1996: 50). In fact, the inevitable counterpart of a 'negative cultivation' that inculcates 'the discipline required to set aside and hold in check the insistent stimuli of daily life so that attention may be free to tarry upon distinctions and discriminations that may be otherwise overlooked' (Goffman, 1951: 301), is the systematic lowering of the thresholds of tolerance for "heavy" foods, "loud" noises or colours, "strong" smells and perfumes, "sweet" flavours or "cloying" textures, in short, for everything that provides an all too "obvious", "easy" or "cheap" source of gratification. This cultivation of distaste perhaps finds one if its clearest expressions in the bourgeois phobia of "crowds", the realization par excellence of the dominant fiction of society as essentially composed of "the masses", an amorphous horde, homogenous and homogenizing, which abolishes difference and distance by subjecting each and every one to its unconcerted movements and rhythms, not to mention to all kinds of unsolicited contacts and sensory impressions (body odour).

Far from leading to a cynical strive for distinction, one could in fact argue that the early exposure to conditions of luxury provides the basis for what is in a sense the most "enchanted" relationship to the body. In fact, more than any other group, the dominant can rely most strongly on the "natural" inclinations of their bodies, their tastes and distastes, in order to be "spontaneously" led to the most distinctive and distinguished properties, starting of course with those that are materialized in the perceptible body itself. Contrary to mechanistic, quasi-Cartesian models of consumption, which often credit different types of products, goods and foods – especially the sweetest, heaviest and fattiest – with an intrinsic power to "tempt" or to "seduce" – i.e. to suspend conscious control and speak directly to bodily impulse and desire (themselves defined in a wholly essentialist manner) – the notions of class-taste and class-habitus serve to underline the fact that such products can only exert a seductive effect on those who already have a taste for them. Conversely, those who have acquired a taste for the light, the refined, the healthy, the pure and the organic (see Chapter 5) tend to "naturally" avoid such products, because they either have "no taste" for them or, better yet, find them completely distasteful.

Without therefore minimizing the time, means and effort that go into the cultivation of the dominant physique, such explicit forms of "body-work" always draw a considerable part of their efficacy from the more opaque action of class-dispositions. It is the latter which endow the dominant relationship to the body with an ease and self-evidence that makes it appear as rooted in nature. This not only sets it apart from those who are at once dispossessed both of the legitimate physical capital, as well as the intrinsic motivation to attain it (i.e. working-class), but also from the anxious, "superficial" and often equally "vulgar" concern with looks and appearance that characterizes members of the *petit-bourgeoisie*. Crucially, the misrecognition of the social foundations of their own distinguished tastes is one of the central factors that contribute to reinforcing the dominant in their own *sociocentrism*. It effectively ensures that *other* ways of perceiving, using and treating the body – i.e. those that are the product of less privileged social conditions – are not only seen as "un-*think*-able", but elicit a response that is often profoundly visceral. In fact, at least one of the reasons why 'aesthetic intolerance can be terribly violent' (Bourdieu, 1984: 56) is because disputes over taste, especially in everything pertaining to the body, are rarely restricted to the dispassionate mode of intellectual disagreement, but more often express themselves in the form of bodily emotion. In this sense, there is a kernel of truth in the maxim "*De gustibus non est disputandum*", since the most unequivocal affirmations of class are precisely those that circumvent deliberation or debate, which are not "discussed", but find their direct expression in the apparently most spontaneous and quasi-automatic of physical reactions. Repulsion, disgust or even vicarious shame are the ultimate expression of an inability to comprehend the tastes of others, of understanding how they could eat "this", wear "that" or do "those things" to their bodies. However, as the following chapter will aim to show, the opposite of course also holds true, namely that for those who are the product of less privileged social conditions and consequently have higher 'thresholds of repugnance' (Elias, 1982), it is often equally difficult to grasp the intensity of the reactions that transgressions against "good taste" can provoke among the dominant. To a less sensitive palate, a less "trained" eye or a less "cultivated" ear such reactions will all too easily appear as disproportionate or even contrived. Small wonder then, that they regard the tastes of the latter with the suspicious eye of (*petit-bourgeois*) resentment, seeing mere "affectation", deliberate "posturing" and "conspicuous" intent in what are most often wholly sincere expressions of cultural antipathy.

Conspicuous simplicity

However, simplicity and naturalness do not only apply to the *manner* in which the most everyday acts are accomplished, but also to the management and presentation of the body itself. Here again, approaches that equate dominant tastes with explicit snobbery and the conscious, conspicuous assertion of difference tend to ignore that so much of the dominant lifestyle is in fact oriented towards subtlety and self-effacement. 'The details of the bourgeois person's mode of being', writes Le Wita, 'are for their part aimed at discretion and neutrality – at "not showing off"' (1994: 70). In this respect, it is often the diametric opposite of the *petit-bourgeois* and especially the working-class relationship to the body. In fact, whereas the latter often tends to be oriented towards the pursuit of *maximum* symbolic effect at *minimal* cost – a principle which can be observed in such areas as clothing (imitation-"brands", ostentatious labels, "flashy" colours, shiny jewellery, etc.) or cosmetics ("strong" perfumes, "heavy" make-up, etc.) – the dominant standards of physical excellence aim to symbolize 'with the fewest "effects" possible the greatest expenditure of time, money and ingenuity' (Bourdieu, 1984: 380).

This leads us to one of the central ambiguities that characterize the dominant relationship to the body. On the one hand, because it is resolutely placed on the side of nature, passion and desire and because it is by definition a "vulgar" object whose own autonomous logic threatens to level social differences (as discussed in Chapter 2), the body requires constant regulation, control and investment. In this manner, it "goes without saying" that agents need to demonstrate the ability for restraint and self-control in such areas as eating, drinking, laughing or blowing one's nose, are capable of displaying a close attention to detail in the minutiae of dress, cosmetics and comportment, in short, cultivate that 'mistrust for letting oneself go in any way' discussed by Nietzsche in the opening quote to this chapter. On the other hand, these necessary investments in physical capital are always constrained by the inherent risk of "overdoing it". In fact, in as much as the dominant norms of propriety demand the symbolic cultivation of the body, at the same time, they also tend to exclude those types of bodily investment that betray a "superficial" or "vulgar" fascination with its appearance and physicality.

Artificially tanned skin, overly developed musculature, brightly dyed or heavily permed hair, highly visible bodily decorations (tattoos, piercings, etc.), heavy make-up, strong perfumes, etc. are all perceived as forms of "over-investment" in the body, which betray a vain concern with its surface, itself taken as a lack of depth and substance, often associated with *petit-bourgeois* pretensions or, *a fortiori*, with working-class carnality. In fact, one of the reasons why the physical capital of dominant social groups is predisposed to function as *symbolic* capital – i.e. as signalling charm, charisma, beauty and "natural" distinction – is that it is the product of a type of cultivation that is inherently self-effacing, concealing the traces of the investments in time and capital that goes into its production. That is why so much of the dominant relationship towards the body is oriented towards being "naturally" cultivated, casually refined, spontaneously distinguished, in short, towards attaining what Le Wita referred to as the state of *mediocritas* or the "happy medium" which she illustrates *a propos* the case of bourgeois dress and cosmetics:

> Any attempt to put into words this nature shaped by culture (in the interests of 'looking natural') will find it very hard to get away from the rhetorical figures of the double negative and the association of opposites: light make-up allowing the texture of the skin and the color of the complexion to show through, natural hair that is nevertheless cut and styled, firm yet relaxed tone

of voice, clear but restrained gestures. Never at the cutting edge of fashion, these women look timeless without ever being out of period, as it were.

(Le Wita, 1994: 68)

It is precisely this focus on the understated, the restrained and the casual that underscores another important aspect of dominant tastes, namely that the 'sought-after distinction does not so much operate in relation to the Other; above all it enables the bourgeoisie to recognize and be recognized by her own people' (ibid.: 67). While more Veblenian interpretations of the logic of distinction tend to stress the role of dominant tastes as intentional instruments of social *exclusion*, explicitly addressed towards those who occupy subordinate positions in social space, they often overlook that, especially from the "indigenous" point-of-view, such tastes primarily serve the function of social *integration*. It is precisely through their capacity to draw and perceive often minute distinctions, to recognize and apply skilful detail in the most mundane of acts that those who occupy dominant social positions signal (without any explicit signifying intention) their shared culture.

Approaches that equate dominant tastes with explicit snobbery in fact all too easily ignore that the legitimate body is the bearer of numerous markers of "class", which tend to pass wholly unnoticed for those who are the product of less privileged social conditions and hence lack the perceptual schemata that would render them susceptible to the significance of such markers in the first place. The logic of objective social distances and the physical segregation of "lifeworlds" that accompanies it tends to ensure that dominated agents only have a partial and quite imperfect knowledge of the products, properties and practices that define the dominant lifestyle. This is what makes strategies of symbolic bluff so inherently risky. Those who aim to project a more prestigious "image" can in fact never be completely certain that the goods, properties and practices they use to construct this image, based on what they *perceive* to be the defining features of the dominant lifestyle, have in fact not already been abandoned by the "truly" distinguished on the basis of their popularization or vulgarization. It is this uncertainty that exposes the upwardly aspiring to the constant risk of either falling short or, instead, of overdoing it producing either 'the awkwardness or arrogance of someone who brings suspicion on his own legitimacy by his too patent need to assert it' (Bourdieu, 1984: 252).

If anything, the conspicuous modesty and simplicity of those who can dispel with conscious strategies of cultural snobbery only tends to reinforce the perception of the dominant as being "innately" or "naturally" distinguished. As Bourdieu insists: 'What is objectionable is not difference, but the conspicuous intention of aloofness. The "natural" difference which defines the bourgeois is the more easily accepted because his "simplicity" proves it is not the product of a negative striving for distinction' (ibid.: 381). The ideological effects of such simplicity are perhaps nowhere as evident as in the dominant uses of all forms of verbal or non-verbal '*hypo-correction*', which Bourdieu subsumed under the heading of 'strategies of condescension'. The latter consist of those types of familiarity and informality which, under the guise of negating objective social differences, have the effect of underlining them, since the objective relationships of force that subtends such differences prevents these forms of familiarity from being reciprocated.

The work of Goffman (1967: 47ff.) and Henley (1977: 94ff.) on the social distribution of the right to touch and to be touched provides a case in point. Both show how in hierarchical social settings, the right to touch the body of others and to do so in an unsolicited manner – patting someone on the back, grabbing them by their shoulder, clutching their arm, etc. – increases with social power, so that superiors may more easily touch subordinates and men may more readily touch women (and male superiors may touch female superiors), but *not* the other way around. It is through these and other gestures of familiarity (addressing subordinates with their surname, closing the physical distance between speakers, etc.) that the dominant are able to reap the profits associated with a symbolic denial of difference (*"she's not stuck up!"*, *"he's a true gentleman"*), while leaving the fundamental principle that 'the profane must not touch the sacred' (Durkheim, 2001 [1912]: 224) fully intact.

'Askesis' and 'aesthesis'

If the analyses presented in the previous chapters enable us to isolate some of the distinctive features of the dominant relationship to the body – i.e. its concern with form and formality, the search for stylistic distinction, its focus on simplicity, restraint and moderation, etc. – they also warn against the use of overly homogenizing or monolithic concepts (often condensed into such qualifiers as "elite", "highbrow", "upper-class" or "bourgeois") to characterize the dominant uses of the body. In fact, the analysis has repeatedly aimed to show that the dominant definition of the "legitimate body" and the appropriate way of caring for, nurturing and presenting it, is itself an object of struggle between class-*fractions* that are unequally endowed with different forms of social power or "capital". Even though they share a number of characteristics, deriving from their shared positions of social power and the distance of necessity that defines their positions in social space, this should not blind the analysis to the fact that the relationship to the body of the culturally and economically dominant fractions of the dominant class are nevertheless informed by different, often diametrically opposed perspectives.

In fact, the same logic that defines the relationship between the classes in terms of the oppositions between Mind and Body, Culture and Nature, Spirit and Matter also subtends the production and perception of differences *within* the dominant class, where it is mapped onto the opposition between their dominated and dominant fractions respectively. Somewhat paradoxically, the tastes of the culturally dominant fractions find their symbolic expression – in their relationship to the body as elsewhere – in a (highly cultivated) celebration of Nature and the natural. In the area of food, as Chapter 5 has attempted to show, their *askesis* is manifested in a taste for the light, the healthy, the pure and unprocessed, the raw and the organic, by an under-consumption of meats and fats and an over-consumption of fish, fruit and vegetables. In cosmetic and sartorial matters, it is expressed in a preference for the "natural look", a refusal of heavy make-up, strong perfume, coloured or "permed" hair, artificial tans, branded clothing, formal dressing, "shiny" jewellery and "flashy" colours, in short, of all the marks that betray an idle fascination with the body's surface and hence with superficiality. Instead, it asserts itself in a choice for "natural" colours, light or no make-up, a preference for simple, casual clothing which often mimics workman's attire (lumberjack shirts, sailor's jackets, etc.) or find its realization in "vintage" or "second hand"-clothing, which satisfies the quest for individuality and originality at an ostensibly low cost (or the *semblance* of low cost).

> The case of second-hand clothing is particularly instructive, because it illustrates how different social groups, in this case the most disadvantaged fringe of the working-class and the culturally richest fractions of the middle- and upper-class, invest different and even opposed meanings in the same type of consumption. While for the former, "buying second-hand" is a result of brute necessity and quickly abandoned as soon as the resources to buy new clothing become available, for the latter it is an elective affinity driven by the search for the most rare and original items ("*it's a unique piece*"). Hence, whereas working-class "choices" for second-hand clothing are always inspired by the intention to find the "newest" items – i.e. those that are least "dated" and bear the least marks of wear – those who are situated towards the culturally dominant pole of social space actively search for the most "vintage" items, namely those which the logic of ageing has rendered unique and endowed with their particular "character". In this manner, when asked if they ever bought "second hand"-clothing 90 per cent of unskilled and 80 per cent of skilled workers claimed they never do, compared to 79 per cent of the office-workers in administrative functions, 68 per cent of those in "front-stage" clerical occupations, 72 per cent of the junior-executives and 70 per cent of the members of the professions (with the women of these fractions being somewhat more inclined to do so than the men). However, it is among the fractions richest in cultural capital, namely the teachers in secondary and higher-education (64 per cent claimed they never bought second-hand) and the academics (44 per cent) that one finds the most avid consumers of second-hand (source: BoS '10). Similar differences are observed in the domain of cosmetics. For instance, the proportion of women who indicated they applied lipstick "daily" or "several times a week" varied from 22 per cent of the female professionals and senior-executives to 8 per cent of the women in higher-education and academic occupations and none of the artists and cultural producers (with the proportion who indicated they "*never*" used lipstick going from 31 per cent to 52 per cent and 42 per cent respectively). Similarly, the number who indicated they use "*eye-shadow*" on a daily or weekly basis varies from 23 per cent of the professionals and executives over 11 per cent of the academics to 14 per cent of the artists, while the use of more subtle, less obvious types of make-up such as "*eye-liner*"

goes from 31 per cent of the former, to 37 per cent and 34 per cent of the academics and artists, respectively. The same logic applies to a practice like "*getting a tan*" with 15 per cent of the female professionals and executives indicated they went to a tanning salon at least once a month or more, compared to 5 per cent of the female academics and 7 per cent of the artists (while 46 per cent, 68 per cent and 62 per cent respectively reported they never went to a tanning salon). An analysis of the average yearly expenditure on jewellery and other types of accessories (watches, cufflinks, etc.) reveals similar differences, with the senior-executives spending an average of 105 euros a year, compared to 113 euros for members of the professions, 63 euros for the academics and 53 euros for the artists and the cultural producers, who in this respect are again much closer to the skilled workers and foremen (50 euros) and the unskilled workers (45 euros).

As already touched upon in Chapter 5, a number of features of the lifestyle of the culturally dominant fractions only become fully intelligible when they are related to their essentially ambivalent position in social space. An "elite" in the eyes of the dominated, they are separated from the latter by their possession of a form of capital that, in turn, assigns them a dominated position within the upper class as a whole. It is this double point-of-reference (i.e. to the lifestyle of the working-classes and that of the economic elites), which predisposes their narratives on the social world to function as 'dual-action devices' (Bourdieu, 1984: 254). In fact, their critique of "materialistic" values, of the excesses of "consumerism", of cultural "homogenization" and "uniformity" are always marked by an indeterminacy that makes them applicable, with equal force, to both the refined hedonism of the temporally dominant (the "fat cats") and the crude materialism of the working-classes (the "couch potatoes"), to the corporate conformism exemplified by the "business-suit" and the "sheep-like conformity" of working-class fashion as embodied in the "track-suit". To this ethic of sobriety and elective austerity, the temporally dominant oppose a relationship to the body that is defined by a hedonistic, yet refined indulgence. Even if they are often forced to invoke, against the crude materialism of the working-class or the pretentiousness of the *petit-bourgeoisie*, the same values of "disinterestedness", "simplicity" and "refinement" that the intellectuals and artists use *against* them, their manner of distinguishing themselves from the vulgar and the profane is based on radically different principles. To the overly "severe" tastes of the cultural elite, who "*don't know how to relax*" and enjoy themselves, they oppose their own 'ethic of fun' (Bourdieu, 1984) which inverts the intellectual table of values by favouring sensuous pleasure over intellectual enjoyment, narcissistic indulgence over ascetic self-denial, gastronomy over aesthetics, cultivation of the body over cultivation of the mind, "haute cuisine" over "haute culture".

The employers and private-sector executives not only have the highest annual expenditure on outdoor-dining (as Chapter 5 already showed), but they also spend more than twice as much on restaurant-visits (1,496 euros or

> 3.3 per cent of their total annual expenditure) than on all of their expenses on "culture" *combined* (631 euros or 1.4 per cent, the category "culture" encompasses the expenditure on books, CDs, DVDs, subscriptions to newspapers and magazines, visits to museums, concerts or theatre, musical instruments and music- and art-classes). On the other extreme of the field of power, the cultural producers and artists not only spend considerably less on restaurants (840 euros or 2.4 per cent of their total expenditure, which is still more than twice as much, in both absolute and relative terms, than the unskilled workers, who have a total expenditure of 399 euros or 1.4 per cent), but their spending on restaurant-visits is also outweighed by their cultural consumption which is considerably higher, in both absolute and relative terms (1,004 euros or 2.9 per cent out of a considerably smaller overall expenditure), than that of the commercial employers and also of the private-sector executives who spend 754 euros (1.9 per cent) on culture and 1,171 euros (3.0 per cent) on restaurant-visits.
>
> (source: EU-HBS '05)

Their expenditure on restaurants and outdoor-dining reveals another crucial aspect of the ways in which the dominant fractions use, perceive and treat their bodies. In fact, whereas the ethos of the dominated fractions often lead them towards the most "spiritual" pursuits and to forms of consumption that are often wholly "symbolic" in nature, that is to say, are most strongly purged of any trace of corporeality (music, literature, etc.), the refined hedonism of the dominant fractions remains much more strongly linked to the body and bodily pleasure. Whether it takes the form of a connoisseurship in wine or fine dining, expresses itself in a taste for "haute couture", luxurious accessories and other forms of bodily decoration or manifests itself in the consumption of high-end services of physical care (spas, wellness-clinics, etc.), their tastes betray a relationship to the body which, despite its high degree of euphemization, remains fundamentally "materialist" in character. If the culturally dominant fractions often derive a considerable degree of subjective pleasure from their capacity for self-denial and the ability to adopt a stoic attitude towards the body – and often do so in the name of "inner" qualities like "character-building", "mental discipline" and "inner well-being" – then the economic fractions tend to distinguish themselves through an attitude of refined indulgence towards their body. Not only do they treat the latter as a precious object with specific needs that deserve (and demand) constant care and attention, but they also invest considerably more in its *perceptible* qualities (clothing, cosmetics, accessories, etc.) making the body into the visible bearer of material value.

Again, the idiom in which the relationships between the dominant and dominated fractions are expressed (and naturalized), draws heavily on the language and imagery of sexual domination. Not only are the intellectual fractions quick to castigate the economic elite for their celebration of "anti-intellectualist" and androcentric virtues like prowess in sports, but they also tend to disqualify their lifestyle and their relationship to the body as "greedy", "wasteful", "destructive", if not "cruel" (foie gras, fur, SUVs, etc.). Conversely, the temporally dominant are equally quick to denounce the "naïve" idealism of artists and intellectuals, the "touchy-feely" concerns that inform their relationship to the body (like those related to environmental or animal-rights, for instance), the "frivolity" and lack of "seriousness" that is expressed in all the markers of a quasi-Bohemian lifestyle (long hair, casual dress, etc.), in short, to discredit them with all the traits that sexist ideology assigns to women. This is even more evident in the qualities – like weakness, frailty and gaucheness – which the dominant vision attributes to the artist's or intellectual's body (recall the classification of male *and* female silhouettes discussed in Chapter 4). Qualities that testify to their inherent *in*-capacity for "real" authority and responsible leadership and to their "natural" predilection for social activities that might have a certain value (like women's work in the symbolic and emotional management of the household), but remain subordinate to the "real" and "serious" work of social domination. Hence, what lies behind these two different definitions of the legitimate body, is two radically different conceptions of the accomplished individual, themselves linked to two opposing world-views and two opposing principles of social domination. On the one hand, temporal power, inner-worldly success, financial achievement, entrepreneurial skill which translates into an ethos of refined hedonism and materialistic pleasure. On the other, outer-worldly prestige, intellectual authority, the assertion of Mind over Matter, thought over desire translating into an ethos of elective austerity and stoic self-control. As the preceding chapters have aimed to show, within this struggle few everyday "choices" are strictly speaking neutral and even the most mundane acts of working with and on the body quickly acquire the status of 'weapons in a vigorous contest between styles of organization' (Douglas, 1996: xiv).

Negative cultivation

While this chapter has aimed to demonstrate that, against overly cynical, Veblenian interpretations of the logic of distinction, the dominant are most often distinguished *despite* themselves, this does not warrant the conclusion that the *inculcation* of this 'sense of distinction' is itself a smooth and flawless process, nor that the ethos of self-discipline and restraint cannot produce potentially pathological outcomes. In fact, it is precisely because this ethos is constructed around the reconciliation of unlikely opposites (natural, yet cultivated; free, yet restrained; individualist, yet conform to the principles of "class", etc.), its internalization is often rife with tensions and contradictions. As Le Wita notes: 'Bourgeois education, like any other kind of apprenticeship, is based on a constant state of tension and restraint meticulously offset against areas of freedom' (1994: 70).

Dominant educational strategies always have to strike an uneasy and fragile balance between cultivating the child's sense of individuality and autonomous expression, while at the same instilling the importance of restraint and self-discipline, between developing its feeling of entitlement and self-importance, while simultaneously inculcating the values of self-denial, modesty and personal achievement.[1] Too much stress on individuality and autonomy and the pedagogic project can become a self-destroying prophecy, leading to a rejection of parental models and the refusal of the inheritance for which their entire upbringing has prepared them. On the other hand, too much focus on self-discipline, restraint and achievement can produce overly integrated, rigid habitus marked by an over-eagerness to succeed and an extreme, even morbid desire to demonstrate their capacity for achievement and self-control. That such extreme forms of self-control often find their privileged expression in agents' relationship to their own bodies is all too dramatically illustrated by the case of *anorexia nervosa*. Hilde Bruch, one of the pioneers in the study of eating disorders, offers a description of anorexics that seems written for the sociologist:

> Most anorexic girls come from upper-middle-class and upper-class homes; financial achievement and social position are often high. The relatively few homes of lower-middle-class or lower-class rating were upwardly mobile and success-oriented. The anorexic daughter of a postal clerk had two older brothers, one a physician, the other a lawyer, who felt they owed their accomplishment to the driving encouragement from their mother. Another girl, the daughter of a blue-collar worker, was the only child in an extended family group, and everybody had contributed to prepare her for a special career. These families were small of size; in my last fifty cases, the average number of children was 2.8. The age of the parents at the time of birth of the anorexic child was rather high: thirty-eight years the average for the fathers, the oldest being fifty-four; and thirty-two for the mothers, with forty-three as the highest age.
>
> (Bruch, 2001: 24)

While the social etiology of eating disorders is by now becoming quite well-established, Bruch also shows that one of the main obstacles to their early diagnosis and treatment is the fact that parents of anorexics rarely notice any abnormalities in their children. In fact, they very often praise them for being exemplary and far surpassing of parental expectations. If the self-destructive tendencies in these "model-children" often go unnoticed until they have reached a quite advanced stage, one could argue that this is precisely because they have internalized the principles of their class-ethos all *too* well and simply take them to their logical and in this case *patho*-logical conclusions.

This is what is in fact suggested by Darmon's (2009) study of the social production of 'anorexic habitus' among the daughters of the Parisian bourgeoisie. Her analysis shows how 'seemingly "typically anorexic" practices, however pathological they may appear, clearly echo their "normal" and class-biased counterparts' and as such reveal a 'close allegiance with specific upper- and middle-class attitudes and values' (2009: 724). She argues, more specifically, that the particular constellation of practices and beliefs that make up the 'anorexic ethos' can itself be understood as an extreme and hypertrophied form of the traditional elements that define the dominant lifestyle and the dominant relationship to the body. The capacity to control impulse and emotion, the insistence on self-discipline in the minutiae of everyday behaviour and physical comportment, the capacity to defer and transcend immediate, animalistic gratifications (especially in matters of food) and, more generally, the refusal of everything associated with substance, the gross and the material in favour of a concern with form, refinement, the spiritual and the intellectual, all these elements are taken up by the anorexic, only to be magnified and projected onto the one aspect of their existence over which they feel they can exert absolute control, namely their own body.

In addition, both Bruch and Darmon note how for anorexics this capacity to achieve self-control is itself suffused with the logic of distinction, expressing a desire among anorexics to elevate and distance themselves from the average, the plain and the common (quite often explicitly associated with the ostentatious lack of self-discipline deemed typical of the working-class body). As one of Bruch's patients put it: 'Since I was given more [a very wealthy, successful background] I feel that more is expected of me, that morally I'm obliged to give more. I feel that I can't just live on an ordinary scale of human endeavour' (Bruch, 2001: 53; also see Bordo, 1993: 203). While the social conditions that favour the development of such pathological forms of self-control hence prove increasingly met as one rises in the social hierarchy, the model of social space that has been advanced throughout the preceding chapters can help us to more accurately define these conditions. In fact, while the rejection of the heavy, the substantial, the material and the functional in favour of the light, the refined, the spiritual and the formal defines the relationship to the body of the dominant class as a whole, it finds its fullest realization among those fractions that embrace asceticism and elective austerity as the ultimate symbol of the assertion of Mind over Matter, spiritual over material values, namely among those richest in *cultural* capital.[2]

> In this manner, the number of respondents who claim to have family-members (parents, children, siblings) or close friends who have suffered from an eating disorder (i.e. anorexia or bulimia) increases sharply as one moves from those with little or no formal education (5 per cent) to those with a master's or postgraduate degree (21 per cent) and from the unskilled workers and farmers (6 per cent), through the office clerks (11 per cent) to the junior-executives (13 per cent), but proves highest among the teachers (16 per cent), the artists and cultural producers (17 per cent) and especially among the academics (27 per cent), especially when compared to those in the professions and the senior-executives (11 per cent, source: BoS '10). Similarly, the figures presented in Table 4.2 *also show a drastic increase* in the proportion of women who qualify as medically "underweight" (i.e. have a BMI less than 18.5) as one rises in the class-hierarchy and especially towards the culturally dominant pole of social space.

Without therefore aiming to account for an extremely complex phenomenon in the matter of a few lines, our analysis merely serves to highlight the "situated" nature of these pathological forms of self-control. While other factors (most notably the logic of sexual domination) are clearly also at work, the results presented in this and the previous chapters do suggest that the conditions that favour (or inhibit) the development of such forms of bodily hyper-control are not randomly distributed across social space. Instead, they find their conditions of possibility and support within a more general ethos that is rooted in the negation of substance in favour of form, the denial of quantity in favour of quality, the assertion of rationality and self-control over impulse and desire, in short, the affirmation of the power of Culture over the blind forces of Nature.

Notes

1 For a similar argument, see Annette Lareau (2003: especially 131ff.) on 'role confusion'.
2 This is further underlined by the fact that anorexics often take extreme pride in their high academic achievements and overall intellectual faculties and that the onset of the disorder is often associated with entry into higher-education (see Bruch, 2001: 58ff.; Darmon, 2009).

8   Tension in relaxation

> Sometimes he is ashamed of his origins; he has learned to 'turn up his nose', to be a bit superior about much in working-class manners. He is often not at ease about his own physical appearance which speaks too clearly of his birth; he feels uncertain or angry inside when he realizes that that, and a hundred habits of speech and manners, can 'give him away' daily.
>
> (Hoggart, 1957: 301)

If the analyses presented throughout the preceding chapters have often rubbed against the limits of what can be meaningfully uncovered by statistics and survey-research, the intrinsic limitations of the latter tend to come fully to the fore when dealing with those who are situated in the central regions of social space. Neither high nor low, dominant nor dominated, refined nor vulgar, the relationship to the body of the middle-classes or *petit-bourgeoisie* is often notoriously difficult to pin down. There are in fact several ways in which this relationship eludes the mechanics of survey-research. First and foremost, there is the inevitable effect produced by the survey (as a synchronic "snapshot") of freezing a given state of the power-struggles between social positions which define the structure of social space at any given moment. If, in general, this often leads the analyst to treat the social world as a simple collection of self-contained and clearly delineated groups and to ignore what each of these groups owes to its (antagonistic) relationships with others, it becomes particularly problematic when studying a set of social positions which, like the middle-classes, derive a large number of their characteristics precisely *from* these relationships (Wacquant, 1992). Being defined as much by the lifestyle of the working-class, *from* which they aim to distinguish themselves, as by that of the dominant class, *towards* which they tend to aspire, the petit-bourgeois relationship to the body only becomes fully intelligible when it is related to these opposites.

This synchronizing effect of the survey not only tends to downplay the importance of these antagonistic relationships, but also freezes the *movements* of various groups throughout social space of which its middle region is in a sense the "crossroads". In fact, what the survey registers as "intermediate" or "middle" positions often prove to be the meeting point, at any given time, of groups that occupy a fairly "stable" position within the *petit-bourgeoisie* (the teachers for instance), those that are caught in a downward trajectory (the small shopkeepers) and those that are propelled in an upward movement (such as those employed in the financial services, like real-estate or insurance). Given that such varied trajectories are themselves constitutive of differences in class-dispositions – like the optimistic, "subversive" dispositions of the upwardly mobile or the pessimistic, "regressive" dispositions of those who are marked by a downward trajectory – the label "middle-class" tends to group agents who are often the product of quite divergent social condition(ing)s.

It is this dynamic character of the middle-classes which also highlights a second limitation of survey-analysis, namely the inherent difficulty of using *established* taxonomies of status to adequately define what are often ill-defined locations in social space. In fact, given that such taxonomies are, at least partly, the *outcome* of the struggle of groups for official recognition (on this point see Boltanski, 1987; Desrosières, 1991), they in a sense always tend to arrive "after the battle", that is, when groups have already succeeded in gaining inclusion into the official (i.e. state-sanctioned) systems of classification. While this essentially applies to *all* social groups, it is especially problematic when trying to delineate those who occupy "intermediate" social positions, that is, categories which are still in the *process of becoming* (mental coach, colour-therapist, sustainability expert, etc.).

Finally, these limitations do not only apply to the process of *locating* groups within a highly dynamic sector of social space, but also to the task of identifying the *particularity* of their practices. In fact, while the survey is an invaluable instrument in helping to gauge the *absolute* probability that a certain class (fraction) is associated with a certain practice, property or opinion, it tends to be more limited in its ability to grasp the specific *modality* of practice, that is, to differentiate the *manner* in which agents consume, appropriate, enact or adhere to such practices, properties and opinions. As already discussed in the case of surveys on household-consumption (see Chapter 5), such differences in modality are nevertheless crucial in aiming to distinguish the relationship to the body of those who have the "means", but lack the "manners" to appropriate certain categories of practices or goods – i.e. the "nouveaux riches", the "parvenus" or the "pedants" of all stripes – from those whose comportment and appearance derive their distinguished value from a long-standing familiarity with these categories. This means that on a wide range of indices, the survey tends to artificially efface or compress some of the central differences between the dominant and *petit-bourgeois* relationship to the body. If one adds to this the ways in which this relationship itself is further differentiated in terms of particular class-fractions endowed with specific *types* of capital, it becomes clear that the term "middle-class" covers quite a mixed bag.

Inner tension

Despite such important limitations, the analysis was nevertheless able to isolate some of the distinctive features of the *petit-bourgeois* relationship to the body.

196 Class bodies

Features that can all be traced back to the fundamental ambiguity that marks those who occupy central regions in the social structure and which have their origin in 'the contradictions between an objectively dominated position and would-be participation in the dominant values' (Bourdieu, 1984: 253). In fact, as one moves from dominated to intermediate positions in social space (i.e. when one crosses the boundary separating the skilled workers from the office clerks), a number of indices converge to show that agents increasingly embrace the dominant definition of bodily appearance and *hexis* and come to perceive and judge their own bodies according to its standards of value. Compared to manual workers (and especially working-class *men*), the office clerks, school-teachers, small business-owners and junior-executives – women *and* men – prove more concerned with the size and shape of their bodies, more readily adopt forms of restraint and self-denial in the name of appearance and health, more often read fashion-, beauty- and lifestyle-magazines or watch television-programmes devoted to these topics (see below) and more actively engage in dieting and exercise. At the same time however, they also tend to express a higher level of dissatisfaction with their bodies. This seems particularly true of those who are situated near the bottom of the middle-class, namely the office clerks (and especially the women of this fraction). Not only are they among those groups who most often state they want to lose weight, who report the widest gap between current and ideal weight and who most often indicate they want to go to the gym to work on their figure, but they also tend to rate themselves lowest in terms of appearance and physical attractiveness.

It is precisely this gap between recognition and ownership, between perceived body and dream body, that seems particularly important in understanding the ways in which members of the middle-class (and middle-class women in particular) come to perceive and evaluate their bodies. In fact, the discrepancy between the body one "has" and the body one "ought to have" can itself be understood as a special case of the more general discrepancy between means and aspirations that characterizes the middle-classes and especially its upwardly aspiring fractions. This chapter will argue, more specifically, that a host of concerns, needs and anxieties that define the *petit-bourgeois* relationship to the body can be traced back to their *intermediate* position in the class-structure, "intermediate" being taken both in the sense of "in-the-middle" or "in-between" (neither high nor low, dominant nor dominated), but also in the sense of being "liminal", "ill-defined" or "unfinished". It will aim to show that this specific position imbues their habitus with a tension that not only makes them particularly sensitive to the importance of "presentation" and "appearance", but also renders them particularly prone to feelings of bodily shame and timidity. It is Norbert Elias who again provides a particularly striking description of this "inner tension" that defines the *petit-bourgeois* habitus:

> They [*the petit-bourgeois*] are frequently, though not always, still unformed in many areas in which members of the upper class are highly developed, and they are so impressed, in their social inferiority, by the affect-control

and code of conduct of the upper-class, that they try to control their own affects according to the same pattern. [...] But on closer inspection this super-ego is in many respects different from its model. It is less balanced and therefore often much more severe. It always reveals the immense effort which individual social advancement requires [...] And this shaping of the super-ego on upper-class models also brings about in the rising class a specific form of shame and embarrassment. [...] It is this peculiar contradiction between the upper class within themselves, represented by their own super-ego, and their incapability of fulfilling its demands, it is this constant inner tension that gives their affective life and their conduct its particular character.

(Elias, 2000: 430–431)

In this particular quotation (and elsewhere in *The Civilizing Process*), Elias in fact comes remarkably close to formulating the principles of what Bourdieu would later coin 'symbolic violence', namely that specific form of social coercion 'which is set up only through the consent that the dominated cannot fail to give to the dominator (and therefore to domination) when their understanding of the situation and relation can only use instruments of knowledge that they have in common with the dominator' (Bourdieu, 2000b: 170). While the effects of this particular type of social domination are by no means restricted to members of the *petit-bourgeoisie* (and increasingly extend into the working-class as the following chapter will aim to show), it is their direct participation in the 'legitimate market in physical properties' (Bourdieu, 1984: 152) that makes them particularly prone to its effects. This can perhaps be illustrated best by comparing the attitudes towards the body of the female office-workers with those of women who are employed in skilled manual labour. In fact, despite the fact that office-workers occupy a more secure and prestigious position in social space than the skilled workers (having higher incomes and higher levels of education), they nevertheless rate themselves lower in appearance than the latter and more often indicate they want to lose weight or change one or more aspects of their body. This apparent contradiction can be accounted for once it is recognized that both groups of women are separated by what is effectively a class-*boundary*. This boundary separates the skilled workers, who occupy a "dominant" or perhaps better stable position within a social universe where the body is still primarily perceived as an *instrument* of labour, from the office clerks, who in turn occupy a dominated position within a social class/field that places a much higher value on physical appearance and self-presentation, that is to say, on the value of the "body-as-sign".

This is in fact one of the crucial differences that distinguish the *petit-bourgeois* from the working-class relationship to the dominant norms of appearance and demeanour. While neither are capable of fully ignoring these norms and countering the effect of symbolic dispossession they exert (as clearly shown by the evaluations of their own appearance presented in Chapter 4), fact remains that they impose themselves to a different degree and in a different manner for each class. Whereas working-class women more often encounter these norms in an "indirect" manner, through their diffusion in entertainment-weeklies or television-programmes for instance, middle-class women are exposed to a more direct scrutiny of their appearance and (hence) are a lot more sensitive to the material and symbolic rewards that are linked to investments in their "body-for-others". Furthermore, while working-class women can still find a limited form of "shelter" from the dominant norms of appearance in alternative sources of social valorization, such as those provided by the domestic and maternal role, such alternatives clash more strongly with the definition of accomplished femininity of women in the middle- and dominant classes (Warrin *et al.* 2008). This means that the gap between recognition and ownership, which typifies the middle-classes as a whole, tends to be widest among those who are situated near its lower fringe.

Body-images

That contemporary forms of anxiety over one's body and appearance are far from universal, but still have quite distinct social origins can perhaps be illustrated best by looking at the role of one of the symbolic agents that is deemed central in universalizing this anxiety, namely the modern "mass media". In fact, the sociological and feminist literature on the body and "consumer culture" (see Bartky, 1990; Featherstone, 1991 or Bordo, 1993) often tends to attribute an inordinate power to advertising, television and magazines in circulating and universalizing (often unrealistic) ideals of feminine beauty and hence of instilling a generalized sense of physical inadequacy among women.[1] However, an analysis of the actual relationship between the consumption of different types of media and women's perception of their own bodies suggests a slightly more complex picture. A first thing to note is that, against monolithic and hyperbolic narratives on the role of "the media", the specific *manner* in which ideal bodily aesthetics are presented tends to differ considerably from one type of media-outlet to the next. So whereas entertainment weeklies, celebrity-magazines and tabloids undoubtedly contribute to the idealization of dominant norms of appearance, they also present these norms as being very much the distinctive hallmark of the "rich and famous" and hence as part of the lifestyle of an unattainable Other. This sets them apart from fashion- and lifestyle-magazines (*Elle, Vogue, Cosmopolitan*, etc.) which – through their beauty tips, dietary guidelines, cosmetic and sartorial advice, etc. – *directly* address their readership and are precisely predicated on the idea that the "ideal body" is very much within the reach of every woman. The same distinction also holds true for television, where there is a clear difference between those forms of "women's"- or "lifestyle"-television which actively instruct their audience on how to attain the legitimate body (*Trinny and Susanna, Extreme Makeover, Queer Eye for a Straight Guy*, etc.) and soap-series, "rom-coms" or "chick flicks" in which the ideal body is presented as an inherent attribute of the distant "celebrity".

The reason for drawing this distinction is that the consumption of these different types of media is itself distributed highly unevenly between the classes

(Table 8.1). Quite tellingly, it is the women of the lower-middle-class (and especially female office clerks) who prove to be among the most avid consumers of periodicals devoted to women's beauty, fitness and health, with nearly half of them choosing them as their *"favourite type of magazine"* (compared to a third of working-class women and less than a quarter of the female professionals and executives). Equally telling is that those women who have the highest probability of embodying the norms of physical attractiveness and who rate themselves highest in appearance, i.e. upper-middle and upper-class women, tend to be *least* interested in those types of media that are directly or indirectly devoted to the management and cultivation of the body. Fashion- and lifestyle-magazines or tabloids account for less than a third of their overall consumption of periodicals (compared to 60 per cent for political or cultural magazines), while only one out of ten regularly tune into those television channels that diffuse the dominant bodily aesthetic, either through their actual programming or through advertising (while more than 70 per cent claim to only watch public-television which devote little or no air-time to either). Even if we narrow the broad categories of television-use down to the consumption of individual *types* of programmes, it becomes clear that those programmes that are devoted specifically to the presentation and transformation of the body – the infamous 'makeover-TV' – are only consumed on a regular basis by a small fraction of women. While such programmes undoubtedly contain a strong element of class racism and have a clear potential for symbolic violence (see Wood and Skeggs, 2011), it should not be overlooked that less than one out of five women, regardless of social position, watch them on a regular basis. More importantly however, when one looks at the actual relationship between women's media-consumption and various indices of body-image and body-size, the results prove far from straightforward (Table 8.2). Not only are there very few differences in terms of how they perceive and judge their bodies between women who intensely consume various types of body-oriented media and those who rarely ever read or watch various forms of health-, beauty- or lifestyle-media, but there is even less indication that regular exposure to such media effectively has an impact on their actual physical size.

> To gauge the impact of the exposure to the ideals of physical beauty as portrayed in visual and printed media, the analysis compared differences in media-preference for different indices of women's relationship to their bodies: First, their general degree of satisfaction with their appearance and weight (score from 0 to 10) as an indicator of women's 'subjective' *perception* of their bodies. Secondly, differences in actual physical size as measured both by average BMI, as well as by the proportion of women who would qualify as medically 'underweight'. If conventional narratives on the role of the media are to be believed, we should expect high exposure to various body-oriented media – and the resulting internalization of their bodily aesthetic – to be associated with consistently lower satisfaction-scores. In addition, if the quite unrealistic ideals conveyed by these media actually manage to shape women's bodies (through such pathological practices as disordered eating), consumption

Table 8.1 Women's consumption of various types of printed and visual media

	Favourite type of magazine				Favourite type of television				
	Doesn't read magazines	Entertainment weeklies and tabloids	Women's weeklies (Elle, Cosmo, etc.)	Other periodicals (politics, culture, etc.)	Doesn't watch TV	Commercial TV	Public TV	Women's and lifestyle TV	N
Working-class	*17*[a]	*36*	33	14	1	*58*	23	*18*	430
Lower-middle-class	11	20	*41*	28	4	35	49	13	934
Upper-middle-class	13	7	25	*55*	5	13	*76*	5	89
Upper class	14	14	23	*48*	9	15	*70*	6	20
Total	15	27	30	28	3	38	44	9	1,473

Type of TV-programmes (% watch 'often' to 'very often')

	Talk shows	News	Soaps	'Makeover'-TV	Celebrity-TV	N
Working-class	23	48	*48*	*18*	*16*	337
Lower-middle-class	31	53	28	15	12	619
Upper-middle-class	31	*64*	10	13	2	43
Upper class	*46*	60	10	14	0	21
Total	29	52	33	16	13	1,020

Source: PaS '09

Note
a This number reads as follows: "17 per cent of working-class women do not read magazines." Figures in italic denote the strongest tendency for that column.

Table 8.2 Relationship between women's media-consumption, body-image and physical size

			Satisfaction with...[a]			
	Weight	Appearance	N	Avg. BMI	% "underweight"	N
	**	n.s.		***		
Doesn't read	6.0[b]	6.8	634	24.9	4.8	159
Celebrity and tabloid	5.6	6.4	566	25.9	0.8	92
Women's weeklies	6.0	6.7	346	25.0	1.9	33
Other periodicals	6.3	7.0	366	24.0	4.5	402
Total	5.9	6.7	1,895	24.9	2.8	1,416

			Satisfaction with...			
	Weight	Appearance	N	Avg. BMI	% "underweight"	N
	***	***		***		
Doesn't watch TV	6.5	6.5	75	22.9	7.7	39
Public TV	6.3	7.0	548	24.4	3.2	624
Commercial TV	5.7	6.9	388	25.4	1.9	535
Women's and lifestyle TV	5.9	6.7	114	25.4	1.6	131
Total	6.0	6.9	1,125	24.9	3.2	1,329

Notes
a Data from SHW '06.
b This number reads as follows: "On average, women who do not or rarely read magazines rate their own weight as 6.0 out of 10."
* $p < .05$, ** $p < .01$, *** $p < .001$, n.s.: non-significant.

of body-oriented media should be linked to low average BMI and a high proportion of women who are underweight. It is important to point out that these indices were drawn from two *different* surveys with the figures for appearance-satisfaction coming from the aforementioned study on well-being (SHW '06), while BMI-figures were based on a survey of cultural consumption (PaS '09). These indicators were compared for women who did not read any magazines and rarely ever watched television (and can hence be said to be most 'sheltered' from these ideals), those who claimed to most often read lifestyle-, beauty- and fashion-magazines and most often watched women's and 'lifestyle'-channels (two types of media that not only explicitly aim to diffuse the dominant bodily aesthetic, but also claim to offer the techniques and 'know-how' to realize it), those who consume tabloids and watch commercial TV-channels (which diffuse this aesthetic in a more 'indirect' manner) and, finally, those who read other types of periodicals or mainly watch public-television (i.e. as media-types that devote little or no attention to the management and modification of the body, either through their actual content or through advertising). As far as overall degree of satisfaction with appearance and weight is concerned, there are little or no differences in satisfaction-scores between women who claim lifestyle-magazines and -television as their favourite and those who don't read magazines or watch TV on a regular basis. The latter even rated themselves slightly lower in appearance than those who watch a lot of commercial or lifestyle-TV. Only as far as television-use was concerned did the analysis show a higher level of dissatisfaction among women who regularly watch commercial or lifestyle-TV compared to those who mainly watched public or no television at all and even then only in terms of weight-satisfaction and not appearance in general. BMI-indicators also provide little evidence for the thesis that regular consumers of body-oriented media effectively try to emulate the aesthetic ideals that these media convey. In terms of average physical size, readers of women's weeklies were not consistently slimmer than women who did not read magazines at all and the lowest BMI was actually recorded among women who read political, cultural or other types of periodicals. Similarly, the women whose physical size comes closest to the dominant ideal portrayed in televised media are actually the women who rarely ever watch TV, while the risk of being "underweight" proved highest among women who do not regularly watch TV or read magazines and lowest among those who consumed printed and visual media that is specifically devoted to the topics of beauty and fitness. Again, this does not provide much evidence for the proposition that modern media are among the prime culprits in producing the type of pathological relationship to the body that is expressed, amongst others, in eating disorders like anorexia or bulimia.

Without therefore denying that television, women's weeklies and advertising play a role in promulgating the dominant bodily aesthetic, nor that they add their own symbolic force to its universalization and legitimation, it would be all too reductionist to credit the 'fashion-beauty complex' (Bartky, 1990) with a quasi-universal power to impose the legitimate definition of the female (and male) body, let alone with the capacity to shape its visible features. The problem with such a view is that it inevitably reduces social agents to the status of passive "recipients" and ignores the fact that media-imagery, however ubiquitous it might be, is itself subjected to a process of active selection and interpretation in accordance with the practical principles of apperception which are transmitted and inculcated, from a very early age onwards, within the family unit. It is these principles which not only help to determine the degree in which the ideals of physical excellence diffused by the media and other symbolic agents come to be viewed as attainable, probable or unrealistic ("*not for the likes of us*"), but also contribute to the demand for the explicit guidelines and "models" that can help realize these ideals. The symbolic efficacy of the norms promulgated by the media is hence in no small part dependent on the degree in which their social and sexual ethos has already rendered agents receptive to such ideals in the first place. Put differently, before all too easily defining media-images as the "cause" of physical anxiety and insecurity, one needs to ask the question of what the "choices" for different types of media already reveals about the practical experience of the body. One could in fact argue that the popularity of magazines devoted to beauty, fashion and lifestyle among women of the *petit-bourgeoisie* – as well as their relative *under*-consumption among other social groups, most notably among upper-class women – is due to the fact that the message and "advice" such magazines convey, appeals most strongly to their sense of cosmetic voluntarism. In fact, without suggesting that the contemporary fascination with appearance, dieting and health (and above all the needs and anxietiescit generates) is somehow exclusive to members of the middle-class, I will argue that there are at least three defining features of the *petit-bourgeois* ethos which make them particularly susceptible to the messages of the beauty- and fitness-industry. First, the *tendency towards asceticism* which goes hand in hand with the development of a strategic, long-term perspective on existence and the body and hence with the type of outlook that is demanded by the products and services this industry puts on offer. Secondly, their *tendency towards moralism* which not only generates the demand for explicit principles and guidelines to action, but also favours a perception of the most wide-ranging aspects of everyday life in terms of "good" and "bad", "right" or "wrong". Thirdly and finally, the *inclination towards a Berkeleian vision of the social world* in which "being" is often equated with "being-perceived" and which makes the *petit-bourgeoisie* particularly sensitive to everything related to image, appearance and self-presentation.

A Protestant aesthetic

The centrality of ascetic dispositions in defining the *petit-bourgeois* ethos was already discussed in Chapter 3. There it was argued that the gap between objective chances and subjective aspirations is particularly pronounced among those who occupy *intermediate* positions in social space. Having considerably better chances of access to the dominant class than those who are situated at the bottom of the class-hierarchy, their aspirations to do so nevertheless tend to outrun their actual resources. This forces the aspiring fractions of the middle-class into the double strategy of restraint and accumulation in which present consumption and present gratifications become systematically geared to the long-term project of upward mobility. There are at least three ways in which the development of this long-term, strategic perspective on experience resonates with the ethic of the contemporary cult of health and fitness.

First, because they are forced to situate their own social aspirations (home-ownership, promotions, etc.) in a more or less distant future, to which they orient and sacrifice their present, the *petit-bourgeois* tend to be among the most ardent believers in the value of deferred gratification which, as the preceding chapters have aimed to show, is the sine qua non of all forms of investment in bodily appearance and well-being. Second, the objective necessity of austerity and accumulation favours a comprehensive rationalization of the various dimensions of their lifestyle, including of course the relationship to the body. In fact, the same Puritan dispositions that incline agents to the rational administration of income and expenditure and to all forms of thrift, accounting and time-management, also have a spontaneous affinity with all those products, programmes and solutions that require them to monitor and calculate their caloric intake or its equivalent in "points" (as in the infamous *Weight Watchers* programme), to subject their exercise and leisure to pseudo-scientific schedules and routines, to monitor and judge their progress in accordance with pre-defined goals and "targets", if not to organize their entire relationship to the body on the model of double-entry bookkeeping in which every indulgence (often "guilty") should be matched with an equal amount of self-denial, every "input" with an equally large "output". Third and finally, the same meritocratic belief in the value of hard work and personal dedication that is inherent in their social aspirations – exemplified, for instance, in the conviction that "education" (in the largest sense of the term) is a central instrument of individual and social salvation – also has its equivalent in the belief in the inherent plasticity and malleability of the body.

> This cosmetic voluntarism can be deduced from a series of statements on the perceived malleability of the body and the importance of investing in appearance. Whereas 40 per cent of unskilled and 36 per cent of skilled workers still agreed with the proposition "*An attractive body with the right measurements is something you have or you don't, there's not a lot you can do about it*", this drops to 29 per cent of the office-workers in traditional administrative functions and 19 per cent of those in 'front-stage' clerical occupations (secretaries, receptionists, etc.), who also most strongly disagreed (64 per cent) with this statement. Similarly, whereas 32 per cent of unskilled workers and farmers subscribed to the opinion "*I don't believe in dieting, some people are naturally thinner than others, that's just the way it is*", this drops to 14 per cent of the traditional office clerks, 12 per cent of the teachers and 10 per cent of those engaged in occupations devoted to Goffmanian labour. Finally, the proportion of respondents who agreed with the statement "*I don't get that some people can be so preoccupied with their*

> *appearance"* drops from 54 per cent of the unskilled workers and farmers and 52 per cent of the skilled workers to 48 per cent of the office-workers in administrative functions, 42 per cent of the teachers to 25 per cent of Goffmanian workers, only to increase again among the academics (42 per cent), the professionals and senior-executives (55 per cent).
>
> (source: BoS '10)

Doxa and orthodoxy

This tendency towards asceticism is closely tied to a second trait that defines those who occupy intermediate positions in social space (and especially its upwardly aspiring fractions), namely their propensity towards moralism. In fact, the importance that the middle-classes attribute to principles, virtue, values and norms, often coupled with an anxious search for explicit guidelines and models of conduct, can itself be understood as a product of the necessity imposed by their social pretensions. Lacking the initial capital to fully realize their ambitions, the *petit-bourgeois* tend to compensate for this absence through the development of ethical rigor and moral discipline, especially in their relationships with those institutions, like the bank or the educational system, that are most central to their social ascent. Thrift, hard work, obedience, legalism, ethical and linguistic hyper-correctness are all examples of 'the guarantees the *petit-bourgeois* offers to these institutions while putting himself entirely at their mercy (as opposed to the owner of real economic or cultural capital) since they represent his only hope of deriving profits from fundamentally negative assets' (Bourdieu, 1984: 337). In fact, if dominant groups can more often give free rein to the objective mechanisms of social reproduction (inheritance law, titles of nobility, etc.) and can hence more easily dispense with an explicit moralization of their practices, the very social pretensions of the *petit-bourgeoisie* – suspended between what they "are" and what they "want to be" – often mean that they can leave little to chance and force them bring the most divergent areas of everyday life under explicit regulation. Since the slightest deviation from the envisioned social career runs the risk of undermining the project of upward mobility and depriving it of its momentum, moral discipline not only has to be inculcated from an early age onwards, but also constantly reinforced:

> Equidistant from the two extreme poles of the field of social classes, at a neutral point where the forces of attraction and repulsion are evenly balanced, the petit bourgeois are constantly faced with ethical, aesthetic or political dilemmas forcing them to bring the most ordinary operations of existence to the level of consciousness and strategic choice.
>
> (Bourdieu, 1984: 345)

Because their own aspirations condemn them to a situation in which they can take little for granted, the middle-classes are often forced to transform *doxa*, the primary experience of the social world as "natural" and self-evident, into *orthodoxy*, an explicit code of ethical principles and moral guidelines. With this in mind one can perhaps re-read Durkheim's observations on the development of 'systematic asceticism' for a particularly evocative description of the *petit-bourgeois* ethos:

> The negative cult [*petit-bourgeois lifestyle*] usually serves as barely more than an introduction to, and a preparation for, the positive cult [*dominant lifestyle*]. But it sometimes escapes that subordination and becomes central, the system of prohibitions swelling and aggrandizing itself to the point of invading the whole of life. In this way systematic asceticism is born; it is thus nothing more than a bloating of the negative cult. [...] They have the same origin, for both rest on the principle that the very effort to separate oneself from the profane [*i.e. the working-class*] sanctifies. The pure ascetic is a man who raises himself above men and who acquires a special sanctity through fasts, vigils, retreat and silence – in a word, more by privations than by acts of positive piety (offerings, sacrifices, prayers, etc.).
>
> (Durkheim, 1995 [1912]: 316)

This ascetic morality, as Durkheim suggests, already contains a strong element of distinction ("*The pure ascetic is a man who raises himself above men*"). In fact, because it tends to judge properties, practices and beliefs not in terms of their direct utility or practical value, but for the degree in which they conform to "principles", moral action is already a form of disinterested action, and as such presupposes a certain distance from necessity. However, unlike the disinterested and gratuitous practices of the dominant, which derive their distinctive value from conditions of real material and cultural privilege, the disinterest of the middle-classes is often wholly situated on the terrain of morality, measuring itself more by its capacity for restraint and restriction in the name of 'norms' and 'values', rather than by the refined assertion of luxury and freedom ("*more by privations than by acts of positive piety*").

It is precisely this importance attributed to virtue and "principles" and especially the tendency to elevate self-denial and privation to the level of ethical virtues that resonates with another aspect of the contemporary beauty- and fitness-industry, namely its tendency to *moralize* the relationship to the body. Several authors (see Stinson, 1981; Turner, 1994; Stearns, 2002) have in fact noted how, despite its obviously secular and "inner-worldly" goals (beauty, charm, sexual desirability, etc.), the discourse of the various experts in health, beauty and fitness remains steeped in an ethical and often quasi-religious terminology. Not only do their various tips, trick and guidelines contribute to dividing the most wide-ranging aspects of everyday life – from cooking to sexuality, child-rearing to skin-care – into the spheres of "good" and "bad", but such guidelines are themselves suffused with the language of "sin", "guilt", "temptation", "indulgence", "sacrifice", "salvation" and "redemption". If such terms have been stripped of their more metaphysical connotations, fact remains that the cultural messages of the various "lifestyle-experts" (themselves delivered with the necessary proselytizing zeal) often draw on remarkably traditional themes. In fact, attaining and maintaining the "sacred" state of a slim and healthy body requires that individuals resist all the "profane" temptations provided by consumer culture, that they display moderation and self-discipline in the face of an abundance of "bad" things and pay for any transgressions ("guilty pleasures") with abstinence, self-denial and self-sacrifice ("*working off those holiday pounds*").

In a sense, this predisposes the products and services offered by the various specialists in bodily management to be perceived and interpreted in *moral* terms – i.e. as pertaining to the "correct" and "appropriate" mode of being and to the definition of the accomplished individual – especially by those who, like the middle-classes, are inclined to read everyday life through a moral lens. In fact, even if the discourse of the contemporary cult of health and beauty often *claims* to emancipate or liberate the body from the bonds of traditional morality (as it pertains to sexuality for instance), one could argue that in reality it has effectively multiplied the sites for moral judgment. Better yet, one could even say that one of the most significant accomplishments of the contemporary health and fitness-industry is that it has managed to transform the act of investing in and working on the body *itself* into a distinct source of moral value. Even if the gap between the body that is and the body that "ought to be" can never be fully closed – and the incessant dialectic of distinction and pretension effectively ensures that it never does – the very *intention* of bringing the body in line with the dominant ideal is already deemed laudable in and of itself ("*the very effort to separate oneself from the profane sanctifies*"). By actively *trying* to realize the legitimate body, by "doing something, rather than nothing", the *petit-bourgeois* already distinguish themselves from the passivity and inertia – always read as a form of *moral* laxity, a "letting oneself go" – of those who, like the working-class, apparently lack the basic self-determination to take up their body as an on-going "project".

Being-perceived

While their propensity towards asceticism and moralism explains part of the appeal that the morality eschewed by the diet- and health-industry exerts on the middle-classes, it is the particular importance that they grant to "appearance" and "image" that tends to make them into its ideal clientele. In fact, nowhere does the question of the relationship between "being" and "seeming", "backstage" and "front stage", "essence" and "appearance" pose itself in such an explicit manner than among those who occupy intermediate positions in the social structure. The very desire for recognition by the dominant – i.e. to "make a good impression" – which is inherent in their social aspirations tends to render the *petit-bourgeois* extremely sensitive to the image they project towards others. As such, it generates a considerable amount of anxiety and self-doubt as to what constitutes the appropriate "norms" of appearance and demeanour which manifests itself, amongst others, in a constant search for guidelines, advice, "tips and tricks". As mentioned above, the relative over-consumption of lifestyle-magazines and -television among the middle-classes can be understood, at least partly, as the result of this desire to "keep informed" and "up-to-date" or, perhaps better, is partly inspired by the fear of appearing "outdated", "out of the loop" or "out of fashion". It is this double insecurity – i.e. with regards to what exactly constitutes the norm within a given social situation *and* the manner in which one's own behaviour measures up to it – that not only imbues their actions and words with a high degree of reflexive self-consciousness, but also inclines them towards all forms of "hyper-correction" in accent, posture or discourse. In fact, contrary to those whose privileged access to the most distinguished practices, products and services enables them to be "naturally cultivated", as well as those whose social conditions foreclose upon the very pretension to enter the symbolic race and hence condemn them to being "naturally natural"; for members of the *petit-bourgeoisie* being "natural" is always problematic, since it is precisely that which – as Richard Hoggart observed in the introduction to this chapter – is liable of "giving them away". It is this constant self-monitoring and self-correcting, the feeling of being "on edge" or "in character" in social situations that form the basis for what Bourdieu (1984: 253) called a 'Berkeleian' (or 'Goffmanian') vision of the social world. Treating being as synonymous with "being-perceived", this vision often tends to reduce everyday social life to a theatrical performance in which every actor is seen as assuming his or her *rôle*, of dissimulating his or her true identity behind a carefully constructed public mask. This tendency to draw a strong distinction between the "front-stage" of public self-presentation and the "backstage" of authentic, natural interaction (often associated with the privacy of the home and a tight-knit conception of the family) is only reinforced by the professional logic of all those occupations (secretaries, hostesses, sales clerks, representatives, etc.) in which the middle-classes have to use their charm, elegance and "image" as professional attributes, that is, have to sell their own image and appearance in order to sell their particular products or services.

However, in as much as this anxious concern with the "body-for-others", is a source of tension and ambiguity (not to mention the basis for the famous *petit-bourgeois* resentment), it is also an important instrument for social ascent. If their social pretensions often earn them the scorn of dominant and dominated alike (both of which are quick to denounce them as "snobbish" or "pedantic"), strategies of symbolic emulation or "bluff" are often one of the few ways that members of the middle-class have at their disposal to transcend the limits inscribed in their social conditions, that is, to overcome the discrepancy between aspirations and chances. As Bourdieu notes:

> Their concern for appearance, which may be experienced as unhappy consciousness, sometimes disguised as arrogance, is also a source of their pretension, a permanent disposition towards the bluff or usurpation of social identity which consists in anticipating 'being' by 'seeming', appropriating the appearances so as to have the reality, the nominal so as to have the real, in trying to modify the positions in the objective classifications by modifying the representation of the ranks in the classification or of the principles of classification.
>
> (1984: 253)

It is precisely this collective belief in the "power of looks" that renders them particularly inclined to appropriate the outward signs of a more prestigious social position and especially eager to invest in all those forms of extra-curricular training that aim to compensate for a lack of inherited capital.

> The proportion of respondents who indicated they had taken extra-curricular classes in diction and verbal expression rises from 5 per cent among the unskilled workers and farmers and 2 per cent of the skilled workers and foremen to 14 per cent of the office-workers in administrative functions, 19 per cent of office clerks in representational functions to 20 per cent of the teachers and reaches its peak among the upper fringes of the middle-class, namely 30 per cent of the junior-executives. Interestingly, this number tends to drop again as one moves to members of the dominant class where a quarter of the artists and cultural producers (24 per cent) and less than a fifth of the academics and professionals (18 per cent) indicated they had ever taken such classes.
>
> (source: BoS '10)

That this optimistic faith in the power of "looks" can quite easily regress to an alienated and unhappy relationship to the body is shown by the manner in which members of the middle-class, and middle-class *women* in particular, experience the process that threatens to erode this very power, namely *ageing*. In fact, the more agents depend on their appearance and self-presentation as a source of labour power, the more they come to experience this process, and hence the gradual deterioration of their physical capital, as a source of considerable anxiety and frustration. Working-class women, who derive little value from their "body-for-others" and can at any rate expect little from investing in it, also tend to be less concerned with the decline of its valued properties throughout the life-course (which is not to say they are completely immune to its effects). Conversely, while women who occupy dominant social positions place more value on bodily *hexis* and appearance, their definition of physical grace and excellence tends to stress authenticity over artificiality, depth over surface and hence privileges the more fundamental and timeless markers of "class" embodied in comportment, speech and manners over the vagaries of superficial beauty. More importantly, their access to less ephemeral sources of social power provides them with forms of symbolic capital (occupational prestige, cultural authority, social standing, etc.) that are less prone to biological decline and present them with better opportunities to "age gracefully" (on this point see Featherstone, 1987 and more recently Dumas *et al.,* 2006).

This is often much less the case for women of the *petit-bourgeoisie* who are most directly dependent on the state of their physical capital and are hence also most by its (biological) decline. Because this fleeting type of capital is condemned to devalue with age, middle-class women are often particularly predisposed to invest in all those techniques (surgical or non-surgical) that are aimed at warding off the most visible effects of ageing. In fact, the same logic that inclines them to appropriate the markers of a higher position in the *social* division of labour, also inclines them to adopt the traits associated with a more prestigious (i.e. younger) position in the hierarchy of age-groups. In a sense, this makes them "doubly" pretentious, especially in the eyes of the dominant who tend to view such desperate attempts to cling onto a more youthful image as the ultimate expression of a lack of taste (*"mutton dressed as lamb"*).[2]

> Whereas 38 per cent of the unskilled workers and farmers agreed with the statement *"Getting older doesn't bother me"* (while only 29 per cent disagreed), this percentage tends to drop as one moves towards the middle-classes and especially towards those occupations which place the largest importance on appearance and self-presentation. So while 39 per cent of the office clerks performing more traditional "backstage"-tasks (administration, accounting, etc.) agreed (while 30 per cent disagreed), this drops to 36 per cent of the teachers (40 per cent disagreed) and reaches its low among women involved in the "front-stage"-labour of presentation and representation, less than a quarter of which agreed (23 per cent), while more than half of them (54 per cent) disagreed. Interestingly, as one moves to women who occupy dominant social positions, the number of women who indicate that ageing doesn't bother them increased again with 40 per cent of female academics and 46 per cent of women in the professions agreeing with this statement, while 37 per cent and 46 per cent, respectively, disagreed (source: BoS '10). Similarly, when looking at the manner in which women *over the age of 40 years old* rate their own appearance (on a scale from 0 to 10), the office clerks (6.6) prove to be closer to the unskilled workers and farmers (6.3) and unemployed women (6.4), than to the junior-executives (7.1), the professionals and senior-executives (7.1) and even rate themselves lower in appearance than the housewives (6.8).
> (source: SHW '06)

The anxiety surrounding the effects of ageing is just one illustration of the fact that for large numbers of women, especially those in employed in occupations entailing Goffmanian labour (sales clerks, secretaries, hostesses, receptionists, etc.), the inherently emancipatory effects of paid employment often come at the price of a host of new concerns. More specifically, the same principle that enables them to escape the most degrading effects of relationships of *economic* dependence and the confinement to domestic life – i.e. their physical properties and "charm" as an autonomous source of labour power – also exposes them to the effects of *symbolic* power and domination. A form of domination that is all the more subtle and effective, because it hinges on the consent of the dominated – i.e. their willingness to be ranked according to the dominant criteria of physical value – and hence has all the appearance of being wholly "self-imposed".

Situating reflexivity

Having arrived at the end of this chapter, we are now perhaps better placed to clarify some of the key-differences between the theoretical perspective that has animated our analyses and the sociological narratives propounded by theorists of "late", "reflexive", "liquid" or "post"-modernity. The main point of divergence does not so much concern the *reality* of phenomena like bodily self-consciousness, anxiety and insecurity or the growing perception of the body as an inherently malleable object open to reflexive management and manipulation. Where our perspective parts ways with such narratives is in their conception of both the social *origins* and *scope* of these phenomena. In fact, whereas the latter postulate that certain key societal transformations – most notably the erosion of the traditional frames of reference provided by State, Religion or Class – have produced a gradual "disembedding" of lifestyle from its traditional conditions of production which have instead given way to the increasingly important role of the individual in reflexively crafting his or her own self-identity. What the preceding chapters have argued (and what the analyses have aimed to show) is that there is not only remarkably little evidence for this purported individualization of the relationship between the individual and his or her body, but also (and perhaps more importantly) that the type of attitudes they view as all but endemic to life in "high" or "reflexive" modernity are themselves disproportionately located in a particular region of social space, namely among the *middle-class*es. The anxious concern with appearance and the "body-for-others", the conception of the body as an on-going project which deserves (and demands) constant maintenance and investment, the uncertainties regarding the "proper" manner of feeding, clothing and caring for it and the search for explicit guidelines, advice and rules regarding its "appropriate" management, all find their ideal conditions of possibility in the tensions, ambiguities and contradictions faced by those who occupy "intermediate" social positions. However, if the specific constellation of features that constitute the *petit-bourgeois* habitus (as outlined in this chapter) make them particularly prone to the symbolic violence that accompanies the imposition of the dominant bodily ideal, bodily self-consciousness and anxiety are by no means exclusive to middle-class men and women. Indeed, the following (and final) chapter will show that they increasingly affect members of the working-class (and especially working-class *women*) as well.

Notes

1 Susan Bordo speaks of 'the central role of media imagery in "spreading" eating and body-image problems across race and class (or sexual orientation)' (1993: xix). Featherstone considers advertising as having 'helped to create a world in which individuals are made to become emotionally vulnerable, constantly monitoring themselves for bodily imperfections which could no longer be regarded as natural' (1991: 175). Similarly, Bauman speaks of 'the formidable power which the mass media exercise over popular – collective and individual – imagination. Powerful, 'more real than reality' images on ubiquitous screens set the standards for reality and for its evaluation, as well as the urge to make the 'lived' reality more palatable (2000: 84).
2 In their study of class-differences in the experience of ageing among elderly Canadian women, Dumas *et al.* (2006) have shown how their upper-class respondents were often quite benign in their judgment of working-class women – which they recognized as lacking the means to "age gracefully" – but proved more hostile towards those women (i.e. from the middle-classes) who had the pretentiousness to perpetuate an image of youth and beauty that was at odds with their actual age.

9 Necessity incarnate

> The body is man's first and most natural instrument.
> (Mauss, 1973 [1935]: 75)

The case of the working-class relationship to the body raises a question that has been lurking at the edge of the analysis as it has unfolded throughout the preceding chapters. If the essence of "class" is acquired in a manner that largely eludes conscious description, that is only transmitted by lasting insertion into a specific class of conditions and that is rooted in a profoundly corporeal knowledge of class-position, then how is one ever to produce an adequate account of the experience that is engendered in that position? In fact, the risk of producing an account which, under the guise of an objective description of the working-class condition, is nothing more than a transmuted form of the intellectual relationship *to* that condition, is perhaps nowhere as real as when describing an aspect of this condition which, like the practical experience of the body, not only shares so much of the incommunicable, but which is also in many ways the *antithesis* of the intellectual relationship to the world (and the body). Purely interpretative or "qualitative" methods might be of little avail here. In fact, even if one were to place oneself in the working-class condition and expose oneself to the experience of necessity that defines it, fact remains that this experience is always grasped through categories of perception and action that are the product of *different* social conditions.

Here as elsewhere, perhaps the only way to escape from this partial perspective is to fully constitute it as such, that is, to re-construct the space of positions that forms the basis for the different and antagonistic points-of-view on the social world. Such an approach is not a way of submitting before a post-modern relativism or 'perspectivism', but, quite to the contrary, hinges on the conviction that only by analysing, classifying and comparing the different perspectives on the body that are engendered in different class-positions, does it become possible to define what is particular to each, including that which animates the "intellectual" perspective. In fact, only by trying to isolate and objectify what distinguishes this particular point-of-view from all others does it become possible to try and transcend the limits it imposes. By doing so, it perhaps becomes possible

Necessity incarnate 213

to more adequately grasp the central paradox that informs the working-class relationship to the body. In fact, whereas no group depends as closely on the body, its strength and its skills in order to ensure their social reproduction, there is also no group that adopts such a stoic attitude towards its needs, its desires and the general degree of "wear and tear" it incurs through its everyday uses. It is this simultaneous *over*-valuation and *under*-protection of the body which Schwartz succinctly captured in the following maxim: 'One does not protect the body, it is the body that protects' (1990: 479). In fact, because they are exposed to conditions of existence that force them to work as much *with* as *against* their bodies, working-class men and women often tend to credit it with an innate "robustness", a natural capacity to incur physical "shock", pain and fatigue and even an intrinsic ability to repair and regenerate itself outside of any deliberate intervention on the part of its owners. This basic belief again underlines how the relationship to the body is part and parcel of one's relationship to the social world and how, more specifically, the feeling of being able to exert control over, to manage and to influence the state of one's own body is but one dimension of the more general feeling of being able to exert control over the totality of one's own existence.

At the risk of repetition, it should be stressed once more how this instrumental and quasi-mechanistic conception of the body is at odds with the development of a therapeutic and aesthetic, that is to say, *autonomous* relationship towards it. In fact, the very reality of manual labour means that agents are forced to expose themselves fully to the forces and frictions of the physical world and hence to the temporary or lasting traces it leaves on the body. To worry about the short- or long-term effects that such exposure might have on the outer appearance or inner well-being of the body is to effectively prevent oneself from fully engaging with the task at hand, to introduce a reticence and reflexivity in an act that demands the complete engagement of the body, its strength and its skills, in short, to reduce its capacity for labour (also see Boltanski, 1971). Conversely, to treat one's body as an object of care and attention, to pay active attention to its signs and signals and to cater to its intrinsic needs presupposes *distance*, which is first and foremost a distance from economic necessity. To this also needs to be added (as Chapter 3 already argued) the manner in which economic insecurity tends to undermine the development of the strategic, long-term dispositions towards the body which form the basis for the entire notion of "medical prevention". In fact, the less the future discloses itself as a field of meaningful possibilities and the more the exigencies of daily life tend to tie agents to an inescapable present, the less they tend to worry about the long-term effects of their present-day actions, let alone to orient such actions in terms of future, abstract and often wholly "negative" gains like health and longevity.

> The number of respondents who agreed with a proposition like "*There's no point in worrying about your health, everyone can get ill*" decreases sharply from nearly half (47 per cent) of unskilled workers and farmers (of whom only 31 per cent disagreed), a third of the skilled workers (34 per cent agree,

32 per cent disagree), less than a fifth of the office clerks (19 per cent) and the junior-executives (16 per cent) to 15 per cent of the professionals and the senior-executives of whom 64 per cent disagreed (source: BoS '10). Similarly, the number of respondents *over the age of 40 years old* who indicated they had gone for a cholesterol check-up in the past five years, goes from 66 per cent of the unskilled workers and farmers, 77 per cent of the office-workers, 85 per cent of the junior-executives, 78 per cent of the professionals and 86 per cent of the senior-executives.

(source: BNHS '04)

Before all too easily (dis)qualifying this practical philosophy of the body as "fatalistic", it should be stressed that it plays a central role in the process by which dominated agents negotiate the necessity that defines their social conditions. More specifically, the belief in the body's innate robustness can be said to fulfil at least two crucial functions. On the one hand, it enables a continuous *over-estimation* of the capacity for sustained activity and exertion and hence helps to satisfy the strictly economic imperative of extracting the maximum potential for labour from the body. On the other, it favours *an under-estimation* of the risk and harm to which the body is exposed and hence provides a rudimentary buffer against the most degrading – in the physical and psychological sense of this term – effects of their everyday living and working-conditions. This philosophy of the body does not only inform the manner in which working-class men and women come to experience their own bodies, but also occupies a central place in their educational strategies and especially in their perception of the physical abilities and needs of their children. In fact, the belief in the inherent resilience of the body perhaps applies *a fortiori* to children's bodies, which are thought to have an even greater capacity for self-protection and self-correction than adults. As already briefly mentioned in Chapter 5, a number of forms of popular "indulgence" towards children, especially in the domain of food and drink (sweets, soft-drinks, etc.), can be traced back to this practical conception of the body as a robust structure. If certain practices and products are being increasingly recognized as "unhealthy" or "bad" (which is one of the effects of the manifold public health-campaigns, often targeted directly at working-class families), their potentially pathological effects are often minimized by the assumption that they will eventually "wear off", that it's good to "have a buffer" or that children will simply "grow out of it".

The labouring body

To try and provide an adequate account of the popular relationship to the body is always to plot a treacherous course between the Scylla of *populism*, which tends to view such tastes as the confident assertion of a "culture-for-itself", ignoring that this "culture" emerges out of conditions of privation and necessity and is as such profoundly marked by the effects of class-domination, and the Charybdis of *miserabilism* which, seeing *only* domination and exploitation, often ignores that the latter can only function and be perpetuated because dominated groups manage to construct a valorizing sense of self-identity from the limited means at their disposal. What both alternatives tend to overlook, is that 'necessity can only function, most of the time, because agents are inclined to fulfil it' (Bourdieu, 1984: 178). One of the key mechanisms that leads dominated agents to not only accept, but actively embrace a dominated condition and the experience of necessity that defines it, was already discussed in Chapter 1. There I argued, following Willis and others, that the scarcity of socially recognized resources (income, educational degree, etc.) leads agents to turn to other sources of status to construct a valorizing sense of self, most notably their *sexual* identity. In fact, one of the things that make it particularly problematic to speak about *the* "working-class" relationship to the body (*in globo*) is that this relationship itself is strongly differentiated along gendered lines. If the reality of economic necessity profoundly shapes the way in which dominated groups come to experience their bodies, this experience tends to take on a quite different shape and hue for women and men. Among the latter, it constitutes the basis for an ethos of virility which, although rooted in economic imperatives, extends well beyond the professional uses of the body.

As Chapter 6 already indicated, economic necessity alone cannot in itself account for the often frenetic desire for physical effort and the agonistic self-assertion through labour that extend well beyond the sphere of paid work. Weight-lifting, boxing, DIY, gardening, moonlighting, etc. are all part of a constellation which Schwartz subsumed under the rubric of practices of 'expenditure' (*dépense*). He used the concept of 'expenditure' to denote a 'way of using physical force that is rooted in the intention of consuming it to the fullest extent. The principle of these practices is not to conserve but to spend and to go to the limit' (1990: 294). Akin to a "potlatch" of physical force, Schwartz argues that, one of the reasons why working-class men often prove so eager to invest in and conspicuously display their physical strength and prowess is ultimately because it constitutes one of the few resources that they *can* spend and spend in quantity. More importantly, it is also the type of resource that forms the basis for an identity that working-class men can claim as being almost *exclusively* their own. As Paul Willis observes:

> Though it is difficult to obtain stature in work itself, both what work provides and the very sacrifice and strength required to do it provides the materials for an elemental self-esteem. This self-esteem derives from an achievement of purpose which not all – particularly women – are held capable of achieving.
>
> (1974: 150)

Charlesworth makes a similar argument, when he notes that:

> Being a 'big strong lad' or a 'good grafter' is a sure mark of people who have been reduced to little because only in conditions of scarcity and the

absence of others forms of competence could capacity to work with one's body be a form of capital, a difference that made a difference.

(2000: 262)

If working-class men so willingly expose themselves to demanding, dangerous and ill-paid working conditions, this is because the latter still provide them with a space for the demonstration of a competence and the accumulation of a type of symbolic capital over which they can assert a quasi-monopoly, namely the capacity for "real" work that requires "real" strength and "real" skills and is hence as much opposed to the mere "window-dressing" that characterizes women's work or the simple "pencil-pushing" performed by upper- and middle-class men. More generally, because virility serves as one of the few distinctive sources of symbolic capital, masculine identity always has its dual point-of-reference in the "posh" and "effete" mannerisms of those who occupy more favourable positions, as well as the "frivolous" and "superficial" concerns of women.

It is precisely this double point-of-reference by which working-class men use virility to not only assert their "natural" superiority over women, but also to invert the dominant table of values (mental work = feminine = inferior/manual work = masculine = superior) which in my view is not adequately captured by Connell's concept of 'hegemonic masculinity' (see Connell, 1987: 183ff.; Connell, 1995: 76ff.). While she is right in pointing out the existence of a hierarchy of masculinities and femininities, her proposition that there is one type of masculinity which does not only asserts itself over women, but also over other types of masculinity to me does not seem to be fully borne out by the evidence. In fact, while she asserts that 'there is no femininity that holds among women the position that hegemonic masculinity holds among men' and that 'actual femininities in our society are more diverse than actual masculinities' (1987: 187), our analysis (especially the classification of bodies presented in Chapter 4) suggests that quite the opposite holds true. Not only did it reveal a larger consensus among women as to what constitutes the ideal feminine physique, but this ideal was also much more readily attributed to upper-class women. Did this not prove to be the case among men, where there was a clear proclivity for a muscular ideal, but this ideal was not clearly associated with a particular group or class.

I would argue that one of the key reasons for such differences is that for women, the 'legitimate market in physical properties' (Bourdieu, 1984: 152) is at once more extensive *and* more unified than for men. This means that, among women, certain physical properties (like slimness, for instance) have a much more uniform value and a much wider currency *across* social space than they do for men. From this it also follows that the imposition of dominant standards of attractiveness is felt much more strongly among the working-class women than it is among men. What this means for the practical experience of the female body will be discussed more fully in the following section. Here I merely want to suggest that as far as men are concerned, there exists a wider plethora of "local" markets with divergent conceptions of accomplished masculinity which, especially in the case of working-class men, provide a degree of protection against the imposition of the dominant lifestyle. It enables them to perpetuate an ethos of virility that is not only materialized in the physical features of the labouring body, but also deposited at the level of bodily *hexis*.

Even if this ethos can sometimes take on the appearance of an "aesthetic" – a cultivation of physical form for form's sake, as in *body-building* – the working-class perception of the male body remains wholly subjected to the functional demands of a functional relationship to the social world, that is, a world in which judgments of physical *form* are, ultimately, judgments of physical *force*. One could even argue, with Charlesworth (2000: 257ff.) and Wacquant (2004: 41ff.), that popular pastimes like weight-lifting or boxing are themselves used as a means of demonstrating and upholding traditional forms of working-class masculinity and this perhaps increasingly more so, given that the institutional basis for this ethos of virility – i.e. stable employment in manual labour – is in a state of accelerated erosion. The on-going precarization of employment that has accompanied processes of large-scale de-industrialization has in fact led to a gradual compression and fracturing of the spaces in which working-class masculinity can assert itself in a positive and valorizing manner (a process which is all too vividly captured by Charlesworth, 2000). Since so much of this ethos of physical and agonistic self-assertion depends on manual labour for its positive expression and valorization, the decline in the availability of this type of labour not only generates *material* insecurity, but also cuts off access to one of the central markets for the demonstration and accumulation of *symbolic* capital (i.e. masculine pride and honour).

More importantly, at the same time that the *positive* foundation for this identity is shrinking, working-class men (and especially the *youngest* generations) increasingly find themselves subjected to the verdicts of social markets that wield quite different (and often opposing) criteria of social value. This seems especially true of the growing importance of the educational system as an arbiter of social status. The judgments of the latter are in fact based on the successful display of precisely those dispositions *against* which working-class masculinity is constructed, namely docility, adherence to pedagogic authority, physical passivity and self-censorship, in short, all the traits that the sexual cosmology of the working-class disproportionately assigns to women. Similarly, if traditional forms of working-class masculinity still have a value on a labour market that is increasingly geared to the demands of a service-economy, it is often in a highly limited and "aestheticized" form. Instead of valuing qualities like strength and endurance in terms of their capacity for physical production and transformation, those service-sector jobs that demand an assertive type of masculinity, like security-clerk or bouncer, often reduce such qualities to their purely *symbolic* dimension, that is, as "signs" that merely indicate the *potential* for violence and confrontation.

A body-for-others

While the capacity for sustained physical exertion and the ability to withstand pain, fatigue or discomfort are central components of popular masculinity, the ethos of self-renunciation that subtends the popular uses of the body is by no means restricted to working-class men. The experience of the body as one's 'first and most natural instrument' (Mauss, 1973: 75) equally structures the manner in which women who occupy the most precarious positions in social space come to use, perceive and judge their bodies. For the latter, however, the dispossession and self-denial that flow from occupying an inferior position in the class-structure is further compounded by the effects of occupying a dominated position in the *sexual* division of labour. If their experience with paid employment already tends to foster an "instrumental" rather than "ornamental" relationship to the body, this experience is only reinforced by the realities of domestic and maternal labour. In fact, one of the corollaries of a sexual division of labour that equates the masculine with the public, the assertive and the extroverted is that working-class women are assigned the quasi-monopoly over the sphere of the private and the introverted, that is, over the material, emotional and symbolic management of the domestic economy.

If their professional uses of the body already encourage its perception as a tool honed towards ends that lie wholly outside of itself, their domestic responsibilities only tend to reinforce such an instrumentalist relation to the body. It is in their roles of mothers and partners that women come to perceive themselves and their bodies as the legitimate provides of pleasure, who systematically place the needs and desires of others before their own. However, one of the key-differences between their professional and domestic roles is the degree of autonomy and control they provide. Contrary to the physically demanding, poorly remunerated nature of the work that is available to them (women remain overrepresented among the most precarious categories of the labour force, see Figure 1.2), the domestic and maternal role, for all the particular hardships it entails, still provides them with one of the few venues for acquiring a sense of independence and personal achievement. Just as working-class men often come to accept harsh working conditions because they still provide them with the basis for a valorizing mode of self-assertion, working-class women often so readily accept the monotony and drudgeries of domestic life, because it not only provides them with a limited sphere of control, but also because it offers a way of ascending to a socially recognized and valorized identity.

An identity of which self-renunciation and self-sacrifice are foundational elements. As their attitudes towards food and dining presented in Chapter 5 illustrate, working-class women tend to systematically value the physical and emotional needs of their family over the more "narcissistic" concerns with the effects of food on the appearance and shape of their own bodies (on this point also see Charles and Kerr, 1988; Warrin *et al.*, 2008). More generally, their specific role as care-takers who sacrifice their own needs and desires in favour of their partners and children tends to produce what Schwartz (1990) coined 'anti-narcissistic' dispositions. The latter are at the basis of a practical conception of the female body in which any form of "pampering" or "mollycoddling" is often seen as an in irresponsible luxury, not only because it implies resources that are at any rate scarce, but also because they imply forms of investment in the self that wholly contradict the ethos of self-renunciation that is one of the central pillars of working-class femininity.

Working-class women not only most often agreed with the proposition that people spend too much time on their appearance, least often invoked beauty and slimness as reasons for engaging in sports, but also prove most inclined to agree with a statement like "*I just want to be dressed neatly that's all*" (78 per cent compared to 50 per cent of the office clerks, 26 per cent of the teachers, 35 per cent of the junior-executives and 54 per cent of female professionals) and least often agreed with the statement "*I often buy fashion-magazines*" (5 per cent compared to 15 per cent of the office clerks, 11 per cent of the teachers and 12 per cent of the junior-executives, although none of the professionals agreed, which seems to support the thesis defended in the previous two chapters). A perhaps even more pertinent indicator of this instrumental orientation towards the body can be found in the differential uses that are made of an item of clothing which perhaps most clearly expresses the subjection of bodily functionality to form, that effectively inhibits the uses of the body as an instrument and instead highlights its importance as a perceptible form or "sign" oriented towards the scrutiny of others and aimed at conveying charm and desirability in its everyday movements, namely *high heels*. Whereas 74 per cent of the unskilled workers indicated they *never* wore high heels during their working-hours, this drops to 38 per cent among administrative office-workers, 32 per cent of those in Goffmanian occupations, 26 per cent of the secondary school-teachers, 24 per cent of the academics and 31 per cent of the senior-executives and members of the professions.

(source: BoS '10)

However, in as much as their domestic role provides the basis for a valorizing self-identity, their doubly dominated position tends to place different and even contradictory demands on their bodies. In fact, precisely because they are tasked with the management of the symbolic capital of the family and the home – what Collins coined 'the Weberian task of transforming class into status group membership' (Collins, 1992: 219) – women are "naturally" predisposed to display an interest in matters of style and appearance. While men still find a minimal defence against the imposition of the dominant definition of appearance in an ethos of virility that devalues everything related to form(ality) as effeminate and hence inferior, working-class women are presented with no such alternatives. If the logic of sexual domination inclines them to judge their bodies in terms of its perceptible qualities, then the logic of social domination excludes them from the resources that are necessary to realize the most valued physique. If the body marked by the realities of manual and/or domestic labour certainly has a distinct "local" value – i.e. derives its *raison-d'être* and its social worth from the primary group of family and close friends – it has little or no value on the broader markets in symbolic goods and properties, where it often serves as the foil *against* which the definitions of middle- and upper-class femininity are constructed (see Skeggs, 1997).

It is precisely the practical recognition of the limited value of their own physical capital which makes working-class women particularly prone to the type of 'socially constituted agoraphobia' which leads them 'to exclude themselves from a whole range of public activities and ceremonies from which they are structurally excluded' (Bourdieu and Wacquant, 1994: 74). Unable (and hence ill-inclined) to realize the dominant norms of appearance and demeanour, they are nevertheless incapable of ignoring the value it assigns to their bodies. If it is indeed true that every habitus 'seeks to create the conditions of its fulfilment, and therefore to create the conditions most favourable to what it is' (Bourdieu, 2000b: 150), it also follows that every habitus will seek to avoid those conditions in which it systematically finds itself questioned, problematized, stigmatized and devalued. Just as the practical recognition of their own devalued cultural competence increasingly condemns them to silence in matters of culture and politics (see Charlesworth, 2000), the awareness of their own stigmatized physique leads dominated agents (and especially working-class women) to withdraw from those spaces in which they are subjected to public scrutiny and to retreat within the security of the primary group which at least provides a basic 'protective capsule' (Goffman, 1963), against the devaluation of their physical capital.

> If women were almost twice as likely as men to agree with the statement "*I often feel uncomfortable when I'm in public places*" (19 per cent compared to 11 per cent), such avowals of public insecurity in turn varied sharply in terms of their own position within the different hierarchies of capital. For instance, whereas more than a third (36 per cent) of women with little or no formal education and a quarter (26 per cent) of those in the lowest income-brackets (an income of less than 1,250 euros a month) agreed with this statement (while 39 per cent and 50 per cent disagreed), this drops to 10 per cent of those with a master's or postgraduate degree and 14 per cent of those with an income exceeding 4,000 euros a month (of whom 70 per cent and 84 per cent respectively disagreed). That such insecurity is not just a simple function of the actual time that women spend outside of the domestic sphere (i.e. in paid employment) is shown by the fact that agreement with this statement varies only slightly between housewives (24 per cent agree) and those who are employed part-time (21 per cent) or full-time (17 per cent). Instead, it appears closely linked to the specific sector of the labour market in which women find themselves. For instance, while 45 per cent of female unskilled workers and farmers agreed with this statement, this drops to 19 per cent of the office clerks – which are themselves strongly divided between those that perform more traditional "backstage"-functions (26 per cent agree) and those whose job entails roles of presentation and representation (only 10 per cent agreed) – over 16 per cent of the junior-executives to 8 per cent of female professionals and executives.
>
> (source: BoS '10)

In fact, when it comes to discussing the ways in which the divisions of class and gender help shape the experience of the "body-for-others", perhaps one of the most remarkable phenomena is the curious historical inversion in the prevalence of a disorder like *agoraphobia*. As a phenomenon that, in the late nineteenth and early twentieth century, was mainly concentrated among women of the bourgeoisie, where it provided the unarticulated expression of all the phantasms and anxieties that were projected onto "the street" as the site of violence, promiscuity and moral depravity typically associated with the unruly working-class (De Swaan, 1981; Reuter, 2008), nowadays it is disproportionately found among women who occupy the most precarious social positions (see Schneier *et al.* 1992 or Ruscio *et al.* 2008).

The transformations in the dominant definition of femininity that have accompanied the increased influx of upper- and middle-class women into the public sphere – where they have discovered, amongst other, the material and symbolic rewards linked to bodily "form" and self-presentation (albeit at the price of a host of new concerns and anxieties) – also mean that women who are situated at the bottom of social space increasingly find themselves measured against standards of appearance and demeanour that are fundamentally at odds with the type of femininity that is produced in conditions of necessity. While all of this has obvious consequences for the manner in which working-class women come to experience their "body-for-others", there is also evidence to suggest that the effects of symbolic dispossession exerted by the imposition of the dominant definition of femininity tend to extend into the most intimate aspects of the relationship to the body, namely those related to its sexual being.

The de-narcissized body

The case of sexuality is of particular interest because it shows how the practical awareness of the value ascribed to his or her body does not only determine the ease or difficulty with which each agent negotiates its "symbolic" appropriation through the objectifying gaze of others, but also its "physical" appropriation within an act which constitutes the ultimate surrender of one's body to another. As such, the case of sexuality can help elucidate the principles that govern the relationship to the body in general. 'In so far as man's [*sic*] sexual history provides a key to his life', writes Merleau-Ponty, 'it is because in his sexuality is projected his manner of being towards the world, that is, towards time and other men' (1969: 158). The logic of social and sexual domination impinges on sexuality by structuring what Merleau-Ponty calls the 'sexual schema', that particular dimension of bodily experience which endows the individual with the capacity of 'projecting before himself a sexual world, of putting himself in an erotic situation, or, once such a situation is stumbled upon, of maintaining it or following it through to complete satisfaction' (ibid.: 156). In fact, the dominant view of the working-class, and working-class *women* in particular, as the site of an uninhibited sexual appetite and promiscuity (nowadays incarnated in the conservative spectre of the "single welfare-mom") tends to obscure the fact that it is precisely those women who occupy the most precarious social positions, who often experience the greatest difficulties in realizing a fulfilling sexuality.

In their large-scale study of the social differentiation in sexual practices and attitudes, Laumann *et al.* (1994: 368ff.) already observed that the incidence of sexual dysfunctions (inability to orgasm, experiencing pain during intercourse, not finding sex pleasurable, lacking interest in sex, etc.) proved inversely related to women's position in the different hierarchies of capital (and was considerably higher than that of men *at any given level*). Similarly, ethnographic studies on working-class intimacy and sexuality (Schwartz 1990: 480ff.; Skeggs 1997: 118ff.) have also drawn attention to the inherent difficulties that working-class women experience in recognizing themselves as sexual beings, that is, as not just the *object*, but also the *subject* of sexual desire. One of the central causes of such a problematic sexual subjectivity is undoubtedly located in a particularly dichotomous and asymmetrical sexual division of labour (see Chapter 1) and, especially, the manner in which its definition of men as the legitimate *recipients* and women as the *providers* of pleasure in turn shapes the division of sexual labour. However, for working-class women, the effects of sexual domination are compounded by those that result from occupying a dominated position in the class-structure. Doubly dominated, their relationship to the body is most clearly marked by the logic of self-renunciation and dispossession that imposes itself on the working-class as a whole.

Schwartz (1990) reads this process of self-renunciation in psycho-analytical terms by arguing that the relationship to the body of working-class women is marked by a gradual process of 'de-narcissization'. Contra psycho-sociological narratives that all too easily equate narcissism with a condition of a-social self-absorption (of which Lasch [1979] undoubtedly provides the paradigm), he argues that a given degree of libidinal self-investment is necessary for agents to ascend to the status of sexual subjects. It is precisely this type of investment, however, which he claims to be particularly problematic for working-class women. Subjected to the twin realities of manual and domestic labour, the care-giving, nurturing, labouring body is primarily experienced as a means to an end, an instrument catering to the pleasure and desires of others, rather than an end in itself, a source of narcissistic pleasure and an object that is itself worthy of the desire of others. In fact, while the ability to subordinate one's own needs and desires to those of others constitutes a fundamental dimension of a valorizing feminine identity, the 'anti-narcissistic' dispositions that are at the basis of this femininity also tend to inhibit the experience of the body as both sexually desiring and desirable. In short, the 'sexual schema' of working-class women has become gradually supplanted by a 'maternal schema':

> To work, to nourish and to reproduce constitute its fundamental postures, tracing their lines as the years go by, imprinting the marks in which one at once reads the dignity of maternal labour and the complete renunciation of the self. Excluded from all circuits of social recognition, the body marked as maternal is certainly not bereft of sense for those who inhabit it, it embodies a feminine destiny for which their entire history and their entire social world have prepared them. However, it has been progressively cut off from any reference to a [body] image that is sexually gratifying, desirable and valorizing.
> (Schwartz, 1990: 480)

Somewhat paradoxically then, in order for agents to "surrender" their body to others in a manner that is both pleasurable and gratifying, they must first be able to fully "occupy" it themselves. This not only requires that they are sexualized through the gaze and actions of others, but are also capable of perceiving *themselves* in sexual terms. If their everyday uses of the body already favour its experience as a *provider* rather than a *recipient* of pleasure, the practical awareness of the value of their own physical capital only further inhibits its perception as an attractive object worthy of the desire of others.

> While the topic of class and sexuality provides material for a study in itself and was therefore deliberately kept beyond the scope of our analyses, the available data nevertheless provide some clues into the unequal distribution of sexual capital. Apart from the results presented in Chapter 4, another indicator can be found in the frequency in which women engage in those types of body-work that are deliberately aimed at enhancing their sexual desirability. For instance, the proportion of women who indicate they shave their legs weekly or more increased from 20 per cent of unskilled workers and 30 per cent of housewives to 54 per cent of office clerks, 51 per cent of the teachers and 63 per cent of the junior-executives. Similarly, those who claim to shave or trim their pubic hair at least once a week or more varies from 21 per cent of housewives and manual workers to 35 per cent of office clerks, 54 per cent of the teachers and 44 per cent of the junior-executives (source: BoS '10). Similarly, the annual expenditure on clothing increases, in both absolute and relative terms, as one rises in the social hierarchy with women's clothing budgets varying from 259.8 euros among farmers (1 per cent of total expenditure), 322.6 euros (1.1 per cent) among unskilled workers, 592.3 euros (1.8 per cent) among office-workers, 714.1 euros (1.8 per cent) among junior-executives to 875 euros (2.1 per cent) among women in the professions. More importantly for the case at hand, the proportion of women's clothing budgets devoted to underwear and *lingerie* also increases from 2.1 per cent (66.3 euros) and 2.3 per cent (51.3 euros) for farmers and unskilled workers to 3.7 per cent (78.7 euros) for office-workers and 4.8 per cent of junior-executives. Quite tellingly, the expenditure on lingerie reaches its peak among those occupations that depend most strictly on the possession of physical and sexual capital, namely among sales clerks (5.8 per cent or 122.9 euros) and among the clerical occupations requiring a high degree of Goffmanian labour, like secretaries and receptionists (5.4 per cent or 113.5 euros).
>
> (source: EU-HBS '05)

These results illustrate how the propensity to *invest* – in the economic and psychological sense of the term – in the value of one's own body already implies the practical recognition of one's own body as "value-*able*", that is, as both worthy and capable of social recognition and desire, which in turn presupposes access to the symbolic markets in which appearance can function as a source of capital. In fact, the degree of "subjective" satisfaction that agents draw from their bodies is linked to the propensity to maintain or increase their physical capital in a relationship of 'circular causality' functioning at once as its *precondition* and its *effect*. Just as the experience of one's own body as attractive, charming and valuable tends to increase the willingness to invest in its value (which in turn reinforces the chances of it being perceived as attractive and valuable, etc.), the practical recognition of one's own body as ugly, deviant, stigmatized and abject, in short, as "worth-*less*" constitutes one of the largest obstacles to such investments.

As discussed in the previous chapter, this is one of the fundamental distinctions that separate the type of physical anxiety experienced by *middle-class* women from the bodily alienation that is most common among women who occupy the most precarious social positions. For the former, who have a more direct experience of the "body-as-sign", this anxiety is essentially rooted in the fear of falling short of standards of appearance that impose themselves in a more tangible and direct manner. If the pressure to conform to the dominant bodily aesthetic is undoubtedly felt much stronger by middle-class women, this is not only because the symbolic or material returns for investing in their physical capital are a lot more tangible, but also because, consequently, the direct penalties for the decline in its value are a lot more severe. It is this principle that often leads to "over-investments" in appearance, which tend to become all the more desperate, the more they have to rely on their charm and beauty as exclusive sources of labour power. This is much less the case for working-class women. In fact, their exclusion from the symbolic markets in which appearance can function as a "capital" not only means that they can expect less tangible rewards from investing in their bodies, but given the absence of professional justifications for such investments, they also risk the scorn of their primary group, who tend to perceive such investments as an attempt to "distinguish" themselves from their own class (i.e. "*Who does she think she is?*"). Furthermore, for women who occupy the most precarious social positions investing in appearance effectively amounts to engaging in *elective* forms of austerity and self-denial which only serve to compound the privations and strictures that are *imposed* by the necessity that defines their social conditions.

Needless to say, this relationship to the body is fundamentally in the nature of a self-fulfilling prophecy: if the exclusion of those spaces in which the body can be experienced as an autonomous source of value inhibits the propensity to maintain or invest in this value, then this in turn tends to produce a body that has little or no value on these markets, which in turn leads agents to exclude themselves from these markets, which further undercuts the sense of investments in physical capital, etc. It should also go without saying that such vicious circles are exceedingly difficult to break through. To do so would not only imply access to the forms of capital that provide the objective basis for the production of the legitimate body, but would also require a profound transformation of class-dispositions that are themselves firmly anchored in the body, whether in the obscurity of quasi-visceral "tastes" or the automaticity of postural schemes. Such a transformation can hence not be reduced to a simple *mental* conversion – i.e. a change of "attitude" and "outlook" or an "awakening of consciousness" – but effectively amounts to little less than a de-socialization and re-socialization of the body.

The "unregulated" body

The preceding chapters have aimed to show that the dominant perception of working-class taste and the type of body it produces, essentially reduces the latter to a state of "anomie" or "non-control". Unrestrained in its appetites, driven by impulse and bodily desire, inherently passive and lethargic, yet prone to violence and aggression, the working-class body is somehow seen as 'being more rooted in, or having more direct affinity with, nature' (Ortner, 1972: 73). In fact, Sherry Ortner's famous thesis that structures of patriarchy are legitimized by representing masculine domination in terms of the dominance of Culture over Nature could easily be extended to virtually *all* of the cardinal power-relationships that define the structure of contemporary social space, *including* those of class. The same logic that invokes the cold-bloodedness of men as a sign of their innate superiority over the emotionality of women, that refers to the sagacity of old age as possessing a natural authority over the blind passions and impulsive energy of youth or that posits the rationality of Western culture as a sign of its supremacy over the primitive and archaic dispositions of Blacks, Arabs, Asians and Latinos (or whoever happens to serve as its mirror-image), also conceives the relationship between the classes in terms of the dominance of Spirit, Mind or Intellect over Matter, Body and Flesh. Whether it applies to their physical features, their tastes or the way in which they use their bodies, the working-class invariably provides the Nature *against* which those who occupy more favourable positions in social space measure their own degree of Culture. This is perhaps most evident in the two traits that the popular imagination most readily associates with the working-class body, namely *muscle* and *fat*, brute force and unbridled appetite, respectively expressing popular masculinity or femininity, the two most tangible expressions of an unrestrained and irrepressible nature.

Crucially, this conception of the working-class body as somehow rooted in a more "direct", less "mediated", "more natural" and hence "less social" relationship to the biological body does not only subtend the everyday perception of class-bodies, but also emerges, albeit in highly transfigured form, in scholarly accounts of this body. Whether it is the epidemiologist who concludes that the unhealthy practices of the working-classes are due to a lack of appropriate information and know-how (i.e. to ignorance), the economist of consumption who observes that the working-class spend more on "basic" necessities, while the dominant classes devote more to "symbolic" goods and services (see Grignon and Grignon, 1980; also Boltanski, 1970) or even the psychologist who ranks eating disorders on an imaginary continuum ranging from the extreme self-control of the anorexic to the complete disinhibition of the obese, their analyses are often informed by the same set of oppositions (mind/body, culture/nature, etc.).

If it is so easy to describe the working-class relationship to the body in entirely negative terms – i.e. as marked by an "absence" or "lack" of – and to slip from the (generally correct) observation that this relation is manifestly at odds with the definition of the legitimate body to the (incorrect) conclusion that this relationship is bereft of *any* logic, this is because the very categories of the social unconscious predispose the analyst to place the working-class body on the side of nature, impulse and desire. It in fact makes all the difference in the world whether one describes the realistic hedonism or practical materialism that defines working-class tastes (in the domain of food as elsewhere) as the simple product of a corporeal *laissez-faire*, the expression of an essentially unregulated relationship to the body *or*, inversely, treats this hedonism as the positive affirmation of an 'ethic of convivial indulgence' which not only tolerates, but *demands* that agents enter 'into the generous and familiar – that is, both simple and free – relationship that is encouraged and symbolized by eating and drinking together' (Bourdieu, 1984: 179). In the former case, the relationship to the body not only appears as "anomic" and anarchic, but also as somehow more "direct" and "unmediated", knowing no other principle than the egoistic and hence a-social logic of bodily impulse and desire. In the latter, it appears as the expression of an *ethos* which is collectively imposed and reinforced, that is to say, endowed with a *social* logic that is acquired in the course of a particular apprenticeship – one "learns" how to drink – and provokes collective sanctions when transgressed (*"he can't hold his liquor!"*). In the first case, indulgence and freedom are equated with the absence of social and self-control, in the latter they are seen as the positive affirmation of such control.

A similar logic can be observed in the dominant interpretation of the working-class relationship to health, personal care and cosmetics. Here again, the (relatively) small amount of time, effort and means that working-class men and women invest in the "outer" and "inner" well-being of their bodies is all too easily attributed to a lack of care and interest or the complete absence of any aesthetic or moral criteria. Such a view again runs the risk of mistaking explicit refusals for simple negligence and acts of "principle" for lack of morals. What hence might appear as a lack of interest in one's appearance is more often an explicit refusal to "pamper" or "mollycoddle" oneself, itself rooted in an ethos of self-renunciation which views the cultivation and display of "anti-narcissistic" dispositions as an integral element of a valorizing identity. If, against all populist inclinations, it should be stressed that this ethos emerges out of conditions of privation and constraint, rather than freedom and choice, this does not imply that it is somehow "less social" in character.

That the popular relationship to the body is not governed by *anomie* can be seen in all those cases in which individuals deviate from the principles of the popular ethos. In fact, if the 'sense of distinction' is highly attuned to any signs that might indicate the vulgarization of a particular property or practice (and hence diminish its distinctive value), which are often quickly abandoned, then the 'sense of necessity' inverts this principle by being equally sensitive to any indices that could betray the intention to distinguish oneself from the primary group. Given the highly compressed nature of the universe of stylistic possibilities, any intentional deviation from the prescribed standards of appearance, dress and demeanour is likely to be perceived as an attempt to be "different", that is to say, "better" than the rest (*"Who does he think he is?"*). Here again, the taste for what is given, that is, for what can be reasonably expected from conditions of privation and restraint functions as a powerful principle of conformity (Bourdieu, 1984: 381). This seems especially true of everything that is concerned with the management and modification of the body. Since, as the preceding chapters have tried to show, dominant techniques of using and managing the body always imply a given degree of self-denial, the willingness to adopt such techniques in conditions that are already marked by privation, can only signal the intention to distinguish oneself. It is this effect of closure that is one of the central principles behind the high degree of uniformity of working-class tastes, the "sheep-like conformism" of the masses that never ceases to inspire the horror of dominant narratives on cultural "homogenization" or "massification".

Stronger still, commonality and communality are not only collectively enforced, but also actively affirmed. This seems to be at least one of the functions of all the forms of ritual slander and symbolic degradation that pervade working-class speech. If the ritual insults that populate popular discourse are often thick with references to the 'material bodily lower stratum' ("fucker", "shithead", "cunt", "slag", etc.), this is because, like the Bakhtinian figure of the grotesque, they serve the dual role of subverting all forms of hierarchy, while underlining commonality and the shared 'involvement in the urgencies and exigencies of a common world that refuses formalities and is uncomfortable with second-names and "small-talk"' (Charlesworth, 2000: 214). As such, they provide the ideal litmus-test of group-membership, since they can only be taken as "offensive" by those who actually think and feel themselves to be better than to undergo such forms of symbolic denigration. To summarize, if the popular relationship to the body can somehow be said to be "more natural", it is so only in a highly *ritualized* sense of the terms "nature" and "natural". What distinguishes the popular from the dominant uses of the body is not their level of "symbolic mediation" or their purported degree of "social-ness", but merely the sign that they affix to the body, that is, positive rather than negative, a means of expression and self-affirmation, rather than an object of censorship and modulation.

Conclusion
The visible and the invisible

> [F]or though to be overlooked, and to be disapproved of, are things entirely different, yet as obscurity covers us from the daylight of honour and approbation, to feel that we are taken no notice of, necessarily damps the most agreeable hope, and disappoints the most ardent desire, of human nature. The poor man goes out and comes in unheeded, and when in the midst of a crowd is in the same obscurity as if shut up in his own hovel [...] The man of rank and distinction, on the contrary, is observed by all the world [...] His actions are the objects of the public care. Scarce a word, scarce a gesture, can fall from him that is altogether neglected. In a great assembly he is the person upon whom all direct their eyes [...] and if his behaviour is not altogether absurd, he has, every moment, an opportunity of interesting mankind, and of rendering himself the object of the observation and fellow-feeling of every body about him.
>
> (Smith, 2002 [1759]: 62)

'Saying that I have a body', writes Merleau-Ponty, 'is a way of saying that I can be seen as an object and that I try to be seen as a subject' (1962: 167). The preceding chapters have aimed to show that the chances of living one's own body in the mode of a *subject*, to be fully in command of one's actions, gestures and words, to "in-habit" and be "as one" with one's body *or*, inversely, of experiencing it as an *object*, reduced to its perceptible qualities, to immanence and facticity, in short, as a "*class*-ified" body are not randomly distributed across social space. I have tried to show that dominant and dominated social groups have a highly unequal probability of finding themselves on either side of this Subject/Object-divide. In fact, contrary to sociological narratives that have hailed (or bewailed) the body as the site of ever-expanding possibilities, options and lifestyle-choices, a blank canvas on which increasingly reflexive individuals can (and *must*) write their own stylized narratives of self, this study has aimed to demonstrate that the body is increasingly the object of one of the most pernicious forms of symbolic violence, namely that specific form of cultural dispossession that leads social agents to break solidarity with their own bodies. A dispossession that is at once symbolic and technical. *Symbolic*, since it increasingly deprives the most disadvantaged of the basic power to impose their own criteria of physical value and instead encourages them to perceive and judge their own bodies in terms of the dominant standards of appearance and demeanour, hence durably instituting a gap between the "body-that-is" and the "body-that-ought-to-be". *Technical*, since it hinges on a devaluation of the conventional ways in which dominated agents use, clothe, feed, adorn and care for their bodies, which are increasingly branded as "irresponsible", "tasteless", "outdated" or "pathological".

A view from nowhere

As such, the practical experience of the body is closely intertwined with what Iris M. Young has coined the logic of 'cultural imperialism', namely the process whereby dominant groups – whether dominant in terms of gender, race, age or class – manage to 'project their own values, experience and perspective as normative and universal' (1990: 123). In fact, because these groups quite literally "embody" the norm, they 'fail to recognize the perspective embodied in their cultural expressions as a perspective' (1990: 60) and instead experience their own point-of-view as seemingly emanating from 'an unmarked, neutral, apparently universal position' (1990: 60). Since their perspective constitutes the official and universally recognized standard, they have the luxury of perceiving their own physical mode of being as wholly self-evident, transparent, unproblematic, in short, as "invisible".

For socially dominated groups, however, quite the opposite holds true. Serving as the foil *against* which the dominant norms of rationality and respectability are constructed, they stand out as dramatically visible, 'marked out, frozen as a being marked as Other' (1990: 60), that is, endowed with properties that render them as fundamentally deviant, abject and inferior. However, at the same time that their bodies are rendered highly visible, those who occupy dominated social positions 'are rendered invisible as subjects, as persons with their own perspective and group-specific experience and interests' (1990: 60). Instead, they find themselves reduced to their stigmatized properties, to their "exterior" which is, somewhat paradoxically, taken as the most tangible evidence of their "interior", that is, of an essence or "nature" that is branded as vulgar, coarse, undisciplined and unregulated. Rather than experiencing their body (and hence themselves) as self-evident and unproblematic, 'victims of cultural imperialism cannot forget their group-identity because the behaviour and reactions of others call them back to it' (ibid.). Forced to internalize the value that the dominant taxonomies ascribe to them, they become effectively 'imprisoned in their bodies' (ibid.).

In fact, whereas it is one of the rarest privileges of dominant groups to be for others what they are for themselves, to function as the "role-models", the "taste-makers" or the "trend-setters", it is the plight of the losers in the struggle for symbolic recognition to be for themselves what they are for others. If the ability to impose the criteria of his own apperception often enables the dominant actor to live his body in the mode of 'an absolute Subject, without an exterior (being his own Other), fully justified in existing, legitimated' (Bourdieu, 1984: 208), then the devaluation of her physical capital by those same criteria often leads the dominated actor to an 'epidermalizing' of her experience (Slaughter, 1977), forced to construct her self-identity in terms of those properties that the dominant vision assigns to her. More specifically, our analysis has aimed to demonstrate that the phenomenological account of the 'lived body', crucial as it is for breaking with intellectualist conceptions of agency and cognition, does not provide a *universal* template of embodiment. Instead, it is itself rooted in quite particular social conditions, namely those of white, higher-educated and upper-class men. As feminist and black scholars like Iris M. Young (2005) and Frantz Fanon (2008 [1952]) have already shown, there is nothing natural about the phenomenologist's "natural attitude" and the primary experience of one's own body and (hence) of the world as self-evident, transparent and unproblematic is not an anthropological invariant, but is itself a *social* privilege. It is the rare freedom granted to those who incarnate the dominant standards of appearance and demeanour. Even though it is true that *no one* can, strictly speaking, claim his or her body exclusively as their own – given how its perception is always mediated by the norms that are inculcated in the course of a situated and dated social trajectory – it does not automatically follow that *everyone* is condemned to experience the type of generic alienation that befalls the body when it is perceived and judged by others. In fact, it is precisely the ability to simultaneously impose and realize their own definition of physical value, that enables the dominant to live their body as the 'materialized coincidence of "is" and "ought"' (Bourdieu, 1984: 339) and hence to treat it with an aloofness that forms the basis for its self-confident and unselfconscious projection towards others. Conversely, it is precisely among those who lack the means to meaningfully realize this definition, that the lived body (*Leib*) often presents itself as a foreign object (*Körper*). Instead of being experienced as "absent" or "invisible", the primary foundation of thematic awareness, the body constantly lurks at the edges of this awareness, where it is quickly drawn out by the tacit or explicit, real or perceived judgments of others. Crucially, this recognition of the gap between current and ideal body itself takes a practical, that is, *embodied* form. The experience of being objectified by the gaze of others is, quite tellingly, expressed in all those sensations that are associated with a lack of control over the body, such as trembling, blushing, stuttering or sweating, which are all 'ways of submitting, however reluctantly, to the dominant judgment, sometimes in internal conflict and "self-division",' which in turn reveal 'the subterranean complicity that a body slipping away from the directives of consciousness and will maintains with the violence of the censures inherent in the social structures' (Bourdieu, 2000b: 169–170).

Expansion and compression

What makes the symbolic imposition of the dominant definition of the body particularly pernicious, is that it affects dominated agents in an aspect of their identity that is not only experienced as the most "natural" and hence the least amenable to conscious control, but which also provides them with one of the few foundations for a truly autonomous definition of class-identity. In fact, as the analyses presented in Chapter 5 have aimed to show, it is especially in the domain of the body and bodily pleasures (such as those provided by eating and drinking) that members of the working-class still manage to carve out a space of freedom and communal enjoyment that is relatively freed from the censorships imposed by dominant morality. That is why, as Bourdieu argues, the 'most fundamental principles of class-identity and unity would be affected if, on the decisive point of the relation to the body, the dominated class came to see itself only through the eyes of the dominant class' (1984: 384). While our analyses do suggest that this is still far from being the completely the case (with working-class *men* in particular often displaying a degree of heterodoxy with regards to the dominant norms of appearance and comportment), they also show that those who are situated at the bottom of social space prove far from immune to the devaluation of their own physical capital. Two factors in particular seem to have played a crucial role in eroding the capacity of working-class culture to function as a 'protective capsule' (Goffman, 1963: 48) against the contemporary stigmatization of their appearance and demeanour. On the one hand, the proliferation of symbolic outlets devoted to diffusing the dominant bodily aesthetic, itself linked to the dramatic expansion in those occupational sectors that cater to the symbolic management and manipulation of the body (beauticians, dieticians, cosmetic surgeons, health and fitness consultants, etc.). In fact, more than any conscious striving towards distinction on behalf of the dominant, it is the action of these Goffmanian 'curator groups' which (ever-eager to expand the need for their products and services) have been instrumental in universalizing the principles of the dominant lifestyle across ever-larger sectors of social space and across an ever-wider range of everyday practices, from cooking to sexuality, weight-control to child-rearing, fashion to interior design. The expansion of the 'legitimate market in physical properties' (Bourdieu, 1984: 152) is in turn accompanied by a compression and fracturing of the semi-autonomous spaces in which working-class men and women are able to impose their own definition of physical value. This process is itself linked to the erosion of the one of the central pillars of working-class identity, namely stable employment and the securities (indissolubly economic and psychological) it provides. In fact, the on-going precarization of manual labour has not only exposed increasingly large fractions of the working-class to the threat of economic insecurity, but also undermined the traditional forms of solidarity (of which trade-unionism is but one expression) which enabled those who occupy dominated social positions to self-confidently assert themselves as a class and, especially, to impose their own definition of the accomplished body. Both of these processes are in turn compounded by the fact that the social conditions for *politicization* – which constitutes one of the few ways of collectively resisting the dominant taxonomies through, for instance, inverting the values they impose ("*black is beautiful*") – are perhaps nowhere as limited as in this particular aspect of social identity. The unequal distribution of the means of production of legitimate political discourse, which in itself increasingly condemns members of the working-class to silence in matters of politics and culture (on this point see Charlesworth, 2000) is here compounded by the fact that such politicization would have to apply to a dimension of existence which, being endowed with all the appearance of "innateness", is itself exceedingly difficult to verbalize, let alone rationalize.

Moreover, unlike the stigmatization of relatively "ascribed" physical traits (skin colour, sex or age for instance), *class*-based physical differences provide a much less stable foundation for the development of an assertive "counter-culture". In fact, whereas critiques of sexual or ethnoracial domination can more easily invoke the unjust and anti-meritocratic nature of social mechanisms of exclusion on the basis of factors over which agents ultimately have little or no control, physical markers of *class* (like the example of body-size and shape discussed in Chapter 4) are more often deemed to be a simple matter of "lifestyle-choice" and hence of individual responsibility. If those who are situated at the bottom of the social hierarchy are endowed with the most devalued and stigmatized physical traits, this is largely because they are thought to lack the intrinsic willpower and self-discipline (not to mention self-respect) to make the proper investments in their appearance and demeanour for which contemporary "consumer culture" provides all the means. Such beliefs are only reinforced by the cosmetic voluntarism preached by the contemporary 'fashion-beauty complex' (Bartky, 1990). In fact, the same agents that help to universalize the dominant norms of appearance also contribute to mystifying the *social* conditions that are necessary for these norms to be meaningfully attained. The advocates of the contemporary cult of slimness and sobriety never cease to highlight how "quick and easy" it is to keep in shape, how following "a few simple steps" is enough to attain the ideal figure, how maintaining a healthy lifestyle is a simple matter of "changing bad habits" or how "being fashionable doesn't have to be expensive". Given that such voluntarist narratives provide the dominant framework within which individuals come to perceive and judge their own bodies, it is no wonder that those who fail to live up to the standards defined by the legitimate lifestyle and the legitimate relationship to the body are increasingly led to individualize, psychologize and pathologize their failure to do so. Instead of viewing their bodies for what they are, namely the product of *class*-dispositions reflecting the limits and opportunities inscribed in a given social position and hence directly tied into the dynamics of domination and exclusion (which would be a first step in collectively reclaiming their identity as a class), they come to view their own bodies and their own tastes as the expression of an innate, immutable and abject nature, in short, come to experience 'a sense of inadequacy [that] often comes from a dispossession that cannot recognize itself as such' (Bourdieu, 1993a: 24). Faced with such a pervasive stigmatization of their lifestyle, dominated agents appear increasingly condemned to oscillate between two, often equally desperate alternatives. On the one hand, the wholly individual attempts at assimilating the principles of the dominant aesthetics. Attempts that are not only liable to be perceived as a form of social treason by the members of their own social group, but are also quickly spotted for what they are by those who possess the legitimate physical capital, namely as cheap copies, second-rank substitutes, an 'imitation of alien models' (Elias, 1982: 313). On the other hand, the choice to remain loyal to the unwritten principles of their class-ethos, which increasingly comes at the price of a symbolic ostracization that can only be (partly) avoided by withdrawing into the relative security provided by the primary group, if not the isolation of the domestic sphere.

It is precisely this particular type of *self*-exclusion which plays a central, if often overlooked role in shaping the dynamics of social reproduction. In fact, the process whereby dominated agents come to exclude themselves from the practices and properties which they are at any rate denied, is itself reinforced by the profound sense of insecurity and inadequacy they experience in the social spaces where these properties and practices circulate. This is especially true of all those situations where, in order to ascend to an officially consecrated mode of social being, they have to offer up themselves and their bodies to the scrutiny of others and which, like the oral exam or the job-interview, are the 'occasion for passing total judgments, armed with the unconscious criteria of social perception on total persons' (Bourdieu and Passeron, 1990: 162). Because they encounter these situations as so many markets in which their physical, linguistic and cultural capital is subjected to devaluation, it is no wonder that the most dispossessed increasingly retrench from public life and the incessant verdicts it exerts. The unequal distribution of physical capital is therefore not only a key factor in the reproduction of relationships of social domination, but also leads those who occupy the most precarious social positions to remove themselves from the public eye and hence from collective consciousness, in short, to render themselves "invisible".

Negative discrimination

Crucially, the process whereby bodies become endowed with unequal value need not imply overt acts of stigmatization or discrimination on behalf of those who occupy more favourable social positions. While explicit forms of class racism have far from disappeared (see Jones, 2012), some of its most effective manifestations are often those in which explicit stigmatization is most strongly euphemized. In fact, the growing social sensitivity to any type of overtly discriminatory behaviour (as embodied in the culture of "political correctness"), means that such discrimination is increasingly expressed in *negative* form, that is, less through explicit defamation and denigration, but rather through disinterest and disregard, the lack of *any* type of attention, positive or negative, a simple failure to acknowledge the stigmatized Other. Studying the incidence of racial exclusion among privileged primary school-children Diane Reay notes: 'The racism of these middle-class children was not manifested in any action, rather it lay in the absences. Paradoxically it was there in what was not there, in the lack of care, lack of contact, lack of recognition' (1995: 367). As a form of social power that only exists by virtue of the recognition of others, *symbolic capital* (prestige, charm, authority, etc.) depends on the constant cues of recognition and affirmation that others provide through their gestures, their postures and above all their *gaze*. In fact, in as much as it is vehicle for objectification and stigmatization (as feminist scholars have amply documented), the gaze of others, especially when expressed in the mode of admiration, adulation, desire (or jealousy) remains a profoundly *valorizing* force. There is already an elementary sense of social consecration in the ability to elicit the attention of others and to be acknowledged through the tacit deference that is present in their embodied cues of recognition. Consequently, one of the most tangible ways in which those who are situated at the bottom of social space come to experience their own lack of value is by being deprived of such recognition, to be ignored, overlooked, treated as a "no body" and hence rendered "invisible" by the indifference they encounter in everyday interaction. If overt forms of class racism can be extremely violent, then the experience of being ignored and deprived of the recognition of others is often no less stigmatizing and dehumanizing and, as Adam Smith pointed out above, 'damps the most agreeable hope, and disappoints the most ardent desire of human nature' (1976: 51). Recent advances in neuroscience and brain-imaging (see Harris and Fiske, 2006) have produced some startling support for Smith's observations. When presented with images of socially marginalized groups (in this case homeless people and drug addicts), test-subjects that were subjected to MRI-scanning showed *no* significant neural activity in that part of the brain (the *medial prefrontal cortex*) that is known to be closely linked to so-called 'social cognition' (i.e. that which organizes the relation to persons, rather than non-human objects, see Forbes and Grafman, 2010), while instead revealing heightened activity in those areas (the *amygdala* and the *insula*) that have been found to be associated with feelings of loathing and disgust. While sociologists should not get to easily carried away by the promises of magnetic resonance, such research does point to one of the more unsettling aspects of the symbolic struggle for social recognition.

In fact, while this struggle provides some with the markers of a consecrated identity that transforms them, in Adam Smith's words, into the 'object of public care', it consigns many to the anonymity of an existence that is deprived of any "noticeable" qualities or is branded with a negative symbolic capital to the point that they no longer appear to be perceived as "human" and instead become reduced to objects (in a quite literal sense) of fear and repulsion. To "ex-ist" is – as the etymology of the word already suggests – to "stand out" and if the struggle for social recognition so often takes the form of a zero-sum-game, this is because prestige, status, fame and authority only exist in and through difference, distance and distinction. Just as every beauty needs her wallflowers, every distinguished figure his plain background, every brilliant elite its anonymous mass, 'every form of the sacred has its profane complement [and] all distinction generates its own vulgarity' (Bourdieu, 1990a: 196), which is simply another way of saying that when everybody (or *every* body) is special, nobody is.

Distinctions in the flesh

Having arrived at the end of this study, we are now perhaps better placed to discuss a point that was raised in the introductory remarks, namely that the advanced division of sociological labour constitutes one of the most formidable obstacles to adequately grasping the relationship between social power and embodiment. In fact, the same divisions that organize the everyday perception of the social world (Mind/Body, masculine/feminine, theoretical/practical, spiritual/ material, etc.) also subtend the traditional hierarchy of sociological research-topics which goes from the "serious" and "grand" themes of politics, economic markets, social structure and inequality down to the more "frivolous" and "superficial" subjects like dieting, sports, family-life, health, relationships or food-preferences. Apart from reproducing, within the organizational structure of the discipline, the very social divisions sociologists should attempt to objectify and analyse in the first place, this hierarchy also tends to obscure the fact that an answer to some of the most pertinent questions raised by political or economic sociology, class-studies or 'critical theory' is increasingly found in the domains that are staked out by sociologists of food, sociologists of the family, sociologists of sports and, of course, sociologists of the body. What our analyses have attempted to highlight, is that some of the most powerful (because most well-hidden) effects of class-domination can be observed precisely in those areas of everyday life – like personal care, clothing or food – where sociologists are often least inclined to look for them. In fact, it is precisely because these aspects of lifestyle (like the domain of primary tastes) are endowed with all the semblance of "innateness" and because they lie outside of the scope of the conventional definition of the "political", they are most susceptible to the imposition of the principles of the dominant lifestyle and the concomitant dispossession this exerts on the dominated. As Bourdieu notes:

> In [this] area, which is completely ignored by political analysis, although it is the site of objectively political action, the dominated groups are left to their own weapons; they are absolutely bereft of weapons of collective defence in order to confront the dominant groups and their 'poor man's psychoanalysts'.
>
> (Bourdieu, 1993a: 24)

In fact, because the vendors of the dominant bodily aesthetic contribute to imposing ideals that find their objective conditions of possibility in the lifestyle and "world-view" of dominant social groups, they engage in a type of symbolic action that is profoundly *political* in nature. Even if they speak the seemingly anodyne language of needs, desires, self-care and self-respect, the various "specialists" in bodily management and self-presentation tend to bank on what is ultimately a 'form of exploitation of people's deprivation which consists of imposing impossible norms and then selling the means – generally ineffective ones – of bridging the gap between these norms and the real possibilities of achieving them' (Bourdieu, 1993a: 24). Under the guise of liberating and emancipating the body, of promoting sensuality and "self-expression", they not only help to produce new types of shame, insecurity and anxiety, but also create new forms of dependence on the products and services only *they* can offer and

Conclusion

thereby effectively trap dominated groups in the illusion of individual control and personal choice. If anything, this study has aimed to show that the sociology of the body, of its social uses and its socially produced features is an integral element of a sociology of social domination, especially when such domination increasingly exerts itself in a mode that by 'substituting seduction for repression, public relations for policing, advertising for authority, the velvet glove for the iron fist, pursues the symbolic integration of the dominated classes by imposing needs rather than inculcating norms' (Bourdieu, 1984: 154).

Methodological appendices

Appendix 1: description of primary and secondary data sources

The bulk of the analyses presented in this study draw on data generated from a number of existing surveys. Table A1.2 provides a full overview of the seven surveys that were used with their abbreviations as used throughout the text. While these surveys offered a fair number of pertinent indices pertaining to the perception, evaluation and management of the body, they nevertheless proved too limited to cover the various aspects of the relationship to the body that this study aimed to explore. To this end I designed my own survey that was geared more closely to the theoretical demands of this particular study. This survey consisted of a 31-page questionnaire which covered a wide array of topics ranging from dieting and weight-concern, food-preferences, cosmetics and adornment of the body (piercings, tattoos, etc.), selection of body-types and satisfaction with various aspects of appearance as well as several attitudes relating to the overall conception of the body, health and appearance. The process of data-collection itself ran from October 2009 until January 2010 and consisted of a two-stage approach. First, the questionnaire was distributed as an online survey through social media such as Facebook and Twitter. The survey itself adopted the principle of "snowball sampling" through which each respondent recruited new respondents from his or her own network of contacts. After a two month-period the initial sample was analysed and compared to a representative sample of the population conducted in the same year (source: PaS '09, see Table A1.2), in terms of its gender-composition, educational, income- and age-differences. Not surprisingly, this sample proved to show an under-representation of men, the lower educated (i.e. those without a degree in secondary education) and of respondents over the age of 60 years old. To help correct this under-representation, the second-stage of the sampling procedure consisted in the dissemination of an identical, but *printed* version of the questionnaire among these specific groups. To this end, questionnaires were distributed among the visitors of two community centres catering to the elderly (one in a large urban centre, one in small provincial town), among the employees of a large public firm (i.e. the national railways) and a large private firm (car-manufacturer) and finally, among the residents of two council estates. Filled-out questionnaires were either collected by the author or sent back via mail. This two-stage approach led to an initial sample of 1,020 respondents. However, after "data-cleaning" (removing duplicate cases, deleting respondents with missing information, etc.), this was reduced to a total of 891 respondents. While the use of a paper-questionnaire managed to attenuate the under-representation of the abovementioned groups, the final sample remains skewed towards an over-representation of women, higher-educated and younger respondents. Despite such limitations, there was enough variation in the sample to provide a tentative outline of the ways in which differences in social position and trajectory shape the relationship to the body. The data-set is labelled as BoS '10 (*Body Survey 2010*) throughout the text.

Table A1.1 Sociographic composition of the sample for *Body Survey 2010*

	BoS '10	N	PaS '09	N
Gender				
Men	41.3	368	49.4	1,453
Women	58.7	522	50.6	1,488
Educational Capital				
Less than HS	16.8	146	36.3	1,010
HS (technical/vocational)	14.5	126	29.0	806
HS (academic/artistic)	8.9	77	8.1	226
Bachelor	29.7	258	18.5	514
Master or postgraduate	30.1	262	8.2	229
Age				
18 to 25 yrs	13.7	120	11.2	330
26 to 40 yrs	42.0	368	24.6	723
41 to 60 yrs	27.7	243	36.2	1,065
Older than 60 yrs	16.6	145	28.0	823
Social class				
Working	12.7	90	34.0	40
Lower-middle	34.5	244	45.1	168
Upper-middle	35.5	251	14.7	115
Dominant	17.4	123	6.2	65

Table A1.2 Summary of secondary data-sets

Name + indicators	Abbreviation	Type	N	Region	Age-group	Institution
1 General Cultural Participation Survey 2003–2004 • *Attitudes towards food and dining* • *Consumption of women's and lifestyle periodicals* • *Television-preferences*	GCPS '03–04	Face-to-face survey	2,907	Flanders	18 to 85 yrs	Policy Research Centre 'Recreatief Vlaanderen'
2 National Health Survey 2004: • *Distribution of BMI* • *Subjective degree of weight-concern* • *Preventive medical techniques*	BNHS '04	Face-to-face survey	11,297	Belgium	18 to 85 yrs	Federal Department of Public Health
3 Time-Budget Survey 2004: • *Time devoted to cooking and eating*	TBS '04	Face-to-face survey/diary of daily activities	1,768	Belgium	18 to 85 yrs	Dept. of Sociology, Research Group TOR, Free University of Brussels
4 Life-Course and Future Perspectives of Young Adults 2004: • *Subjective definition of the future* • *Attitudes on gender-roles*	LFPA '04	Postal survey	4,666	Belgium	18 to 36 yrs	Dept. of Sociology, Research Group TOR, Free University of Brussels
5 Participation Survey 2009: • *Frequency of sporting-practices* • *Type of sporting-practices* • *Reasons for sports*	PaS '09	Face-to-face survey	2,907	Flanders	18 to 85 yrs	Policy Research Center Culture, Youth and Sports

continued

Table A1.2 Continued

Name + indicators	Abbreviation	Type	N	Region	Age-group	Institution
6 European Union – Household Budget Survey 2005: • *Expenditure on food and restaurants* • *Expenditure on clothing, lingerie and accessories*	EU-HBS '05	Face-to-face survey/diary of household-expenditure	6,400	Belgium	18 to 99 yrs	Federal Department of Economy and Labour
7 Survey on Happiness and Well-being 2006: • *Satisfaction with appearance, weight and sexuality* • *Consumption of lifestyle- and reality-television*	SHW '06	Postal survey	4,487	Belgium	18 to 81 yrs	Dept. of Sociology, Research Group TOR, Free University of Brussels

Appendix 2: constructing social space

This section deals with the theoretical rationale behind the particular indicators of social position that were used throughout this study. Ideally, the adequate construction of social space and class-fractions would have to draw on a wide variety of indicators of both cultural and economic capital in their various guises (level of education, number of art objects owned, value of house, number of cars, etc.) of the type presented in Bennett *et al.*'s (2009) study of class and lifestyle in Britain or Prieur *et al.*'s (2008) study of class-differentiation of tastes in Denmark. Needless to say, such indices are rarely ever available for one single survey, let alone across *different* surveys in a manner that would allow for systematic comparison. In the absence of such indicators, *occupational category* proved the only means of locating differentiate individuals on the basis of both capital-*volume* and capital-*composition*. With this in mind, it seems crucial to stress the wholly provisional character of the taxonomy presented here. While an attempt was made to construct classes that were as homogenous as possible with regards to the basic structuring principles (i.e. capital-volume and -composition), the available surveys differed widely in their ability to construct a taxonomy that would capture their effects. In general, the degree of refinement of this taxonomy was dependent, first, on the availability of an "open"-coding of occupational status for that particular survey and, second, on its sample size and hence the degree in which it allowed for fine-graded distinctions of social position, while still enabling the analysis to produce (statistically) meaningful results. This proved to be the case, for instance, for the *National Health Survey 2004* which enabled us to produce the most detailed classification. Inversely, while our own survey wielded and open coding of occupational status and theoretically allowed for a more fine-graded classification of social position, the small sample-size (N = 891) effectively rendered such a classification meaningless (especially when trying to account for additional principles of intra-class variation such as gender or age). The most rudimentary classification distinguished between "working", "middle" and "lower" class-positions (see Table A2.1) corresponding to the three broad conceptions of the body outlined in Chapters 7 to 9. The category "middle-class" was further differentiated into a "lower" and "upper"-fringe and this for two reasons. First, to highlight the fact that the relationship to the body already changes quite considerably as one moves from the working- to the middle-classes, in this case from skilled workers and foremen (the upper fringe of the working-class), to the office-workers (the lower fringe of the middle-classes) which have similar (and often slightly *lower*) incomes than the skilled workers (albeit slightly higher levels of education), but clearly differ from the latter in their overall management of the body (as discussed in Chapter 8). Secondly, to illustrate the differences *within* the middle-classes, between those who are situated close enough to the dominant class to organize their practices accordingly, such as the junior-executives. Both the middle and dominant classes were then further divided into class-fractions on the basis of the capital-composition of the positions they group together. Situated near the economically dominant pole of the 'lower-middle-class' are the shopkeepers and the owners of small private businesses who are marked by fairly high incomes, albeit which are diametrically opposed, in terms of capital-structure to the teachers in primary education. A similar logic was used to further differentiate the broad and heterogeneous category of "office-workers" into those fractions that are engaged in more traditional, administrative functions and those that are engaged in tasks of symbolic presentation and representation, what Collins (1992) coined 'Goffmanian labour' (i.e. secretaries, receptionists, hostesses, etc.). Compared to those engaged in more "backstage" administrative functions, the occupational activities of these "front-stage" clerical workers not only depend more intensely on their *physical* capital as a direct source of labour power, but also require a minimal possession of cultural capital as embodied in forms of etiquette and comportment which, as Collins himself argues, makes them more receptive to the dominant standards of appearance and demeanour. The 'upper-middle-class' was differentiated in a similar manner. Near the economically dominant one finds agents engaged in various types of "financial services", such as real-estate agents, insurance brokers, traders and mid-level bankers. Unlike the shopkeepers and small business-owners, who tend to be marked by a downward trajectory owing to the concentration of corporate capital, those that are engaged in these types of services tend to be marked by an upward trajectory owing to such transformations as the "financialization" of capitalism and the privatization of the housing-market. Situated at the dominated pole of the dominant class one finds the "artists and cultural producers" which includes those groups that are directly or indirectly engaged in symbolic production such as writers, actors, photographers, journalist, curators and art critics. Situated more towards the dominant pole of the field of power (having higher average incomes) are the "academic and scientific occupations" which includes professors, junior- and senior-lecturers and senior-researchers. The category "professions" groups positions that could be qualified as "intermediate" in that they combine the possession of a highly specialized type of cultural capital (acquired through extensive periods of schooling) with relatively large incomes and includes lawyers, notaries, architects, doctors, surgeons and psychiatrists. Situated near the dominant pole are the senior-executives in large private firms and finally the commercial employers who are the owners of large-scale corporations. The final class scheme is highly similar to the Norwegian *Oslo Register Data Class Scheme* (ORDC, see Hansen et al., 2009) and the recent efforts by Atkinson and Rosenlund (2014) to construct a similar model for the United Kingdom.

Table A2.1 A taxonomy of social position

Dominant	**Dominant**	Commercial employers	Commercial employers	EC+
		Professions	Senior-executives	
			Professions	
			Academic and scientific occupations	
			Artists and cultural producers	CC+
	Upper-middle	Junior-executives	Financial services	EC+
			Junior-executives	
			Socio-medical services	
			Teachers secondary education	CC+
Middle	**Lower-middle**	Shopkeepers and small business-owners	Shopkeepers and small business-owners	EC+
		Office-workers	Office-workers (administration)	
			Office-workers (presentation and representation)	
			Teachers primary education	CC+
	Working	Skilled workers and foremen	Skilled manual (incl. foremen)	
			Semi-skilled manual	
Working		Unskilled workers	Unskilled manual	
			Farm workers	

Appendix 3: figure rating scale

In order to gain a better understanding of the relation between 'perceived' and 'ideal' body, I employed the help of a visual artist (R. Carremans) to construct a diagram representing different figures. The main reason for developing such a diagram is that existing instruments, like the *Figure Rating Scale* (see Stunkard, Sorensen and Schulsinger, 1983) or the *Contour Drawing Rating Scale* (Gray and James, 1995), have some important limitations from the theoretical point-of-view of this study. Leaving aside the rather poor aesthetic quality of these diagrams, their most important drawback is the fact that they hinge on the assumption that differences in body-shape (and especially the logic according to which they are perceived and evaluated) can indeed be expressed in the form of a continuous 'scale' ranging from the leanest to the largest physique. While this logic seems to hold true for the perception of *women*'s bodies for whom, as the analysis has tried to show, "large" and "small" are invested with quite unequivocal differences in social value, this does not necessarily apply to the perception of men's bodies. First, because a "slender" physique does not constitute the same source of symbolic capital for men as it is does for women. Secondly, because men who are "large" are not only *not* exposed to the same degree of social stigmatization, but "being large" can itself take two quite different, namely a very corpulent *or* a very muscular physique. Curiously enough however, the available rating-scales do not include explicitly *muscular* body-types among their range of male silhouettes and hence ignore this distinction which, as Monaghan (2007) has shown, is nevertheless central to men's understanding of masculinity and self-identity. I therefore opted to construct a diagram that presented a wider variety of masculine body-types including muscular as well as corpulent figures, without thereby necessarily assuming the existence of an underlying "linear" construct (which all too often appears dictated by the requirements of statistical technique than by any actual theoretical impetus). Obviously, the 11 somatotypes provided by each diagram by no means pretend to exhaust the entire spectrum of morphological differences. Such an endeavour would no doubt require closer to 110 figures (not to mention a great deal of positivistic courage). Instead, the ultimate goal of these diagrams is to provide a range of figures that is varied enough to capture meaningful *differences* in class morphology, while at the same time being general enough to allow for a reasonable level of statistical aggregation. Figure A3.1 represents the diagrams of male and female silhouettes in the *exact order and format* in which they were presented to respondents (although colour and shading might differ slightly from the version used in the questionnaires).

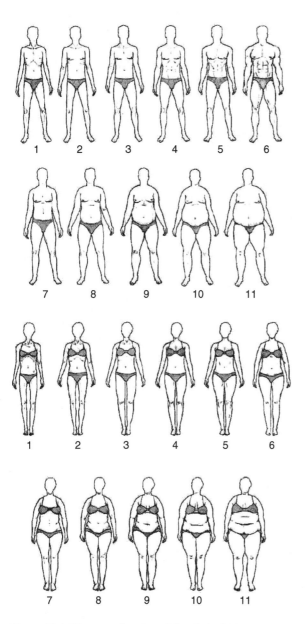

Figure A3.1 Diagram of male and female body-types
Source: BoS '10

Appendix 4: additional tables and figures

Table A4.1 Indices of dieting and weight-concern by gender, educational capital, professional status and social class

	R weighs him-/herself...				Weight-gain before R would notice (kg)[a]		Weight-gain before R goes on diet (kg)		Ideal weight (kg)		Difference ideal and current weight (kg)[c]	
	...daily or weekly (%)		...occasionally or never									
	♂	♀	♂	♀	♂	♀	♂	♀	♂	♀	♂	♀
Educational capital					n.s	**	*	*	n.s.	*	*	**
Less than HS	21	25	27	29	5.8	5.4	10.0	13.3	74.9	62.2	5.9	6.1
HS (technical/vocational)	19	37	40	28	5.7	5.2	8.2	7.7	77.0	59.8	7.6	6.2
HS (academic)	20	40	48	17	6.9	3.5	12.3	5.3	76.1	60.5	5.3	6.1
Bachelor	18	48	36	14	4.2	4.0	7.4	5.0	75.5	61.6	4.7	5.7
Master	28[b]	35	26	21	4.5	2.9	6.5	4.3	75.8	59.6	5.9	4.5
Professional status												
Unemployed	–	–	–	–	–	–	–	–	–	–	–	–
Housework	–	–	–	19	–	2.8	–	7.5	–	61.7	–	4.9
Social class						**	–	*	n.s.	**	*	**
Working	19	43	36	19	5.0	4.5	9.2	6.9	75.7	60.5	6.7	5.8
Lower-middle	19	44	30	19	5.5	3.3	8.6	5.7	76.2	61.8	5.5	6.2
Upper-middle	24	42	34	17	4.2	3.3	7.4	5.1	76.3	61.6	6.0	5.8
Dominant	29	34	31	25	4.4	3.1	6.2	4.4	75.2	58.2	5.0	3.8
Total	22	33	33	21	5.0	3.9	8.1	6.2	75.8	60.8	5.8	5.7

Notes

a All figures have been adjusted for age-differences.
b Numbers in italic denote the highest score for that particular indicator.
c This column only contains the difference for those who indicated that their current weight was equal or higher than their ideal weight.
n.s. = non-significant, *** $p < .005$, ** $p < .010$, * $p < .05$, n.a. = number of observations too low to make meaningful inferences.

Table A4.1 Continued

	Number of times R went on a diet				Lost kg and maintained weight-loss		Lost and regained several kgs		Lost and back at original weight (or more)		N^a	
	Never (%)		Several times									
	♂	♀	♂	♀	♂	♀	♂	♀	♂	♀	♂	♀
Educational capital												
Less than HS	83	48	6	31	40	24	30	40	30	36	10	38
HS (technical/vocational)	59	43	27	39	28	32	38	36	44	32	18	44
HS (general)	77	50	18	29	25	21	38	26	38	53	8	19
Bachelor	66	36	19	52	32	39	27	34	41	27	37	92
Master	60	42	23	44	26	38	38	29	36	33	42	86
Professional status												
Unemployed	n.a.	n.a.	n.a.	n.a.	n.a.	n.a.	n.a.	n.a.	n.a.	n.a.	2	14
Housework	n.a.	67	n.a.	8	n.a.	2.8	n.a.	7.5	n.a.	61.7	0	8
Social class												
Working	75	38	14	40	36	21	27	25	36	35	11	24
Lower-middle	70	41	18	45	26	37	39	31	35	32	23	96
Upper-middle	63	32	19	53	29	37	35	33	36	30	49	76
Dominant	62	48	26	36	35	47	30	28	35	25	20	32
Total	67	42	19	41	29	32	32	33	29	34	116	287

Source: BoS '10

Note
a This N only applies to those who indicated they have been on a diet.

Table A4.2 Selection of current, ideal and most disliked body by gender and social class (%)

	Figures											N
	1	2	3	4	5	6	7	8	9	10	11	
MEN												
Working-class												**46**
Current	0.0	6.4	10.6	6.4	14.9	2.1	14.9	23.4	17.0	4.3	0.0	
Ideal	0.0	0.0	4.3	10.9	41.3	21.7	17.4	4.3	0.0	0.0	0.0	
Most disliked	13.0	0.0	0.0	0.0	0.0	0.0	0.0	2.2	0.0	0.0	84.8	
Lower-middle-class												**72**
Current	0.0	0.0	16.2	13.5	9.5	1.4	20.3	25.7	5.4	5.4	2.7	
Ideal	0.0	0.0	4.2	19.4	41.7	19.4	8.3	4.2	2.8	0.0	0.0	
Most disliked	8.2	0.0	0.0	0.0	0.0	0.0	0.0	0.0	1.4	4.1	84.9	
Upper-middle-class												**134**
Current	2.2	1.5	6.7	11.2	9.7	2.2	26.1	25.4	11.9	2.2	0.7	
Ideal	0.0	0.0	3.1	18.3	46.6	16.8	9.9	4.6	0.8	0.0	0.0	
Most disliked	11.2	0.0	0.0	0.0	0.7	2.2	0.0	0.7	0.7	0.7	83.6	
Upper class												**53**
Current	0.0	0.0	11.1	11.1	13.0	1.9	24.1	20.4	11.1	3.7	3.7	
Ideal	0.0	0.0	1.9	18.5	46.3	16.7	5.6	7.4	1.9	0.0	0.0	
Most disliked	5.7	0.0	0.0	0.0	0.0	1.9	0.0	0.0	0.0	3.8	88.7	

WOMEN

												N
Working-class												39
Current	0.0	0.0	7.7	15.4	5.1	23.1	17.9	23.1	5.1	2.6	0.0	
Ideal	0.0	5.1	15.4	30.8	30.8	15.4	2.6	0.0	0.0	0.0	0.0	
Most disliked	15.8	0.0	0.0	0.0	0.0	0.0	0.0	0.0	5.3	0.0	78.9	
Lower-middle-class												164
Current	0.6	2.4	4.9	12.2	17.1	25.6	20.7	7.9	4.3	1.8	2.4	
Ideal	0.0	3.1	17.2	44.8	19.0	12.9	1.8	1.2	0.0	0.0	0.0	
Most disliked	12.8	0.6	0.0	0.0	0.0	0.0	0.0	3.0	3.0	1.8	78.0	
Upper-middle-class												112
Current	0.0	2.7	4.5	10.7	23.2	25.0	13.4	9.8	4.5	2.7	3.6	
Ideal	0.9	1.8	18.8	45.5	23.2	7.1	1.8	0.9	0.0	0.0	0.0	
Most disliked	11.6	0.0	0.0	0.0	0.0	0.0	0.0	0.0	0.9	0.0	87.5	
Upper class												64
Current	0.0	0.0	4.7	21.9	35.9	18.8	15.6	3.1	0.0	0.0	0.0	
Ideal	0.9	1.8	18.8	45.5	23.3	7.1	1.8	0.9	0.0	0.0	0.0	
Most disliked	10.9	0.0	0.0	0.0	0.0	0.0	1.6	4.7	0.0	0.0	82.8	

Notes

Significance-tests (Cramer's V): class x current body men = 0.182 (n.s.), class x ideal body men = 0.126 (n.s.), class x most disliked body men = 0.117 (n.s.), class x current body women = 0.197 (*), class x ideal body women = 0.139 (n.s.), class x most disliked body women = 0.143 (n.s.).

Table A4.3 Selection of class bodies by social class (%)

	Male silhouettes												
	1	2	3	4	5	6	7	8	9	10	11	?	N
Working-class													
Unemployed man	0.0	6.4	10.6	6.4	14.9	2.1	14.9	23.4	17.0	4.3	15.4	12.8	78
Manual worker	1.2	0.0	1.2	6.1	8.5	18.3	13.4	32.9	8.5	1.2	0.0	8.5	82
Businessman	0.0	0.0	12.5	11.3	10.0	6.3	16.3	11.3	13.8	7.5	2.5	8.8	80
Artist	9.0	14.1	15.4	9.0	9.0	0.0	3.8	11.5	14.1	1.3	12.8	9.0	78
Lower-middle-class													
Unemployed man	2.2	3.1	5.3	1.8	1.3	0.4	4.9	12.8	20.8	18.6	10.6	18.1	226
Manual worker	0.4	0.9	1.8	5.7	13.7	17.6	13.7	20.3	11.0	2.6	0.4	11.9	227
Businessman	0.0	1.3	6.6	10.2	11.5	1.8	18.6	15.0	16.8	8.0	0.4	9.7	226
Artist	6.7	17.4	23.7	8.5	4.0	0.9	10.7	8.0	3.1	0.4	0.0	16.5	224
Upper-middle-class													
Unemployed man	1.7	2.5	4.6	0.8	1.7	1.3	5.0	14.2	23.0	18.8	9.2	17.2	239
Manual worker	0.0	0.8	3.3	5.4	16.3	14.2	16.7	18.4	12.6	2.1	0.0	10.0	239
Businessman	0.0	1.7	7.5	8.3	6.7	1.7	16.7	21.7	21.3	3.3	1.7	9.6	240
Artist	9.7	23.9	26.1	7.6	2.9	1.3	5.9	5.9	2.9	2.1	0.0	11.8	238
Upper class													
Unemployed man	0.9	2.6	2.6	0.9	0.0	0.0	10.4	13.9	21.7	16.5	12.2	18.3	115
Manual worker	0.0	0.9	2.6	6.9	15.5	12.1	16.4	19.8	14.7	0.9	0.0	10.3	116
Businessman	0.9	0.9	5.2	12.9	4.3	0.9	14.7	22.4	19.0	6.0	1.7	11.2	116
Artist	3.5	25.2	31.3	5.2	3.5	0.0	6.1	7.0	3.5	0.0	14.8	3.5	115

	Female silhouettes												
	1	2	3	4	5	6	7	8	9	10	11	?	N
Working class													
Unemployed woman	1.3	1.3	1.3	2.7	1.3	9.3	8.0	14.7	16.0	20.0	9.3	14.7	75
Manual worker	0.0	0.0	1.3	3.9	21.1	30.3	21.1	9.2	2.6	1.3	0.0	9.2	76
Businesswoman	0.0	9.3	16.0	28.0	21.3	10.7	4.0	1.3	0.0	0.0	0.0	9.3	75
Artist	5.3	12.0	17.3	14.7	10.7	5.3	10.7	8.0	2.7	0.0	0.0	13.3	75
Lower-middle-class													
Unemployed woman	1.4	0.9	2.7	3.2	3.6	4.5	15.4	13.1	16.3	9.0	11.8	18.1	221
Manual worker	0.4	2.2	4.9	6.2	9.8	25.8	18.2	12.9	4.9	1.8	0.9	12.0	225
Businesswoman	0.4	5.4	12.1	37.5	25.0	6.3	3.6	0.0	0.4	0.0	0.4	8.9	224
Artist	4.5	12.6	22.1	10.8	10.4	9.0	10.4	1.8	1.4	0.5	0.5	16.2	222
Upper-middle-class													
Unemployed woman	2.5	2.5	3.3	0.4	2.1	4.2	14.6	12.1	16.7	14.2	11.3	16.3	240
Manual worker	0.0	0.4	2.5	2.1	10.4	22.1	27.1	15.0	7.1	1.3	0.4	11.7	240
Businesswoman	0.0	3.3	16.2	25.3	27.0	10.4	4.6	1.7	0.8	0.0	0.4	10.4	241
Artist	5.0	14.3	21.8	10.5	13.9	8.8	6.3	2.5	1.3	0.8	0.4	14.3	238
Upper class													
Unemployed woman	0.9	5.1	0.9	0.0	1.7	7.7	17.1	15.4	15.4	11.1	8.5	16.2	117
Manual worker	0.9	2.6	1.7	4.3	12.9	19.8	15.5	16.4	7.8	3.4	0.0	14.7	116
Businesswoman	0.0	2.6	17.1	29.9	25.6	8.5	5.1	0.0	0.0	0.0	0.0	11.1	117
Artist	4.3	12.8	17.9	18.8	6.0	9.4	5.1	4.3	2.6	0.9	0.0	17.9	117

Notes

Significance-tests (*Cramer's V*): class x unemployed man = 0.114 (n.s.), class x manual worker = 0.111 (n.s.), class x businessman = 0.146 (n.s.); class x artist = 0.170 (*), class x unemployed woman = 0.136 (n.s.), class x manual worker = 0.147 (n.s.), class x businesswoman = 0.146 (n.s.), class x artists = 0.136 (n.s.).

Table A4.4 Annual average household-expenditure on food (upper class)

	Artists and cultural producers		Academic and scientific occupations		Professions		Senior-executives		Commercial employers	
	EUR	% of total food exp.	EUR	% of total food exp.	EUR	% of total food exp.	EUR	% of total food exp.	EUR	% of total food exp.
Avg. total expenditure on food (EUR)	**5,218**		**6,695**		**6,565**		**7,075**		**7,066**	
Domestic consumption	4,262		5,179		5,201		5,609		5,188	
Outdoor consumption	956		1,516		1,364		1,466		1,878	
Proportion of total expenditure (%)	**17.0**		**17.3**		**17.1**		**17.6**		**17.0**	
Domestic consumption	13.9		13.4		13.5		13.9		12.5	
Outdoor consumption	3.1		3.9		3.6		3.7		4.5	
Type of food										
Meat	**688**	**13.2**	**815**	**12.2**	**848**	**12.9**	**1,112**	**15.7**	**984**	**13.9**
Beef	101	1.9	94	1.4	96	1.5	158	2.2	79	1.1
Pork	28	0.5	47	0.7	42	0.6	64	0.9	63	0.9
Chicken and other poultry	83	1.6	97	1.4	96	1.5	131	1.9	160	2.3
Veal	21	0.4	27	0.4	16	0.2	22	0.3	45	0.6

Table A4.4 Continued

Type of food	Artists and cultural producers		Academic and scientific occupations		Professions		Senior-executives		Commercial employers	
	EUR	% of total food exp.	EUR	% of total food exp.	EUR	% of total food exp.	EUR	% of total food exp.	EUR	% of total food exp.
Bacon	17	0.3	21	0.3	23	0.4	26	0.4	28	0.4
Delicatessen	207	4.0	229	3.4	264	4.0	335	4.7	311	4.4
Minced meat, hamburgers, sausages	86	1.6	130	1.9	130	2.0	147	2.1	117	1.7
Fish and shellfish	**262**	**5.0**	**265**	**4.0**	**261**	**4.0**	**313**	**4.4**	**225**	**3.2**
Fresh fish	156	3.0	141	2.1	127	1.9	187	2.6	145	2.1
Canned, frozen, smoked fish	80	1.5	88	1.3	101	1.5	100	1.4	49	0.7
Vegetables	**381**	**7.3**	**409**	**6.5**	**445**	**6.8**	**439**	**6.2**	**393**	**5.6**
Fresh vegetables	276	5.3	265	4.0	277	4.2	288	4.1	235	3.3
Potatoes	67	1.3	92	1.4	86	1.3	89	1.3	91	1.3
Canned vegetables	21	0.4	31	0.5	60	0.9	38	0.5	27	0.4
Dried, frozen vegetables	11	0.2	12	0.2	18	0.3	20	0.3	32	0.5
Fruit	**325**	**6.0**	**318**	**5.0**	**336**	**5.1**	**376**	**5.5**	**374**	**6.5**
Fresh fruit	281	5.4	268	4.0	295	4.5	327	4.6	334	4.7
Canned, dried, frozen fruit	41	0.8	38	0.6	35	0.5	46	0.7	38	0.5
Bread	**206**	**3.9**	**258**	**3.9**	**241**	**3.7**	**289**	**4.1**	**292**	**4.1**
Milk and milk products	**183**	**3.5**	**243**	**3.6**	**221**	**3.4**	**245**	**3.5**	**228**	**3.2**
Cheese	**232**	**4.4**	**301**	**4.5**	**368**	**5.6**	**350**	**4.9**	**305**	**4.3**

Table A4.4 Continued

Type of food	Artists and cultural producers		Academic and scientific occupations		Professions		Senior-executives		Commercial employers	
	EUR	% of total food exp.	EUR	% of total food exp.	EUR	% of total food exp.	EUR	% of total food exp.	EUR	% of total food exp.
Eggs	**23**	**0.4**	**26**	**0.4**	**31**	**0.5**	**28**	**0.4**	**32**	**0.5**
Pasta	**26**	**0.5**	**42**	**0.6**	**41**	**0.6**	**38**	**0.5**	**34**	**0.5**
Rice	**9**	**0.2**	**11**	**0.2**	**8**	**0.1**	**9**	**0.1**	**9**	**0.1**
Fats	**75**	**1.4**	**74**	**1.1**	**97**	**1.5**	**95**	**1.3**	**84**	**1.2**
Butter	24	0.5	27	0.4	27	0.4	30	0.4	31	0.4
Margarine	12	0.2	22	0.3	23	0.4	33	0.5	31	0.4
Oil	38	0.7	24	0.4	45	0.7	30	0.4	21	0.3
Ready-made meals	**337**	**6.5**	**494**	**7.4**	**425**	**6.5**	**356**	**5.0**	**392**	**5.5**
Cakes, pastries, cookies	**249**	**4.8**	**293**	**4.4**	**302**	**4.6**	**341**	**4.8**	**349**	**4.9**
Chocolate, ice-cream, sugar	**202**	**3.9**	**338**	**5.0**	**235**	**3.6**	**294**	**4.2**	**238**	**3.4**
Alcohol	**504**	**9.7**	**616**	**9.2**	**660**	**10.1**	**565**	**8.0**	**674**	**9.5**
Beer (lager)	70	1.3	30	0.4	25	0.4	46	0.7	61	0.9
Beer (other)	55	1.1	76	1.1	49	0.7	53	0.7	21	0.3
Wine	281	5.4	360	5.4	441	6.7	295	4.2	299	4.2
Champagne, sparkling wine	11	0.2	44	0.7	51	0.8	44	0.6	166	2.3
Aperitifs	30	0.6	50	0.7	31	0.5	51	0.7	27	0.4
Liquor (whiskey, brandy, etc.)	32	0.6	34	0.5	37	0.6	51	0.7	79	1.1
Soft-drinks	**100**	**1.9**	**120**	**1.8**	**148**	**2.3**	**178**	**2.5**	**124**	**1.8**
Fruit and vegetable juice	**61**	**1.2**	**60**	**0.9**	**72**	**1.1**	**83**	**1.2**	**44**	**0.6**
Coffee	**36**	**0.7**	**36**	**0.5**	**46**	**0.7**	**55**	**0.8**	**25**	**0.4**
Tea	**23**	**0.4**	**21**	**0.3**	**8**	**0.1**	**16**	**0.2**	**8**	**0.1**
Restaurants	**704**	**13.5**	**1,138**	**17.0**	**1,135**	**17.3**	**1,201**	**17.0**	**1,564**	**22.1**
Fast-food and take-away	**108**	**2.1**	**257**	**3.8**	**157**	**2.4**	**153**	**2.2**	**222**	**3.1**

Source: EUR-HBS '05

Table A4.5 Annual average household-expenditure on food (middle-class)

	Teachers primary and secondary education		Office-workers		Shopkeepers and small business-owners		Junior-executives	
N (households)	522		799		110		530	
Avg. total expenditure on food (EUR)	**5,499**		**4,782**		**4,388**		**6,167**	
Domestic consumption	4,598		3,923		3,510		4,898	
Outdoor consumption	901		859		878		1,269	
Proportion of total expenditure (%)	**17.0**		**17.3**		**19.4**		**19.1**	
Domestic consumption	14.2		14.2		15.5		15.4	
Outdoor consumption	2.8		3.1		3.9		3.7	
Type of food	EUR	% of total food exp.	EUR	% of total food exp.	EUR	% of total food exp.	EUR	% of total food exp.
Meat	**876**	**15.9**	**803**	**16.8**	**792**	**18.0**	**938**	**15.2**
Beef	102	1.9	100	2.1	134	3.1	118	1.9
Pork	53	1.0	48	1.0	52	1.2	57	0.9
Chicken and other poultry	108	2.0	88	1.8	62	1.4	110	1.8
Veal	22	0.4	16	0.3	14	0.3	25	0.4
Bacon	24	0.4	24	0.5	26	0.6	24	0.4
Delicatessen	253	4.6	238	5.0	245	5.6	274	4.4
Minced meat, hamburgers, sausages	128	2.3	118	2.5	106	2.4	135	2.2
Fish and shellfish	**233**	**4.2**	**174**	**3.6**	**209**	**4.8**	**229**	**3.7**
Fresh fish	135	2.5	95	2.0	112	2.6	134	2.2
Canned, smoked, salted fish	73	1.3	54	1.1	78	1.8	68	1.1
Fish preparations	25	0.5	25	0.5	19	0.4	28	0.5

continued

Table A4.5 Continued

Type of food	EUR	% of total food exp.	EUR	% of total food exp.	EUR	% of total food exp.	EUR	% of total food exp.
Vegetables	**379**	**6.9**	**313**	**6.5**	**266**	**6.1**	**390**	**6.3**
Fresh vegetables	230	4.2	189	4.0	178	4.1	252	4.1
Potatoes	91	1.7	82	1.7	58	1.3	90	1.5
Canned vegetables	33	0.6	26	0.5	19	0.4	27	0.4
Dried, frozen vegetables	18	0.3	13	0.3	10	0.2	0.0	0.0
Fruit	**296**	**5.4**	**238**	**5.0**	**261**	**5.9**	**310**	**5.0**
Fresh fruit	261	4.7	204	4.3	229	5.2	272	4.4
Canned, dried, frozen fruit								
Bread	**255**	**4.6**	**223**	**4.7**	**203**	**4.6**	**257**	**4.2**
Milk and milk products	**204**	**3.7**	**181**	**3.8**	**147**	**3.4**	**235**	**3.8**
Cheese	**271**	**4.9**	**212**	**4.4**	**182**	**4.1**	**268**	**4.3**
Eggs	**26**	**0.5**	**21**	**0.4**	**22**	**0.5**	**22**	**0.4**
Pasta	**30**	**0.5**	**25**	**0.5**	**15**	**0.3**	**33**	**0.5**
Rice	**9**	**0.2**	**8**	**0.2**	**6**	**0.1**	**9**	**0.1**
Fats	**88**	**1.6**	**78**	**1.6**	**84**	**1.9**	**90**	**1.5**
Butter	**33**	**0.6**	**26**	**0.5**	**34**	**0.8**	**32**	**0.5**
Margarine	30	0.5	28	0.6	29	0.7	30	0.5
Oil	22	0.4	21	0.4	21	0.5	24	0.4

Mayonnaise and other sauces	**41**	0.7	**41**	0.9	**27**	0.6	47	0.8
Cakes, pastries, cookies	5.3	241	5.0	191	4.4	305	4.9	5.3
Chocolate, ice-cream, sugar	4.4	199	4.2	162	3.7	252	4.1	**4.4**
Ready-made meals	**5.4**	**299**	**6.3**	**182**	**4.1**	**376**	**6.1**	**5.4**
Alcohol	**520**	**9.5**	**361**	**7.5**	**370**	**8.4**	**530**	**8.6**
Beer (lager)	45	0.8	34	0.7	24	0.5	33	0.5
Beer (other)	50	0.9	24	0.5	35	0.8	45	0.7
Wine	293	5.3	183	3.8	160	3.6	292	4.7
Champagne, sparkling wine	35	0.6	26	0.5	36	0.8	28	0.5
Aperitifs	35	0.6	27	0.6	57	1.3	48	0.8
Liquor (whiskey, brandy, etc.)	49	0.9	43	0.9	24	0.5	62	1.0
Soft-drinks	**146**	**2.7**	**143**	**3.0**	**114**	**2.6**	**155**	**2.5**
Fruit and vegetable juice	63	1.1	53	1.1	31	0.7	70	1.1
Coffee	66	1.2	60	1.3	76	1.7	70	1.1
Tea	**44**	**0.8**	**39**	**0.8**	**55**	**1.3**	**44**	**0.7**
Restaurants	756	13.7	633	13.2	642	14.6	1,005	16.3
Fast-food and delivery	**91**	**1.7**	**110**	**2.3**	**83**	**1.9**	**154**	**2.5**

Source: EU-HBS '05

Table A4.6 Annual average household-expenditure on food (working-class)

		Unemployed		Farmers and farm workers		Unskilled manual workers		Skilled manual (incl. foremen)	
N (households)		393		22		477		373	
Avg. total expenditure on food (EUR)		**3,209**		**4,106**		**4,751**		**4,984**	
Domestic consumption		2,801		3,765		4,107		4,326	
Outdoor consumption		408		340		645		656	
Proportion of total expenditure (%)		**17.9**		**17.8**		**18.7**		**18.3**	
Domestic consumption		15.6		16.3		16.1		15.9	
Outdoor consumption		2.3		1.5		2.6		2.4	

Type of food	p	EUR	% of total food exp.	EUR	% of total food exp.	EUR	% of total food exp.	EUR	% of total food exp.
Meat	***	**570**	**17.8**	**907**	**22.1**	**961**	**20.2**	**1,002**	**20.1**
Beef	***	75	2.3	128	3.1	128	2.7	146	2.9
Pork	***	37	1.2	61	1.5	64	1.3	68	1.4
Chicken and other poultry	n.s.	58	1.8	95	2.3	86	1.8	93	1.9
Veal	n.s.	6	0.2	5	0.1	18	0.4	17	0.3
Bacon	***	15	0.5	41	1.0	24	0.5	28	0.6
Delicatessen	***	156	4.9	257	6.3	274	5.8	281	5.6
Minced meat, hamburgers, sausages	***	94	2.9	90	2.2	149	3.1	141	2.8
Fish and shellfish	n.s.	**104**	**3.2**	**150**	**3.7**	**159**	**3.3**	**177**	**3.6**
Fresh fish	*	52	1.6	77	1.9	80	1.7	96	1.9
Canned, smoked, salted fish	n.s.	39	1.2	50	1.2	50	1.1	56	1.1
Fish preparations	*	13	0.4	23	0.6	29	0.6	24	0.5
Vegetables	n.s.	**381**	**11.9**	**270**	**6.6**	**313**	**6.6**	**329**	**6.6**
Fresh vegetables	**	143	4.5	173	4.2	178	3.7	188	3.8
Potatoes	***	63	2.0	52	1.3	94	2.0	92	1.8
Canned vegetables	***	24	0.7	28	0.7	29	0.6	33	0.7
Dried, frozen vegetables	**	10	0.3	11	0.3	12	0.3	12	0.2
Fruit	*	**151**	**4.7**	**194**	**4.7**	**222**	**4.7**	**223**	**4.5**
Fresh fruit	n.s.	127	4.0	175	4.3	198	4.2	194	3.9
Canned, dried, frozen fruit	*	21	0.7	15	0.4	23	0.5	27	0.5

		Unemployed		Farmers and farm workers		Unskilled manual workers		Skilled manual (incl. foremen)	
Bread	***	160	5.0	272	6.6	272	5.7	278	5.6
Milk and milk products	n.s.	149	4.6	183	4.5	195	4.1	195	3.9
Cheese	**	144	4.5	238	5.8	212	4.5	220	4.4
Eggs	*	21	0.7	19	0.5	23	0.5	25	0.5
Pasta	n.s.	23	0.7	22	0.5	27	0.6	26	0.5
Rice	n.s.	7	0.2	7	0.2	7	0.1	10	0.2
Fats	***	56	1.7	103	2.5	87	1.8	85	1.7
Butter	**	19	0.6	36	0.9	28	0.6	29	0.6
Margarine	***	16	0.5	40	1.0	33	0.7	29	0.6
Oil	n.s.	19	0.6	26	0.6	23	0.5	19	0.4
Mayonnaise and other sauces	***	31	1.0	48	1.2	44	0.9	43	0.9
Cakes, pastries, cookies	*	136	4.2	211	5.1	257	5.4	237	4.8
Chocolate, ice-cream, sugar	n.s.	134	4.2	235	5.7	205	4.3	216	4.3
Ready-made meals	***	211	6.6	184	4.5	273	5.7	249	5.0
Alcohol	***	275	8.6	239	5.8	303	6.4	423	8.5
Beer (lager)	**	37	1.2	45	1.1	48	1.0	59	1.2
Beer (other)	*	20	0.6	27	0.7	36	0.8	37	0.7
Wine	***	129	4.0	108	2.6	111	2.4	201	4.0
Champagne, sparkling wine	*	21	0.7	0	0.0	19	0.4	26	0.5
Aperitifs	n.s.	22	0.7	16	0.4	25	0.5	31	0.6
Liquor (whiskey, brandy, etc.)	*	18	0.6	34	0.8	44	0.9	42	0.8
Soft-drinks	***	108	3.4	118	2.9	179	3.8	171	3.4
Fruit and vegetable juice	n.s.	39	1.2	43	1.0	51	1.1	50	1.0
Coffee	***	46	1.4	63	1.5	76	1.6	74	1.5
Tea	***	9	0.3	13	0.3	6	0.1	8	0.2
Restaurants	*	286	8.9	256	6.2	493	10.4	547	11.0
Fast-food and delivery	***	65	2.0	84	2.0	93	2.0	69	1.4

Source: EU-HBS '05

Notes
* $p < .05$, ** $p < .01$, *** $p < .001$, n.s.: non-significant.

Table A4.7 Total time devoted to meals (5 weekdays)

	Preparation	Dining	Total time	N
Sig. (*p*)	<0.005	<0.005	<0.005	
Commercial employers	1 h 20 m	12 h 55 m	14 h 05 m	12
Professions	1 h 37 m	10 h 15 m	11 h 53 m	16
Junior-executives	2 h 36 m	10 h 50 m	13 h 26 m	162
Office clerks	3 h 13 m	10 h 01 m	13 h 14 m	593
Shopkeepers and small business-owners	2 h 16 m	9 h 47 m	12 h 03 m	107
Skilled workers	3 h 05 m	9 h 16 m	12 h 21 m	325
Unskilled workers	4 h 29 m	8 h 57 m	13 h 26 m	294

Source: TBS '04

References

Abbott, A. (1995) 'Things of Boundaries', *Social Research*, 62 (4): 857–882.
Alexander, J.C. (1987) *Twenty Lectures. Sociological Theory since World War II*, New York: Columbia University Press.
Alexander, J.C. (1995) *Fin de Siècle Social Theory: Relativism, Reduction and the Problem of Reason*, London: Verso.
Atkinson, M. (2008) 'Triathlon, Suffering and Exciting Significance', *Leisure Studies*, 27 (2): 165–180.
Atkinson, W. and Rosenlund, L. (2014) 'Mapping the British Social Space: Towards a Bourdieusian Class Scheme', *Working Paper School of Sociology, Politics and International Studies*, University of Bristol.
Bakhtin, M. (1984) *Rabelais and his World*, Bloomington: Indiana University Press.
Ball, K. and Mishra, G.D. (2006) 'Whose Socioeconomic Status Influences a Woman's Obesity Risk? Her Mother's, Her Father's or Her Own?', *International Journal of Epidemiology*, 35 (1): 131–138.
Barlösius, E. (1999) *Soziologie des Essens. Eine Sozial- und Kulturwissenschaftliche Einführung in die Ernährungsforschung*, Munich: Juventa.
Barthes, R. (1972) [1957] *Mythologies*, New York: Noonday Press.
Barthes, R. (1961) 'Pour une Psycho-sociologie de l'Alimentation Contemporaine', *Annales*, 16 (5): 977–986.
Bartky, S.L. (1990) *Femininity and Domination: Studies in the Phenomenology of Oppression*, London: Routledge.
Bauman, Z. (2000) *Liquid Modernity*, London: Polity Press.
Beck, U. and Beck-Gérnsheim, E. (2002) *Individualization. Institutionalized Individualism and its Social and Political Consequences*, London: Sage.
Bennett, T., Savage, M., Silva, E.B., Gayo-Cal, M. and Wright, D. (2009) *Culture, Class, Distinction*, London: Routledge.
Berger, P.L. and Luckmann, T. (1966) *The Social Construction of Reality. A Treatise in the Sociology of Knowledge*, New York: Anchor Books.
Bernauer, J.W. and Rasmussen, D. (1988) *The Final Foucault*, Boston: MIT Press.
Boltanski, L. (1969) *Prime Education et Morale de Classe*, Paris: Cahiers du Centre de Sociologie Européenne.
Boltanski, L. (1970) 'Taxinomies Populaires, Taxinomies Savantes. Les Objets de Consommation et leur Classement', *Revue Française de Sociologie*, 11 (1): 34–44.
Boltanski, L. (1971) 'Les Usages Sociaux du Corps', *Annales*, 26 (1): 205–233.
Boltanski, L. and Thévenot, L. (1984) 'Finding One's Way in Social Space', *Social Science Information*, 22 (4/5): 631–680.

References

Bordo, S. (1993) *Unbearable Weight. Feminism, Western Culture and the Body*, Los Angeles: University of California Press.

Bourdieu, P. (1974) 'Avenir de Classe et Causalité du Probable', *Revue Française de Sociologie*, 15 (1): 3–42.

Bourdieu, P. (1977a) *Outline of a Theory of Practice*, Cambridge: Cambridge University Press.

Bourdieu, P. (1977b) 'The Economics of Linguistic Exchanges', *Social Science Information*, 16 (6): 645–668.

Bourdieu, P. (1978) 'Sports and Social Class', *Social Science Information*, 17 (6): 819–840.

Bourdieu, P. (1979) *Algeria 1960*, Cambridge: Cambridge University Press.

Bourdieu, P. (1984) *Distinction. A Social Critique of the Judgment of Taste*, Cambridge: Harvard University Press.

Bourdieu, P. (1985) 'The Social Space and the Genesis of Groups', *Theory and Society*, 14 (6): 723–744.

Bourdieu, P. (1988) *Homo Academicus*, Stanford: Stanford University Press.

Bourdieu, P. (1986) 'The Forms of Capital', in: Richardson, J.E. (ed.) *Handbook of Theory of Research for the Sociology of Education*, New York: Greenword Press: 241–258.

Bourdieu, P. (1989) 'Social Space and Symbolic Power', *Sociological Theory*, 7 (1): 14–25.

Bourdieu, P. (1990a) *In Other Words. Essays Towards a Reflexive Sociology*, Stanford: Stanford University Press.

Bourdieu, P. (1990b) *The Logic of Practice*, Cambridge: Polity.

Bourdieu, P. (1990c) *The Love of Art. European Art Museums and Their Public*, Cambridge: Polity.

Bourdieu, P. (1990d) 'Time Perspectives of the Kabyle', in: Hassard, J. (ed.) *The Sociology of Time*, New York: Saint Martin's Press: 219–237.

Bourdieu, P. (1993a) *Sociology in Question*, London: Sage.

Bourdieu, P. (1993b) *The Field of Cultural Production. Essays on Art and Literature*, New York: Columbia University Press.

Bourdieu, P. (1994) 'Le Corps et le Sacré', *Actes de La Recherche en Sciences Sociales*, 104 (1): 2.

Bourdieu, P. (1996), *Physical Space, Social Space and Habitus*, Vilhelm Aubert Memorial Lecture offered at the University of Oslo.

Bourdieu, P. (2000a) 'Making the Economic Habitus. Algerian Workers Revisited', *Ethnography*, 1 (1): 17–41.

Bourdieu, P. (2000b) *Pascalion Meditations*, Stanford: Stanford University Press.

Bourdieu, P. (2002) *Masculine Domination*, Stanford: Stanford University Press.

Bourdieu, P. (2008) *The Bachelor's Ball: The Crisis of Peasant Society in Béarn*, London: Polity.

Bourdieu, P., Boltanski, L. and Chamboredon, J.C. (1963) *La Banque et sa Clientèle*, Paris: Rapport de CSE.

Bourdieu, P., Chamboredon, J.C. and Passeron, J.C. (1991) *The Craft of Sociology. Epistemological Preliminaries*, New York: Walter de Gruyter.

Bourdieu, P. and Passeron, J.C. (1990) *Reproduction in Education, Society and Culture*, London: Sage.

Bourdieu, P. and Wacquant, L. (1992) *An Invitation to Reflexive Sociology*, Cambridge: Polity.

Brillat-Savarin, J.A. (1975 [1826]) *Physiologie du Gout*, Paris: Hermann.
Brubaker, R. (2004) 'Rethinking Classical Theory. The Sociological Vision of Pierre Bourdieu', in: Swartz, D.L. and Zolberg, V. (eds) *After Bourdieu*, Amsterdam: Kluwer: 25–64.
Bruch, H. (1973) *Eating Disorders. Obesity, Anorexia Nervosa and the Person Within*, New York: Basic Books.
Bruch, H. (2001) *The Golden Cage. The Enigma of Anorexia Nervosa*, Cambridge: Harvard University Press.
Bufton, S. (2003) 'The Lifeworld of the University Student: Habitus and Social Class', *Journal of Phenomenological Psychology*, 34 (2): 207–234.
Burwood, S. (2008) 'The Apparent Truth of Dualism and the Uncanny Body', *Phenomenology and the Cognitive Sciences*, 7: 263–278.
Buytendijk, F.J.J. (1974) *Prolegomena to an Anthropological Physiology*, Pittsburgh: Duquesne University Press.
Cahnman, W.J. (1968) 'The Stigma of Obesity', *The Sociological Quarterly*, 9 (3): 283–299.
Canguilhem, G. (1978 [1966]) *On the Normal and the Pathological*, Dordrecht: D. Reidel Publishing.
Cassirer, E. (2000) *The Logic of the Cultural Sciences*, New Haven: Yale University Press.
Charles, N. and Kerr, M. (1988) *Women, Food and Families*, Manchester: Manchester University Press.
Charlesworth, S.J. (2000) *A Phenomenology of Working-Class Experience*, Cambridge: Cambridge University Press.
Collins, R. (1992) 'Women and the Production of Status Cultures', in: Lamont, M. and Fournier, M. (eds) *Cultivating Differences. Symbolic Boundaries and the Making of Inequality*, Chicago: University of Chicago Press: 213–231.
Connell, R.W. (1987) *Gender and Power. Society, the Person and Sexual Politics*, London: Polity.
Connell, R.W. (2000) *The Men and the Boys*, New York: Allen & Unwin.
Connell, R.W. and Wood, J. (2005) 'Globalization and Business Masculinities', *Men and Masculinities*, 7 (4): 347–364.
Coser, L.A. and Coser, R.L. (1963) 'Time Perspective and Social Structure', in: Gouldner, A.W. and Gouldner, H.P. (eds) *Modern Sociology. An Introduction to the Study of Human Interaction*, New York: Harcourt Brace: 638–647.
Cregan, K. (2005) *The Sociology of the Body: Mapping the Abstraction of Embodiment*, London: Sage.
Crossley, N. (2001) *The Social Body. Habit, Identity and Desire*, London: Sage.
Crossley, N. (2003) *Reflexive Embodiment in Contemporary Society*, London: Open University Press.
Crossley, N. (2004) 'Fat is a Sociological Issue', *Social Theory & Health*, 2: 222–253.
Csordas, T.J. (ed.) (1994) *Embodiment and Experience. The Existential Ground of Culture and Self*, Cambridge: Cambridge University Press.
Darmon, M. (2009) 'The Fifth Element: Social Class and the Sociology of Anorexia', *Sociology*, 43 (4): 717–733.
De Saussure, F. (1966) [1907] *Course in General Linguistics*, New York: McGraw-Hill.
De Swaan, A. (1981) 'The Politics of Agoraphobia: On Changes in Emotional and Relational Management'*, Theory and Society*, 10 (3): 359–385.
Defrance, J. (2003) *Sociologie du Sport*, Paris: La Découverte.

DeJong, W. (1980) 'The Stigma of Obesity: The Consequences of Naive Assumptions Concerning the Causes of Physical Deviance', *Journal of Health and Social Behavior*, 21 (1): 75–87.

Desrosières, A. (1991) 'How To Make Things Which Hold Together', in: Wagner, P., Wittrock, B. and Wittley, R. (eds.), *Discourses on Society. The Shaping of the Social Science Disciplines*, Dordrecht: Kluwer: 195–218.

Dewey, J. (1922) *Human Nature and Conduct*, New York: Henry Holt and Company.

Douglas, M. (1996a [1970]) *Natural Symbols. Explorations in Cosmology*, London: Routledge.

Douglas, M. (1996b) *Thought Styles. Critical Essays on Good Taste*, London: Sage.

Douglas, M. and Isherwood B. (1979) *The World of Goods. Towards an Anthropology of Consumption*, London: Routledge.

Dumas, A., Laberge, S. and Straka, S.M. (2006) 'Older Women's Relation to Bodily Appearance: The Embodiment of Biological and Social Conditions of Existence', *Ageing & Society*, 25: 883–902.

Durkheim, E. (2001 [1912]) *The Elementary Forms of Religious Life*, Oxford: Oxford University Press.

Durkheim, E. (2005 [1914]) 'The Dualism of Human Nature and its Social Conditions', *Durkheimian Studies*, 11 (1): 35–45.

Durkheim, E. (2013 [1895]) *The Rules of Sociological Method (2nd Edition)*, Basingstoke: Palgrave Macmillan.

Elder, G.H. (1969) 'Appearance and Education in Marriage Mobility', *American Sociological Review*, 34 (4): 519–533.

Elias, N. (1978) *What is Sociology?*, New York: Columbia University Press.

Elias, N. (1982 [1939]) *The Civilizing Process. Vol. II: State Formation and Civilization*, Oxford: Blackwell.

Elias, N. (1983) *The Court Society*, New York: Pantheon.

Elias, N. (2000 [1939]) *The Civilizing Process. Sociogenetic and Psychogenetic Investigations*, Oxford: Blackwell.

Elias, N. and Dunning, E. (1986) *Quest for Excitement. Sport and Leisure in the Civilizing Process*, Oxford: Blackwell.

Elster, J. (1985) *Sour Grapes: Studies in the Subversion of Rationality*, Cambridge: Cambridge University Press.

Engels, F. (2009 [1845]) *The Condition of the Working-Class in 1844*, Middlesex: The Echo Library.

Fanon, F. (2008 [1952]) *Black Skin. White Masks*, London: Pluto.

Featherstone, M. (1987) 'Leisure, Symbolic Power and the Life Course', in: Horn, J.D. and Tomlinson, A. (eds) *Sport, Leisure and Social Relations*, London: Routledge: 113–138.

Featherstone, M. (1991) 'The Body in Consumer Culture', in: Featherstone, M., Hepworth, M. and Turner, B.S. (eds) *The Body: Social Process and Cultural Theory*, London: Sage: 170–196.

Featherstone, M. and Hepworth, M. (1991) 'The Mask of Ageing and the Postmodern Life Course', in: Featherstone, M., Hepworth, M. and Turner, B.S. (eds) *The Body: Social Process and Cultural Theory*, London: Sage: 371–389.

Fischler, C. (2001) *L'Homnivore. Le Goût, la Cuisine et le Corps*, Paris: Odile Jacob.

Fogel, R.W. (1994) 'Economic Growth, Population Theory and Physiology: The Bearing of Long-Term Processes on the Making of Economic Policy', *Economic Review*, 84: 369–395.

Forbes, C.E. and Grafman, J. (2010) 'The Role of the Human Prefrontal Cortex in Social Cognition and Moral Judgment', *Annual Review of Neuroscience*, 33: 299–334.

Freud, S. (1961 [1930]) *Civilization and its Discontents*, New York: W.W. Norton.

Freund, P.E.S. (1988) 'Bringing Society into the Body', *Theory and Society*, 17 (6): 839–864.

Freund, P.E.S. and McGuire, M.B. (1995) *Health, Illness and the Social Body*, New Jersey: Prentice-Hall.

Fussell, S.W. (1991) *Muscle. Confessions of an Unlikely Body-Builder*, New York: Poseidon Press.

Galton, F. (1884) 'The Weights of British Noblemen during the Last Three Generations', *Nature*, 29: 266–268.

Giddens, A. (1991) *Modernity and Self-Identity. Self and Society in the Late Modern Age*, Stanford: Stanford University Press.

Giddens, A. (1992) *The Transformation of Intimacy. Sexuality, Love and Eroticism in Modern Societies*, London: Polity Press.

Goffman, E. (1951) 'Symbols of Class Status', *British Journal of Sociology*, 2 (4): 294–304.

Goffman, E. (1963) *Stigma. Notes on the Management of Spoiled Identity*, Harmondsworth: Penguin Books.

Goffman, E. (1967) *Interaction Ritual. Essays on Face-to-Face Behavior*, New York: Pantheon.

Gombrich, E.H. (1985) *Meditations on a Hobby Horse. Essays on the Theory of Art*, London: Phaidon.

Goudsblom, J. (1995) 'Elias and Cassirer, Sociology and Philosophy', *Theory, Culture & Society*, 12 (3): 121–126.

Gray, M.A. and James, J. (1995) 'Development and Validation of a New Body-Image Assessment Scale', *Journal of Personality Assessment*, 64 (2): 258–269.

Grignon, C. and Grignon, C. (1980) 'Styles d'Alimentation et Goûts Populaires', *Revue Française de Sociologie*, 21 (4): 531–569.

Halbwachs, M. (1912) *La Théorie de l'Homme Moyen. Essai sûr Quêtelet et la Statistique Morale*, Paris: Felix Alcan.

Hansen, M.N., Flemmen, M. and Andersen, P.L. (2009) 'The Oslo Register Data Class Scheme (ORDC). Final Report from the Classification Project', *Memorandum 1, Department of Sociology and Human Geography*, University of Oslo.

Hargreaves, J. (1987) 'The Body, Sports and Power Relations', in: Horn, J.D. and Tomlinson, A. (eds) *Sport, Leisure and Social Relations*, London: Routledge: 139–159.

Harris, L.T. and Fiske, S.T. (2006) 'Dehumanizing the Lowest of the Low. Neuroimaging Responses to Extreme Out-Groups', *Psychological Science*, 17 (10): 847–853.

Henley, N.M. (1977) *Body Politics. Power, Sex and Nonverbal Communication*, Englewood Cliffs: Prentice-Hall.

Henslin, J.M. and Biggs, M.A. (2007) [1993] 'Behavior in Pubic Places: The Sociology of the Vaginal Examination', in: Henslin, J.M. (ed.) *Down to Earth Sociology: Introductory Readings*, New York: Free Press: 229–241.

Hoggart, R. (1957) *The Uses of Literacy. Aspects of Working-Class Life with Special Reference to Publications and Entertainments*, Harmondsworth: Penguin Books.

Jeffery, R.W., Epstein, L.H., Wilson, G.T., Drewnowski, A., Stunkard, A.J. and Wing, R.W. (2000) 'Long-Term Maintenance of Weight-Loss: Current Status', *Health Psychology*, 19 (1): 5–16.

Jones, O. (2012) *Chavs: The Demonization of the Working Class*, London: Verso.

Jordan, S. (2001) 'From Grotesque Bodies to Idle Hands. Idleness, Industry and the Laboring Classes', *Eighteenth Century Life*, 25: 62–79.
Kantorowicz, E.H. (1957) *The King's Two Bodies. Studies in Medieval Political Theology*, Princeton: Princeton University Press.
Kay, J. and Laberge, S. (2002) 'The "New" Corporate Habitus in Adventure Racing', *International Review for the Sociology of Sport*, 37 (17): 17–36.
Kleinman, A., Brodwin, P.E., Good, B.J. and Del Vecchio-Good, M.J. (1994) 'Pain as Human Experience: An Introduction', in: Del Vecchio-Good, M.J. and Brodwin, P.E. (eds) *Pain as Human Experience: An Anthropological Perspective*, Berkeley: University of California Press: 1–28.
Kramer, F.M., Jeffery, R.W., Forser, J.L. and Snell, M.K. (1989) 'Long-Term Follow-Up of Behavorial Treatment for Obesity: Patterns of Weight Regain among Men and Women', *International Journal of Obesity*, 13 (2): 123–136.
Lahire, B. (2011) *The Plural Actor*, London: Polity Press.
Lamm, H., Schmidt, R.W. and Trommsdorff, G. (1976) 'Sex and Social Class as Determinants of Future Orientation (Time Perspective) in Adolescents', *Journal of Personality and Social Psychology*, 34 (3): 317–326.
Lamont, M. (1992) *Money, Morals and Manners*, Chicago: University of Chicago Press.
Lamont, M. (2000) *The Dignity of Working Men. Morality and the Boundaries of Race, Class and Migration*, Chicago: University of Chicago Press.
Lareau, A. (2003) *Unequal Childhoods. Class, Race and Family Life*, Berkeley: University of California Press.
Lasch, C. (1979) *The Culture of Narcissism: American Life in an Age of Diminishing Expectations*, New York: Norton.
Laumann, E.O., Gagnon, J.H., Michael, R.T. and Michaels, S. (1994) *The Social Organization of Sexuality. Sexual Practices in the United States*, Chicago: University of Chicago Press.
Le Goff, J. (1980) *Time, Work and Culture in the Middle Ages*, Chicago: University of Chicago Press.
Le Wita, B. (1994) *French Bourgeois Culture*, Cambridge: Cambridge University Press.
Leder, D. (1990) *The Absent Body*, Chicago: University of Chicago Press.
Leibel, R.L. (1990) 'Is Obesity Due to a Heritable Difference in "Set Point" for Adiposity?', *Western Journal of Medicine*, 153 (4): 429–431.
Leibniz, G.W. (2006 [1715]) 'Briefwechsel mit Samuel Clarke', in: Dünne, J. and Günzel, S. (eds) *Raumtheorie. Grundlagentexte aus Philosophie und Kulturwissenschaften*, Frankfurt-am-Main: Suhrkamp: 58–73.
Levins, R. and Lewontin, R. (1985) *The Dialectical Biologist*, Cambridge: Harvard University Press.
Lhuissier, A. and Regnier, F. (2005) 'Obésité et Alimentation dans les Catégories Populaires: Une Approche du Corps Féminin', *INRA-Sciences Sociales*, 20 (3/4): 1–4.
Lizardo, O. (2006) 'The Puzzle of Women's Highbrow Culture Consumption: Integrating Gender and Work into Bourdieu's Class Theory of Taste', *Poetics*, 34 (1): 1–23.
Lupton, D. (1994) 'Food, Memory and Meaning: The Symbolic and Social Nature of Food Events', *The Sociological Review*, 42 (4): 664–685.
Lupton, D. (1996) *Food, the Body and the Self*, London: Sage.
Mannheim, K. (1968 [1936]) *Ideology and Utopia*, London: Routledge.
Mannheim, K. (1972 [1928]) 'The Problem of Generations', in: Kecskemeti, P. (ed.) *Karl Mannheim: Essays*, London: Routledge: 276–322.

Martin, J.L. (2000) 'What Do Animals Do All Day? The Division of Labor, Class Bodies and Totemic Thinking in the Popular Imagination', *Poetics*, 27: 195–231.

Martin, J.L. (2003) 'What is Field Theory?', *American Journal of Sociology*, 109 (1): 1–49.

Marx, K. (2007 [1844]) *Economic and Philosophic Manuscripts of 1844*, New York: Dover.

Mauss, M. (1974 [1934]) 'Techniques of the Body', *Economy and Society*, 2 (1): 70–88.

McCall, L. (1992) 'Does Gender Fit? Bourdieu, Feminism and Conceptions of Social Order', *Theory and Society*, 21: 837–867.

McLaren, L. (2007) 'Socioeconomic Status and Obesity', *Epidemiological Reviews*, 29: 29–48.

McNay, L. (1999) 'Gender, Habitus and the Field. Pierre Bourdieu and the Limits of Reflexivity', *Theory, Culture & Society*, 16 (1): 95–117.

Mennell, S. (1991) 'On the Civilizing of Appetite', in: Featherstone, M., Hepworth, M. and Turner, B.S. (eds) *The Body: Social Process and Cultural Theory*, London: Sage: 126–156.

Merleau-Ponty, M. (2005/1962) *Phenomenology of Perception*, London: Routledge.

Molarius, A., Seidell, J.C., Sans, S., Tuomilehto, J. and Kuulasmaa, K. (2000) 'Educational Level, Relative Body Weight, and Changes in Their Association Over 10 Years: An International Perspective From the WHO MONICA Project', *American Journal of Public Health*, 90 (8): 1260–1268.

Monaghan, L.F. (2007) 'Body Mass Index, Masculinities and Moral Worth: Mens' Critical Understanding of Weight-for-Height', *Sociology of Health and Illness*, 29 (4): 584–609.

Murakami, H. (2008) *What I Talk About When I Talk About Running*, New York: Alfred Knopf.

Najman, J.M. and Smith, G.D. (2000) 'The Embodiment of Class-Related and Health-Inequalities. Australian Policies', *Australian and New Zealand Journal of Mental Health*, 24 (1): 3–4.

Nietzsche, F. (1968 [1885]) *The Will to Power*, New York: Vintage Books.

Nisbett, R.E. (1972) 'Hunger, Obesity and the Ventromedial Hypothalamus', *Psychological Review*, 79 (6): 433–453.

Offer, A. (2006) *The Challenge of Affluence. Self-Control and Well-Being in the United States and Britain since 1950*, Oxford: Oxford University Press.

O'Neill, J. (2004) *Five Bodies. Re-figuring Relationships*, London: Sage.

O'Rand, A. and Ellis, R.A. (1974) 'Social Class and Social Time Perspective', *Social Forces*, 53 (1): 53–62.

Orbach, S. (2010) *Fat is a Feminist Issue*, New York: Random House.

Ortner, S.B. (1972) 'Is Female to Male as Nature is to Culture?', *Feminist Studies*, 1 (2): 5–31.

Ostrow, J.M. (1981) 'Culture as a Fundamental Dimension of Experience: A Discussion of Pierre Bourdieu's Theory of Human Habitus', *Human Studies*, 4: 279–297.

Passeron, J.-C. and de Singly, F. (1984) 'Différences dans la Différence: Socialisation de Classe et Socialisation Sexuelle', *Revue Française de Science Politique*, 34 (1): 48–78.

Paulle, B., van Heerikhuizen, B. and Emirbayer, M. (2012) 'Elias and Bourdieu', *Journal of Classical Sociology*, 12 (1): 69–93.

Peterson, R. and Simkus, A. (1992) 'How Musical Tastes Mark Occupational Status Groups' in Lamont, M. and Fournier, M. (eds) *Cultivating Differences. Symbolic*

Boundaries and the Making of Inequality, Chicago: University of Chicago Press: 152-186.

Plessner, H. (1975) *Die Stufen des Organischen und der Mensch. Einleitung in die Philosophischen Anthropologie*, New York: Walter De Gruyter.

Polanyi, M. (2009) *The Tacit Dimension*, Chicago: University of Chicago Press.

Prieur A, Rosenlund, L. and Skjott-Larssen, J. (2008) 'Cultural Capital Today. A Case Study from Denmark', *Poetics*, 38 (1): 45–71.

Reay, D. (1995) 'The Employ Cleaners To Do That. Habitus in the Primary Classroom', *British Journal of Sociology of Education*, 16 (3): 353–371.

Reay, D. (2002) 'Shaun's Story. Troubling Discourses of White Working-Class Masculinities', *Gender and Education*, 14 (3): 221–234.

Reuter, S. (2008) '(Re)Gendering Panic. Towards a Critical Sociology of Agoraphobia', *Women's Health & Urban Life*, 5 (1): 48–74.

Rothblum, E.D. (1994), 'I'll Die for the Revolution, But Don't Ask Me Not to Diet: Feminism and the Continuing Stigmatization of Obesity', in: Fallon, P., Katzman, M.A. and Wooley, S.C. (eds) *Feminist Perspectives on Eating Disorders*, New York: Guilford Press: 53–76.

Ruscio, A.M., Brown, T.A., Chiu, W.T., Sareen, J., Stein, M.B. and Kessler, R.C. (2008) 'Social Fears and Social Phobia in the United States. Results from the National Comorbidity Survey Replication', *Psychological Medicine*, 38: 15–28.

Ryle, G. (2000 [1949]) *The Concept of Mind*, London: Penguin.

Sallaz, J.J. and Zavisca, J. (2007) 'Bourdieu in American Sociology, 1980–2004', *Annual Review of Sociology*, 33: 21–41.

Sapir, E. (1949) *Selected Writings of Edward Sapir in Language, Culture and Personality*, Berkeley: University of California Press.

Scheper-Hughes, N. and Lock, M. (1987) 'The Mindful Body: A Prolegomenon to Future Work in Medical Anthropology', *Medical Anthropology Quarterly*, 1 (1): 6–41.

Schneier, F.R., Johnson, J., Hornig, C.D., Liebowitz, M.R. and Weissman, M.M. (1992) 'Social Phobia. Comorbidity and Morbidity in an Epidemiological Sample', *Archives of General Psychiatry*, 49 (4): 282–288.

Schwartz, O. (1990) *Le Monde Privé des Ouvriers*, Paris: Presses Universitaires de France.

Shakespeare, W. (2006) *The Merchant of Venice*, New Haven and London: Yale University Press.

Shilling, C. (2003) *The Body and Social Theory*. London: Sage.

Simmel, G. (1965) *Essays on Sociology, Philosophy and Aesthetics*, New York: Harper & Row.

Simmel, G. (1997 [1907]) 'Sociology of the Senses', in: Frisby, D. and Featherstone, M. (eds) *Simmel on Culture: Selected Writings*, London: Sage: 109–130.

Skeggs, B. (1997) *Formations of Class and Gender,* London: Sage.

Skeggs, B. (2005) 'The Making of Class and Gender through Visualizing Moral Subject Formation', *Sociology*, 39: 965.

Slaughter, T.F. (1977) 'Epidermalizing the World. A Basic Mode of Being Black', *Man and World*, 10 (3): 303–308.

Smith, A. (2002 [1759]) *The Theory of Moral Sentiments*, Cambridge: Cambridge University Press.

Sobal, J. and Stunkard, A.J. (1984) 'Socioeconomic Status and Obesity: A Review of the Literature', *Psychological Bulletin*, 105 (2): 260–275.

Sobal, J. (1995) *The Medicalization and Demedicalization of Obesity*, in: Maurer, D. and Sobal, J. (eds) 'Eating Agendas. Food and Nutritition as Social Problems', New York: Aldine de Gruyter, 67–90.

Speakman, J.R. (2007) 'A Nonadaptive Scenario Explaining the Predisposition to Obesity', *Cell Metabolism*, 6 (1): 5–12.

Stearns, P.N. (2002) *Fat History. Bodies and Beauty in the Modern West*, New York: New York University Press.

Stempel, C. (2005) 'Adults Sports Participation as Cultural Capital. A Test of Bourdieu's Theory of the Field of Sports', *International Review for the Sociology of Sport*, 40: 411.

Stunkard, A.J., Sorensen, T. and Schulsinger, F. (1983) 'Use of the Danish Adoption Register for the Study of Obesity and Thinness', in: Kety, S.S., Rowland, L.P, Sidman, R.L. and Matthysse, R.L. (eds) *Genetics of Neurological and Psychiatric Disorders*, New York: Raven Press.

Synnott, A. (1993) *The Body Social: Symbolism, Self and Society*, London: Routledge.

Taylor, C. (1993) 'To Follow a Rule…', in: Calhoun C., LiPuma, E. and Postone, M. (eds) *Bourdieu: Critical Perspectives*, Chicago: University of Chicago Press: 45–60.

Trostle, J.A. and Somerfeld, J. (1996) 'Medical Anthropology and Epidemiology', *Annual Review of Anthropology*, 25: 253–274.

Turner, B.S. (2005/1995) 'Aging and Identity. Some Reflections on The Somatization of the Self' in: Featherstone, M. and Wernick, A. (eds) *Images of Aging. Cultural Representations of Later Life*, London: Routledge: 249–263.

Turner, B.S. (1996) *The Body and Society: Explorations in Social Theory (Second Edition)*, London: Sage.

Valverde, M. (1998) *Diseases of the Will. Alcohol and the Dilemmas of Freedom*, Cambridge: Cambridge University Press.

Vandebroeck, D. (2015) 'Classifying Bodies, Classified Bodies, Class Bodies', in: Coulangeon, P. and Duval, J. (eds) *The Routledge Companion to Bourdieu's Distinction*, London: Routledge: 227–254.

Veblen, T. (1952 [1899]) *The Theory of the Leisure Class. An Economic Study of Institutions*, New York: New American Library.

Warrin, M., Turner, K., Moore, V. and Davies, M. (2008) 'Bodies, Mothers and Identities: Rethinking Obesity and the BMI', *Sociology of Health and Illness*, 30 (1): 97–111.

Wacquant, L. (1992) 'Making Class: The Middle Clas(ses) in Social Theory and Social Structure', in: McNall, S.G., Levine, R. and Fantasia, R. (eds) *Bringing Class Back In*, Boulder: Westview Press: 39–64.

Wacquant, L.C. (1993) 'Bourdieu in America: Notes on the Transatlantic Importation of Social Theory', in: Calhoun, C., LiPuma, E. and Postone, M. (eds) *Bourdieu: Critical Perspectives*, Chicago: University of Chicago Press: 235–262.

Wacquant, L.C. (2004) *Body & Soul. Notebooks of an Apprentice Boxer*, Oxford: Oxford University Press.

Wacquant, L. (2010) 'Crafting the Neoliberal State. Workfare, Prisonfare and Social Insecurity', *Sociological Forum*, 25 (2): 197–220.

Weber, M. (1978 [1956]) *Economy and Society. An Outline of Interpretive Sociology*, Berkeley: University of California Press.

Weiss, E.C., Galuska, D.A., Kahn, L.K., Gillespie, C. and Sardula, M.K. (2007) 'Weight Regain in U.S. Adults Who Experienced Substantial Weight Loss, 1999–2002', *American Journal of Preventive Medicine*, 33 (1): 34–40.

Wilkinson, R.G. (1996) *Unhealthy Societies. The Afflictions of Inequality,* London: Routledge.
Willis, P. (1977) *Learning to Labor. How Working Class Kids Get Working Class Jobs,* New York: Columbia University Press.
Wittgenstein, L. (2001 [1949]) *Philosophical Investigations,* Oxford: Blackwell.
Wood, H. and Skeggs, B. (eds) (2011) *Reality Television and Class,* London: Palgrave Macmillan.
Young, I.M. (1990) *Justice and the Politics of Difference,* New Jersey: Princeton University Press.
Young, I.M. (2005) *On Female Bodily Experience. Throwing like a Girl and Other Essays,* Oxford: Oxford University Press.
Zborowski, M. (1952) 'Cultural Components in Responses to Pain', *Journal of Social Issues,* 8 (4): 16–30.
Zborowski, M. (1969) *People in Pain,* San Francisco: Jossey-Bass.

Index

Page numbers in *italics* denote tables, those in **bold** denote figures

Abbott, Andrew 15
advertising 151, 198–9, 202, 211n1, 236; *see also* lifestyle-media
age 4, 56, 59, 124, 171; homology of class and 31, 62, 209–10, 225; sports-participation and *160*, 161–3, 173; satisfaction with appearance and 79–81, 209–10
agoraphobia 220–1; *see also* symbolic violence
Alexander, Jeffery 25, 54, 75, 182
anorexia *see* eating disorders
appearance 11, 30, 55, 78–9, 89–90, 98, 115, *116*, 128, 130, 139, 196, *201*, 229; as embodied class 52–3, 108, 114, 124, 184, 195, 229–32, 237; gender and 28–9, 32–3, 81, 164, 167–8, 219; middle-classes and 101, 110, 183, 194, 196–9, 203–11, 224; working class and 101, 108, 213, 218–21, 223, 226; *see also* physical capital
asceticism 77, 90, 108, 178n1; cultural capital and 25, 96, 147–8, 188, 192; health and 72, 142; middle-classes and 76–7, 203–7; in sports 173, 175–6; *see also* hedonism self-control, time-perspective

Bakhtin, M. 61, 227
Barlösius, E. 128
Barthes, R. 139, 143–4
Bartky, S. 27, 198, 202, 232
Bauman, Z. 78, 211n1
'being-perceived' *see* appearance
Biggs, M.A. 16
bluff 54–5, 125, 185, 208; *see also* snobbery

body image: current versus ideal 111, **112**, **113**, 114–17, *116*, 229–30, *246*, *248*, *249*; gender and 27, 63, 114–15, 216; media-consumption and 198–203, *200*, *201*
body mass index 92, *93*, *97*, *99*, *100*, 102, **104**, **105**, 111, 125n2, 192, 199, *201*, 202; *see also* overweight, obesity
body weight *see* body mass index, slimness, obesity, overweight
Boltanski, L. 7, 9, 49, 68–73, 79, 83n2, 121, 143, 178, 195, 213, 225
Bordo, S. 27, 89–91, 192, 198, 211n1
Bourdieu, P. 1–7, 18–26, 28–9, 31–2, 34–8, 40–1, 44–50, 52–4, 62, 64, 73–9, 82, 83n2, 84n3, 94, 96, 107, 111, 115, 117–18, 125, 127, 129, 133, 136, 139, 143–4, 147, 151, 154, 157–8, 162, 171–2, 178, 181–5, 188, 196–7, 205, 208, 215–16, 220, 226–36
Brillat-Savarin, J.A. 87–8
Bruch, H. 136–7, 191–2, 193n1
bulimia see eating disorders

Cahnman, W.J. 89, 124
Canguilhem, G. 87, 103
capital: cultural 24, 29, 32, 34, 77, 132, 136, 148, 154, 187, 192, 205, 233, 242; economic 21, 33–4, 77, *93*, *99*, 142, 148–9, 241; sexual 223; social 20, 37n4, 132, 146, 157, 174; volume and composition **20**, 21–2, **34**, 96, 147–9; *see also* physical capital, social space
capitalism 4, 83, 90, 242
Cassirer, E. 36n3
Charles, N. 108, 146, 154, 218

272 Index

Charlesworth, S.J. 5, 31, 52, 61, 125, 136, 139, 144, 159, 215, 217, 220, 227, 232
children 28, 42, 72, 76, 126, 191–2, 218, 233; attitudes towards food and 136–7, 146; conceptions of health and 214; inculcation of class- and gender-differences 63, 190–2
class position: probable versus actual 22–3, 44; sociology of the body and 4–5, 78, 90–1, 210–11; worldview and 22, 49–52, 81–3, 229–30; *see also* capital, dominant class, middle classes, social space, working classes
classification 16, 19, 23, 30, 60, 81–2, 83n2, 208; body-types and 118–24, **119, 120**, 169, 190, 216; habitus and 48, 53, 143; surveys and 2, 8, 195, 241
clothing 29–30, 50, 53, 81, 125, 157, 184, 187, 189; high heels 219; lingerie 223; second-hand/vintage 187
Collins, R. 28, 33, 219, 242
Connell, R. 27–8, 31, 33, 35, 62–3, 216
Cregan, K. 10, 36n1
Crossley, N. 3, 49, 64n1, 90, 98
cultural imperialism 229; *see also* symbolic violence

Darmon, M. 5, 90, 191–2, 193n2
de-narcissization *see* sex
Defrance, J. 156
DeJong, W. 89, 124
Dewey, J. 41–3, 64n1
dieting 49, 53, 55, 79–80, 83, 87–90, 196, 235, 237; social distribution of 98, *99–100*, 101, 203–4, *246, 247*; success of 106–10; *see also* obesity, overweight, self-control
distinction 46, 61–2, 114, 128, 171, 177, 207, 226, 234; conscious strategies of 110–11, 181–2, 185, 231; as 'negative cultivation' 181–2, 190–2; self-control as 64, 184, 191–2, 206; statistical averages and 103–6; types of 24–7, 186–90; *see also* dominant class
dominant class: ageing and 81, 209–10, 211n2; dominant versus dominated fractions 21–2, 24–7, 33–6, 96–8, *97*, 147–50, 173–4, 186–90; masculinity and 34–6, 189–90; sense of distinction and 54, 181–2, 190–2, 226; sports and 174–5; *see also* distinction
Douglas, M. 3, 5, 12n3, 60, 75, 110, 156, 182, 190

drinks: beer 145, 150, *254, 257, 259*; champagne 150, *254, 257, 259*; coffee 126, *254, 257, 259*; soft-drinks 142, 214, *254, 257, 259*; spirits 150, *254, 257, 259*; wine 128, 145, 150, 189, *254, 257, 259*
Dumas, A. 81, 209, 211n2
Durkheim, E. 15, 17, 19, 59, 65n4, 77, 177, 178n1, 186, 206

eating disorders 88–90, 137, 191–2, 225
Elias, N. 15–19, 36n1, 61, 64, 82, 157–8, 163, 183, 196–7, 233
elite *see* dominant class
embodiment: class and 46–52, 54, 182–3; gender and 27–8, 51, 62–3, 219; phenomenology and 41–3, 46, 48, 50, 57–8, 65n3, 115, 117, 230; reflexive character of 52, 55–6; social theory and 4, 6, 11, 16, 56–7, 84n4; visceral dimension of 38–9, 44, 56–9, 61, 63–4, 65n3, 129, 183; *see also* habitus
Engels, F. 88
epidemiology 91, 94–5, 98, 109, 225
ethos 25, 31, 33, 35, 49–52, 62, 70–2, 82, 110, 133, 137, 139, 144, 149–50, 157, 159, 161, 173, 176, 178, 189–93, 203, 206, 217–19, 226, 233

Fanon, F. 230
fashion *see* clothing
fashion-beauty complex 202, 232
Featherstone, M. 4, 90–1, 111, 161, 198, 209, 211n1
femininity: appearance and 27, 198; class-identity and 29–34, 123, 198, 216, 218–19, 222, 225; dominant definition of 101, 108, 209, 220–1; embodiment and 27–8, 51, 63, 65n3, 144–5, 219; sports and 164, 167–8; *see also* gender, masculinity
fields 8, 18–21, 24–5, 35, 39, 47, 75, 189, 197, 205, 242; *see also* social space
figuration 16–19, 82; *see also* fields, social space
Fischler, C. 139
Fogel, R.W. 125n2
food: aestheticization of 128–9; body techniques and 143–7; culinary exoticism and 131–3; depression and 137–8; as primary luxury 136–7; time devoted to 145–6, *260*; *see also* food-types
food-types: bananas 143–4; beef 131, *140–1*, 143–4, 146; fish 128, 131,

142–4, 148, 187, *253*, *255*, *258*; fruit & vegetables 142, 148, 187; pork 131, 142, *252*, *255*, *258*; steak 128, 130–1, 133, *135–6*, *140–1*, 144, *153*
Foucault, M. 50
Freud, S. 17, 43
Freund, P.E.S. 6, 56, 58

Galton, F. 88, 125n2
gender 4, 27, 59, 62, 89, 215, 220, 229, 237, *238*; homologies of class and 32–4, **34**, 171; objectification of the body and 27–8, 63, 122, 216; *see also* femininity, masculinity
Giddens, A. 3, 19, 78, 84n4, 89–90, 98
Goffman, E. 51, 53–5, 89, 124, 125n3, 182, 186, 220, 231
Goffmanian labour 28, 204–5, 210, 219, 223, 242
Gombrich, E.H. 126–8
Grignon, C. & C. 136, 225

habit 41–3, 64n1, 64n2
habitus 5, 18–19, 35, 64n1, 74–5, 94, 108, 182, 190–1; class position and 22, 196, 211, 220; as classifying principle 183: embodiment and 44–6; as mode of consumption 143–7; as unifying principle 49–50; *see also* embodiment, ethos, hexis
Halbwachs, M. 11n2, 103
Henley, N. 4, 27, 51, 186
Henslin, J.M. 16
health 6, 9, 88, 94, 107, 167, 169, *170*, 203, 206–7, 225, 231–2, 235, 237; class-differences in attitudes towards 71–3, 133, 137, 142, 146, 148, 213–14, 226; survey-research and 9, 91, 225; time-perspective and 67–70, 79–81, 139, 196, 213
health-campaigns 107, 133, 214; *see also* epidemiology, health
hedonism 82–3, 136–9, 149, 188–90, 226
hexis 33, 51–2, 55, 115, 117, 121, 125, 158, 196, 209, 217; *see also* ethos, habitus
Hoggart, R. 37n7, 194, 208
hysteresis 75, 108–10, 151, 154

inequality 63, 75, 88, 162, 235; *see also* class position, gender

Kantorowicz, E.H. 60–1
Kay, J. 35
Kerr, M. 108, 146, 154, 218

Lahire, B. 39, 45
Lamont, M. 24, 62
Lareau, A. 193n1
Lasch, C. 222
Laumann, E.O. 221
Le Goff, J. 81
Le Wita, B. 145, 183–5, 190
Leder, D. 57, 59
Leibniz, G.W. 22
lifestyle-media 54, 79–80, 84, 84n5, 108, 133, 196, 198–203, *200*, *201*, 207–8, 219
lived body *see* embodiment
Lupton, D. 108, 128, 133, 137, 151, 154

McCall, L. 32
McNay, L. 108, 155
Mannheim, K. 45, 66
Martin, J.L. 39, 118
Marx, K. 40, 130
masculinity 27–9, 51, 63, 144, 167, 225, 244; as symbolic capital 30–1, 68, 216–18; class-identity and 31–3, 35, 122–3, 168, 217; eating and 128, 144–5; sports and 164, 167, 171–3; *see also* gender, muscularity
maternal schema 222; *see also* femininity
Mauss, M. 3, 11n2, 43, 143, 212, 218
Mennell, S. 88
Merleau-Ponty, M. 5, 41–3, 46, 48, 50, 56–8, 64n1, 221, 228
middle classes **20**, 23–4, 72, 115, 124, 154, 205–6; appearance and 101, 168, 207–10, 211n2; asceticism and 72, 76–7, 148, 150, 176, 196, 203–5; statistical analysis and 96, 146–7, 194–5, 241
modernity 4, 78, 84n4, 89–91, 98, 210–11
Monaghan, L.F. 111, 244
Murakami, H. 177
muscularity 39, 111, 114, 121, 167–9, *170*, 216, 225, 244

Najman, J.M. 69
narcissism 188, 218, 221–2, 226
Nietzsche, F. 181

obesity 87–90, 98, 125n2, 137; epidemic of 88, 91–5; genetic explanations of 106–8; as stigma 89, 123–4; *see also* overweight
Offer, A. 83, 117
Orbach, S. 107, 137

overweight 88–90, 115; social distribution of 95–6, *97*, *116*; stigmatization of 89, 103, 114, 117, 123–5, 233–4, 244; *see also* obesity

pain 58, 66–9, 71–2, 83n1, 163, 177, 213, 217, 222; *see also* health
Peterson, R. 25
petit-bourgeoisie *see* middle classes
physical capital 31, 111, 114–15, 162, 174, 183–4, 209, 219–20, 223–4, 230–3, 242
physiognomy 64, 98, 118, 125, 127
physique *see* appearance
Polanyi, M. 49

Reay, D. 33, 37n6, 233
reflexivity 2, 9, 55, 78, 210–11, 213
restaurants 132, *134*, 142, 149–50, *152*, 188–9, *254*, *257*, *259*
Ryle, G. 41–2, 64n1

Sapir, E. 41–2
Schwartz, O. 29–30, 136, 138, 159–61, 213, 215, 218, 222
self-control 2, 17, 90, 173, 225; distinction and 28, 64, 184, 190–2; as moral property 82, 124, 155, 226; time-perspective and 79, 81–2; *see also* asceticism
set-points 106–7, 109
sexual schema 221; *see also* sexuality
sexuality 2, 15–16, 138, 206–7, 221–4
Shakespeare, W. 61–2
Shilling, C. 3, 78, 84n4, 89–91
Simmel, G. 38, 60, 118, 129
Skeggs, B. 37n6, 122, 199, 219
Slaughter, T.F. 230
slimness 95, 117, 125, 137, 168, 216, 219, 232; *see also* dieting, self-control
Smith, A. 228, 234
Smith, G.D. 96
snobbery 183, 185; *see also* bluff, distinction
Sobal, J. 88–9, 91
social mobility: asceticism and 72, 76–7, 175–7, 203–5; durability of class tastes and 48–9, 151–6, *152–3*; morality and 205–7; sexual dispositions and 32–3; *see also* hysteresis, middle classes
social space 18–27, **20**, 28, 52, 241–2, *243*; absence in research of 24–6, 98; embodiment of 50, 52, 55, *93*, 96, *97*, 117, 129–30; sexual dimension of 30–6, **34**, 189–90; *see also* capital, fields

sports and exercise: aestheticization of effort 163, 173–7; age- and class-differences in *160*, 161–2, *165–6*; gender and 164, 167–71, 173; as psychological release 157, 163; reasons for 167–9, *170*, 173–5
sports-types: basketball 158, *166*, 172; boxing 158, *165*, 171, 215, 217; football/futsal 157, 164, *165*, 171–5; golf 157–8, *165*, 173–5; jogging/running 157, 161, *165*, 169, 173–6; mountain biking/cycling 164, *165*, 167, 176; swimming 158, *166*, 169, 174–6; tennis 157–8, *165*, 172–5; triathlon 158, 164, 175–7; volleyball *166*, 172; walking *166*; weight-lifting 166, 168, 171, 215, 217
Stunkard, A.J. 88, 91, 244
survey-research; differential meaning of practices and 143–4, 146–7, 156–7, 172–3; partial constructions of object 8–10, 94–5; synchronizing effect of 151, 175–6, 194–5
symbolic violence 5, 197, 199, 211, 228; *see also* cultural imperialism

taste 11, 25, 36, 46–8, 52–4, 103, 124, 133, 147–8, 175, 186; classification struggles and 26, 50, 127, 170, 177, 190, 209–10, 225–6; differentiation of the senses 128–30; distaste and 39, 127, 131, 182–3, 234; incorporated principle of classification 44, 47–8, 109–10, 128, 143–4, 154, 181–2, 232; *see also* distinction, drinks, food, hysteresis
Taylor, C. 51
Thévenot, L. 83n2, 121
time-perspective: bodily investment and 79–81, 169, 184, 203–4, 226; food-attitudes 139, 145–6, *260*; health-views and 66–73; Pierre Bourdieu on 73–7, 84n3; self-control and 81–3, 203–4
time use-surveys *see* survey-research
transcendence/negation 62–3
Turner, B.S. 3, 4, 10, 12n3, 70, 78, 83, 89

Valverde, Mariana 124
Veblen, T. 55, 64n2
vegetarianism 148

Wacquant, L. 5, 21, 24, 36, 36n3, 40, 56, 73, 194, 217, 220
Weber, M. 2, 19, 23
Wilkinson, R. 53, 58

Willis, P. 30–2, 215
Wittgenstein, L. 125
working classes: dominant bodily aesthetic and 33, 209, 216, 219–21, 230–6; food and 130–9, 144–5; gender-divisions within 30–3, 132, 144, 197, 215–21; instrumentalization of the body and 133, 136, 159–61, 214–15; sports and 159, 161–2

Young, I.M. 27–8, 51, 65n3, 229–30

Zborowski, M. 66–8, 72, 83n1

Taylor & Francis eBooks

Helping you to choose the right eBooks for your Library

Add Routledge titles to your library's digital collection today. Taylor and Francis ebooks contains over 50,000 titles in the Humanities, Social Sciences, Behavioural Sciences, Built Environment and Law.

Choose from a range of subject packages or create your own!

Benefits for you
- Free MARC records
- COUNTER-compliant usage statistics
- Flexible purchase and pricing options
- All titles DRM-free.

Benefits for your user
- Off-site, anytime access via Athens or referring URL
- Print or copy pages or chapters
- Full content search
- Bookmark, highlight and annotate text
- Access to thousands of pages of quality research at the click of a button.

Free Trials Available
We offer free trials to qualifying academic, corporate and government customers.

eCollections – Choose from over 30 subject eCollections, including:

Archaeology	Language Learning
Architecture	Law
Asian Studies	Literature
Business & Management	Media & Communication
Classical Studies	Middle East Studies
Construction	Music
Creative & Media Arts	Philosophy
Criminology & Criminal Justice	Planning
Economics	Politics
Education	Psychology & Mental Health
Energy	Religion
Engineering	Security
English Language & Linguistics	Social Work
Environment & Sustainability	Sociology
Geography	Sport
Health Studies	Theatre & Performance
History	Tourism, Hospitality & Events

For more information, pricing enquiries or to order a free trial, please contact your local sales team:
www.tandfebooks.com/page/sales

 The home of Routledge books

www.tandfebooks.com